Contemporary Influences of C.G. Jung's Thought

Contemporary Psychoanalytic Studies

VOLUME 24

The titles published in this series are listed at *brill.com/cps*

Contemporary Influences of C.G. Jung's Thought

Edited by

Ilona Błocian
Andrew Kuzmicki

BRILL
RODOPI

LEIDEN | BOSTON

Cover illustration: *Silhouette of People Standing Near Tree Under the Moon,* by Gerd Altmann. Retrieved from www.pexels.com. Used under the CCo License.

Library of Congress Cataloging-in-Publication Data

Names: Błocian, Ilona, editor. | Kuzmicki, Andrew, editor.
Title: Contemporary influences of C.G. Jung's thought / edited by Ilona Błocian, Andrew Kuzmicki.
Description: Leiden ; Boston : Brill, [2018] | Series: Contemporary psychoanalytic studies, ISSN 1571-4977 ; VOLUME 26 | Includes bibliographical references and index.
Identifiers: LCCN 2018042514 (print) | LCCN 2018043931 (ebook) | ISBN 9789004336636 (eBook) | ISBN 9789004336629 (pbk. : alk. paper)
Subjects: LCSH: Jung, C. G. (Carl Gustav), 1875-1961. | Jungian psychology. | Psychoanalysis.
Classification: LCC BF109.J8 (ebook) | LCC BF109.J8 C66 2018 (print) | DDC 150.19/54092--dc23
LC record available at https://lccn.loc.gov/2018042514

Typeface for the Latin, Greek, and Cyrillic scripts: "Brill". See and download: brill.com/brill-typeface.

ISSN 1571-4977
ISBN 978-90-04-33662-9 (paperback)
ISBN 978-90-04-33663-6 (e-book)

This book is printed on acid-free paper and produced in a sustainable manner.

Contents

List of Figures and Tables VII
List of Contributors IX

Introduction 1
Ilona Błocian and Andrew Kuzmicki

1 Jung in the Academy and Beyond: The Fordham Lectures – 100 Years Later 11
Joseph Cambray

2 Aspects of Descartes' and Pascal's Diverging Psychological Standings as Regards Knowledge That Find Expression in the Differences of the Freudian and Jungian Methodological Approaches to Psychology 35
Miriam Gomes de Freitas

3 On Problem Solving – C.G. Jung's and M. Heidegger's Perspectives 71
Maria Kostyszak

4 Is a Jungian Analysis Scientific? 86
Robert Segal

5 Collective Memory and Common Imagination – Archetypes in the Perspective of the Theory of Sign 96
Anna Olejarczyk

6 The Idea of Culture Image Confronted with Psychoanalytic Tradition 116
Ewa Kwiatkowska

7 Is the Jungian Concept of "Image" Still Relevant in a Modern Psychoanalytic Perspective? 135
Alessandra De Coro

8 Jung and Social Thought: “The Undiscovered Self” 152
Ilona Błocian

9 In a Secular Age: Weber, Taylor, Jung 169
Roderick Main

10 Non-fixed Multiple Perspectives in the Japanese Psyche: Traditional Japanese Art, Dream and Myth 193
Megumi Yama

11 Subject Drop and the Japanese Ego 216
Norifumi Kishimoto

12 Developing Jung’s Theory of Mind in the Light of Evolutionary Psychology 228
Andrew Kuzmicki

13 The Contributions of C.G. Jung and Eugen Bleuler to Psychiatry: Schizophrenia Then and Now 253
Michael Escamilla

14 A Discourse on the Textual-Psychoidal Duality in the Novel *Thorn and Laurel* [“Cierń i laur”] by Wladyslaw Lech Terlecki 269
Zbigniew Bitka

15 Evidence for the Effectiveness of Jungian Psychotherapy: A Review of Empirical Studies 304
Christian Roesler

16 How Can We Objectify a Study on Analytical Psychology? 318
Jolanta Kowal

Index 353

Figures and Tables

Figures

2.1 *Las Meninas.* Painter: Velázquez (1656). Illustration is in the public domain. No permission needed. Retrieved from Wikipedia 38

2.2 *Malkunst.* Painter: Vermeer (1666). Illustration is in the public domain. No permission needed. Retrieved from Wikipedia 39

10.1 *Two models of Japanese consciousness and Westerner's consciousness.* Artist: [Megumi Yama]. Retrieved from: H. Kawai, *Boseishakai Nihon no Byori* (*Pathology of Japan as a Society of Maternity*), Tokyo: Chuokoron-sha, 1976. Used with permission from the copyright holder 197

10.2 *Rakuchu-Rakugai-zu* (*left wing*) *Uesugi version.* Copyright holder: Yonezawa City Uesugi Museum. Retrieved from: https://commons.wikimedia.org/wiki/File:%E6%B4%9B%E4%B8%AD%E6%B4%9B%E5%A4%96%E5%9B%B3%E5%8F%B3.jpg. Illustration is in the public domain. No permission needed 198

10.3 Rakuchu-Rakugai-zu (left wing) Zooming-up. Uesugi version. Copyright holder: Yonezawa City Uesugi Museum. Retrieved from Yonezawa City Uesugi Museum. Used with permission 199

10.4a. *Palace of Versailles.* Photographer: Luca Volpi (Goldmund100). Retrieved from https://upload.wikimedia.org/wikipedia/commons/a/a4/Park_of_Versailles_main_view.jpg. Used with permission of the author 201

10.4b *The palace and gardens of Schönbrunn in Vienna.* Photographer: Gryffindor. Retrieved from: https://commons.wikimedia.org/wiki/File%3ASchloss_Schoenbrunn_August_2006_406.jpg Illustration is in the public domain. No permission needed 201

10.5a *The Katsura Imperial Villa.* Photographer: Megumi Yama (author). Retrieved from Megumi Yama. Used with permission from the copyright holder 202

10.5b *The Katsura Imperial Villa.* Photographer: Megumi Yama (author). Retrieved from Megumi Yama. Used with permission from the copyright holder 202

10.6 *Map of the Katsura Imperial Villa.* Designer: The Imperial Household Agency. Retrieved from: http://sankan.kunaicho.go.jp/english/guide/institution_katsura.html. Illustration is in the public domain. No permission needed 203

10.7 *Genji Monogatari Emaki.* Published by the Tokugawa Museum in Nagoya, Japan, 1937. Retrieved from: https://en.wikipedia.org/wiki/Genji_Monogatari_Emaki#/media/File:Genji_emaki_azumaya.jpg. Illustration is in the public domain. No permission needed 208

10.8 *The gradual transition from the "nothing" to the concrete.* Designer: Megumi Yama. Yama, M. (2013) "Ego consciousness in the Japanese psyche: culture, myth and disaster." Journal of Analytical Psychology, 58, 52–72. Used with permission from the copyright holder 211
11.1 *The train came out of the long tunnel into the snow country.* Artist: Ena Kishimoto. Retrieved from Ena Kishimoto. Used with permission 218
11.2 *Got through the long border tunnel, was a snow country.* Artist: Ena Kishimoto. Retrieved from Ena Kishimoto. Used with permission 219
12.1 *Different factors "shaping" the conscious and unconscious processes.* Designer: Andrew Kuzmicki. Retrieved from Andrew Kuzmicki. Used with permission from the copyright holder 238
12.2 *Integrating scheme of conscious and unconscious processes from Jungian perspective.* Designer: Andrew Kuzmicki. Retrieved from Andrew Kuzmicki. Used with permission from the copyright holder 238
12.3 *Integrating scheme of conscious (Antonio Damasio).* Designer: Andrew Kuzmicki. Retrieved from Andrew Kuzmicki. Used with permission from the copyright holder 241
12.4 *Integrating scheme of conscious and unconscious processes – C.G. Jung vs. A. Damasio.* Designer: Andrew Kuzmicki. Retrieved from Andrew Kuzmicki. Used with permission from the copyright holder 243
16.1 The stages of research process (from Remenyi, 2013) 327
16.2 Title: Animus. Photographer: Jolanta Kowal. Retrieved from Jolanta Kowal. Used with permission from the copyright holder 330

Tables

16.1 Comparison of quantitative and qualitative research 324
16.2A Matrix of experts' answers 329
16.2B Answer matrix for every competent judge. Assessment of judge number 1 331
16.2C Assessment of judge number 2 333
16.3 The algorithm of "ambigous objects" – The statistical procedures to choose pictures for projective method 341
16.4 Descriptive statistics for saturation of picture 1 with symbolism of each archetype 344
16.5 Wilcoxon (paired samples) sequence test 345
16.6 Friedman's ANOVA and Kendall's coefficient of concordance 346
16.7 Pearson's correlation coefficient r for picture 2 (number N = 13) 347
16.8 Variables in concentration 1 (pictures) with the highest and at most moderate variability 347

Contributors

Robert A. Segal
is Sixth Century Chair in Religious Studies, University of Aberdeen. He came to the United Kingdom from his native United States in 1994. He taught at Lancaster University, England, and since 2006 has taught at Aberdeen. He writes and teaches on theories of myth and religion and also on Gnosticism. Among the works he has written or edited are *The Poimandres as Myth* (1986), *Joseph Campbell* (rev. 1990), *The Gnostic Jung* (1992), *Jung on* Mythology (1998), The *Myth and Ritual Theory* (1998), *Theorizing about Myth* (1999), *The Blackwell Companion to the Study of Religion* (2000), *30-Second Mythology* (2012), and *Myth: A Very Short Introduction* (rev. ed. 2015).

Miriam Gomes Freitas
is a brazilian medical doctor, specialist in psychiatry. She finished medical school in 1973, then she moved for a year to Paris, to the Neurology Department in the Salpetrière where prof. F Lhermitte was the chair person. From 1974 to 1980 she attended the C.G. Jung Institut in Zürich where she worked analytically with prof. C.A. Meier, M.M. Pope and had supervision with Dr. M. Jacoby, C.T. Frey and I. Baker. From 1980 she had her own Jungian praxis in Porto Alegre, RS, Brazil.

Her field of interest is wide. It includes art, philosophy, psychiatry, social psychology and Jewish studies – specially Spinoza, W. Benjamin and L. Wittgenstein. She is also a painter and writer. She writes poetry and wrote and directed a few theatre plays.

Maria Kostyszak
is a scholar in the Institute of Philosophy at the Wrocław University, Poland. She has written four books and over forty articles. Her books: *B. Pascal and B. Spinoza- Comparison of Philosophical Approaches, Martin Heidegger-Handwork of Thinking, The Essence of Technology – the Voice of Martin Heidegger, The Quarrel with Language – Criticism of ontotheology in F. Nietzsche's, M. Heidegger's and J. Derrida's writings*. At present her field of research embraces philosophy of technology with the particular emphasis on transformation of ethics. She is focused on examining chances and conditions to liberate human thinking from the present dominance of instrumental reason.

Joseph Cambray
Ph.D., is Provost at Pacifica Graduate Institute; he is Past-President of the International Association for Analytical Psychology and has served as the U.S.

Editor for *The Journal of Analytical Psychology* and is on the Editorial Boards of the *Journal of Analytical Psychology*, *The Jung Journal: Culture and Psyche*, and *Israel Annual of Psychoanalytic Theory, Research and Practice*. He was a faculty member at Harvard Medical School in the Department of Psychiatry at Massachusetts General Hospital, Center for Psychoanalytic Studies; and former President of the C.G. Jung Institute of Boston. Dr. Cambray is a Jungian analyst in Santa Barbara, CA. His numerous publications include the book based on his Fay Lectures: *Synchronicity: Nature and Psyche in an Interconnected Universe* and a volume edited with Linda Carter, *Analytical Psychology: Contemporary Perspectives in Jungian Psychology.*

Alessandra de Coro

is a Jungian analyst (IAAP) and Associate Professor of Dynamic Psychology in Faculty of Psychology at the University of Rome "La Sapienza", Italy, where she is the head of the Department of Dynamic and Clinical Psychology.

She published several books: "Dynamic psychology. The clinical theories", / "Psicologia dinamica. Le teorie cliniche" [Italian], 2007. "Empirical research in psychotherapy" / "La ricerca empirica in psicoterapia" [Italian], 2004. Psicologia Dinamica: i modelli teorici (Laterza, Roma 2010) (co-author with F. Ortu), in English: Dynamic Psychology: Theorical Models.

Anna Olejarczyk

is an assistant professor in the Faculty of Philosophy in University of Wroclaw, Poland. She works on the fields of semiotics, hermeneutics, and theory of discourse and is very keen to explore the modern reception of Plato's philosophy, especially in French and German tradition. She published (and co-edit) eight books on modern reception of Plato and the concept of possible worlds. She cooperate with four philosophical and interdisciplinary multiannual projects ("Colloquia Platonica", "Possible Worlds", "Mythopeia", and "Phronesis"). Her recent works consider the ontology of discourse. Her hobby is tutoring the students from science Club of Philosophical Psychology "Parusia."

Ewa Kwiatkowska

is a researcher in the Institute of Sociology at the Wrocław University, Poland. She deals with the problem of the border of contemporary theories and philosophy of culture, especially with metatheory of contemporary humanities with research on myth and theory of images. At the moment she works on her new book concerning different contemporary interpretations of images in verious fields and applies different approaches.

Christian Roesler

is Professor of Clinical Psychology at the Catholic University of Applied Sciences in Freiburg, Germany; a Jungian psychoanalyst in private practice in Freiburg and a member of the faculties of the C.G. Jung Institutes in Stuttgart and Zurich. He specializes in work with couples and families and in interpretive research methods. His research and publications cover such areas as analytical psychology and contemporary sciences, couples counselling, postmodern identity construction, narrative research, and media psychology.

Roderick Main

Ph.D., is a professor in the Department of Psychosocial and Psychoanalytic Studies at the University of Essex, UK, where he is also Director of the Centre for Myth Studies. He is the author of *The Rupture of Time: Synchronicity and Jung's Critique of Modern Western Culture* (Brunner-Routledge, 2004) and *Revelations of Chance: Synchronicity as Spiritual Experience* (SUNY, 2007), editor of *Jung on Synchronicity and the Paranormal* (Routledge/Princeton, 1997), and co-editor of *Myth, Literature, and the Unconscious* (Karnac, 2013).

Ilona Błocian

is an accociate professor in the Faculty of Philosophy in University of Wrocław, Section of Philosophical Anthropology, Poland. Her interests are: philosophy of psychoanalysis, history of the unconscious conceptions, philosophy of myth, anthropology and psychology of religion, philosophy and anthropology of image. Subjects of publications: Jung's conceptions of the unconscious, definitions of the archetype notion, Freud's and Jung's conceptions of evil, mythopoetic function of the unconscious, psychoanalysis and myth, relation between myth and philosophy, basic images in Jungian and French philosophical anthropology. She is the author of *Psychoanalytical Interpretations of Myth. Freud, Jung, Fromm,* co-ed. *Myth Studies. The Contemporary Presence of Myth; Myth Studies. Philosophical and Sociological Aspects of Myth.* Minor: *Jung's Conception of Myth. The Schellingian Influence.*

Megumi Yama

Ph.D., is a professor in the faculty of Humanities at Kyoto Gakuen University in Japan, where she teaches clinical psychology and depth psychology. She also engages in clinical work as a psychotherapist, mainly based on Jungian thought. She was educated in clinical psychology at Kyoto University under Professor Hayao Kawai. Her interest is in images and words; what is taking place in the invisible silence, seemingly "nothingness." She deals with the theme byexploring clinical materials, formative art, myth, literature and Japanese culture.

Her recent interest is focused on Haruki Murakami's process of creative work. She has written many articles and books including translations both in English and Japanese.

Norifumi Kishimoto
is the head of the Department of Palliative Medicine at the Takatsuki Red Cross Hospital, Osaka, Japan. He is an internist specialized in palliative medicine and psychotherapy. He is one of the founders of the Japan Association of Jungian Psychology. He published several books: *Cancer and Psychotherapy*(1999), *Palliative Mind* (2004), *Palliative Care from the Perspective of Narratology*(2015), all in Japanese. He also translated Jungian books into Japanese: *Christopher's Dream* (Robert Bosnak), *Anatomy of Psyche* (Edward Edinger), *and Awakening Woman* (Nancy Qualls-Corbett and Leila McMackin).

Michael Escamilla
is a professor of psychiatry and director of the Center of Excellence in Neuroscience at the Paul L. Foster School of Medicine, Texas Tech University Health Sciences Center, in El Paso Texas. He is an internationally renowned psychiatric researcher in the area of genetics of schizophrenia and bipolar disorder. He is also a Jungian analyst, recently graduated from the Jung Institute in Zurich. His current scholarship is focussed on neurosciences and how these relate to both genetics and Jungian depth psychology.

Andrew Kuzmicki
Ph.D., an editor of Polish Online Journal of Analytical Psychology (JungPoland.org), a psychotherapist and a member of IAJS. His interests are: the mind-body problem, human development seen from the perspective of the psychoanalytical theory of C.G. Jung with his concept of an individuation, but also seen from the perspective of the wider filed of the consciousness studies. Some of the subjects of his publications were: Jung's concept of the Self, the collective unconsciousness, archetypes and the concept of individuation with its archetypal dimension. He published several books: "The Symbolism of the Self in the Theory of C.G. Jung" ("Symbolika Jaźni C.G. Junga" [Polish], 2008), "Psychology and Philosophy of C.G. Jung" ("Psychologia i filozofia C.G. Junga" [Polish], 2013), "Individuation – Literature – Culture" ("Indywiduacja – literatura – kultura" [Polish], 2013).

Jolanta Kowal
Ph.D., in economic sciences, Jungian analyst, assistant professor in the Institute of Psychology of Wrocław University, Poland. She is a member of

scientific associations: AIS, PLAIS (President), Polish Statistical Association, International Association for Analytical Psychology, and Polish Association for Analytical Psychology (President). Her research interests include analytical psychology, cross-cultural research and its implementation in organization and management, information systems, research methodology, psychology of management. Jolanta published papers in Jung Journal: Culture & Psyche, The Electronic Journal of Information Systems in Developing Countries, Journal of Business and Economic Management, Journal of Global Information Technology Management, Lecture Notes in Business Information Processing, and in a numerous conference proceedings including AMCIS, HICSS, ICTM, EMCIS, INDIN, and ECMLG. Jolanta acted as the conference and track co-chair in AMCIS, ICTM, INDIN, and ECMLG. She is member of editorial boards of the Economy-Market-Education (GRE) journal and Polish Journal of Applied Psychology (PJAP), and associated research editor of Cambridge Scholars Publishing. Jolanta has reviewed for ITD, EJISDC, JBEM, JGTIM, Telematics and Informatics, and LNBIP.

Zbigniew Bitka

is a of the "Wandering towards the end of suffering. Archetypal and symbolic themes in the prose of Jerzy Krzysztoń" (STUDIES AND MONOGRAPHIES No. 304), Opole 2001; and co-author of books in Theatre studies: "People and Puppets" Opole 2007 and "The Elements of Theatre" Opole 2017. Associate Professor at the Institute of Polish and Cultural Studies at Opole University. Member of the Polish Association for Analytical Psychology.

Research interests: modern historic prose analysed through archetypal criticism, hermeneutics and psychoanalysis. Literary Director of the Puppet and Actor Theatre in Opole, author of theatrical screenplays.

Introduction

Ilona Błocian and Andrew Kuzmicki

The theory of C.G. Jung is a multidimensional form of thought and it can provoke many different evaluations from various points of view: sometimes it is read and re-read in a kind of apology, sometimes in a refutation of some of his theses. Researchers notice his erudition, his philosophical knowledge and consciousness of the philosophical base and consequences of his own conception; they usually also indicate his influences upon the modern mind, therapists, and patients. Hereby P. Bishop mentioned that Jung "is one of the most influential figures in twentieth-century intellectual thought."[1]

M.L. von Franz notes that Jung's theory concerns the whole of man, and goes beyond the border of psychology, reflecting its influences and echoes in the very wide-ranging domains of science and philosophy.[2] This theory does not have an established place in the history of ideas; there is ambivalence in the trials to recognize it. Some of its aspects are certainly evaluated as rather philosophical and not purely scientific; Jung had declared that his concepts had only an auxiliary role to play and it had not been his aim to find some ordered system of thought.[3] He considered a direct primeval experience as focusing his own attention and research efforts. Jung expressed these kinds of statements prolifically underlining his phenomenological attitude;[4] however, it also induced the question about the degree to which he was attached to its consequences and whether it was specifically connected with some metaphysical core of his thought. His theory can rather be considered as a specific compound of wide philosophical perspectives and references to speculative philosophical structures of thoughts,[5] ideas inherited from scientific evolutionary theories and a dialogue with contemporaneously developing psychological debates of his time.

1 P. Bishop, *The Dionysian Self: C.G. Jung's Reception of Friedrich Nietzsche*, Monographien und Texte zur Nietzsche-Forschung, Bd. 30 (Berlin; New York: W. de Gruyter, 1995), 1.

2 M.L. von Franz, *C.G. Jung: son mythe en notre temps* (Paris: Buchet/Chastel, 1988), 15.

3 Ibid. 21; About problems rising in practical use of theory also in ibid., v. x, 1070–1071.

4 R. Brooke, *Jung and Phenomenology* (London, New York: Routledge, 1991).

5 Jung had himself indicated a philosophical heritage of the unconscious conception: in thought of G. Leibniz, C.G. Carus, A. Schopenhauer and E. von Hartmann. Among the others R. Noll underlined Romantic Naturphilosophie as playing the most important role in Jung's thought sources (R. Noll, *The Jung Cult: Origins of a Charismatic Movement* [Princeton, N.J: Princeton University Press, 1994]). It is very well presented in H.F. Ellenberger, *The Discovery of the Unconscious. The History and Evolution of Dynamic Psychiatry* (London, 1994).

 | DOI:10.1163/9789004336636_002

Jung made multiform trials to understand direct experiences of the psyche, including numinous ones that he undertook with phenomenological sensitivity for inner experiences and their structures. R.D. Romanyshyn observes Jung as freeing psychology "from the unacknowledged remnants of its Cartesian heritage" and, in his conception, "latent phenomenological significance."[6]

Jung's theory has many different aspects concerning its structural layers and sources of his thought: (1) The philosophical speculative kernel going far beyond the limits of science; it is connected with German idealism[7] and Romantic philosophy including the basis of the "idea of the unconscious" as an unknown sphere and order of reality that he develops more than any other psychoanalyst; (2) The psychological basis: the observations of human behaviour in some boundary situations: neurosis, psychosis, mental disturbances, creative processes, dreams etc. The theory of the unconscious enables the connection of these phenomena and renders them comprehensible;[8] and (3) The anthropological perspective and evolutionary grasp of the cumulative character of changes in the human body and psyche. There is also evidence of an influence of a socio-anthropological conception of the collective imagination and its representations upon his thinking.

There are also the others' grasps of multiplicity in Jung's theory (R. Noll); it is some "combination of six separate but interconnected theories": (1) the theory of the complex, (2) psychological types, (3) vitalism of the phylogenetic unconscious (revised), (4) the collective unconscious, (5) archetypes of the collective unconscious, and (6) the individuation theories.[9] It is paramount to understand that interconnection introduces some difficulties and – sometimes – an antithetical tension. Brooke observes that even secondary sources in analytical psychology fall "into the same epistemological eclecticism and difficulties as Jung himself."[10] There is also another interpretation of such a tension between sources and dimensions of his theory: Jung was an empiricist; however, his basic assumptions were metaphysical.[11]

---

6 R.D. Romanyshyn, "Foreword", in *Jung and Phenomenology*, ed. R. Brooke (London; New York: Routledge, 1991), XV–XVI. R. Brooke added: Jung "established his own position in the name of phenomenology"; "understanding Jung as a phenomenologist is central to understanding Jung."

7 Bishop, *The Dionysian Self*, 10.

8 L.L. Whyte, *The Unconscious Before Freud* (London, 1960); Ellenberger, *The Discovery of the Unconscious. The History and Evolution of Dynamic Psychiatry*; B. Dobroczyński, *Ciemna strona psychiki: geneza i historia idei nieświadomości*, 3rd ed. (Kraków: Wydawnictwo Uniwersytetu Jagiellońskiego, 2001).

9 Noll, *The Jung Cult: Origins of a Charismatic Movement*, 9.

10 Brooke, *Jung and Phenomenology*, XVII.

11 R.C. Smith, "Empirical Science and Value Assumptions: Lessons from C.G. Jung", *Journal of Religion and Health* 16, no. 2 (1977): 102–09.

The notion of the "unconscious" was used by psychologists (W. Wundt in the early phase of his thought development, P. Janet [*les idées fixes subconscientes*], A. Binet); the observation of some different mental states leads to the question about the connections between them, and opens a perspective of one basic sphere of the psyche that manifests through them. Jung merged the speculative philosophical thesis about the existence of the unconscious and the observations of certain classes of human behaviour: dreams, creativity/creative processes, mental disturbances. The idea of a connection caused many difficulties and accusations of the whole psychoanalytic movement for the speculations leading far beyond empirical data and founding a "new mythology" (L. Wittgenstein[12]). It is therefore possible to put a question about "the censure of the speculative" (S. Shamdasani[13]) and there appears a problem – how speculative a psychological theory can be. That aspect of psychoanalysis also influenced many trials to associate it with the empirical contents of other theories. Its internal multiplicity of views and interpretations, and its inherent state of immanent "dissociation" has provoked debates.[14] It seems, however, from the point of view of the history of ideas, that Jung's theory was a trail to connect many separate elements. It can be understood not only as a form of psychological theory but also as a kind of philosophy with its conception of man; his ideas about cognition, nature, mind and matter; and his contribution to the context of discovery in science and the philosophy of science.[15]

There is also a separate question about Jung's position in the domain of activity of his ideas in contemporary philosophy and science regarding the problem of the division of sciences. From a monistic point of view in the philosophy of science many of his ideas can be regarded as rooted in an observation basis and connected with observation notions but a lot of them can also be considered as speculative, leading beyond empirical data. From dualistic point of view in the philosophy of science Jung created a specific form of hermeneutic perspective and tried to connect it with Darwinian and psychological aspects of his thought.

---

12 L. Wittgenstein, *Lectures and Conversations on Aesthetics, Psychology, and Religious Belief* (Oxford, 1970).

13 S. Shamdasani, "Introduction. The Censure of the Speculative", in *Speculations after Freud: Psychoanalysis, Philosophy, and Culture*, ed. S. Shamdasani and M. Münchow (London, New York: Routledge, 1994).

14 "Contemporary psychoanalysis is in a state of dissociationdue to the multiple claims upon its identity" ibid., XI.

15 A. Motycka, *Nauka a nieświadomość: filozofia nauki wobec kontekstu tworzenia* (Wrocław: Leopoldinum, 1998); W. Detel, "Nauka", in *Filozofia: podstawowe pytania*, ed. E. Martens and H. Schnädelbach (Warsaw: Wiedza Powszechna, 1995).

In various fields of contemporary studies or research – including psychology, anthropology, philosophy, sociology etc. – ongoing discussions regarding the validity and value of C.G. Jung's theory of the human psyche and its relationship to the world are slowly gaining momentum. At the same time this theory is among the most quoted and commented on among contemporary psychological theories. Jungian concepts and assumptions are used today in many areas where the scientists and thinkers seek to build bridges between psychology and other areas of our knowledge.

A paradox, however, remains that, despite such clear resonance with disciplines engaged in reflection on consciousness and the environment, this approach seems not to be fully employed by contemporary academic society. Very often Jungian theory is treated rather as solely of historical interest and not as a theory worthy of further development.

To address this problem, we wish to propose in this book a collection of papers that can fill this explicit gap. The papers presented below aim to give the reader some insights or reflections which will articulate and discuss the key Jungian concepts and findings that seem to have stood the test of time and have been proven valuable from the point of view of contemporary knowledge, including the scientific discourse.

Thus the proposed book is directed not only to Jungian scholars, and Jungian analysts, psychologists and psychiatrists, but also to the other people fascinated by the insights of C.G. Jung – for students, thinkers, and researchers representing other general areas: philosophy, anthropology, sociology, cultural studies, political science, biology, medicine etc. A major task of the book will be to outline the contemporary – direct or indirect – usefulness and applicability of Jung's ideas at the beginning of the twenty-first century while simultaneously making a critical review of this theory.

We would like to invite the reader of our book to add us to those who use Jung's concepts in their theoretical studies or practice in various areas and disciplines. The well-known application of these concepts in psychotherapy, philosophical anthropology, the study of symbolic life, or in conjunction with theoretical physics have been frequently discussed; however, we also realize that there is still room for further studies. We hope, then, that there is still an entire range of other disciplines that could be integrated into an interdisciplinary approach towards Jungian conception and we would like to add our efforts from this book to this multidisciplinary or multilingual discourse.

The book is a volume of the collected works of sixteen different authors. They reflect the contemporary meaning of C.G. Jung's theory on many fields of scientific activity and in a different cultural context: Japanese (M. Yama, N. Kishimoto), South American (M. Gomes de Freitas), and North American

(J. Cambray), as well as European: English (R. Segal, R. Main), Italian (A. De Coro), and Polish (A. Olejarczyk, E. Kwiatkowska, et al.). The authors consider a specific milieu of Jung's theory and his influence or possible dialogue with contemporary ideas and scientific activity. His ideas are interpreted in his possible dialogue with cognitive and evolutionary psychology (psychology of the mind), with religious studies and the question of the scientific character of his works, with sociology and social philosophy, and with the question of his theoretical tools for modern humanistic interpretation of art works or literary texts.

The order of the papers in the book reflects a logical order of the following issues: paradigms, the relation between the notion of archetype and image, psychological and sociological aspects of Jung's theory, his theory of the mind, the application of his conceptual tools to understand phenomena of literature, and in the question of effectiveness of his psychotherapy in empirical studies.

Jung's theory, and his relations with Freud are thus confronted with a question of a philosophical basis of given psychological constructs (M. Gomes de Freitas); with Cartesian and Pascalian philosophies or the Romantic attitude toward knowledge and science of A. von Humboldt (J. Cambray); Heideggerian ideas of *Verwindung* (M. Kostyszak); with ideas of E. Durkheim, M. Mauss, and H. Hubert (R. Main); with H. Marcuse, H. Arendt or E. Fromm's critique of contemporary status of the individual (I. Błocian); modern semiotics of U. Eco (A. Olejarczyk) or – inter alia – W. Bucci's model of mind (A. De Coro).

The book is addressed to scholars, students and people interested in the relation between the theory of Jung and contemporary sciences and humanities. It contains studies concerning social sciences, humanities studies and psychology (empirical studies); it is a proposal for psychologists, psychiatrists, philosophers, sociologists, and researchers in religious or literary studies.

The volume has international character – 16 authors come from 7 different countries: the USA, the UK, Brazil, Poland, Italy, Japan and Germany. Their texts confront the theory of Jung with contemporary science but also their socio-cultural environment. It is especially very clear in the texts of Japanese authors – one of them even compares the attitude toward "ego" in Japanese and Western cultures.

Jung's theory was and still is very popular; however, there are not many studies confronting it with contemporary science and, putting the question in a manner by which we can understand Jung nowadays, how can we read his hypothesis, statements, and constructs now? There is a need to understand the contemporary world and science with Jung's theory with its multidimensional aspects of psychology, social philosophy, conception of myth, art, psychotherapy etc.

There are several focuses in the whole theoretical perspective of the book. The first part of the book is devoted to confronting the problem of the philosophical and scientific character of Jung's thought. It contains the texts of M. Gomes de Freitas, J. Cambray, M. Kostyszak and R. Segal. The authors consider a Pascalian perspective of Jung's psychology in confrontation with a Cartesian one, which is followed by S. Freud. The most important aspects of these analyses are a possibility to grasp a philosophical basis of psychological theories. Pascal's perspective is more interesting from a contemporary philosophy point of view: it is a non-essentialist way of thought, and does not deny the meaning of doubts and hesitations; it is more open for the importance of empirical data and a pragmatic dimension of knowledge. One can also find these features of thought in Jung's theory in opposition to Freud's research of a perfectly certain foundation of cognition connected with arbitrary rejections of doubts. The text of J. Cambray has presented some new aspects of grasp of science in the example of A. von Humboldt. Cambray has argued that it is a stereotypical idea of Romanticism antiscientific attitude or mysticism only. Jung is a successor of that kind of philosophy researching nature and understanding the complexity and mutual dependence between mind and nature.

Thus, the conclusions from analyses and interpretations of M. Gomes de Freitas and J. Cambray overlap to some extent, because they present the dimensions of Jung's thinking, which allow him to combine observational data, to grasp real human experience, and simultaneously, to confront it with psychological knowledge in constructing his own theory. This is also the context of Jung's declarations of an empirical attitude.

M. Kostyszak has compared Jung's idea of development – understood as an "overgrowing" of the problem – with the Heideggerian category of *Verwindung* pointing at European "one-sidedness" and treating rationality as the most perfect way of cognition; however, it also has its limits and practical disadvantages such as excesses of voluntarism. Both researchers share a critical attitude towards unilateral rationality. The authors continue to discuss a broader understanding of science and rationality, emphasized by M. Gomes de Freitas, J. Cambray and M. Kostyszak. R. Segal's text remains contrasting in conclusion to these voices and polemic to Jung's theory's scientific status.

R. Segal presents his own perspective of understanding Jung's theory. He argues that it cannot be considered as scientific in the domain of religious studies because it is overwhelming: an archetype can be found for any given character or thing in any myth; his analyses are made *ex post facto*.

In these three papers, the authors try to understand science in a specific meaning; they observe the changes in the scientific paradigms; they evaluate Jung's theory as a successor of non-dogmatic, non-essentialist, pragmatic and an open-for-psychological-phenomenology grasp of science; however, R. Segal considers it as rather non-scientific in the classic perspective of the scientific order of explaining phenomena. His criticism of Jung's conception of science goes in the directions that K. Popper established for the whole of psychoanalysis – the statements in this theory were formulated on an overly generalized level, and it seems that there are no phenomena that it would not attempt to explain.

The next papers are of the three authoresses: A. Olejarczyk, E. Kwiatkowska and A. De Coro. They try to understand the problem of the archetype-image relation; however, they research the problem from different scientific perspectives: modern semiotics, theory of discourse (A. Olejarczyk), culture studies, cultural anthropology and iconic turn (E. Kwiatkowska) and a relation between psychoanalysis and cognitive psychology, cognitive sciences (A. De Coro). The authoress of the first paper deals with philosophical roots, the Platonic and Neo-Platonic layer of Jung's notion of archetype and its cultural activity in the collective memory and common imagination. An archetype of the hero and a cultural process of heroisation are considered as examples for the collective activity of the unconscious. The main question in the second paper is an application of "psychoanalytical thinking" in cultural studies and in new images studies, in the context of Warburg, Benjamin or Boehm works. The interesting perspective from that point of view is an iconic interpretation of the unconscious as an anthropological basis with some specific features: mnestic aspects of images, their energy and relation between images and symptoms (image as a symptom).

A. Olejarczyk and E. Kwiatkowska try to show the applicability and usefulness of Jung's image-archetype theory of unconsciousness to studies of the phenomena of culture. Alessandra De Coro compares the Jungian theory of image with W. Bucci's studies' links between verbal and sensory representations and Multiple Code Theory with an underlining of emotional informational processes. Both authors emphasize the aspects of psychic activity related to the emotional sphere and the activity of memory. These phenomena also draw the attention of Jung. They seem to be pivotal for individual and social life and they are also researched by modern scientists (G. Boehm, W. Bucci).

The next four papers concern social aspects of Jung's conception.

This is a transition to the issues of relation between Jung's theory and the social phenomena of the modern world and to their sociological research and reflections in the history of social thought. The problems are researched not in terms of images and archetypes that are active in cultural phenomena as in the texts of E. Kwiatkowska and A. Olejarczyk but in social phenomena such as mass processes, totalitarianism and authoritarianism. The authors also present different ways of understanding the basic dimensions of social human existence in different cultures. Jung himself gave such comparisons. The bases of his many texts are devoted to the cultures and religions of the Orient.

Articles of I. Błocian and R. Main formulate a question of a connection between Jung's conception and social philosophy (Fromm, Marcuse, Arendt) or sociology (Durkheim, Weber). M. Yama and N. Kishimoto realize the importance of the transcultural application of Jung's conception in its most basic structures as the different attitudes towards human ego or self in Western and Eastern cultural circles. The collective character of an archetype and unconscious notions and a question of their social aspect are considered in the first article. Jung had analyzed social problems of modern and contemporary Western societies in the perspective of his own conception of evil; many of his analyses are social critiques of "mass society", "mass man", "absolute/totalitarian state" and a "logic of great numbers" accusing them of losing of individual value. His critique resonates with the Marcusean "one-dimensional man" or the mercantile personality of Fromm, forming a psychological type of defense of the individual. R. Main underlines the social character of many problems that had focused the attention of Jung: health, education, religion, nationality. He observes that Jung's psychology is evaluated as based on social perspective (Durkheim's, Weber's type). There are reasons to understand Jung's thought as interesting for sociology, for example, in contemporary analyses of relation between fundamentalism and projection mechanism.

M. Yama considers the contemporary meaning of division between "West" and "East" in Jung's "dialogue with the Orient"; globalization and the Internet can make this division doubtful but they act on a very superficial level. In the Japanese psyche, a dual process of life was formed: the modern, "Western ego" and traditional way of life; it requires new ways of psychotherapy that the author presents in the example of a thirty-year-old patient and his psychotherapeutic experience. N. Kishimoto considers many different ideas of grammatical differences in languages (A. von Humboldt, E. Sapir, B. Lee Whorf, Deutscher). He also mentions here the Whorfian thesis from cognitive psychology, that the mother language pays attention to certain aspects of the world, forming "habits of mind", memory, perception, associations, etc. Kishimoto refers to Jung's concept of ego but also to his own clinical practice.

Jung's theory was embedded in observation, psychotherapy, and psychological and psychiatric research. They were the initial sphere of his analysis of social or historical-cultural issues. This axis of his theory concerns articles by A. Kuzmicki and M. Escamilla. The first author focuses on Jung's notion of consciousness; the second – on mental on mental disorders and the way of understanding schizophrenia. A. Kuzmicki considers consciousness and its role in the functioning of the mind. He formulates a lot of questions about the genesis of consciousness and its connection with the neuro-physiological level of the organism; psychoanalysis grasps the phenomenon of being conscious with a hidden level of biological drives and unconscious processes manifested in involuntary, automatic behaviour. The author points out the research of B. Bridgeman, research on quick reactions in sport and mental cognitive skills of the pygmy chimpanzees. He complements Jung's theory of mind with A. Damasio's concept of the "proto-self." M. Escamilla examines the early period of Jung's work (1900–1912), and his cooperation with psychiatrist E. Bleuler in Burghölzli Hospital in order to indicate the importance of their experiences with schizophrenia and the Word Associations Test. Escamilla compares Jung's and Bleuler's view upon that disease with current theories and research findings.

A lot of Jung's work is devoted to the interpretation of specific phenomena of culture, works of art and literature. This is a perspective corresponding to the grasps of E. Kwiatkowska and A. Olejarczyk. Z. Bitka underlines the archetypal and mythological levels of the artist's imagination. He leads hermeneutic reflection on the archetypal contents in L. Terlecki's historical novel, *Cierń i laur* (*A Thorn and a Laurel*). The novel contains historical, mythical and psychoanalytical contexts. It has a specific "casket composition", which results in an ambiguous weave of chthonic symbols.

The last two papers reflect an intention of verifying Jung's theory through examining its practical applications and operational usefulness in scientifically oriented research. The papers concern objectifications and empirical investigations of Jung's theory.

Ch. Roestler gives a lot of examples of empirical research examining the effectiveness of Jungian psychotherapy. He refers here to the research that was undertaken in Zurich, Berlin and San Francisco. As he underlines in his paper, the effectiveness of Jungian psychotherapy has been proved on many levels: reduction of symptoms, positive changes of the patients' personality structure and desired changes in their everyday conduct.

J. Kowal shows how to effectively apply the methods of statistics in the area of qualitative Jungian research. She also gives the reader the possibility to verify the methodological efficiency of her approach, providing a very detailed description of the research she conducted using this methodology.

We believe that all papers gathered in this book reflect the polyvalence of Jung's theory from a contemporary perspective and can help the reader to identify the influences of his theory in many different areas: psychology, philosophy, sociology, psychotherapy etc.

Hereby it can be recognized how Jung's thought can be re-read nowadays.

References

Bishop, P. *The Dionysian Self: C.G. Jung's Reception of Friedrich Nietzsche*. Monographien und Texte zur Nietzsche Forschung, Bd. 30. Berlin ; New York: W. de Gruyter, 1995.

Brooke, R. *Jung and Phenomenology*. London, New York: Routledge, 1991.

Detel, W. "Nauka." In *Filozofia: podstawowe pytania*, edited by E. Martens and H. Schnädelbach. Warsaw: Wiedza Powszechna, 1995.

Dobroczyński, B. *Ciemna strona psychiki: geneza i historia idei nieświadomości*. 3rd ed. Kraków: Wydawnictwo Uniwersytetu Jagiellońskiego, 2001.

Ellenberger, H.F. *The Discovery of the Unconscious. The History and Evolution of Dynamic Psychiatry*. London, 1994.

Motycka, A. *Nauka a nieświadomość: filozofia nauki wobec kontekstu tworzenia*. Wrocław: Leopoldinum, 1998.

Noll, R. *The Jung Cult: Origins of a Charismatic Movement*. Princeton, N.J: Princeton University Press, 1994.

Romanyshyn, R.D. "Foreword." In *Jung and Phenomenology*, edited by R. Brooke. London ; New York: Routledge, 1991.

Shamdasani, S. "Introduction. The Censure of the Speculative." In *Speculations after Freud: Psychoanalysis, Philosophy, and Culture*, edited by S. Shamdasani and M. Münchow. London, New York: Routledge, 1994.

Smith, R.C. "Empirical Science and Value Assumptions: Lessons from C.G. Jung." Journal of Religion and Health 16, no. 2 (1977): 102–09.

Von Franz, M.L. *C.G. Jung: son mythe en notre temps*. Paris: Buchet/Chastel, 1988.

Whyte, L.L. *The Unconscious Before Freud*. London, 1960.

Wittgenstein, L. *Lectures and Conversations on Aesthetics, Psychology, and Religious Belief*. Oxford, 1970.

CHAPTER 1

Jung in the Academy and Beyond: The Fordham Lectures – 100 Years Later

Joseph Cambray

Abstract

C.G. Jung was one of the pioneers of depth psychology, initially working in close collaboration with Sigmund Freud. In 1912 he delivered nine lectures at Fordham University on the "Theory of Psychoanalysis." These lectures came at the high water mark of Jung's first period of academic life and are closely linked with the early rise of psychoanalysis; in particular they represent Jung's differentiation from Freud. Soon after he was to resign his position at the University of Zurich (in 1914) and not fully resume academic work until 1933. In between these periods Jung underwent the inner experiences that led to his production of *The Red Book*. Both of Jung's academic periods are marked by what he identified as a scientific approach. However, examination and comparison of these periods reveal a shift in emphasis on what constitutes science for Jung. In this chapter we will look in detail at this shift and how the experiences leading to *The Red Book* were integral to this change. The importance of the scientific tradition associated with the German Romantic movement is key to understanding this transition, though it came without much formal acknowledgement by Jung. Finally we will explore the resurgence of interest in and re-valuation of this same tradition in some branches of contemporary science, especially epigenetics. Thus Jung's work will be contextualized within a trajectory of this alternative, romantic expression of science which is regaining a place in the modern academy.

Keywords

German Romanticism – Jung – Freud – Psychoanalysis – inner experience – scientific approaches – history of science

 | DOI:10.1163/9789004336636_003

1 Introduction

In March 1912 C.G. Jung received an invitation from the American physician Smith Ely Jelliffe (1866–1945), a medical editor and pioneer American psychoanalyst who was a clinical professor at Fordham Medical College. The offer was to present a series of lectures for the International Extension Course in Medicine in September 1912 along with a number of other medical experts from around the world. At this date Jung and Freud were still on friendly terms, though this was to be a year of significant difficulties between the two, and barely a year and half before their termination of relations. By the end of April 1912 Jung had sent off part two of *Wandlungen und Symbole der Libido* (later translated as *The Psychology of the Unconscious*) to his publisher without first getting Freud's input. Then in May Freud visited the ailing Binswanger in Kreuzlingen without contacting Jung, for which he felt snubbed – the so-called "Kreuzlingen gesture" – a symptom of the growing alienation between the two men. In September Jung gave nine lectures at the medical school of Fordham University under the title "The Theory of Psychoanalysis." A number of points differentiating himself from Freud were made in these lectures, especially Jung's views on the libido theory. Jung's nine lectures were published initially in the inaugural volumes of the *Psychoanalytic Review* (in the first five issues of Volumes 1 and 2, from 1913 to 1915) co-edited by Jelliffe and William Alanson White who had also been an instructor in the same course.

The invitation to Jung was based on his scientific contributions; especially to the emerging field of psychoanalysis, in particular the word association experiments and his studies on "dementia praecox." While he was in transit to Fordham University an honorary doctorate of law was conferred on Jung (on September 11 by Fordham University) – his second, as he had received his first honorary doctorate from Clark University in 1909; the American scientific and medical communities clearly valued his research efforts. Soon after arrival (September 18th) he was interviewed by the New York Times and a long article was published in the magazine section on Sunday, September 29, including a photo-portrait. The text was reprinted in *C.G. Jung Speaking*.[1] For the 37 year old Jung this must have seemed a new height of success.

The audience of his lectures consisted of eighty-eight psychiatrists and neurologists, American physicians who were especially interested in learning about his clinical approach and analytic techniques. In addition to these lectures Jung also held a number of individual consultations, small discussion

1 C.G. Jung, *C.G. Jung Speaking: Interviews and Encounters*, ed. W. McGuire and R.F.C. Hull (Princeton, N.J: Princeton University Press, 1977), 11–24.

groups and larger clinical demonstrations. He also lectured at Bellevue Hospital, the New York Psychiatric Institute and gave a presentation to the New York Academy of Medicine, all within the space of a ten day stay in New York, a whirlwind tour.[2]

I will not go through the content of Jung's lectures as other contributors to this volume will be exploring them. The full text can be found in volume four of his *Collected Works*, recently released as a paperback monograph in the Philemon Series with a valuable introduction by Sonu Shamdasani. My focus instead will be on the type of scientific writing Jung was involved with here, and going forward for the remainder of his career in the context of various traditions of science writing available. As Jung's biographer Deirdre Bair rightly notes about these lectures:

> The nine lectures employ the same writing pattern and exhibit the same scientific precision as the writings on word association and dementia praecox that established his international reputation. They are more "Freudian" than "Jungian" in style, for each begins with a thesis, develops it with logical consistency, and ends with a convincing summation. They are classical in the Freudian sense, with none of the Jungian circularity that pervades most of his other writing.[3]

However, the "circularity" Bair refers to, could more accurately be read as "non-linear" and reflect an aspect of Jung's new approach which needs to be reappraised.

The Fordham lectures should be seen as the acme of Jung's writing style based on the idea of scientific objectivity that held sway in the intellectual culture of the time. However, the foundations of the certainty (in the world, and in Jung himself) that still prevailed in 1912 had already begun to crack and crumble: quantum theory and relativity were emerging to reshape scientific thought, though they were still nascent; the first theory of continental drift in earth sciences was proposed by Alfred Wegner but was ridiculed; technologically, the grandiose and iconic Titanic sinks (on April 15) while *The White Star Line* claimed it was "designed to be unsinkable"; the world order itself was also about to be severely challenged, as in less than two years the outbreak of "The Great War" (WWI) would alter the fate of nations.

2 D. Bair, *Jung: A Biography* (Boston: Little, Brown and Co, 2003), 229–30.

3 Ibid., 230.

2 The First Phase of Scientific Writing in Jung's Career

As I written elsewhere the 19 year old Jung had two similar dreams which he felt were crucial in deciding on a career in the sciences.[4] These dreams are recorded in *Memories, Dreams, and Reflections* (MDR). In both he enters a woods and makes a remarkable discovery: in the first the bones of prehistoric animals, in the second "a circular pool with the strangest and most wonderful creature, a *round animal, shimmering in opalescent hues … It was a giant radiolarian …* [which] aroused in me an intense desire for knowledge, so that I awoke with a beating heart."

Jung goes on to say: "These two dreams decided me overwhelmingly in favor of *science*, and removed all my doubts."[5] The lure of archeology, paleontology, zoology and biology is evident in his framing of the dreams. As a young man he was reading these fields as potential career choices rather than as explicit metaphors for exploration of psychological depth; later they would become significant expressions for archaic and core aspects of the psyche. For the 19 year old Jung the visionary inner world and the scientific were already intertwined and mutually interacting.

Soon after the dreams Jung entered the medical school of Basel University, in April 1895. He quickly joined the Basel section of the Swiss student fraternity, Zofingiaverein, and gave his very first lecture to this group in November 1896; it was entitled "The Border Zones of Exact Science."[6] Jung's eclectic tendencies were already in evidence in this first lecture as he ranges over topics in physics (gravitation, ether, conservation of energy, the newly discovered X-rays), chemistry (atomic and molecular theory), biology (Darwinism, mechanistic versus vitalistic theories, origin of life) and even a dash of psychology by the end (the entry of hypnotism into German science). His final plea is "to allow the immaterial to retain its immaterial properties."[7] The scientific content is of student quality, many of the exciting developments of the previous several decades are not included, yet his intuitions are strong, he is searching for important questions and revealing the limits of the science he has been taught.

Upon completion of his medical studies, Jung secured a position at the University Psychiatric Hospital and Clinic of Zürich, the Burghölzli Hospital,

4 J. Cambray, "Jung, Science, and His Legacy", *International Journal of Jungian Studies* 3, no. 2 (2011): 110–24.

5 C.G. Jung, *Memories, Dreams, Reflections* (New York: Pantheon Books, 1961), 85.

6 C.G. Jung, "The Border Zone of Exact Science", in *The Zofingia Lectures,* ed. W. McGuire, The Collected Works of C.G. Jung: Supplementary Volume A (Princeton, NJ: Princeton University Press, 1983).

7 Ibid., 19.

under its director, Dr. Med. Eugen Bleuler at the end of 1900. The hospital at this time was focused on humane patient care, likely the first milieu model in-patient psychiatric facility in the world. In contradistinction to Emil Kraeplin's strictly biological view of "dementia praecox", Bleuler held to a view combining biological and hermeneutic elements in the etiology of these conditions – at the time the only major European psychiatrist to do so.[8] By 1908 Bleuler coined the term schizophrenia and then proceeded to expand Kraeplin's dementia praecox into a class of illnesses, the "group of schizophrenias."[9] The Burghölzli under Bleuler is of course where Jung conducted the research that won him international acclaim.

In 1905 Jung qualified as a lecturer (*Privatdozent*) in psychiatry at the University of Zürich. As an instructor he injected lively cultural and historical dimensions into his material and developed a large following. His research interests predominated and students came to observe and some to study at the Burghölzli from around the world, including many of those who would go on to become prominent psychoanalysts (Karl Abraham, Ludwig Binswanger, Sandor Ferenczi, Ernest Jones, A.A. Brill etc.). In this period Jung was operating within the standard scientific paradigm of the times, with a strong focus on objective observations with precise measurements; the subjective aspects of the research was almost wholly focused on internal dynamics in the mental world of the patients, to be described in clinically objective terms.

Jung retained his university position until April 1914, at which time he voluntarily resigned it. The internal changes behind this decision were already brewing in 1912 but did not openly appear in his Fordham Lectures. Those lectures should be seen as an expression of his dedication to scientific objectivity, written in the idiom prevalent amongst his medical and scientific colleagues. However, in his writing of part two of the *Psychology of the Unconscious*, an alteration in writing style had become evident. Deirdre Bair observes Jung's discomfort with this:

> he said it "embarrassed" him because it went against his grain, referring to all his medical training and previous writings that his peers considered models of scientific objectivity. But he had no choice and was compelled to write it down as he heard it spoken inside himself.[10]

8 P. Hoff, "Private Lecture on the History of the Burghölzli Hospital", 2011.

9 E. Bleuler, "Dementia Praecox or the Group of Schizophrenias", in *Handbuch Der Psychiatrie*, ed. G. Aschaffenburg, trans. J. Zinkin (New York: International Universities Press, 1950). Originally published as *Dementia Praecox Oder Gruppe Der Schizophrenien* (Leipzig, Vienna: Deutike, 1911).

10 Bair, *Jung: A Biography*, 224–25.

Since having access to Jung's *Red Book*, we can now understand this was just the prelude to a much more profound change he was about to undergo based on his internal experiences. Before turning to that transformation, I would like to say a bit more about the state of science in 1912.

3 Science Around 1912: A Selection

The need for a new theory of matter and energy had already been apparent from the turn of the century, starting with Max Planck's work on black body radiation, which showed light was quantized. Attempts, however, to describe the atom remained stymied in classical, mechanistic accounts. In 1897 J.J. Thompson, Lord Kelvin, had shown that the supposed smallest particle of matter, the atom, in fact was comprised of components, when he discovered the electron in his work on cathode rays. He proposed the "plum pudding" model of the atom (negatively charged electrons embedded in a uniform sea of positive material). His former student Ernst Rutherford disproved this model, showing the positively charged portion of the atom was indeed quite small; by 1912 he had advanced the miniature solar system model of the atom. The new image was still wholly classical. However, this same year Rutherford had a young, visiting scientist in his laboratory, Niels Bohr. The next year, 1913, Bohr was to radicalize our views of matter by bringing quantum physics into the vision of the atom. The full articulation of a quantum theory of matter required almost 15 more years of intensive research but in retrospect 1912–1913 can be seen as a major turning point.

Similarly the theory of relativity, the cornerstone of modern cosmology, was not fully articulated at this time. Einstein had proposed the special theory of relativity in 1905 and was working towards the inclusion of gravitation. By 1911–12 Einstein had revived a prediction about the deflection of light rays by massive objects such as the sun and described the curvature of space-time. His calculations were not complete until he was in possession of the full general theory in 1915; the predictions were spectacularly verified by observations made during a solar eclipse in 1919 by Arthur Eddington, making front page news around the world.

In 1911 the Olduvai Gorge in the Great Rift Valley of Tanzania was discovered along with an abundance of fossils, which beginning in 1913 would eventually lead to a much richer view of hominid evolution than was currently held. Franz Boas published *The Mind of Primitive Man* (1911), in which he cogently argues for cultural plurality, showing the interdependence of biological, linguistic, and cultural traits of any people result from their historical developments, which includes environmental as well as cultural forces. Boas here echoes one of his heroes, Alexander von Humboldt, and similarly brings a strong humanistic, anti-racist perspective to cultural anthropology. Boas had of course been at the Clark University festivities in 1909 along with Jung, Freud, William James and a host of others; Shamdasani has devoted several pages to the influence Boas exerted on Jung as well as the limits of this.[11] In 1912 Émile Durkheimpublished *The Elementary Forms of the Religious Life* which further explored religious phenomena from the perspective of sociology, speaking of a collective consciousness and discussed totemism. Jung later drew on two of Durkheim's students, Hubert and Mauss, in discussing his formulation of archetypes acknowledging these two had formulated the idea of "categories of the imagination" from their ethnographic work.[12] Jung's notion of the collective unconscious also seems to have been formed partially in counterpoint to Durkheim's collective consciousness.[13] Jung first used the term in a 1916 lecture "on the unconscious and its contents."[14] In brief, at the time of Jung's Fordham lectures the fundamental, scientific view of the world was undergoing radical transformations and this majorly impacted his own conceptualizations.

The next year was one of personal trauma and exploration for JungAs we now know in some detail, following within a month of his severance of ties with Freud in October 1913, Jung underwent a series of inner experiences that were to make him into the figure we largely know today. With the publication in 2009 of his Red Book, we can now see the evidence of this transformation.

4 The Red Book and a New View of Science

The processes already underway in the writing of part two of the *Psychology of the Unconscious* burst forth in a much more powerful way in October-November 1913. As we know Jung experienced waking visions in which he saw "a terrible flood that covered all of the northern and low-lying lands between the North Sea and the Alps ... yellow waves, swimming ruble, and the death of

11 S. Shamdasani, *Jung and the Making of Modern Psychology* (Cambridge: Cambridge University Press, 2003), 276–78.

12 C.G. Jung, "The Archetypes and the Collective Unconscious", in *The Collected Works*, ed. G. Adler and R.F.C. Hull, vol. 9i (Princeton: Princeton University Press, 1940), § 153.

13 S.F. Greenwood, "Émile Durkheim and C.G. Jung: Structuring a Transpersonal Sociology of Religion", Journal for the Scientific Study of Religion 29, no. 4 (1990): 482–95.

14 D. Tresan, "Collective Unconscious", in *International Dictionary of Psychoanalysis*, ed. A. de Mijolla (New York: Thomson Gale, 2005).

countless thousands"; once it was a sea of blood.[15] Although he feared for his psychological stability, he intentionally entered into and recorded this material along with other fantasies and dreams during the period from November 1913 through April 1914. This came to form the basis for his method of "active imagination", the deliberate engagement with the unconscious through direct exploration of internal image and affect, a forerunner of the contemporary use of analytic reveries in assessing activations in the interactive field.

Realizing the importance of this archaic material for his own psychological development, Jung wrote down the fantasies and dreams along with his reflections. Reworking drafts, elaborating and refining commentaries, he gradually produced a calligraphic volume bound in red leather in the fashion of a medieval, illuminated manuscript, *Liber Novus*.

By the end of April 1914 he had resigned as president of the International Psychoanalytic Association and from his position on the medical faculty of Zürich University. Clearly he was facing a crisis in his life; much of what he had embraced no longer sustained him. Although he had a series of dreams from April into June 1914 that he ultimately found healing, it was not until August 1st 1914 that he felt released from the feeling of being endangered by "an overcompensated psychosis."[16] The onset of World War I gave him the conviction that his experiences were not wholly personal but had an objective dimension to them. However, this placed him on the horns of a seeming impossible dilemma: was this madness or prophecy? His struggle to work through this and other conundrums posed by his internal experience was formative; it is what made Jung "*Jung*." By 1916 he was able to write his essay on "The Transcendent Function" in which he detailed his innovative approach to the unconscious, especially as accessed through active imagination.

In Jung's grappling to fully enter the inner dialogues, emergent phenomena became evident in the deep background of his thought. While descriptions of complex systems were unavailable to Jung, a qualitative appreciation of phenomena of this type could be found in the biological literature of the time that he was reading, as evident in his examples of archetypal analogies from instincts found in nature. The logic of emergence can be readily found in *The Red Book*, e.g., "if you marry the ordered to chaos you produce the divine child, the supreme meaning beyond meaning and meaninglessness."[17] Jung wrestled

15 C.G. Jung, *The Red Book: Liber Novus*, ed. S. Shamdasani, trans. S. Shamdasani, M. Kyburz, and J. Peck (New York: W.W. Norton & Company Inc., 2009), 231.

16 C.G. Jung, *C.G. Jung Analytical Psychology: Notes of the Seminar Given in 1925 by C.G. Jung*, ed. W. McGuire (Princeton: Princeton University Press, 1989), 44.

17 Jung, *The Red Book: Liber Novus*, 235.

to stay poised on this edge of order and chaos as he descended into depths of imagination.

In the epilogue to the *Red Book* Jung writes: "My acquaintance with alchemy in 1930 took me away from it. The beginning of the end came in 1928, when Wilhelm sent me the text of the 'Golden flower,' an alchemical treatise. There the contents of this book found their way into actuality and I could no longer continue working on it."[18] In *MDR* Jung also identifies a deeply meaningful synchronistic occurrence at this moment: his painting of "a mandala with a golden castle in the center" having a curiously Chinese feeling about it, just prior to receipt of this Taoist manuscript from Richard Wilhelm who had translated it while in China.[19] The text eventually was published as *The Secret of the Golden Flower* with a commentary by Jung accompanying Wilhelm's German translation, subsequently translated into English by Cary F. Baynes and found in Jung's *Collected Works*, volume 13.[20] The corresponding castle painting is found on page 163 of the *Red Book*, marking where Jung was in his composition of the Red Book when this definitive event occurred.

As his confrontation with the unconscious drew to a close, the confrontation with the world began. Shamdasani comments, "In retrospect he described the *Red Book* as an attempt to formulate things in terms of revelation. He had hope that this would free him, but found that it didn't. He then realized that he had to return to the human side and to science. He had to draw conclusions from the insights."[21]

The timing of Jung's original formulation of the concept of synchronicity is highly significant here. The term first emerged in Jung's dream seminars in 1928 (i.e., near the time he received the Golden Flower text) where meaningfully coincident clusters of dreams and images were also being discussed. I have suggested it was Jung's formulation of this new idea, which became a redemptive "third" position beyond his prophecy-madness dilemma that was the real exit from the Red Book.[22] By taking the synchronistic exit, Jung was attempting a transformation in culture from a theological to a psychological ground. In contemporary parlance, synchronicity became a conceptual means

18 Ibid., 360.

19 Jung, *Memories, Dreams, Reflections*, 197.

20 C.G. Jung, "Commentary on 'The Secret of the Golden Flower'", in *The Collected Works*, ed. G. Adler and R.F.C. Hull, vol. 13 (Princeton: Princeton University Press, 1967), 1–56.

21 Jung, *The Red Book: Liber Novus*, 219.

22 J. Cambray, "The Red Book: Entrances and Exits", in *The Red Book: Reflections on C.G. Jung's Liber Novus*, ed. T. Kirsch and G. Hogenson (London, New York: Routledge, 2013), 36–53.

for discussing emergent phenomena, and as George Bright has commented is the basis for the Jungian analytic attitude.[23]

My thesis is that the experiences involved in producing the *Red Book* fundamentally altered Jung, including his vision of science and scientific writing. In this vein at the encouragement of his friend, Professor Fierz, Jung wrote to the president of the ETH in May 1933 to resume his public lectures but now wanted to speak about "the general subject of modern psychology, so this could not be within the medical faculty"; his request was granted and he began in October 1933.[24]

In the years following his exit from the *Red Book* project he developed a relationship with Wolfgang Pauli, one of the star physicists who gave birth to modern quantum theory. They had a long correspondence, available in English as *Atom and Archetype* in large part due to Beverley Zabriskie. Together they authored *The Interpretation of Nature and the Psyche* a book containing Jung's essay on Synchronicity, though this was much later, in 1952. Pauli's critique of Jung's use of science in his understanding of objectivity in quantum theory is important. As science historian Suzanne Gieser notes, Pauli:

> compared Jung's way of describing the unconscious with the classical field concepts of physics.... Jung still used a mode of description which did not take the new epistemological situation revealed by quantum physics satisfactorily into account ... he still had a tendency to treat the unconscious as a field that may be observed without considering the influence of the observation.[25]

I believe Jung vacillated on this point as he was trying to meld subjective experience into objective observation, though he was seeking to bring a form of objectivity to seemingly subjective experiences, rather than solely trying to include subjective factors in objective observation. In this project he was unconsciously drawing on an older, discarded scientific tradition, i.e., from German Romanticism, that he could not let himself directly claim.

23 G. Bright, "Synchronicity as A Basis of Analytic Attitude", *Journal of Analytical Psychology* 42, no. 4 (1997): 613–35.

24 A. Graf-Nold, "C.G. Jung's Position at the Eidgenössische Technische Hochschule (ETH), the Swiss Federal Institute of Technology, Zürich", in *Jung History*, vol. 2, 2, 2007, 12–15.

25 S. Gieser, *The Innermost Kernel* (Berlin, Heidelberg, New York: Springer, 2005), 245.

5 German Romanticism and Science

In response to the French and English domination in science during the 17th and 18th century, which was increasingly aligned with governmental agendas, German scientists developed a more individual, less nationally oriented form of science in the latter half of the 18th century. In contradistinction to the analytic, reductive methods of the Enlightenment, the German scientists retained an older, holistic perspective, which also was congruent with the emerging Romantic Movement.

Closer to Jung's education and cultural affinity, the scientific aspects of German Romanticism have generally not been considered in his works beyond philosophical implications. The scientific contributions themselves have largely been ignored, or demeaned until recently. A small but growing scholarly interest in the German Romantics' has been developing over the last several decades. The intertwining of science and art in ways that generate intuitive knowledge about systems of nature is regaining attention, providing an alternative vision with an interest in the science of wholes. As Andrew Cunningham and Nicholas Jardine note in their introduction to their edited volume on *Romanticism and the sciences*:

> The stereotype of the Romantic sciences as speculative, fantastic, mystical and ill-disciplined, and their alleged defeat by the empirical natural sciences, are polemical constructs rather than the fruits of unbiased historical research.[26]

The collection of essays they offer provides a useful, broad introduction to the range of accomplishments of the Romantic scientists. For the purpose of this essay, I will skip over the obvious and well-known figure of Goethe but instead will use the life and work of Alexander von Humboldt (1769–1859) as an example I have explored elsewhere.[27]

Alexander, a traveler and scientist and his brother Wilhelm, a renowned linguist and humanist, are both memorialized by Humboldt University in Berlin. Alexander developed personal friendships with numerous scientist and philosophers, including Goethe who was 20 years his senior. When Alexander was

26 A. Cunningham and N. Jardine, eds., *Romanticism and the Sciences* (Cambridge, New York: Cambridge University Press, 1990), 7–8.

27 J. Cambray, "Romanticism and Revolution in Jung's Science", in *Jung & Science*, ed. R. Jones (Hove / New York: Routledge, 2014).

20 years old and studying at Göttingen, he met Georg Forster, who was by that time a best-selling author with his 1777 travelogue and scientific narrative, *A Voyage Round the World*, based on sailing with James Cook on his second Pacific voyage. Forster brought the young Humboldt along with him on a trip across Europe to London, where they met with the great British naturalist, Sir Joseph Banks. This trip was life altering for Humboldt and a prelude to his great adventures in Latin America.[28]

Before turning to his trek in South America, it should be noted that although Humboldt is only mentioned once in Jung's *Collected Works* volume 5 (originally in Part II of the *Psychology of the Unconscious*, Hinkle p. 352) where Jung makes reference to a South American Indian libido symbol that he found in Humboldt's final work *Cosmos*, there is good reason to consider deeper influence.[29] Alexander von Humboldt is the person responsible for the Jung family living in Switzerland. Briefly Karl Gustav Jung-Frey, a native of Mannheim Germany, arrived in Basel via Paris in 1822 to take up a professorship in medicine at the University there, becoming Swiss in the process, due to a letter from Humboldt to the Burgermeister of Basel recommending him for the post.[30] Andreas Jung, C.G. Jung's grandson, has provided a detailed account of how this occurred: as a young man Karl Jung was involved in German unification politics and was unjustly imprisoned then exiled without trial; he went to Paris where he found Humboldt who "wanted to make up for what his government did to me in a series of injustices. The unforgotten, gracious man kept his word!" which was to help Karl Jung obtain the professorship.[31] With such a family story directly tied to his namesake, it is not much of a leap to imagine Humboldt's life and works may have held attractions for Jung in unreported ways. One path by which this may have occurred is through Humboldt's scientific travel narrative, itself a clear work of German Romantic science.

Before traveling to Latin America Humboldt had already established himself as a plant geographer with his first significant publication in 1793 was based on his work in the mines around Freiberg. Even at this early date he argues "plants should not be studied in isolation but as an integral part of the environment in which they are found."[32] His holistic-environmental views were later adopted by Ernst Haeckel when he coined the term ecology – Haeckel's artistic

28 G. Helferich, *Humboldt's Cosmos* (New York: Gotham Books, Penguin Group Inc., 2004), 10–11.

29 C.G. Jung, "Symbols of Transformation", in *The Collected Works*, ed. G. Adler and R.F.C. Hull, vol. 5 (Princeton: Princeton University Press, 1956), § 481 & n.

30 Bair, *Jung: A Biography*, 10.

31 A. Jung, "The Grandfather", *Journal of Analytical Psychology* 56, no. 5 (2011): 661.

32 Helferich, *Humboldt's Cosmos*, 343.

renditions of marine creatures was also to unconsciously impact the imagery of Jung's *Red Book*.[33] The empiricism Humboldt learned from Forster was deliberately "combined with enthusiastic recording of emotional responses and subjective impressions" as when studying the morphology of landscape.[34] Humboldt was a well accomplished, respected scientist in Europe before setting off on his travels.

Humboldt together with the botanist Aimé Bonpland obtained permission and royal support from the Spanish Crown for a scientific expedition to Spanish America. In 1799 they left on a voyage that took them to Venezuela and from there inland by canoe to explore the Orinoco River. Collecting specimens, discovering many new species of plants, insects and animals, they also demonstrated the existence of the Casiquiare Canal: a unique, natural link between the Orinoco and Amazon River systems. They made astronomical observations and took data on geomagnetism. However, as Humboldt details in his travel memoirs they also suffered many (mis)adventures, such as experimenting on themselves with electric eels (being severely shocked in the process), of having their pet Mastiff eaten by jaguars, of nearly drowning in capsizes, of becoming violently ill and of enduring seemingly limitless torture of biting insects in the rainforest. At times there is an inferno-like quality to the narrative, so intense that the reader feels the emotions of the travelers.

After a trip to Cuba to recover their health and to explore that island, the next phase of their travels took them through New Granada (including modern day Columbia and Ecuador) and Peru. In addition to river travel and rainforests they also trekked through the Andes Mountains, with tremendous ascents at the limits of human capacities – they set the world record at the time for height, 19,286 feet, unaided by artificial sources of oxygen. This gave them the opportunity to study the diversity of life, especially plant life at differing altitudes and climates as they ascended from rainforest to snow-capped mountain. In an important essay that came from these observations Humboldt sought to link plant geography, as he termed it, to cultural forms:

> the man who is sensitive to the beauties of nature will ... find there the explanation of the influence exerted by the appearance of vegetation over Man's taste and imagination. He will take pleasure in examining what is constituted by the "character" of the vegetation and the variety

33 Cambray, "The Red Book: Reflections on C.G. Jung's Liber Novus", 36–53.

34 M. Nicolson, "Alexander von Humboldt and Vegetation", in *Romanticism and the Sciences*, ed. A. Cunningham and N. Jardine (Cambridge, New York: Cambridge University Press, 1990), 171.

> of sensation it produces in the soul of the person who contemplates it. These considerations are all the more significant because they are closely linked to the means by which the imitative arts and descriptive poetry succeed in acting upon us... What a marked contrast between forests in temperate zones and those of the Equator, where the bare slender trunks of the palms soar above the flowered mahogany trees and createmajestical portico arches in thesky... How does this ... appearance of nature, rich and pleasant to a greater or lesser degree, affect the customs and above all the sensibility of the people?[35]

Historian of science Margarita Bowen incorporating a quote from Humboldt remarks: "'the apparently impassible gulf between thought and being, the relationship between the knowing mind and perceived object' was seen by Humboldt as the locus of the sciences. Science is mind applied to nature."[36] Hence sciences in Humboldt's definition would make central what Jung termed the psychoid.

Humboldt's scientific travelogue, his multi-volume *Personal Narratives* (1819–1829) was a source of inspiration to numerous scientists including the father of Geology, Charles Lyell as well as Charles Darwin. For a young Darwin, Humboldt was a hero; he brought volumes of the *Personal Narratives* aboard the Beagle (and Captain Fitzroy also had a full set). In a letter to his closest friend the botanist and explorer Sir Joseph Dalton Hooker, Darwin wrote "I believe that you are fully right in calling Humboldt the greatest scientific traveller who ever lived" (Darwin, 1887, 6 August 1881). In his Beagle Diary Darwin wrote: "I am at present fit only to read Humboldt; he like another Sun illumines everything I behold."[37]

The nearly solitary journey into the unknown, at great personal risk and expense, for the purpose of seeking knowledge of the interior, can be viewed as a highly informative precursor to some of Jung's own responses to the experiences that he crafted into *The Red Book*. From this vantage, *The Red Book* can be viewed as a scientific contribution in line with the travel narrative reports of a romantic scientist such as Humboldt, the unknown territory moving from the external physical world to the interior, psychological, similar to the way that some of the Romantics moved back and forth between inner and outer worlds.

35 Ibid., 172.

36 M. Bowen, *Empiricism and Geographical Thought: From Francis Bacon to Alexander von Humboldt* (Cambridge: Cambridge University Press, 1981), 257.

37 R.J. Richards, *The Romantic Conception of Life: Science and Philosophy in the Age of Goethe* (Chicago, London: The University of Chicago Press, 2002), 514.

Humboldt's last great project was his five volume *Cosmos: A Sketch Of A Physical Description Of The Universe* (1866). A lifetime's passion that began as a young man, when he started to formulate the idea of writing a comprehensive treatise on the physical description of the entire universe, it took his travels, a series of 61 lectures at Berlin University on the whole of the physical sciences and then almost two decades of writing to produce the first several volumes.[38] As scholar Laura Dassow Walls remarks: "Historians credit Humboldt's lectures with jump-starting German science, which went on to surpass even the French in brilliance ... in its power to raise and educate the many."[39] In its scope *Cosmos* was perhaps the last work of its kind, with one scientist attempting a total description of the world, displaying his essential vision that nature is a single unifying force in which "Everything is related"[40] which Gerhard Müllernotes emphasizes interrelationship or interrelatedness, making Humboldt's perspective the direct background to environmental sciences[41] and a forerunner to Jung's field theory with its intensely relational quality[42] as well as the relational paradigm in psychoanalysis.

The initial volumes of *Cosmos* were immensely popular and influenced generations of scientists. In the first volume, published in German in 1845, Humboldt focuses on the outer world, an "objective journey through the external world of the senses."[43] The second volume, also in German, published in 1847, shifts to a focus on "an inner or 'subjective' journey through mind, 'the inner, reflected intellectual world.'"[44] As Walls observes, for Humboldt this shift to the subjective is not what we would normally understand as a psychological exploration: "but something more Wordsworthian, the emergence and growth of mind-in-nature, 'the reflection of the image impressed by the senses upon the inner man, that is, upon his ideas and feelings.' The second volume thus journeys through time – historical time, from the earliest civilizations."[45]

38 Helferich, *Humboldt's Cosmos*, 320–23.

39 L. Dassow Walls, *The Passage to Cosmos: Alexander von Humboldt and the Shaping of America* (Chicago, London: The University of Chicago Press, 2011), 216; also see her note 11.

40 Helferich, *Humboldt's Cosmos*, 323.

41 G.H. Müller, "Wechselwirkung in the Life and Other Sciences: A Word, New Claims and a Concept around 1800 ... and Much Later", in *Romanticism in Science: Science in Europe, 1790–1840*, ed. S. Poggi and M. Bossi (Dordrecht, Boston, London: Kluwer Academic Publishers, 1994), 1 and n. 1 & 2.

42 J. Cambray, *Synchronicity: Nature and Psyche in an Interconnected Universe*, Fay Lecture Series (College Station, TX: Texas A & M University Press, 2009), Chap. 2.

43 Dassow Walls, *The Passage to Cosmos*, 221.

44 Ibid.

45 Ibid.

The first section of volume II is entitled "Incitements to the Study of Nature" referring to "the image reflected by the external world on the imagination"; it offers an ecologically-based archeology of civilization and mind as formed in response to the natural environment with the life-forms, especially plants, present. The second section of this volume is titled: "History of the Physical Contemplation of the Universe. Principal Causes of the Gradual Development and Extension of the Idea of the Cosmos as a Natural Whole."[46] In its attempts at a poetics of nature Richards see Humboldt's explicit intention as arguing: "the natural historian had the duty to re-create in the reader – through the use of artful language – aesthetic experiences of the sort the naturalist had himself undergone in his immediate encounter with nature."[47] When examined carefully, I believe this volume can be seen as a holding a worldview which Jung will reformulate in terms of an objective psyche and the collective unconscious. Humboldt's views even more closely anticipate ideas to be found in the work of Jungian analyst James Hillman, with his "poetic basis of mind" and his attention to the *anima mundi* (the soul of the world).[48]

Humboldt's project in creating a vision of *Cosmos* involved marrying scientific measurement and precision to artistic, aesthetic experience. In his words:

> It is by a separation and classification of phenomena, by an intuitive insight into the play of obscure forces, and by animated expressions, in which the perceptible spectacle is reflected with vivid truthfulness, that we may hope to comprehend and describe the *universal all* (τὸ πάν) in a manner worthy of the dignity of the word *Cosmos* in its signification of *universe*, *order of the world*, and *adornment* of this universal order.[49]

In the grand vision of *Cosmos*, Humboldt seeks to weave a coherent unity of nature, self, and nation or "race" (in his study of human differences, Humboldt is one of the first Western scientists to challenge the notion of difference in human groups being due to inherent traits; his views are remarkably democratic for his age and this is part of what won him Boas' admiration). According to Walls this synthesis "is a necessary part of the *Bildung*, or growth

46 A. von Humboldt, *Cosmos: A Sketch of a Physical Description of the Universe*, trans. E.C. Otté, B.H. Paul, and W.S. Dallas, 5 vols. (New York: Harper and Brothers Printing, 1866); All the volumes available on-line by the Biodiversity Heritage Library at: http://www.biodiversitylibrary.org/bibliography/32462.

47 Richards, *Romantic Conception of Life*, 521.

48 J. Hillman, *Re-Visioning Psychology* (New York: Harper and Row Publishers, 1975), xi.

49 Humboldt, *Cosmos: A Sketch of a Physical Description of the Universe*, vol 1, 79.

and integration of the self in the world... One could call what he was after *grounded imagination.*"[50]

The cosmological vision Humboldt is seeking through his study of the physical universe in fact bears resemblance to Jung's late life cosmological musing. As I have written about elsewhere, Jung's goal in his Synchronicity monograph – to supplement the triad of classical physics (space, time and causality) with a fourth principle, synchronicity – is founded on a cosmogonic insight.[51] In response to the articulation of the "big bang" model of the universe of the astrophysicists of his day, Jung sought to locate a pattern forming tendency emerging from an originary singularity that he identifies as synchronicity. At that time, there was no complexity theory available. Starting from Jung's intuitions I suggest his work on synchronicity deserves reconsideration, and some modification in terms of modern theory. Thus the phase transitions proposed in the immediate wake of the big bang which are the ultimate source of all of known physics are now understood in terms of symmetry breaking that leads to increasing complexity.[52] Patterns of increasing complexity emerged as the early universe cooled and evolved; much later in cosmic time this same propensity leads to the origins of life and to the psyche. All of these key events occur through phase transitions that are associated with self-organizing systems that yield new, higher level/emergent properties. Therefore through this late argument Jung at his most far-reaching places the origins of the psyche in the same milieu as belongs to the origins of the physical universe; mind and even the imagination are thereby most fundamentally grounded in nature. In making this link, it should be noted that Jung is hardly a consistent writer: he draws on many sources and over the course of his long life his views alter as his understandings change. As I have argued elsewhere, his views on topics such as symmetry breaking vacillate; my interest is pursuing the edges of his thought, which is where influences outside consciousness often enter, rather than his definitive, unconflicted statements.[53]

As you also may recall, while working on *The Red Book* Jung reported an internal struggle around defining what he was doing, seeing it as neither art nor science; his conscious conclusion was that it was "nature."[54] His mistrust

---

50 Dassow Walls, *The Passage to Cosmos*, 223.

51 J. Cambray, "Cosmos and Culture in the Play of Synchronicity", in *The Playful Psyche Entering Chaos, Coincidence*, ed. S. Wirth et al., vol. IV, Creation Jungian Odyssey Series (New Orleans: Spring Journal, Inc., 2012), 133–47.

52 K. Mainzer, *Symmetry and Complexity: The Spirit and Beauty of Nonlinear Science* (London, New Jersey: World Scientific, 2005), 147–58.

53 Cambray, *Synchronicity*, 57–67.

54 Jung, *Memories, Dreams, Reflections*, 186.

of the aesthetic dimension to his work is captured by his irritable dismissal of the inner voice that was insisting he was doing art: "I recognized it as the voice of a patient, a talented psychopath who had a strong transference to me" together with his fear of his vulnerability to her suggestions.[55] This struggle peaked following receipt of a letter from this woman who stressed "the fantasies arising from my unconscious had artistic value and should be considered art."[56] Jung's subsequent emotional distress provoked a rupture in the mandala he was working on: "part of the periphery had burst open and the symmetry was destroyed."[57] As mentioned such symmetry breaking is essential to emergence, and Jung was both fascinated and repelled by such breaks, making then backing away from them.[58] In *The Red Book* the broken mandala can be seen to reflect the inauguration of a transformative process stemming from an activation of the unconscious[59] and taking him to ground that is analogous to that of the scientist of the German Romantic tradition.

6 Reemergence of Holistic Studies in Contemporary Science

With the advent of high speed computers and the capacity for advanced simulation of systems that had been considered beyond scientific modeling, new possibilities have opened up in the last two decades. In particular exploration of non-linear dynamical systems has become a topic of accelerating interest. Such systems exhibit complex spatial and temporal evolution. The accuracy of the simulations performed on many of these systems has opened up the field of complexity studies. Some of the most intriguing examples come from what is termed complex adaptive systems, as they exhibit the capacity for self-organization with emergent properties (irreducible to properties of the component parts). These studies necessarily form an interdisciplinary branch of science, drawing on multiple disciplines. The results have proven useful at multiple levels, i.e., they tend to be "scale-free" and even include human activities, such as understanding traffic patterns, fluctuations in stock-markets and so forth. This has helped to spark a renewed interest in holistic perspectives thereby rekindling a major concern of the German Romantic scientists, now with enhanced scientific rigor.

---

55 Ibid., 185.
56 Ibid., 195.
57 Ibid.
58 Cambray, *Synchronicity*, Chap. 3.
59 Cambray, "The Red Book: Reflections on C.G. Jung's Liber Novus", 44–45.

One set of applications is geared towards understanding the mind-body relationship. Cognitive and neuro-scientist have begun to generate more integrated views of the role of emotions, images and imagination in the formation of the mind, for example in the writings of Antonio Damasio among many others.[60] Similarly, there has been a turn towards revaluing the importance of aesthetics in the emergence of the mind, e.g., in the work of the visual neurologist V.S. Ramachandran and the new field of neuroesthetics.[61] The return to scientific research of topics at the heart of German Romanticism such as subjectivity, affect and imagination suggest the possibility for reevaluation of this older tradition as holding some necessary perspective if a paradigm shift towards scientific holism is to accomplished. Perhaps as a part of this reconsideration the tendency for oscillations between reductionism and holism may decrease in a manner that allows both approaches to be held in tension in any on-going discourse.

In another paper I offer a further example from the ecological perspective the emerged out of the work of the German Romantic scientists: epigenetics.[62] The concept itself is derived from the much older term "epigenesis" which referred to a developmental theory whereby "an individual is developed by successive differentiation of an unstructured egg rather than by a simple enlarging of a preformed entity."[63] The self-organizing tendencies felt to be in response to environmental pressures inherent in the theory of epigenesis caught the imagination of the romantic scientists and as historian of science Stefan Willer comments "[t]his is why *generation* in an epigenetic view could become closely linked to *genius* and furnish a leading model for philosophical and poetical productivity."[64]

The concept went in and out of fashion over the course of the 19th century, but was largely dismissed as genetics came to dominate, especially through the work of August Weismann. Weismann persuasively argued that once an egg was fertilized nothing essential was added; he linked this with the Darwinian

60 A.R. Damasio, *The Feeling of What Happens* (New York: Harcourt Inc., 1999); *Looking for Spinoza: Joy, Sorrow, and the Feeling Brain* (New York: Harcourt Inc., 2003); *Self Comes to Mind* (New York: Pantheon Books, 2010).

61 V.S. Ramachandran, *The Tell-Tale Brain* (New York: W.W. Norton & Company Inc., 2011).

62 Cambray, "Jung, Science, and His Legacy."

63 *The American Heritage® Medical Dictionary* (Houghton Mifflin Company, 2007).

64 S. Willer, "Epigenesis' in Epigenetics: Scientific Knowledge, Concepts, and Words", in *The Hereditary Hourglass. Genetics and Epigenetics, 1868–2000*, ed. A. Barahona, E. Suarez-Diaz, and H.-J. Rheinberger, Preprint 392 (Berlin: Max Planck Institute for the History of Science, 2010), 17.

evolution but now in the service of genetics, severing development from heredity.

This view was not significantly modified in the scientific community until the work of C.H. Waddington who coined the term "epigenetics" in 1940. Nevertheless, this new field, despite greatly reduced modest claims, no longer an entire theory of inheritance but just a description of the way environmental effects act on and modify an individual's genetic program of development, were often met with scorn.

It has not been until the current century with the completion of the human genome project that the limits of a genetic approach alone for understanding organisms have become widely recognized in the scientific community. A key element in the theory of epigenetics is that there are classes of heritable modifications which are not involved in alterations of DNA bases or their sequences. Within a decade of this resurgence there has been an explosion of interest and applications of epigenetic research, for example to various disease and ageing processes such as the origins of different cancers.[65] Similarly some psychological issues, especially multigenerational trauma have been recognized to have epigenetic components. The reintroduction of the impact of the environment on hereditary processes does herald a return to the importance of ecology in discussions of evolutionary biology in line with German Romantic scientific concerns with "organic memory."

A host of recent studies have begun to document epigenetic influences on biological transmission of traumatic memory. For example, writer Nessa Carey recently published a book with numerous accounts of empirical research verifying epigenetic mechanism at work in various human situations.[66] A particularly poignant example she cites is on the victims of the Dutch Hunger Winter (November 1944 until May 1945), when the German authorities halted food supplies in the portion of the Netherlands that they occupied at this late stage of the Second World War. This tragic situation gives a clearly delineated time frame for this famine. Epidemiologists have been able to study the impact on pregnant mothers and their newborns as detailed records survive due to the excellent healthcare system in place at the time. The findings have been quite surprising:

> If a mother was well-fed around the time of conception and malnourished only for the last few months of the pregnancy, her baby was likely to be

65 S.F. Gilbert and D. Epel, *Ecological Developmental Biology: Integrating Epigenetics, Medicine, and Evolution* (Sunderland MA: Sinauer Associates, Inc., 2009).

66 N. Carey, *The Epigenetics Revolution* (New York, Chichester: Columbia University Press, 2012).

> born small. If, on the other hand, the mother suffered malnutrition for the first three months of the pregnancy only ... but then was well-fed, she was likely to have a baby with normal body weight.... The babies who were born small stayed small all their lives, with lower obesity rates than the general population [despite availability of ample food].... the children whose mothers had been malnourished only early in pregnancy, had higher obesity rates than normal. Recent reports have shown a greater incidence of other health problems as well, including certain tests of mental activity.... Even more extraordinarily, some of these effects seem to be present in the children of this group, i.e., in the grandchildren of the women who were malnourished during the first three months of their pregnancy.[67]

In this case researchers have begun to identify specific epigenetic biochemical markers not found with same sex siblings who were not exposed to the famine. Furthermore, the researchers acknowledge: "[a]n additional contribution of other stressors, such as cold and emotional stress, cannot be ruled out, however. Our study provides the first evidence that transient environmental conditions early in human gestation can be recorded as persistent changes in epigenetic information."[68]

Although these results are primarily concerned with biological mechanism of transmission of environmentally generated trauma, they do open the possibility of serious consideration of the impact of the psychological environment on unconscious memory transmission. With this Jung's notion of a collective unconscious deserves a careful reexamination. More generally Jung's writing in the aftermath of his Red Book experience when contextualized against the background of romantic science offers a way to return to a vision that has largely been lost in the academy outside literature.

References

Bair, D. *Jung: A Biography*. Boston: Little, Brown and Co, 2003.

Bleuler, E. "Dementia Praecox or the Group of Schizophrenias." In *Handbuch Der Psychiatrie*, edited by G. Aschaffenburg, translated by J. Zinkin. New York: International Universities Press, 1950. Originally published as *Dementia Praecox Oder Gruppe Der Schizophrenien* (Leipzig, Vienna: Deutike, 1911).

67 Ibid., 2–3.

68 B.T. Heijmans et al., "Persistent Epigenetic Differences Associated with Prenatal Exposure to Famine in Humans", *Proceedings of the National Academy of Sciences* 105, no. 44 (2008): 17046–48.

Bowen, M. Empiricism and Geographical Thought: From Francis Bacon to Alexander von Humboldt. Cambridge: Cambridge University Press, 1981.

Bright, G. "Synchronicity as A Basis of Analytic Attitude." *Journal of Analytical Psychology* 42, no. 4 (1997): 613–35.

Cambray, J. "Cosmos and Culture in the Play of Synchronicity." In *The Playful Psyche Entering Chaos, Coincidence*, edited by S. Wirth, I. Meier, J. Hill, and N. Cater, Vol. IV. Creation Jungian Odyssey Series. New Orleans: Spring Journal, Inc., 2012.

Cambray, J. "Jung, Science, and His Legacy." *International Journal of Jungian Studies* 3, no. 2 (2011): 110–24.

Cambray, J. "Romanticism and Revolution in Jung's Science." In *Jung & Science*, edited by R. Jones. Hove / New York: Routledge, 2014.

Cambray, J. *Synchronicity: Nature and Psyche in an Interconnected Universe*. Fay Lecture Series. College Station, TX: Texas A & M University Press, 2009.

Cambray, J. "The Red Book: Entrances and Exits." In *The Red Book: Reflections on C.G. Jung's Liber Novus*, edited by T. Kirsch and G. Hogenson. London, New York: Routledge, 2013.

Carey, N. *The Epigenetics Revolution*. New York, Chichester: Columbia University Press, 2012.

Cunningham, A., and N. Jardine, eds. *Romanticism and the Sciences*. Cambridge, New York: Cambridge University Press, 1990.

Damasio, A.R. *Looking for Spinoza: Joy, Sorrow, and the Feeling Brain*. New York: Harcourt Inc., 2003.

Damasio, A.R. *Self Comes to Mind*. New York: Pantheon Books, 2010.

Damasio, A.R. *The Feeling of What Happens*. New York: Harcourt Inc., 1999.

Dassow Walls, L. *The Passage to Cosmos: Alexander von Humboldt and the Shaping of America*. Chicago, London: The University of Chicago Press, 2011.

Gieser, S. *The Innermost Kernel*. Berlin, Heidelberg, New York: Springer, 2005.

Gilbert, S.F., and D. Epel. *Ecological Developmental Biology: Integrating Epigenetics, Medicine, and Evolution*. Sunderland MA: Sinauer Associates, Inc., 2009.

Graf-Nold, A. "C.G. Jung's Position at the Eidgenössische Technische Hochschule (ETH), the Swiss Federal Institute of Technology, Zürich." In *Jung History*, Vol. 2. 2, 2007.

Greenwood, S.F. "Émile Durkheim and C.G. Jung: Structuring a Transpersonal Sociology of Religion." Journal for the Scientific Study of Religion 29, no. 4 (1990): 482–95.

Heijmans, B.T., E.W. Tobi, A.D. Stein, H. Putter, G.J. Blauw, E.S. Susser, P.E. Slagboom, and L.H. Lumey. "Persistent Epigenetic Differences Associated with Prenatal Exposure to Famine in Humans." Proceedings of the National Academy of Sciences 105, no. 44 (2008): 17046–49.

Helferich, G. *Humboldt's Cosmos*. New York: Gotham Books, Penguin Group Inc., 2004.

Hillman, J. *Re-Visioning Psychology*. New York: Harper and Row Publishers, 1975.

Hoff, P. "Private Lecture on the History of the Burghölzli Hospital", 2011.

Humboldt, A. von. *Cosmos: A Sketch of a Physical Description of the Universe*. Translated by E.C. Otté, B.H. Paul, and W.S. Dallas. 5 vols. New York: Harper and Brothers Printing, 1866.

Jung, A. "The Grandfather." *Journal of Analytical Psychology* 56, no. 5 (2011): 653–73.

Jung, C.G. *Analytical Psychology: Notes of the Seminar Given in 1925 by C.G. Jung*. Edited by W. McGuire. Princeton: Princeton University Press, 1989.

Jung, C.G. *C.G. Jung Speaking: Interviews and Encounters*. Edited by W. McGuire and R.F.C. Hull. Princeton, N.J: Princeton University Press, 1977.

Jung, C.G. "Commentary on 'The Secret of the Golden Flower.'" In *The Collected Works*, edited by G. Adler and R.F.C. Hull, Vol. 13. Princeton: Princeton University Press, 1967.

Jung, C.G. *Memories, Dreams, Reflections*. New York: Pantheon Books, 1961.

Jung, C.G. "Symbols of Transformation." In *The Collected Works*, edited by G. Adler and R.F.C. Hull, Vol. 5. Princeton: Princeton University Press, 1956.

Jung, C.G. "The Archetypes and the Collective Unconscious." In *The Collected Works*, edited by G. Adler and R.F.C. Hull, Vol. 9i. Princeton: Princeton University Press, 1940.

Jung, C.G. "The Border Zone of Exact Science." In *The Zofingia Lectures,* edited by W. McGuire. The Collected Works of C.G. Jung: Supplementary Volume A. Princeton, NJ: Princeton University Press, 1983.

Jung, C.G. *The Red Book: Liber Novus*. Edited by S. Shamdasani. Translated by S. Shamdasani, M. Kyburz, and J. Peck. New York: W.W. Norton & Company Inc., 2009.

Mainzer, K. Symmetry and Complexity: The Spirit and Beauty of Nonlinear Science. London, New Jersey: World Scientific, 2005.

Müller, G.H. "Wechselwirkung in the Life and Other Sciences: A Word, New Claims and a Concept around 1800 … and Much Later." In *Romanticism in Science: Science in Europe, 1790–1840*, edited by S. Poggi and M. Bossi. Dordrecht, Boston, London: Kluwer Academic Publishers, 1994.

Nicolson, M. "Alexander von Humboldt and Vegetation." In *Romanticism and the Sciences*, edited by A. Cunningham and N. Jardine. Cambridge, New York: Cambridge University Press, 1990.

Ramachandran, V.S. *The Tell-Tale Brain*. New York: W.W. Norton & Company Inc., 2011.

Richards, R.J. The Romantic Conception of Life: Science and Philosophy in the Age of Goethe. Chicago, London: The University of Chicago Press, 2002.

Shamdasani, S. *Jung and the Making of Modern Psychology*. Cambridge: Cambridge University Press, 2003.

The American Heritage® Medical Dictionary. Houghton Mifflin Company, 2007.

Tresan, D. "Collective Unconscious." In *International Dictionary of Psychoanalysis*, edited by A. de Mijolla. New York: Thomson Gale, 2005.

Willer, S. "Epigenesis' in Epigenetics: Scientific Knowledge, Concepts, and Words." In *The Hereditary Hourglass. Genetics and Epigenetics, 1868–2000*, edited by A. Barahona, E. Suarez-Diaz, and H.-J. Rheinberger. Preprint 392. Berlin: Max Planck Institute for the History of Science, 2010.

CHAPTER 2

Aspects of Descartes' and Pascal's Diverging Psychological Standings as Regards Knowledge That Find Expression in the Differences of the Freudian and Jungian Methodological Approaches to Psychology

Miriam Gomes de Freitas

Abstract

This paper is not a discussion of R. Descartes nor B. Pascal's philosophies. It is a comparative evaluation of their different psychological attitudes when facing the crisis of representation and the scientific methods therein derived. This paper argues that the dubious character of human knowledge, the changing means of coping with new unstable realities (social, cultural, political, economical and scientific) of the modern world are no longer answered by the "thaumazein/wonder" of the Greeks." The dogmatic aspiration is described as an anxiety response to outside facts that unsettle the feeling of control over a world in transformation. In the struggle to overcome uncertainty Descartes' "Meditations" proposes a new ground for knowledge. "Meditations" can be read as a terror tale, told by someone loosing control over an unsteady world. Through the "intuitus" Descartes manages to re-introduce the Absolute, no longer projected unto a Godhead but introjected into human reason, carrying similar divine powers. On the same period, Pascal gives a different answer to shared contestations over the nature and possibility of knowledge. Although one cannot define "space" nor "time" we can do a lot with our imperfect concepts, writes Pascal. Even ignoring what space is, he argues, we can do geometry. The paper proceeds to a further examination of the differences between cartesian and pascalian psychological attitudes facing the moving, uncertain character of the modern world and consequent restrictions set to knowledge generating different methodological strategies. Second, the paper establishes a connection between the scientific dogmatic aspirations of Freudian theory and the cartesian trend at variance with the Jungian method. Pascal and Jung share an acceptance of the vulnerabilities of human knowledge. Different methodological approaches to the unconscious are shaped by different epistemological attitudes.

 | DOI:10.1163/9789004336636_004

Keywords

Descartes – Pascal – Freud – Epistemology – Methodology – Philosophy – Intuition – Human Knowledge – Unconscious

1 Methodological Considerations

The domain we are focusing on is a complex system. The following reflections are not conceived through an essentialist perspective. Hence, there is no claim of an ontological identity between the compared elements. The domain under consideration lies in a threshold zone between psychology and philosophy, a zone in itself of difficult definition due to the subtle interactions that preclude a clear divide as well as a simple merge (just like what happens at the encounter zone between body and soul). This domain is better approached as a liquid mass where the waters of psychology and philosophy get together. I shall limit the borders of that body of water by four different "lands." They are Descartes D, Pascal P, Freud F, Jung J.

I shall not explore the hinterlands, as for instance a philosophical investigation of P and D could be compared, neither will I analyze F and J (theories) in detail. Our target is the moving waters. I shall try to discern how much the composition of the rivers of the P land share similarities with the waters from J, and how the waters of D present a similar pattern to those of the F land. We are dealing with non-linear dynamics prone to the phenomena of turbulence where mixing is thorough, though irregular, because turbulence occurs at all scales at the borders between psychology and philosophy. Turbulence transforms D's encounter with F, or P's encounters with J. Turbulence ensures that two adjacent points in a complex system will eventually end up in very different positions after some time has elapsed. Hence, no hope to find F faithfully copying D, or J copying P because at this hybrid zone specific contents are dissolved, although the pattern of structural dynamics subsists. Phenomena of turbulence are best approached through their fractal properties. Hence, I would describe my method as a search for the fractal properties of that complex, dynamic system. This means a search for a moving pattern with recurring elements distributed among the four authors. As a fractal, it admits no whole-number dimension, just fractions, in this case, "aspects" of the four constituents of the domain examined. However, as a fractal it is not just a fragment, but also a carrier of the whole itself.

2 Historical Conditions of the Seventeenth Century

The seventeenth century is the cultural scenario for coming to terms with revolutionary discoveries and socio-political transformations. Humankind had just learned with Copernicus' (1473–1543) and Galileo's (1564–1642) discoveries that the senses cannot grasp the world. Giordano Bruno (1548–1600) was burned at the stake for upholding, amongst other ideas, the new Copernican cosmology; and although Galileo might have been condemned, yet nevertheless the earth turns around the sun. The Church and tradition no longer have a monopoly over the truth. The telescope defeats our eyes, reality defeats our senses, the world defeats old established truths. Columbus, Magellan and Cabral extended the world beyond the geographical and cosmological limits set by tradition, just as Luther (1483–1546) affirmed the individual reason beyond traditional interpretations. Both res extensa and res cogitans surpass known fixed limits. Machiavelli (1469–1527) had already emancipated politics from theology and moral philosophy. As science controls nature for humankind's benefit, Machiavelli proposed that the rulers should control fortune for their own benefit.

This is no longer a sacred world owned by kings and the Church. In the Middle Ages, two-thirds of the land of Europe belonged to the Church but now the bourgeois man starts to own land. This is tantamount to "own" his destiny, holding possession of his fate. In the socio-political arena, the project of the bourgeois man counteracts medieval mentality, transferring the weight from guilds and fealty to a class of independent individuals. The crisis in science, society, culture and politics produces a paradoxical scenario, where man is defeated by his senses but becomes a conqueror by his will and practical endeavors. Technology rides to the rescue, extending man's senses to domains hitherto unexplored. The over-valuation of technology may lead to technocracy, whereas human self-consciousness wavers between impotence/omnipotence, creating new and complex ethical challenges.

Although there's a wide diversity of tendencies, the stability of a lost world where everything has a fixed place is a shared experience provoking different reactions. With one single mathematical equation Newton pulls together the movement of celestial bodies and the gravity force ruling the earth. Thus, the scission of the Aristotelian universe between the fixed abode of celestial bodies and the sublunar world is dissolved. The grasp of reality by the senses and tradition is undermined. Literature, painting, music, all arts register critical aspects of the representation crisis in this new world. From Cervantes (1547–1616) and Shakespeare (1564–1616) to Quevedo (1580–1645), Calderon de

FIGURE 2.1 *Las Meninas*. Painter: Velázquez (1656). Illustration is in the public domain. No permission needed. Retrieved from Wikipedia.

la Barca (1600–1681), and Milton (1608–1674) epistemic questions are found in their writings.

Foucault[1] calls attention to the painting *Las Meninas* (Fig. 2.1) of Velázquez (1656) as "the representation of representation," when the notion of representation becomes a problem. This theme is also presented by Vermeer's *Malkunst* (Fig. 2.2) in the same period (1666).

1 M. Foucault, *The Order of Things: An Archaeology of the Human Sciences* (London: Routledge, 2002).

FIGURE 2.2 *Malkunst.* Painter: Vermeer (1666). Illustration is in the public domain. No permission needed. Retrieved from Wikipedia.

3 Dialogue with the Contemporary World

One encounter between the seventeenth century and the exploration of the unconscious in the nineteenth and twentieth centuries by Freud and Jung lies in the notion of inquiry and travel into new domains ruled by unknown criteria. This time, inner domains, not external, shatter the boundaries and the rationality of an ancient world, the safe world of consciousness' guidelines and bourgeois self-affirmation. The threads of a still greater convulsion in the crisis of representation were woven throughout these centuries with implacable results. The consciousness upheaval resulting from the confrontation with the unconscious is rather the tip of an iceberg of challenging cultural, scientific and sociopolitical dimensions. It coheres, for instance, with the impossibility of an absolute scale of time (Einstein) and sets man at the edge of chaos, in terms of unpredictability.

To remain within epistemology, the Borges parable retold by Baudrillard[2] leads to what he calls the "precession of simulacra", appropriately referring to a change in the orientation of the earth's rotational axis as in the cosmological precession of the equinoxes. This is a powerful metaphor inscribed in the dense sphere of meanings generated by Copernicus' model denying the earth's immobility.[3] As with the questions resulting from it, Baudrillard's proposition is rooted in the possible or impossible connection of our episteme to reality. Borges' story, not by chance called *On exactitude in Science*, tells of an emperor who wanted a map as large as his Empire so exact that it would wholly and perfectly recover and represent it. Eventually, the Empire crumbled and just the map was left. In Baudrillard's version, people lost all contact with reality and lived on the map. Once the aspiration to connect our episteme to the real in a permanent, essentialist mode, as was Descartes' target, failed, reality is replaced by versions of reality.

The narcisic wound suffered by skeptical non-assumed dogmatic aspirations (of incontrovertibly knowing the world) has consequences. It became the psychological motor behind man's capitulation before the impossibility to construe the authority of truth or of science in ontological terms. An easy answer is to cancel the question away: because I cannot state the relation between reality and my theories in a final, apodictic, manner the relation doesn't exist.[4] The last centuries still didn't heal this wound. In Baudrillard's fable contemporary societies abandoned the search for reality, finding contentment in a cartography of signs. Picking a version of his choice, man is still able to see things through a God's eye point of view. Different contemporary philosophies are witnesses to these facts. Almost all the history of philosophy, from early beginnings to our day, passes through this question. A list would include all the names catalogued in the History of Philosophy. When the significants of

2 J. Baudrillard, *Simulacra and Simulation*, trans. S.F. Glaser (Michigan: The University of Michigan, 2006), 1.

3 Relating macro to microcosmos, on a symbolic level it's possible to see "earth" as connected to ego consciousness and the basis of reality. Therefore, any consciousness of the alteration of its movements shatters the foundations of reality.

4 This is the solution proposed by R. Rorty (1931–2007), in his *Philosophy and the Mirror of Nature* (New Jersey: Princeton University Press, 1979).

culture and media assume such a major role in reality's versions, providing twenty-first century man with an attractive agenda of signs and reassuring cartographies, the task of "brush our standings against the grain" becomes, at least, enthralling.

4 The Relation between Theoretical Models and Facticity: "*Eppur si muove*"

Seventeenth century sciences acknowledged the apories arising from the epistemic challenges of connecting the theoretical models to their objects. The issue with Galileo was precisely about the realistic connection between theoretical models and facticity. As long as Copernicus' discoveries remained "just a model" there was no great challenge to the intellectual status quo supported by the Church and her understanding of Revelation. With his invention of the telescope Galileo insisted that Copernican views were not "just a model" but a truthful description of reality. He was then admonished by Cardinal Bellarmine[5] to discuss Copernicus' model "hypothetically" rather than "absolutely" (i.e. realistically). Although probably legendary, Galileo's words "Eppur si muove – and yet it (the earth) moves", upon leaving the Inquisition confrontation, sealed the realistic claims that eventually led him to condemnation.

In 1633, when learning about Galileo's condemnation, Descartes (1596–1650) confesses to Mersenne his fear of publishing *The World*, a work ready for publication, adhering to the Copernican view. Instead, Descartes sets to write the *Discourse on the Method* (1637), his first published work, then *Meditations* (1639–1640). Parts of *The World* were published only after Descartes' death; other parts were lost. A main feature of *Meditations* is the centering on ideal contents of personal consciousness rather than on an independent external reality. For Descartes, only a foundational philosophy of the subject could root science on solid ground. How this inward orientation expresses Descartes' response to his fear of the Inquisition as well as his personal idealistic leanings disavowing empirical reality, remains a matter of speculation. As regards Pascal, his fear of

5 "This view of the inherent limitations of mathematical astronomy, that its "hypotheses" were no more than calculations devices making no claim on truth, was of course not original with Bellarmine. It went back to medieval natural philosophy and perhaps further, being prompted by the Aristotelian separation between physics and mathematics as well as by the evident inconsistency with one or another of the "two chief world systems" of that earlier day, the mathematical astronomy of Ptolomy and the physical astronomy of Aristotle.' McMullin in P. Machamer, *The Cambridge Companion to Galileo* (Cambridge: Cambridge University Press, 1998), 279.

the Church didn't limit his philosophy. He even joined the heretic group at Port Royal defying the Pope's authority over Jensenius' writings.

5 Towards a Typology of Epistemologies

A different world is a different perceived reality, meaning a different psychology, implying a different anthropology and a different epistemology, because each epistemology reflects not just how man gets to know things, but defines what the specific conception of man sustaining knowledge processes is. This can be read in the reverse sense: each different epistemology implies a different anthropology, and then, of course, a different psychology which means a different perceived reality and a different world as well. In this typology of epistemologies Descartes and Freud, associated to a shared pattern of psychological attitudes, assume and reflect different philosophical and anthropological positions as well as different scientific methodologies from those of Pascal and Jung. I'll try to describe these two types of epistemologies, one being the D-F and other the P-J type. Many other names could be added to these two types, with subgroups and nuances and distinct types as well. An undertaking alien to the present task. Relevant to this description is the Wittgensteinian concept of "family resemblance."[6]

6 Patterns of the Historical Context Mirrored through Epistemic Patterns

Descartes' work is a pivotal point in the consciousness of the crisis of representation that marks the rise of modernity and within it, the rise of the bourgeois individual. In a certain sense, his epistemology is the convergence point of different threads woven throughout the transformations of the medieval world. Historical dimensions are translated into philosophical standings, sustaining Cartesian epistemology, an epistemology historically cogent with his time. Descartes' epistemology is in tune with the ascendant class, representing one of the mainstream tendencies up to our days. Any definition of modernity

6 As proposed by L. Wittgenstein in his *Philosophical Investigations* when explaining what languages are through the image of "game." There is not one element common to all games but rather a network of similarities trespassing and overlapping in detail or in the whole. It can be described as a morphology (a pattern, a type) of interrelations dynamically conceived, generating a methodology that coheres with its living, complex subject (L. Wittgenstein, *Philosophical Investigations,* trans. G.E.M. Anscombe [Oxford: Basil Blackwell, 1958]).

must take Descartes into account. It reflects one possible reaction to the representation crisis, not the exclusive one but a significant one.

Under the cover of an apotheotic affirmation of individual subjectivity we find the reactive formation of a man ready to dismiss the empirical data defeating his senses. Senses that proved so misleading that can no longer provide a solid ground for knowledge. Descartes retires to his mind. Universalized and hyperbolic, doubt turns into the tool of certainty, again a reactive formation: that which he fears (doubt) becomes the very tool to cancel itself: doubt defeats doubt clearing the ground for certainty. For the individual shattered in his convictions, truth becomes less important than certainty, an accusation directed to Cartesian epistemology by many commentators. The senses' impotence turns into mind omnipotence at the service of the subject's peace. Descartes "implodes" doubt by rationally and methodically facing up to all its possible traps: the skeptical, the dreaming, madness, the evil genius. Eventually he appeases his anxiety[7] although at a great price: the dissolution of the empirical. Confronting Aristotle and Aquinas, he leans back to Plato and Augustin. Descartes "swallows" God injecting divine certainty into reason through the intuitus, and stabilizes anxiety. When facing up to his doubts, Descartes is as courageous as he was when accepting the invitation of the Swedish queen to become her mentor. He hesitated, knowing it would be a difficult task on account of his health and the tough Swedish climate. Eventually Descartes succumbed to the power of the empirical as did his ideal theory. Unable to cope with the hardships imposed by the queen[8] and the tough climate, Descartes died in Sweden. As if his mental omnipotence blurred the consciousness of his physical limitations. As his episteme, so his life.

Many philosophers, such as Spinoza, Pascal, Leibniz, Newton, Hume, Vico and others, defy Descartes' positions. Here Walter Benjamin's concept of history is useful by brushing history against the grain[9] we find the buried possible pasts (or past answers) defeated by the victorious ones. Other tendencies as F. Bacon, Vico, Pascal, Locke, Berkeley, Newton and Hume still inform aspects

7 Freud distinguishes between three major types of anxiety: a) realistic anxiety, the anxiety towards the external world; b) moral anxiety, towards the superego; c) neurotic anxiety, as regards the passions of the ego. Anxiety is not necessarily negative, as it can be a motor towards creative work and practical solutions (S. Freud, *Inhibitions, Symptoms and Anxiety*, ed. J. Strachey (New York: W.W. Norton & Company Inc., 1977).

8 The queen required that Descartes, who used to write and meditate throughout the night, give his lessons to her at dawn, before breakfast. His health did not resist the stress; Descartes survived less than a year in Stockholm.

9 W. Benjamin, *Selected Writings*, vol. 4 (Cambridge MA, London: Harvard University Press, 2003), 390.

of contemporary attitudes passing through Kant, Fichte, Schleiermacher, J.S. Mill, Hegel, Dilthey, Husserl, Heidegger and many others. We can see Hume and Descartes as complementary, each one a side of the same coin in the historical transformations of two old tendencies: Aristotelic empiricism and Platonic rational idealism. There are different branches to this double rooted tree, from the theology of mathematics, to an empirical positivism associated to Bacon's extreme developments, to historicism and hermeneutics, passing through Vico, from a diversity of phenomenologies to techno-centrism. There are a number of other contemporary tendencies, each one displaying a different blend of the two radical, quite always opposing starting points, Plato and Aristotle.

7 Bourgeois Subjectivity

We can discern in Descartes an emphasis on the recently acquired power of the individual to determine and to own his ground. Descartes takes possession of reason as a ground just as the bourgeois now possesses land, ground wrestled away from tradition and the Church. Descartes' emphasis on "solid ground possession" assumes the pattern of an ownership of individual subjectivity. This image is applied in the First Meditation, versus traditional, inherited opinions. Ownership becomes a fundamental metaphor for ideas and subjective ground (ego identity). We could say that Descartes' epistemic typology philosophically translates the rise of the bourgeois subject through individualism as *EGO cogito, ergo sum.*

Principia Philosophiae[10] affirms: "Accordingly, the knowledge, I THINK, THEREFORE I AM, is the first and most certain that occurs to one who philosophizes orderly." This expresses the power to conquer the real and the certainty that bourgeois subjectivity, constituted through the new sociopolitical conditions, achieves through ego efforts, from his sole hyperbolic sense of existence. What the bourgeois possesses derives from what he individually IS, he "makes" himself, rather than is made through family inheritance or through class. Self-conscious of a successful existence, bourgeois subjectivity views itself as autonomous. The bourgeois owes his success exclusively to himself. He is the historical (and epistemic) "parvenu."[11] Hence, Descartes emphasizes

10 R. Descartes, *The Selections from The Principles of Philosophy*, trans. J. Veitch (South Dakota: Nuvision Publications, 2008).

11 A French expression for someone who suddenly becomes someone better or achieves a better social position without being quite ready for it.

"private" in his possession of a firm ground: his method insists on "my private" reason, not someone else's reasons, "my private ideas", not someone else's opinions. Through doubt Descartes cleans himself from acquired opinions and reaches a stable point, which is no other than his individual, subjective reason. "I first cleared away everything doubtful like the sand"[12] or:

> I realized how many false opinions I had accepted as true from childhood onwards, and that, whatever I had since built on such shaky foundations, could only be highly doubtful. Hence I saw that at some stage in my life the whole structure would have to be utterly demolished, and that I should have to begin again from the bottom up if I wished to construct something lasting and unshakeable in the sciences. First Meditation.[13]

So desires Freud: to establish a firm and permanent structure in the science of Psychoanalysis.[14] In the rather early *History of the Psychonalytical Movement* (1914), just after his rupture with Jung, Freud[15] writes:

> For psychoanalysis is my creation; for ten years I was the only one occupied with it, and all the annoyance which this new subject caused among my contemporaries has been hurled upon my head in the form of criticism.[16]

In the *Discourse of Method*, Descartes writes:

12 R. Descartes, *Meditations on First Philosophy With Selections from the Objections and Replies*, trans. M. Moriarty (Oxford: Oxford University Press, 2008), Replies 7, AT 7:537.

13 Ibid., para. 17.

14 Freud insists on the scientific character of his discoveries, from the first to his last work, whereas Jung's claims to science are rather pale as compared to Freudian ones; and not as pervasive, restrict mainly to his early works. The denial of a scientific character to psychoanalysis does not imply a denial of its meaningfulness. This would be as absurd as to say that the only meaningful dimension of human life is Science. Philosophy suffers from the same "complex" as psychology in relation to Science, when desiring to uphold "scientific" value and to establish her jurisdiction over Science itself. Wittgenstein denounces this presumption of Philosophy.

15 Although saying it is "really a matter of indifference" whether the history of psychoanalysis started with Breuer's cathartic method or only with his modification of the same, nonetheless Freud spends long paragraphs explaining their differences and claiming the discovery of psychoanalysis for himself (S. Freud, *History of the Psychonalytical Movement in The Basic Writings of Sigmund Freud*, ed. A.A. Brille [New York: Random House, 1938], 933–36).)

16 Ibid., 933.

> And when I noticed how many different opinions learned men may hold on the same subject, despite the fact that no more than one of them can ever be right, I resolved to consider as false any opinion which was merely plausible.[17]

Descartes continues:

> This is why I gave up my studies entirely as soon as I reached the age when I was no longer under the control of my teachers. I resolved to seek no other knowledge than that what I might find within myself, or perhaps, in the great book of nature.[18]

Here the "perhaps" is a concession to empiricism, but an Aristotelian empiricism which is an empiricism at the service of theory and not the other way round as for Pascal and Jung: where theory is at the service of pragmatic, existential realism. The different senses between theory and praxis insinuate themselves as an element in the fractal pattern distinguishing D-F type epistemologies from the P-J types. In an early letter to Fliess, May 30, 1896, Freud writes:

> It may be taken as a recognized fact that neurasthenia is a frequent consequence of an abnormal sexual life. The assertion, however, which I wish to make and to test by observations is that neurasthenia actually can only be a sexual neurosis.[19]

First comes the assertion Freud wishes to make, then the testing. This wouldn't be questionable if acknowledged, as discussed below.[20] The problem is Freud's pretension that his desired assertion was suggested from empirical material when much before his theory was finished, the sexual etiology was already a "wished assertion" to be confirmed.

Freud echoes the Cartesian "private" epistemic aspirations pattern by refusing to read philosophy (the "learned men" denied by Descartes), in order to keep his "own ideas" unmixed with external material. In the *History of the*

---

17 R. Descartes, *Discourse on Method*, trans. L. Lafleur (New York: Macmillan, 1960), 46.

18 Ibid., 49.

19 J.M. Masson, ed., *The Complete Letters of Sigmund Freud to Wilhelm Fliess, (1887–1904)* (Cambridge MA: Harvard University Press, 1985), 39.

20 An experience is a question put to nature, says Galileo. There's no neutrality in science. What is problematic with Freud is his pretension of no bias and on that account taking all his "findings" as ontology.

Psychoanalytical Movement, after rejecting some influence of Schopenhauer that was applied to his findings, Freud writes:

> ...in former years, I had taken more pleasure in reading philosophical authors. In later years I denied myself the great pleasure of reading Nietzsche's works, with the conscious motive of not wishing to be hindered in the working out of my psychoanalytical impressions by any preconceived ideas.[21]

Descartes and Freud set themselves as Robinson Crusoe, in ideal isolation. They rest in a sort of godlikeness, pretending to be unique creators of a new unique world (view) produced from within. Their "robinsonade" is consistent with the denial of history which is a hallmark of essentialist ontologies.

In a contrary move, Jung tries to preserve the history of his ideas when recycling ancient names for new conceptual usages, like "archetype", "anima/animus", "persona" whereas Freud pretends to invent everything anew, even when he is borrowing old concepts and current ideas. Pascal also sustains his *Thoughts* with that of ancient precursors. Although a radical Christian and very critical of Judaism, Pascal acknowledges and borrows from Hebrew Tradition, quoting the *Talmud* and the *Midrash* humbly recognizing the historical formation of his religion. On this line, Jung, conscious that he is no Robinson arriving at Psychology Land, insists on drawing attention to its historical condition. Jung gives the historical itinerary of his concepts, endorsing contingency and conceptual transformations implied by non-essentialist claims.

These different epistemological attitudes of Jung and Freud become apparent in the reading of the Jungian house dream,[22] with its historical layers: Jung sees in this image the expression of the historical formation of his own psyche, whereas Freud reads it as a "wish fulfilment", an expression of subjective occult desires (in this dream, Jung's supposed desires for Freud's death) and not an objective presentation of some aspect of reality as proposed by Jung's reading. Those are two different approaches to the "manifest", i.e. the empirical particular presentation of the proposition (the dream). For Jung it expresses a content intrinsically related to it, that can only be understood inside its particular presentation and the actual situation of the dreamer. For Freud, it shows the ideal being of the doctrine, loosely connected to the dream image, expressing (1) The ontology of the Freudian unconscious, the Id, ruled

---

21 Freud, *History of the Psychonalytical Movement in The Basic Writings of Sigmund Freud*, 9.

22 C.G. Jung, *Memories, Dreams, Reflections*, trans. R. Winston and C. Winston (New York: Vintage, 1989), 158–59.

by the pleasure principle whose sole activity is to desire; hence the dream necessarily as a wish fulfillment and (2) Inescapably submitted to the censorship distortions and/or obliteration of its unconscious content. Owing to Freud's negative conception of unconscious contents, the appearance of human skulls in the dream expresses a death repressed wish. Thereby Freud dissolves the empirical presentation of the dream into its "essential" components, the latent, which goes back to the ideal contents of psychoanalytical doctrine. In the same manner, Descartes dissolves the wax[23] into its essential components, i.e. the "innate" ideas constituting the wax essence. Therefore one can fairly say that in D-F epistemology "innate ideas" and "ideal elements of the doctrine" share the same structural dynamics in relation to knowledge with a common aim: to obscure and/or cancel empirical manifestations and their difficulties.

The Second Meditation stresses self-affirmation. Mind recognizes that although it can doubt the existence of everything it is impossible that it does not exist itself, moreover through its innate, God given notions it is impossible to fail. "I am I exist is necessarily true each time that I pronounce it, or that I mentally conceive it", writes Descartes. Thus the subjective world of the individual holds total sovereignty over being and existence. For Descartes this is warranted by God, for Freud by the doctrine. It's enough to mentally conceive it and then proceed to some empirical proofs, whereby a satisfactory link between empirical reality and theories is severely distorted at the knower's choices.[24] As regards Descartes, the consequences of his dismissal of empirical material is expressed in the poor results of his physics and biology, although

23 In the so-called "wax thought experiment" (Second Meditation) Descartes dissolves all the empirical properties of a piece of wax into its "essential idea" (the latent content of what a wax piece essentially is). Descartes says that all physical properties of the wax (the manifest appearance) are contingent and mutable therefore not suitable for certain knowledge.

24 "Frege rightly associates psychologistic logic with epistemological idealism (…) psychologistic definitions of concepts lead to logical incoherence and epistemological absurdity. By using the ambivalent notion of an idea to define concepts, the distinction between what is perceptible and what is objective is lost at an early stage and ultimately the actual or perceptible is treated as constituted of ideas. If all thinking consists of creating, connecting, and altering ideas, if subjects and predicates are like ideas, then the notion of subjectivity and with it truth, disappear. Thus misapprehension in logic leads to epistemological idealism and hence, with perfect consistency, to solipsism. But the idea of the moon is not the moon, and the number one is not the idea I have of it. The examination of ideas is part of psychology, but the examination of concepts, or of numbers or of anything else that belongs to the domain of the objective, be it Platonistic or perceptible it is not insight and illusion." (P.M.S. Hacker, *Wittgenstein on Philosophy and the Metaphysics of Experience* [Oxford: Clarendon Press, 1972], 34–35).

in relation to abstract thinking, Descartes' mathematical work with algebra is outstanding. Pascal's physics and his careful experiences with vacuums remain till today as models of pragmatic endeavors. Pascal never denied the value of abstract thinking. However he saw it limited to abstract dimensions, as mathematics, impossible to be applied to regions beyond the limits of man's reason. Pascal refused the certainty of reason's proofs of God's existence rejecting the application of reason to the infinite beyond man's limits. A position similar to Wittgenstein's. As E. Mortimer writes:

> A modern man, starting out for his office, may glance at his wrist-watch, tap the barometer, slip into the nearest tobacconist's shop for a purchase, and receive his change from the cash machine, board an omnibus and presently sit at his desk. How remote might seem the French geometer who got mixed up with Jansenism before Versailles was built! Yet Pascal originated that barometer, invented that calculating machine, was the first man to think of an omnibus and to organize a line of public vehicles, and was perhaps the only man before the twentieth century habitually to wear a wrist-watch.[25]

8 Freud and the Surgeon Image

Freud makes a very extensive use of the surgeon image in order to represent psychoanalytical work. He returns to this image several times in his writings. In *Five Lessons on Psycho-analysis*, 1910; in *The Future Prospects of Psycho-analytic Therapy*, 1910; *About teaching*, 1919; *Recommendations to Physicians Practising Psycho-analysis*, 1912; *Turnings in the Ways of Psycho-analytic Therapy*, 1924. In these writings the image appears connected to psychoanalytical technique. Through this image Freud intends to express the neutrality and impassible attitude that best fits the analyst and the aseptic quality required of his technique. However, other elements become apparent. I propose a thought experiment around Freud's surgeon image. Let us suppose the analysand, in the couch, immobilized like a wax figure, receiving the analytical Cartesian wax treatment. What could be expected from the analytical procedure? Arguably all the psychological material produced is to be analytically reduced to its "essential" elements, in order to fulfill the requirements of an efficient episteme. Arguably, those cannot but be the primary processes of the repressed

25 E. Mortimer, *Blaise Pascal, The Life and Work of a Realist* (London: Hertford and Halow, 1959), 12.

unconscious. Now, the contents of the so-called "primary processes", are, inescapably, the essential ideas of the Freudian doctrine, ontologically conceived. These essential ideas have the same structural dynamics as the "innate" ideas in Descartes' episteme. The commitment to innate ideas might place Freud in a rational tradition that goes back to Plato in the measure that essential knowledge derives from ideas of the intellect and not from the senses. Freud epistemically treats the manifest as but a shadow of the latent. Although claiming to be an empiricist, at the moment Freud dissolves the manifest content of psychological facts into latent contents, he is unmasking the true and the real behind the shadows in Plato's cave. There's also some similarity with Plato's recollection as regards the discovery (or re-discovery) of the real truths of the unconscious. As Descartes in his wax thought experiment, Freud digs out from the wax figure immobilized in the couch what is the essential nature of psychic life. Seeing this thought experiment through the perspective of innate ideas we could say that whereas in Descartes we find an ontology of thought in Freud there is an ontology of the doctrine.

9 P-J Alternative

The "natural light" of Pascal is not the same as the Cartesian "intuitus." Whereas Descartes pretends to attain the "essence" of what is known, acquiring a totalitarian, ontological grasp on his subject, thereby producing indubitable, dogmatic knowledge through the intuitus; Pascal's "natural light" produces an intuitive, incomplete knowledge of primitive ideas, like light, space, time, movement, number, with no possible grasp of their essential being. However Pascal doesn't fall into the abyss of his ignorance neither does he fall prey to skepticism. In Thought 72 we find:

> For in fact what is man in nature? A Nothing in comparison with the Infinite, an All in comparison with Nothing, a mean between nothing and everything (…) Let us then take our compass, we are something, and we are not everything. The nature of our existence hides from us the knowledge of first beginnings which are born of the Nothing; and the Littleness of our being conceals from us the sight of the Infinite. Our intellect holds the same position in the world of thought as our body occupies in the expanse of nature. Limited as we are in every way, this state which holds the mean between two extremes (two Infinites) is present in all our impotence. (…)This is our true state; that's what makes us incapable of certain knowledge and of absolute ignorance (…) Let's therefore not

> look for certainty and stability. Our reason is always deceived by fickle shadows; nothing can fix the finite between the two Infinites, which both enclose and fly from it.

With an epistemology consistent with his anthropology, Pascal avoids the temptation to fall in with the extremes: no certainty but no absolute ignorance either. Pascal understands that the skeptical demand for certain knowledge, rejecting limited knowledge, in fact expresses the skeptical aspiration to dogmatic certainty. Perhaps this capacity of holding his ground between extremes is one of the main aspects defining his difference from Descartes who aspired for a pure single conception at a time, since contradictions and paradoxes might breed doubt. Ernest Mortimer emphasizes how Pascal was able to entertain simultaneous propositions which appeared incompatible.[26] So is Jung in his conception of the Self as *Coincidentia Oppositorum*, the masculine and feminine co-existence in every individual and the ego/shadow/persona diversities.

Incapable of holding the middle, the skeptical falls to one of the extremes (certain knowledge is impossible, therefore no knowledge is possible), whereas Descartes falls to the other (certain knowledge is granted by the intuitus, therefore unbeatable certainty is attainable). In his *Thoughts*, Pascal unmasks Descartes' epistemology as the other side of the skeptical coin, calling him "useless and uncertain."[27] Pascal holds a position of equilibrium, a man able to stand his ground between infinite extremes without falling into inflation or despair. Consistent with his anthropology Pascal confesses that although incapable of defining what space is, he can do geometry; although mathematics is unable to define its objects of study, numbers, it solves problems with them.[28] Pascal is not dismayed by the fact that he cannot give essential definitions. Jung expresses a similar epistemic humility and courage. Accepting the "something" actually possible in knowledge and daring to further his investigations without falling into the essentialist trap, Jung proceeds in P mode. Spirit is one of Jung's themes. Rejecting the metaphysical lustre of the spiritual dimension, Jung[29] examines the different uses of the word "spirit" without ever proposing an essential definition. As Pascal in relation to space, Jung is not appalled at his inability to hold a totalitarian grip on the essential nature of

26 Mortimer, *Blaise Pascal, The Life and Work of a Realist.*

27 B. Pascal, *Thoughts*, trans. W.F. Trotter (New York: E.P. Dutton & Co., 1958), 78.

28 Wittgenstein has a similar outlook: we may be able to find our way in a city, although unable to draw a detailed map.

29 C.G. Jung, "The Archetypes and the Collective Unconscious", in *The Collected Works*, ed. G. Adler and R.F.C. Hull, vol. 9i (Princeton: Princeton University Press, 1968), 207–54.

"spirit." Unpretentiously, Jung seizes the pragmatic traces of spiritual reality for his psychological investigations. Jung's approach is pragmatic and of the same nature as Wittgenstein's approach to essential definitions: they are impossible, let us then investigate the use of the words.

This seems to be the pragmatic, non-dogmatic, realistic counterposition to idealism shared by P-J epistemic typology. It reveals a different psychological attitude as those of D-F epistemologies in similar historical conditions. Freud capitulates at the confrontation with the spiritual, precisely on account of his epistemic and anthropological bias. Unable to hold a middle ground between complementary extremes, Freud submits the spiritual realm to biology as a by-product of the physical, which he pretends to know. Limited as he is in the imperfect, finite state which holds the mean between two extremes – matter and spirit, the two Infinites defying human impotence and knowledge challenges – Freud tries to escape his true state by canceling the aporetic nature of his scanty, though possible knowledge of one of the extremes. Unable to possess the spiritual dimension in its "essence", Freud upholds the other extreme (the biological, the physical, the material) as an exclusive solid basis to ground his doctrine, reducing the uncertain spirit to the supposedly solid foundation of the physical.

Epistemologies of the P-J type produce a knowledge that renounces a totalitarian appropriation of the object because they reject the skeptical demands of apodictic truth. It is a type of knowledge able to cope with the anxiety of being unable to find an Absolute ground (be it the intuitus, the transcendental subject or a doctrine). P-J epistemologies yield a brand of knowledge that accepts doubt and restriction, strong enough to stand up to turbulence at the edge of chaos, mature enough to face up to the "the eternal silence of these infinite spaces"[30] of its own ignorance. It doesn't anesthetize the subject as in Freud's surgeon metaphor, nor proposes an èpoché, putting the world into brackets.[31] The fundamental move here is not to dissolve the wax (as Descartes' thought experiment in Second Meditation), refraining from degrading the

30 Pascal, *Thoughts*, 208.

31 Epistemologies of the D-F type support many historical versions, another one is Husserl's enthronement of the transcendental subject – and consequent èpoché of the empirical – a doctrine which Husserl, correctly calls an "egology" as the idealist standings imply an inflation of the ego. Compensatory or not, this typology aims at a dogmatic, totalitarian adventure that is only possible when the world and otherness are ignored. Taking Descartes' Meditations as his starting point, Husserl falls victim to logical absolutism withdrawing into the transcendental subject. No surprise that Wittgenstein's pragmatic and realistic philosophy, in tune with P-J epistemic typology, turns against this brand of phenomenology.

empirical in order to conquer the essence. If ever an "essence hunter" gets somewhere, what is found cannot but be the essence of his own dogmatic whims. The idealist position implies an inflation of the subjective ego.

10 The Intuitus and the Doctrine, the Symbol and the Unknown

P-J and D-F epistemologies are associated with very different anthropologies. Freud and Descartes share the fantasy of a pure research subject, neutral, scientific, purified from subjective prejudice. Whereas Descartes bases his innate ideas in the intuitus, the promised omniscience of the divine seal given to man, Freud bases his warrant seal in the objectivity of the doctrine he discovered. In this sense, Freudian doctrine becomes like a region of pure consciousness that has little to do with the dynamics of the given, i.e. the empirical material. From this region the "surgeon" may act upon the dormant subject. "Doctrine" in Freud plays the same epistemic role as the innate ideas for Descartes. For both, only the being of the idea is alive and active when confronting empirical facts. Like all idealists, Freud degrades the empirical. He does it through the latent/manifest split. The universal (the latent) is radically split from the particular (the manifest). The latent is the ideal secured by the doctrine. The doctrine, from his first works on hysteria to the last one presents three pillars: sexual etiology, formation of the unconscious through repression, the importance of childhood sexuality.[32] These play the role of the innate ideas to which everything in psychological life – individual or collective, healthy or pathological – is to be reduced. Therefore D-F and P-J account for two different epistemological types when facing the unknown. One, born out of a mixture of anxiety and compensatory omnipotence secures the means to hold a stable ground of certainty in the realm of ideas, be it through the intuitus or the doctrine. The other, acknowledges its own ignorance although not giving up the investigation, accepting limited knowledge. Without totalitarian pretensions, P-J epistemologies catch what they can afford.

For Jung, the link to the unknown is the symbol, through the symbol there is no way out to escape to a predictable "latent." The unknown in the symbol is received with no recourse to a doctrine, precisely because what is to be revealed is not exclusively universal and therefore not pre-arranged in any possible catalogue of known essences. The unknown in the symbol is the unique dialogue of the universal (that's why collective material is conjured up to help the understanding) within one particular, empirical historical situation here

32 These are three possible dynamics, however not the exclusive ones of psychic life.

and now. A possible mistake here is to reify the symbolic contents, hypostha-zising them into a doctrine of essences and ontologies where the symbolic image becomes but a catalogue item within an individuation program. Were it so, a symbol would have a permanent meaning, thereby dissolving itself, turning into a "sign", according to Jung's definition. The symbol is only a symbol in the dialogue with the here and now, exclusively through the here and now, conjured up by the here and now. It is a messenger of the unattainable extremes that inhabit and envelop human finitude. Being a synthetic unity inseparable from the here and now, a symbol may die and resurrect in distinct collective or individual conditions and although manifestly "the same" deliver different messages throughout different historical conditions, both individually and collectively. Because the symbol is the best expression for an unknown content its appearance produces a complex system that can be treated as a fractal: we never see wholeness, there are limits everywhere, it comes from regions Infinite, provoking the shock between the unknown but knowable and/or the unknown unknowable. However, as a fractal, the symbol portrays wholeness.

11 Free Association and Amplification

As regards the psychological facts presented (dreams, fantasies, symptoms, life history and reports), Freud develops a technique with a structural dynamics similar to Descartes' chains of reasoning. In the *Discourse of method*, Descartes proposes the following:

> Those long chains of reasoning, simple and easy as they are, of which geometricians make use in order to arrive at the most difficult demonstrations, had caused me to imagine that all those things which fall under the cognizance of man might very likely be mutually related in the same fashion.[33]

There's an affinity with the long chains of free association of the Freudian technique that proceed in a psychologically continuous sequence. The F-D affinity is based on a conception of the smoothness of rationality ruling over empirical roughness, suppressing the discontinuity and surprises provoked by contingency. Freudian free association aspires to be "deductive."[34] Jung rebels

33 R. Descartes, *Discourse on Method and Meditations on First Philosophy*, trans. E.S. Haldane (Kansas: Digireads Publishing, 2005), 10.

34 In the *Tratactus* Wittgenstein writes about deduction: "each logical truth, bears its own warrant upon its face, shows by itself that it is a tautology." (6.127 b) That's why there is no

against the continuity of the association chain, proposing the technique of amplification that works through discontinuous elements around the psychological fact investigated, set as a focal point. Though discontinuous, the associated elements are closely connected and mutually supportive, some overlapping. In this manner, the amplification technique breaks the continuity of a mechanistic, linear, uni-causal chain by this creating the possibility of grasping the historical core.

A similar epistemic position is found in the "reason of effects" proposed by Pascal. Take one proposition (the psychological fact investigated is a proposition) and derive from it the greatest possible number of elements. As Pascal shows in *Thoughts* the derived elements are not conceived as links of the implacable necessity of a linear chain of logical deduction, but form a discontinuous arrangement of pros and cons; different elements, although each of them united to a focal point, the central proposition. The central point is illuminated by the reason (the rationality, the logic) of the multiplicity of discontinuous and even contradictory effects produced; understood as complimentary assessments of the focal proposition. In J's method, the reason of the effects is given by the amplification through both collective and personal associations each one connected to the focal point, instead of being drawn by a single final point. We don't live in a linear world, linearity is incredibly rare in this world and the linear chain of associations fit the ideal deductive method of mathematics. P-J epistemology is realistic and nominalistic, mirroring empirical discontinuity and the aporetic nature of induction, D-F is idealist and essentialist mirroring deduction.

12 The Smoothness of the Ideal versus the Roughness of the Empirical

The notion of discontinuity and roughness of the empirical versus an ideal smoothness and continuity of pure logic is also a theme in Wittgenstein.[35] I would say this is a theme of realistic standpoints against idealist ones.

Discontinuity is a central feature of P-J epistemology. The association experiment is based precisely in the blockade of the association, not in its

unique inferential order among the propositions of logic (6.127 a) and why the proof of logical conclusions from logical premises is merely a useful device for facilitating recognition of tautology in difficult cases. Proof in logic is quite different from proof by means of logic.

35 When describing the requirements of an ideal logic Wittgenstein writes: "We have got onto slippery ice where there is no friction and so in a certain sense the conditions are ideal, but also, just because of that, we are unable to walk. We want to walk, so we need friction. Back to the rough ground!" (Wittgenstein, *Philosophical Investigations,* 46).

flowing. It is there, at the moment that the flowing is obstructed that the unknown emerges. The edge of chaos is announced by a "stop signal" manifest as an instant of mute hesitation foreboding a fearful confrontation with either what we do ignore or what we rather ignore. The association experiment is based on the turbulence created by the shock between what is known and what is unknown, be it repressed or never known. Jung takes a symbolic standing towards the association experiment as well as towards all manifestations of psychic life, normal or pathological, collective or individual, like dreams, symptoms, the transference, art, culture, religion, mythology etc. One could fairly say that the symbol is the central category of Jung's thinking. A similar move occurs with Freud, whose central category also covers the fullness of psychic life. However, on account of different anthropologies the central Freudian category is the latent/manifest split.

13 About Neutrality

Descartes' preconditions for thinking clearly and distinctly are set in the First Meditation:

> I have delivered my mind of every care (and am happily agitated by no passions) and since I have procured for myself an assured leisure in a peaceable retirement, I shall at least seriously and freely address myself to the general upheaval of all my former opinions.

Delivered, free, with no passions, Descartes looks for peaceful neutrality, cleaning himself from all agitation. This psychological attitude may be associated with the apparently "neutral", emptied social terrain (free from guilds, without inheritance, delivered from the oppressive weight of tradition and the Church) upon which bourgeois subjectivity builds its successful existence. Neutrality's requirements fit well the pattern of a unique first creator, sure of his omnipotence and ready to display omniscience, dispensing any counsel from his angels or ministers. We find a similar attitude in Freud: like the surgeon who removes all emotions from himself. In Freud's image, the object becomes a dead element whereas the subject mind appears as the all knower with absolute certainty and ideal purity. Although consciously proposing himself as an empiricist, in this image Freud betrays himself. The surgeon image is an example of the transcendental subject notion, as the exclusive active power working over "dead material", or at least, reduced to wax immobility. The transcendental subject creates his own knowledge universe, establishing his scientific world in a clean, empty space, no longer populated by passions nor by some inherited ideas. Hence, no inheritance to claim, no tradition to fetter one's foresight, no guild to belong only the one he is ready to inaugurate. In 1914, Freud sets to write his *History of the Psychonalytical Movement*. This was Freud's early market cry for the subject promotion shared with Descartes in the scientificization and absolutization of the possibility of subjective knowledge ruling over facticity. In the above-mentioned letter to Fliess, Freud presents what is his obsessive etiology for psychopathology showing how the idea, "an assertion I want to make", came before the facts. But with the theoretical tools Freud provided for himself, his wished assertion hovers above the empirical. Censorship and resistance, repression, condensation and displacement allow for empirical falsifications to fit the doctrine, any empirical fact qualifies to "test" the ideas prescribed by the doctrine.

The ideal standing shared by D-F epistemologies leads to radical practical consequences, distinct from the realistic pragmatic quality of the P-J types. Jung writes in *Memories, Dreams, Reflections*:

> Analysis is a dialogue demanding two partners. Analyst and patient sit facing one another, eye to eye; the doctor has something to say, but so has the patient.[36]

Certainly that's not the case for an anaesthetized subject and no neutrality is pre-supposed for the analyst. Here one can read the pragmatic seal on factual observation. For P, the whole of physics is a science of facts; not for D, where experiences are at the service of "reason." J is closer to P when approaching unconscious material as a science of facts. This supposes no neutrality, because there can be no ideal, pure rational observation of facts. As Galileo proposes, "An experience is a question put to nature", because simply to observe without a determined perspective leads nowhere. To put a question is to direct the orientation of what is being observed in a specific, determined manner. Pascal follows Galileo in his understanding that science cannot be a gratuitous observation of facts, it consists rather in building up the conditions for meaningful experiences which excludes a neutral position, ab initio. Science is not neutral, it is defined by the particular question and perspective man chooses for his observation. K. Popper follows this tenet and all contemporary science stresses the impossibility of neutral observation, including the observer's frame of reference in the observation. From Galileo to Einstein or quantum physics, science remains a particular question put to nature, producing particular

36 Jung, *Memories, Dreams, Reflections*, 131.

technologies designed to answer specific inquires; from Pascal's glass tubes designed for his vacuum experiments to the contemporary particle colliders. No sign of neutral observation. The more objective a knowledge process styles itself, by ignoring its own particular perspective and reference frame, the more subjective it becomes. The problem with Freudian theory is not so much the bias but the fact of ignoring the bias, which is ontologically understood and set as a metaphysical condition.

14 The Inseparability of Theory and Praxis

The issue of neutrality and of a passive subject comes to life in the psychoanalytical choice of the couch. Fordham[37] comments on Jung's disinclination toward the couch as articulated during one of the *Tavistock Lectures* (1935):

> Though Jungian analysis can be very much like that conducted by psychoanalysis there was one respect in which Jung was very emphatic that it should be different: analysts should sit in full view of their patients. From this position, he claimed, the patient can witness his effect on his analyst and the analyst will not be able to detach himself from the patient. He states: "I reject the idea of putting the patient upon a sofa and sitting behind him. I put my patients in front of me and I talk to them as one normal human being to another, and I expose myself and react with no restriction.[38]

On the other hand, following Freud, Fordham expresses a strong preference for the use of the couch. In his book *Jungian Psychotherapy: a study in Analytical Psychology* published in 1978, he enumerates six reasons for its use, which he believes brings "specific advantages."[39] These include: the patient's comfort and relaxation; facilitation of regressive states; easier access to the unconscious; intensification of the transference; awareness of somatic occurrences; and an increase in the analyst's capacity to attend to the clinical process. That regression should be facilitated is already a feature of the doctrine with its emphasis on infantile sexuality showing that the setting is not neutral at all but faithfully follows a doctrine. That an intensification of the transference should

37 M. Fordham, *Jungian Psychotherapy: A Study on Analytical Psychology* (London: Karnac Books, 1990).

38 Ibid.

39 Ibid., 68–69.

be desired is a piece of the doctrine as well as a means to enhance the power of the analyst over the analysand. The transference neurosis repeating childhood elements is essential to the Freudian method. From the opposite side of this episteme, in lecture five of the *Tavistock Lectures,* Jung writes:

> One always has to answer people in their main function, otherwise no contact is established. So, in order to be able to show my patients that their reactions have arrived in my system, I have to sit opposite them so that they can read the reactions in my face and can see that I am listening. If I sit behind them, then I can yawn, I can sleep, I can go off on my own thoughts, and I can do what I please. They never know what is happening to me, and then they remain in an auto-erotic and isolated condition which is not good for ordinary people.[40]

One cannot fail to perceive the seal of Freud's theory in the technique of his choice, autoeroticism being a blueprint of all psychic life, a pervasive, universal content and an essential feature of the transference neuroses rejected by Jung. For Freud, even symptoms are considered as autoerotic forms of satisfaction.

15 Latent/Manifest and the Symbolic

Because truth has its home in the proposition itself, as in mathematics, the concrete instantiation of the empirical loses ground to the supra-temporal being of the idea hence construing reason (in Freud's case, the rationality of the theory, its ideality or ideal being) on an ontological basis. Similar to the wax thought experiment of the Second Meditation where Descartes strips the wax of all empirical being, retaining only its ideal being, Freud posits a split between the latent and the manifest content (not only in the dream but throughout all psychological life, healthy or unhealthy, personal or collective); whereby he strips the empirical material (dream images, slips of the tongue, mishaps, memory blocks, associations, extending the projection of this scission into his interpretation of collective facts, like the developments of civilization, ethnology, culture, art and religion) to unmask the ideal content revealed by the doctrine, consisting of repressed sexuality (the fundamental ideal content), ontologically understood. The tools used are defenses and censorship where repression and resistance are means to entirely deface the manifest thus immunizing the

40 C.G. Jung, "The Tavistock Lectures", in *The Collected Works*, trans. G. Adler and R.F.C. Hull, vol. 18 (Princeton: Princeton University Press, 1980), para. 321.

doctrine from further experiential falsification. As a pseudo scientific dogma, the ideal contents of the doctrine are saved from verification failures by the addition of *post hoc* arrangements making them compatible with facticity.

Therefore, Freud writes that the manifest (the empirical appearance) is not important, what is fundamental are the mechanisms of condensation and displacement, the dream work in itself. But the dream work is the universal, whereas the particular is the manifest. Censorship causes the rejection of evidence, reducing the particular to the universal, a typical idealist procedure. Freud affirms that the significant factors are the dynamics dissolving the manifest into the latent, thereby translating the apories of empiric into the apodictic ideal being of the doctrine. Hence, psychoanalytical observation turns into an exercise of suspicion where the analyst needs to catch what is hidden, although already pre-formulated by the doctrine. Like Descartes, Freud has an instrumental role for "doubt" in his episteme. In contrast, for Jung analytical observation is an exercise of exploration to discover what is not known because the symbol is the central category of his thinking. As Jung writes, the symbol is the best expression for an unknown content. The empirical material has to be preserved in its pristine presentation because it really is "the best possible presentation" for what is not known; hence the doorway to it, the very means to all possible knowability of the unconscious. Therefore, "stick to the image", which means respect facts (an image is a fact), never falsifying empirical material or "doubting" its objective presentation.

16 Structural Dynamics of Conceptual Networks

The Freudian negative evaluation of the unconscious collides with the positive Jungian approach, thereby setting a fundamental distinction between what is supposed to be the best policy in the interface relations of unconscious/consciousness expressed through the differences of the conceptual network connected to the interface. The transcendent function, writes Jung, arises from the union of conscious and unconscious content. As the connector between known/unknown, it is the operator of the symbolic. This function is welcome on account of the fundamentally positive Jungian evaluation of the unconscious as the creative source organized by the Self, which is nothing less than God's image in man. Thus the transcendent function and its child, the symbol, present a vital, creative value, associated with "integration of unconscious contents", viewed as a favorable matter. The Jungian synthetic agencies are supposed to fulfill psychic life furthering the integration of unconscious contents. On the other hand, an examination of Freud's doctrine shows that all the interface activity between consciousness and the unconscious is performed by restrictive concepts. This is perfectly consistent with the negative Freudian approach to the unconscious as shaped mainly by repression on account of the opposition between its ruling principle – the amoral pleasure principle – and the demands of morality, real life, and civilization. Jung's positive perspective on the unconscious as the field of archetypes and instincts joins Pascal's evaluation. In Thought 411 Pascal writes:

> Despite all our miseries which press upon us and grip us by the throat, we have an instinct which we cannot repress, and which raises us up.

For Freud "instinct" abases man and repression is fundamental for growth and civilization.

A J-F comparison of the structural dynamics of phenomena at this interface will necessarily present a distinctive disposition based on their very distinct underlying approaches to the unconscious. To expect a similar evaluation of the interface phenomena in Freud and Jung would be incoherent, not to say extravagant, on account of their fundamentally diverse appreciation of the unconscious. In terms of the structural dynamics displayed by concepts, in Jung we find a transcendent function and the symbol, whereas in Freud there is censorship and a compromise formation. Therefore Jung may write, according to his premises of a creative, positive unconscious: "My life is a story of the self-realization of the unconscious."[41] Jungian theory also provides a consistent conceptual network able to bring about the integration of consciousness and unconscious. In agreement with his theory, Freud would say: my life is a story of the self-repression of the unconscious. Each specific theoretical move engenders a specific practical move as well, the separation between theory and practice being a misconception inherited from the Greek world.

This is consistent with major distinctive aspects of P-J and D-F epistemological types. Censorship is no less an act of violence than is D's thought experiment with the wax. Descartes also holds that metaphysical inquiry (inquiry at A pole) is necessarily in conflict with the senses (B pole) as proposed in his Replies 2, AT 7:156–57.[42] On their structural dynamics functioning D-F epistemologies cancel one of the systems (ideal/doctrine suppressing the empirical) becoming uni-causal and reductionist. The contents of so-called A or B poles are specific to D or to F, however, the conflictive pattern leading to the

41 Jung, *Memories, Dreams, Reflections*, 3.

42 Descartes, *Meditations on First Philosophy With Selections from the Objections and Replies*, 2 AT 7:156–57.

absolutism of the ideal holds a fractal pattern. Different from the extreme positions of D-F, Pascal sets man in the center of two unknown Infinites with no expectation to cancel either of the extremes, only to hold the mean, accepting the limits of his finite being. So does Jung.

17 Neutrality and the Reason of the Effects (Amplification): A Return to the Central Proposition

Consistent with the image of the surgeon, master of his emotions, Freud summons to life the anesthetized subject in the use of the couch. This image is not gratuitous. It is consistent with the defacement of the empirical through the latent/manifest split canceling any activity at the analyzed pole. Although the analysand does all the talk, the doctrine doesn't tolerate anything that cannot be grasped by its ideal contents, since there are no symbolic dimensions to bring up unknown, creative contents. The pathway to new contents is obstructed in favor of old known truths delivered by the doctrine. Reduced to dead matter by the absolutism of the doctrine the passive subject in the couch reveals the idealistic brand of the D-F epistemic type. Hence, the Freudian analytical scenario tells the opposite of what it means, submitted as it is to the latent/manifest rule: the impassible and phlegmatic attitude of the analyst (the manifest) opposes the emotional, talkative analysand (the manifest). Applying the latent/manifest split, the situation is reversed: the apparently active analysand becomes muzzled by the doctrine and the manifestly passive analyst becomes the only active pole, master of all signification. It is the analyst who bestows meaning to the analysand's words, uncovering his psychic life. Fordham writes that Freud saw the couch as creating a "closed" system for analysis (defined by separation between analyst and patient), whereas Jung's own approach to analysis was based on an "open system in which the analyst participated." J's epistemology is much closer to contemporary science where the observer participates in the experiment, his particular position being fundamental for the results whereas Freud's ideal neutrality is a leftover of the scientific positivistic conservatism of the nineteenth century. The ideal purity of the neutral subject is an artifact of a conception of reason that supposes rationality as a realm beyond good and evil, immunized against all the contingencies and defilements of the empirical. Protected by the dogmatic theology of the intuitus or of the doctrine, D-F epistemologies refrain from resting on "the heart." And that's precisely where Pascal sets the source of his primitive, fundamental, although non-essentialist notions like light, time, space, number, movement. Those are notions beyond definition, grounding all possible knowledge, although always surrounded by infinite unknowable abysses never to be conquered by apodictic certainty.

18 P's Heart

The heart is the seat of the "light of nature." Contrary to the rational "nous", Aristotle"s designation of the faculty that allows for knowledge of first principles, Pascal calls it "heart." Pascal doesn't choose a static organ, but an agitated, concrete one, alien to ideal aseptic serenity. He chooses the organ which beats according to our emotions. The common misunderstanding of Thought 277 that "the heart has its reasons, which reason does not know" misses the point of what heart Pascal is talking about. It's not the red heart of the over sentimental nor the blue one of the eighteenth and nineteenth centuries' romanticism, a compensatory tendency for the dry rationality of a certain version of the Enlightenment, related to Cartesian rational idealism. P's heart is the biblical heart, the heart of King Solomon. Solomon doesn't ask for ready-made wisdom, but for an organ capable to produce it. Solomon asks for a "wise heart" (*lev hacham*) in order to judge his difficult people. Immediately after God grants his desire, the Torah describes an application of the wisdom it produces in the famous judgment of the two mothers and a single surviving baby.[43] Unsure of where lies the truth, Solomon is unwilling to favor the wrong side, delivering an unfair judgment. Hence the king resorts to neutrality as a truth guardian: half baby for each mother. Eventually, the truth appears. We don't know if the one who chooses to give away the baby's possession to preserve his life is the biological mother. Anyway, this is the woman, whose heart's judgment reveals the true rationality of motherness.

What is at work here is the living movement of the wise heart. After the first beat generating the equitable, neutral decision, the heart empties itself to be filled again by another flow of understanding thereby summoning a new turn of knowledge and understanding, amplifying its scope. Many effects can be extracted from the rationality of this situation. One is related to the discontinuous flow of the heartbeat, where one judgment is added to another, juxtaposed, even opposed, but always aiming at the central proposition delineating the truth whose radiation starts to concentrate around a focal point,

43 The call for a neutral, aseptic wisdom according to the rules of a surgery room is a sort of an ideal positivism transposed from science into ethics. Ethical positivism is a pervasive tendency of our culture manifest under a perverse polymorphous variety that attains its culmination in the multiple presentations of "political correctness."

showing the reason of the effects. The living dynamics of the heartbeat is very distinct from the deductive inertia of a linear chain, developing as a sequence inexorably attracted to a single point, like to a black hole.[44] Like the heartbeat, knowledge is a living process, unfriendly to static dogmas. Another of the effects (consequences) of the wise heart's reasons is that there is no wisdom in neutrality as there is no neutrality in wisdom. At best, neutrality is a means to a shaking of appearances, a first beat, soon to empty itself, a provoker of knowledge, yielding a more objective appreciation of what is not known but insinuates itself at the verge of the next beat. Neutrality is a procedure immediately to be abandoned as truth emerges from contingency and dynamic, historical processes revealing the hidden aspects of its living radiance.[45] Thought 282 states: "Although reasoning with our souls, the knowledge of first principles comes from the heart", i.e. from the body. The parallelism between the Jungian feeling function proposition as a rational function of judgment and the P biblical heart is another expression of the commensurateness of their shared epistemic typology.

In his sexuality theory Freud finds "truth", a truth that keeps itself permanent, amid the changing presentations of the empirical (whose contradictions he solves with post-hoc arrangements); from his first works to the last one. Only this "truth" is the abiding and the stable. By this move, Freud pushes "ideality" over the empirical. No matter what Freud declares about his empiricism it is the ideal context alone that gives a unified validity to his findings, therefore, an ideal validity. Like Aristotle and Descartes, Freud uses empirical data to serve his ideas, whereas in P and J the theory is at the service of empirical material and pragmatism. Whereas Descartes intends to produce a proof of God's existence, Pascal does not even try to demonstrate God's reality. His Wager Argument[46] is exclusively pragmatic aiming at human existence and not at God's ontology. For both Pascal and Jung God is a pragmatic, existential proposition, although each one derives different consequences from his particular brand of pragmatism. The heart, as a physical organ translates the notions arising from the light of nature, from the infinite regions beyond our limits producing the

---

44 "Free association means that you open yourself to any amount and kind of associations and they naturally lead you to your complexes." (Jung, "The Tavistock Lectures", para. 171). The linear deductive chain attracted to a single energy point.

45 Truth is historical and therefore, dynamic and contingent. As Pascal writes: "Justice and truth are two such subtle points, that our tools are too blunt to touch them accurately. If they reach the point, they either crush it, or lean all round, more on the false than on the true." Therefore, only the living, historical heart, may aspire to understand the subtle movements of truth and justice, through the constant emptying and filling itself again and again, beat after beat. Truth is an activity.

46 Pascal, *Thoughts*, 184–241.

fundamental ground for our epistemic survival. It is the heart's rationality that mediates the basic, fundamental illuminations needed for our life, although we shall never achieve total knowledge. The heart translates these illuminations into pragmatic, existential wisdom,[47] as indispensable epistemic tools in a survival kit. The heart's rationality is the moderator between eternity and time, infinite and finite filtered through our historical condition: a life beat surrounded by infinite abysses everywhere.

19 Anthropologies at the Edge of Chaos

In Thought 282, Pascal writes:

> We know truth, not only by the reason, but also by the heart, and it is in this last way that we know first principles; and reason, which has no part in it, tries in vain to impugn them. The skeptics, who have only this for their object, labour to no purpose. We know that we do not dream, and however impossible it is for us to prove it by reason, this inability demonstrates only the weakness of our reason, but not, as they affirm, the uncertainty of all our knowledge. For the knowledge of first principles, as space, time, motion, number, is as sure as any of those which we get from reasoning. And reason must trust these intuitions of the heart, and must base them on every argument.

With "reasons of the heart" Pascal endorses different rationalities. So does Jung when subscribing to the notion of an organizing principle with its own rationality intrinsic to the unconscious.

The rationality of the unconscious has a self-regulating function for both the individual and the collective. The relations between different rationalities (the unconscious as a whole has its proper rationality and there are specific

47 The whole of the modern Existentialist movement may be considered to stem from Kierkegaard's blunt protest against the Hegelian Absolute: "Put me in a system and you negate me, I'm not a mathematical symbol. I am." There is something peculiarly modern in the very ring of this appeal from abstraction to experience. We should hardly expect to find any parallel to it from a century earlier than the nineteenth, and it would seem specially unlikely from the age of Descartes and Spinoza. But listen to Pascal: "Man is full of needs. He will only turn where they can all be satisfied. Someone may say of me, "He is a good mathematician", but I do other things. He is taking me for a proposition. Jean-Paul Sartre cries today: "L'homme est une passion inutile!" Pascal was before him with "Quelle chimère est donc que l'homme!" and his conception of the néant is precisely echoed in the most sombre passages of the French existentialists; but Pascal has something to put beside it, or rather inside it." (Mortimer, *Blaise Pascal, The Life and Work of a Realist*, 13).

rationalities for each complex and archetype) are not necessarily hostile but rather complementary, except in the case of tyrannic aspirations, when one complex, archetype or consciousness tries to rule dimensions beyond its own scope, excluding or simply deranging a fair interplay between the two systems, consciousness and unconscious. Such a conception is very different from the disorganization (the a-rationality) of the Freudian Id that can only be dealt with through repression on account of Freud's limited notion of "reason" mainly related to the principle of reality centered in the ego. This conception is connected to a one-sided version of "pure reason" developed throughout the Enlightenment which has one of its sources in the Cartesian, flawless reason of idealism.

Although aware of the limits of reason, Pascal and Jung don't fall prey to irrationalism. In Thought 253 Pascal writes: "Two extremes: to exclude reason, to admit reason only." It is the one-sided adherence to one extreme that leads to irrationality. In such a case, it is remarkable how much irrationalism clings to unfettered rationalism and how much subjectivity is produced from unrestrained claims to objectivity. The most coherent position is to understand truth and knowledge according to the epistemic capacities of non-omniscient agents, incapable of a God's eye view of facts, in the middle of extreme possibilities. At best, a bird's eye view, as suggested by Wittgenstein. Or else, a symbolic perception of the turbulence created by the shock between known/unknown, with a glimpse at the edge of chaos: the non predictability and utter unknowability of the other side of the border invading this side of the border, unknown, however knowable. Plausibly, the border is exclusively approachable from within its limits given by our particular frame of reference, never from the outside, in a hypothetical "angelic position" of some hypothetical transcendental subject. Better to accept the consummate symbolic character of all knowledge, within a particular frame of reference, and its permanently moving horizon, our limits. Simply because reference frame and horizon are inseparable.

Since not only our historical perspectives but our eyes as well and the world we live in are in constant change so are the multiplicities of horizons surrounding our knowledge processes. The expansion of our horizons accompanies our knowledge expansion, and with them, more of our ignorance becomes evident. But, as Pascal writes in Thought 395, although "we have an incapacity of proof, insurmountable by all dogmatism. We have an idea of truth, invincible to all scepticism." And this idea of truth comes to us, through the heart, the light of nature born out the unknown Infinite that surrounds man through a beating, concrete organ. It is the consciousness of how these unknown infinities pragmatically touch man, beyond any demands of rational proofs, recognizing the impossibility to grasp their ontologies, that which defines the specific brand of Pascal's anthropology as inseparable from his (existential, not essentialist) epistemology. Therefore epistemology and anthropology are connected through this glimpse to the edge of chaos, the horizon limits of man's knowledge and being. About man's disproportion, in Thought 72, Pascal writes:

> Let man then contemplate the whole of nature in her full and grand majesty, and turn his vision from the low objects which surround him. Let him gaze on that brilliant light, set like an eternal lamp to illumine the universe; let the earth appear to him a point in comparison with the vast circle described by the sun; and let him wonder at the fact that this vast circle is itself but a very fine point in comparison with that described by the stars in their revolution round the firmament. But if our view be arrested there, let our imagination pass beyond; it will sooner exhaust the power of conception than nature that of supplying material for conception. The whole visible world is only an imperceptible atom in the ample bosom of nature. No idea approaches it. We may enlarge our conceptions beyond all imaginable space; we only produce atoms in comparison with the reality of things. It is an infinite sphere, the centre of which is everywhere, the circumference nowhere. In short it is the greatest sensible mark of the almighty power of God, that imagination loses itself in that thought.

In a similar vein, Jung writes:

> The decisive question for man is: Is he related to something or not? That is the telling question of his life. Only if we know that the thing which truly matters is the infinite can we avoid fixing our interest upon futilities, and upon all kinds of goals which are not of real importance. Thus we demand that the world grant us recognition for qualities which we regard as personal possessions: our talent or our beauty. The more a man lays stress on false possessions, and the less sensitivity he has for what is essential, the less satisfying is his life. He feels limited because he has limited aims, and the result is envy and jealousy. If we understand and feel that here in this life we already have a link with the infinite, desires and attitudes change. In the final analysis, we count for something only because of the essential we embody, and if we do not embody that, life is wasted. In our relationships to other men, too, the crucial question is whether an element of boundlessness is expressed in the relationship.[48]

48 Jung, *Memories, Dreams, Reflections*, 325.

Like Pascal, Jung is not interested in ontological proofs of what lies beyond the edges of man's limits. For P-J epistemologies and anthropologies the fundamental question is existential and pragmatic. There are no idealistic speculations about essentialist ontologies or dogmatic certainty.

20 Conclusions

On account of his pragmatism Jung yields a method and not a body of truths, whenever he insinuates some truth it is better to leave it alone, understanding it as "subjective", intrinsically born out from the application of his methodology to his own world experience – inner and outer. Jung's results are to be read as a structural dynamics description, where contents are better understood as "functions" like Self, ego, anima/animus, persona, shadow, but never ontologically, as essentialist contents. On the other hand, Freud proposes a body of truths and a very dubious method although with technical subtleties unattained by Jungian psychology and praxis in general. The unawareness of his particular reference frame, masked as "neutrality' produces a fatal flaw in Freud's work; thereby taking for ontology what is historical and for scientific ground his own subjective mind, a feature of the D-F epistemological type. Differently, Jung is very aware of the contingent, historical dimension of any theory. Jung writes:

> But I am perfectly aware of the merits of Freud and I do not want to diminish them. I know that what Freud says agrees with many people, and I assume that these people have exactly the kind of psychology that he describes. (…) I consider my contributions to psychology to be my subjective confession. It's my personal psychology, my prejudice that I see psychological facts as I do. I admit that I see things in such and such a way. But I expect Freud and Adler to do the same and confess that their ideas are their subjective point of view. So far as we admit our personal prejudice, we are really contributing towards an objective psychology.[49]

As described above, the means to such a fallacy is the dissolution of the empirical through the latent/manifest split, resulting in the being of the idea (the doctrine) as the exclusive ontological guarantor of facticity. This is inseparable from turning psychology and the psychoanalytical method into a doctrine, hence prone to dogmatic applications. Psychology is an activity bound to man's existence, and each life is unique.

49 Jung, "The Tavistock Lectures", para. 275.

Freud and Jung might well be approached through the central categories of their thinking. Freud according to the latent/manifest split and Jung through the symbol. An examination of the Freud-Fliess correspondence shows how since the nineties Freud already had his sexuality doctrine as the ideal content of psychoanalysis, although unfinished and unpolished in details. Many contradictions can be found between the latent (the contents exposed in his intimate correspondence with Fliess) and the manifest, official version as described by Freud in *The History of the Psychoanalytic Movement*. As regards Jung we could see his work as "the best expression of something he doesn't know." His psychology is always at the edge of chaos, unable to deliver an individuation program because it implies unique conditions of dynamic complex existential situations for unique individuals. As Pascal writes in Thought 351:

> Those great spiritual efforts, which the soul sometimes assays, are things on which it does not lay hold. It only leaps to them, not as upon a throne, forever, but merely for an instant.

Pascal and Jung share an acceptance of the vulnerabilities and contingency of human knowledge. Freud, in a truly Cartesian struggle over certainty – strives to keep the solid ground of dogma through un-assumed epistemic commitments of a body of truths, associated to a consonant methodology. P-J epistemologies are historical and existentialist whereas D-F are ideal and essentialist. In Freud there's an absolutism of the doctrine, of the ideal being of the doctrine, as well as with Descartes. What for Freud is ontology, for Jung is historical, as presented by the different readings of the house dream.[50] Truth is an activity, so is psychology, there is no permanent body of truths, but a historical, existential process, unique for each individual. The condition every knowledge requires is not so much freedom from doubts and restriction, as freedom from adulteration of our human condition: the appropriation of an Absolute as bottom ground of all knowledge. Be it an idea, doctrine, reason, or any single understandable cause.

References

Baudrillard, J. *Simulacra and Simulation*. Translated by S.F. Glaser. Michigan: The University of Michigan, 2006.

Benjamin, W. *Selected Writings*. Vol. 4. Cambridge MA, London: Harvard University Press, 2003.

50 Jung, *Memories, Dreams, Reflections*, 158–59.

Descartes, R. *Discourse on Method*. Translated by L. Lafleur. New York: Macmillan, 1960.

Descartes, R. *Discourse on Method and Meditations on First Philosophy*. Translated by E.S. Haldane. Kansas: Digireads Publishing, 2005.

Descartes, R. *Meditations on First Philosophy With Selections from the Objections and Replies*,. Translated by M. Moriarty. Oxford: Oxford University Press, 2008.

Descartes, R. *The Selections from The Principles of Philosophy*. Translated by J. Veitch. South Dakota: Nuvision Publications, 2008.

Fordham, M. *Jungian Psychotherapy: A Study on Analytical Psychology*. London: Karnac Books, 1990.

Foucault, M. *The Order of Things: An Archaeology of the Human Sciences*. London: Routledge, 2002.

Freud, S. *History of the Psychonalytical Movement in The Basic Writings of Sigmund Freud*. Edited by A.A. Brille. New York: Random House, 1938.

Freud, S. *Inhibitions, Symptoms and Anxiety*. Edited by J. Strachey. New York: W.W. Norton & Company Inc., 1977.

Hacker, P.M.S. *Wittgenstein on Philosophy and the Metaphysics of Experience*. Oxford: Clarendon Press, 1972.

Jung, C.G. *Memories, Dreams, Reflections*. Translated by R. Winston and C. Winston. New York: Vintage, 1989.

Jung, C.G. "The Archetypes and the Collective Unconscious." In *The Collected Works*, edited by G. Adler and R.F.C. Hull, Vol. 9i. Princeton: Princeton University Press, 1968.

Jung, C.G. "The Tavistock Lectures." In *The Collected Works*, translated by G. Adler and R.F.C. Hull, Vol. 18. Princeton: Princeton University Press, 1980.

Machamer, P. *The Cambridge Companion to Galileo*. Cambridge: Cambridge University Press, 1998.

Masson, J.M., ed. *The Complete Letters of Sigmund Freud to Wilhelm Fliess, (1887–1904)*. Cambridge MA: Harvard University Press, 1985.

Mortimer, E. *Blaise Pascal, The Life and Work of a Realist*. London: Hertford and Halow, 1959.

Pascal, B. *Thoughts*. Translated by W.F. Trotter. New York: E.P. Dutton & Co., 1958.

Rorty, R. *Philosophy and the Mirror of Nature*. New Jersey: Princeton University Press, 1979.

Wittgenstein, L. *Philosophical Investigations*. Translated by G.E.M. Anscombe. Oxford: Basil Blackwell, 1958.

CHAPTER 3

On Problem Solving – C.G. Jung's and M. Heidegger's Perspectives

Maria Kostyszak

Abstract

The article concerns the problem of the one-sidedness of European culture dominated by consciousness (Jung) and by technology (Heidegger). The vicious impact of that one-sidedness blurs adequate recognition. People overpowered and subjected by it imagine they are open to multisidedness. In fact they are more and more closed. Jung's travels around the world helped him to describe precisely limitations of the Eurocentric culture. Heidegger's analysis of poietic language in art pointed to different possibilities of existence than those dictated by instrumental reason dominating in technology. The comparison of these two thinkers aimed at emphasizing the necessity of cooperation between psychology and philosophy. Apart from differences between idioms of these two areas, their interdisciplinary research could contribute to some mental transformation.

Keywords

Heidegger – Jung – European culture – technological progress – logos – mythos – consciousness – thinking – problem-solving

1 Introductory Remarks

We live in the times of specialization, thus our awareness of the great difference between languages – in this case between the psychological language and the philosophical one – sometimes stops the mere possibility of proper comparison or exchange of experiences between the fields. We can endlessly debate on the immense as well as minute differences of the concepts, meanings and points of departure of separate humanistic domains. However, when man considered as an individual or as humanity is in a critical state, we should

 | DOI:10.1163/9789004336636_005

refer – here Jung's and Heidegger's convictions overlap – to some unity, even in spite of differences.

Contemporary philosophy, due to its immanent development and also due to revolutionary discoveries of psychoanalysis in the twentieth century, progressed into more diligent studies of particular features of existence instead of concentration on abstract ideas. It does not mean that the logical instruments of formalization and generalization can be avoided, but they have to cooperate with the empirical and psychological data. The traditional philosophical hierarchy, conveying the truth that general concepts are more important, and are of real interest for professional philosophers, is gradually replaced by "different sensibility." Susan Sontag explained the presence of irony and autoirony as one of the features of postmodernist authors. They are aware of their subjective points of view, nevertheless, some of them do not want to resign the attempts to embrace general perspective. Thus irony directed to some "dogmatic" assertions has become the characteristic sign of "different sensibility."

Remembering the difference between the code of philosophy and the codes of psychology, I shall nevertheless try to combine both fields, pointing to little differences but also to big similarities. Especially when you deal with a living human being, and not with regularities of general mechanisms. A human being undergoing numerous influences, many of them hidden and not conscious, cannot be explained ultimately by the set of assertions. The adequate explanation acquires the form rather of a labyrinth shaped by biological, psychological and cultural conditions than a simple system of theses.

C.G. Jung, after many years of different experiences and his medical practice concluded once that real human problems are unsolvable, that a slightly melancholic remark does not necessarily leave us with empty hands and frustration, because he added: the real problems can be overgrown. That remark seems to me to possess some quality of universality. That is why I decided to juxtapose two perspectives: that of Jung and of Heidegger to examine the possible meanings of that, not self-evident, concept of overgrowing real problems.

In the case of Heidegger, his criticism of metaphysical tradition was so severe that he postulated at first an overcoming of metaphysics (*Ueberwindung*), then, after understanding how impossible it seemed to be, he reformulated the imperative into *Verwindung* (overgrowing). Gianni Vattimo developed the idea in the direction of the gradual return to health after some illness.[1] Instead of

1 G. Vattimo, *The Adventure of Difference: Philosophy after Nietzsche and Heidegger*, trans. T. Harrison and C.P. Blamires (Baltimore: Johns Hopkins University Press, 1993).

violent war against ontotheological principles, we have to overgrow them, being aware that they still operate and have an influence on us.[2]

There is no complete analogy between these two – Jungian and Heideggerian – types of recognition of problems and their projects of solution, but certain similarities and common features of both perspectives may be pointed out.

2 Recognition of the Problem of One-Sidedness

In my first step I will refer to Jung's memories of his travels contained in the collection *Memories, dreams and recollections* gathered by Aniela Jaffe.[3] An eighty-four-year-old psychoanalyst describes five different places he visited in the past: northern Africa, a village of Pueblo Native American Indians (the United States), tropical Africa (Kenya, Uganda), India and Ravenna (Italy). In fact he remembers and describes meetings rather than places: meetings with different cultures and worldviews, but also meetings with the desired parts of the totality of a human being which was experienced by Jung as reduced and underdeveloped in Europe. These dramatic confessions of the old man point to the fact that Jung felt one-sidedness of the domination of consciousness of the European man as his own fate. Thus in Africa he felt the regenerating return to the source of early time, where nothing changes and nothing passes, as if present forever.[4]

His theoretical conceptions and the whole practice show how complex psychic intricacies can be resolved due to acquiring a more panoramic perspective or a different point of viewing and interpreting one's situation. The notorious fear of death was overgrown by Jung himself, by his creating the myth that dead persons need the living in order to get more understanding. Only living bodies, although limited and finite, may possess more knowledge about the things necessary for the full experience of life. His sermons to the dead had as a source of inspiration his conviction that we are useful. They, according to Jung, need us. When he tells the story of the origin of these *Sermons*

2 M. Heidegger's criticism of metaphysics also included his critique of the psychoanalytical causal and objectifying approach to a human being. He expressed his opposition to such an objectifying approach in lectures he delivered at the University of Zurich and in Zollikon; M. Heidegger, *Zollikon Seminars: Protocols, Conversations, Letters*, ed. M. Boss, trans. R. Askay and F. Mayr (Evanston IL: Northwestern University Press, 2001).

3 C.G. Jung, *Memories, Dreams, Reflections*, ed. A. Jaffe, trans. C. Winston and R. Winston (London: Random House, 1961).

4 Ibid., 267–69.

to the Dead he is 83 to 84 years old,[5] in my opinion he may be more sincere and frank about true reasons why European culture does not allow people to enter bravely into such serious problems with their individual creativity. Constant and engaged effort is also necessary, but hope of outgrowing difficulties appears to be the main source of energy for transformation. Otherwise the change is almost impossible, because the habits form a solid protective structure not to be so easily overgrown by any perspective change. What seems to be fundamental here is the rule that one needs to leave, at least for a moment, the closed circle of one's illusions and to find the conditions of the interaction of the self with its surroundings, but what must be emphasized is that it has to happen without the self's resignation of itself. When relations are built with the premeditated absence of oneself, which sometimes makes the whole process of building easier, psychic disaster seems to be lurking from afar. Absence of the self as it takes revenge after some time destroying what seemed to be development of an individual.

Some impulses supporting successful individuation must be recognized and the integration of consciousness with the subconscious gradually achieved. What C.G. Jung examined in reference to individual development has been always interconnected with the whole culture. Jung's travels to Africa, Asia and to the Native American Indians were inspired by his wish to perceive and understand the European perspective from outside. Our assumptions and axioms could be revised when confronted with entirely different worldviews. That was, according to me, Jung's attempt to solve the problem of European one-sidedness and the lack of balance that had fatal consequences for human psychosomatic health. Jung's form of interdisciplinarity consists in his brave connecting elements of psychotherapy with research on myths, literature, alchemy, art, philosophy etc. He was also preparing the dialogue with the Far East form of spirituality, although he realized that the typical Westerner requires first some inner spiritual transformation before he can successfully apply Eastern forms of spiritual growth.

M. Heidegger at the beginning of his development tried to transcend classical philosophy with its dualistic paradigm which opposed truth and falsehood (Greek: *aletheia*, German: *Unverborgenheit*), time and eternity, oneness and plurality and such like. His philosophical narrative was constructed around the idea to arouse respect and gratitude towards everything that is (Being). From that point of view, science and technology, both being born in Europe by philosophical thinking, are now seen as ruling tyrannically over everything in

5 Ibid., 336–39.

a profound, metaphysical way.[6] That thesis was considered to be problematic. Not all researchers on the role of science and technology in the contemporary world are so pessimistic as Heidegger seemed to be.[7] He underlined the fact that at first technology was only the instrument that could be treated as neutral. It was possible to use it or not, as the case could be. Human beings had the power to decide about using technological innovations for human benefit. In the course of time, however, according to Heidegger, the essence of technology, together with the authority of science and rationalistic dominance, step by step began to limit and repress those human capabilities which are connected with the meditative side of human behavior. Heidegger calls it the "forgetting of being" or the "rapid expelling of Mnemosyne" (cf. *Being and Time* (1927), *Was heisst Denken?* (1954)). He formulates a postulate to rethink "the essence of technology" in an interrogative way, so that we were not slaves of the power that we do not even approach understanding.

In order to make it possible – approaching the essence of technology – he examines how in the European tradition "thinking" was understood, and he objects to the exclusively conceptual understanding, reducing the many faceted process of combining the past and the future into some simplified scheme. Instead, he postulates a profound revision of the sources and purposes of thinking, as a creative but individual activity of body and soul together (psychocorporeal), in cooperation with the environment conceived as the cultural, social and biological milieu, cooperation based on memory. That problem leads him to offer some transformations of philosophical language, reconfiguration of interrelations among concepts that construct culture and finally reinvention of the way of being that would regenerate Europe. Spiritual decline is according to Heidegger a main European problem and a symptom of a dangerous situation. Under such threat we should seek various ways of rescue. The so-called pessimism of Heidegger, although he considered optimism and pessimism as inadequate forms of approach to the totality of what is, was connected with the awareness that the thorough change that is needed cannot be achieved easily. Nevertheless he attempted to sketch the conditions that should be fulfilled to "overgrow"[8] – internally – the problem of technology. The solution may be the

6 Cf. M. Heidegger, *The Question Concerning Technology and Other Essays*, trans. W. Lovitt (New York: Harper and Row, 1977); In more actual articulation it is called control or monitoring. Cf. A. Kępińska, *Sztuka w kulturze płynności* (*Art. in the culture of fluidity*) (Poznań: Wydaw. Galerii Miejskiej "Arsenał", 2003).

7 Cf. J.K.B. Olsen, S.A. Pedersen, and V.F. Hendricks, eds., *A Companion to the Philosophy of Technology* (Wiley-Blackwell, 2009).

8 Here I use the Jungian term „to overgrow the problem" instead of solving it, because in my attempt to juxtapose these two thinkers, I underline similarities in their attitude. That does

sort of advice one could direct to the individual, but in *Gelassenheit* it is formulated as a sort of agenda for the whole of humanity.[9] The philosopher here recommends not to negate technology, but also not to become too dependent on it. The attitude he calls, following Meister Eckhart, releasement (*Gelassenheit*), may be interpreted as achieving deeper peace inside before we enter the adventure with technology. Being aware, that is the luxurious program for only those who are not wholly dependent with the conditions of their life on technology, he could appeal to such a direction as better for humanity in future.[10]

3 Psychological and Philosophical Preparing Steps towards Solution

Anchoring oneself in great inner peace seems to be a postulate of both thinkers. In their interpretation such peace does not mean insensitivity to the size of misfortunes all over the world. They rather make us aware that simple conformism to the conditions that govern at present may become a great threat to the inner development of the individual.

The sense of cooperating between psychological and philosophical idioms may be exposed when we consider the problem of relation between the ego and its world. When the ego grows too big – philosophy helps to cure that form of pathology. That discipline of knowledge and of distance teaches of the great achievements of humanity gained due to systematic training of wider than egoistic and egocentric thinking. Contemporary reference to Far East philosophical and religious traditions also helps in the process of overcoming too strong and big an ego. On the other hand, when the ego becomes, in the story of life, too small and weak, psychology may help a lot. The two representatives about whom we are speaking here, C.G. Jung and Heidegger, appealed straight towards the individual human being. But, at the same time, they knew that relations between an individual and a culture consist in reciprocity. They

---

not mean we could obscure numerous differences between them and between philosophical and psychological language.

9 M. Heidegger, "Conversation on a Country Path about Thinking", in *Discourse on Thinking*, trans. J.M. Anderson and E.H. Freund (New York: Harper and Row, 1966). Originally published as *Gelassenheit* (1959).

10 When we realize we are living on the planet of slums (Cf. M. Davis, *Planet of Slums* [London; New York: Verso, 2007]) Heidegger's theory of technology seems even more elitist. That's why in anthologies and companions devoted to the problem of technology, he is respected mainly for formulating the question concerning technology. His specific solutions and suggestions (especially undertaking the dialogue with the essence of technology from the standpoint of art) are rather considered as too romantic and abstract. Cf. Olsen, Pedersen, and Hendricks, *A Companion to the Philosophy of Technology*.

both found cultural conditions in Europe to be blocking individual growth and all their thoughtful efforts served unblocking, opening the living character of that mutuality. They adopt different textual strategies: Jung writes about great historical or fictional figures to give us patterns, Heidegger, through detailed analysis of *Dasein* (individual awareness) adds nobility to it.[11] In previous philosophy, the particular story of a person was rather neglected in favour of the story of totality. Heidegger continues S. Kierkegaard's understanding of existence as the gradual process of becoming a singular person through choices and constant reflection on them.[12]

Jung writes about Gilgamesh. He dreamt something that he treated as a warning. Because Gilgamesh treated his dreams seriously he was able to escape the gods' revenge. Jung remarks that in Europe, very common prejudice against dreams takes place among many other symptoms of undervaluation of the human soul in general. Splendid development of science and technology finds its counterbalance in the awesome deficiency of wisdom and of introspection. He adds that religious doctrine speaks about the immortal soul, but it does not find "too many warm words towards real human psyche",[13] which would be condemned for ever, if the special act of Divine Grace would not prevent it. These two factors, among many others, but especially they, are responsible for the common undervaluation of psychic life. On the other hand, Jung appreciates the positive function that religion can play in social life.[14] According to his interpretation, Protestantism annihilated the mediation of the Church. The enormous potential of energy was liberated which immediately flew in the old channel: the channel of curiosity and pursuit of conquests, in such a way that Europe has become mother of dragons – reports Jung – that devoured the greater part of the earth. Since these days Protestantism has become the place of the incubation of schisms but at the same time the mother of science and technology, which have absorbed human consciousness to such an extent that it forgot about the unpredictable powers hidden in unconsciousness. The war catastrophe of 1914 and all the spiritual disturbances that happened after it have aroused serious doubts and misgivings about the spiritual state of mind of the white man. According to Jung, people in Europe were deeply convinced before the First World War that the world could be improved by means

11 Cf. M. Heidegger, *Being and Time*, trans. J. Macquarrie and E. Robinson, re-trans. by Stambaugh J., Albany: State University of New York Press, 1962 (London: SCM Press, 1996). Originally published as *Sein und Zeit* (New York: Harper & Row, 1962).

12 S. Kierkegaard, *Bojaźń i drżenie* (*Fear and Trembling*), trans. J. Iwaszkiewicz (Warsaw, 1972).

13 C.G. Jung, *Psychologia i religia* (*Psychology and Religion*), trans. J. Prokopiuk (Warsaw: Wydawnictwo KR, 1995), 20.

14 Ibid., 63.

of rational instruments. The author of *Aion* is disappointed, that instead of learning from the experience of before the war illusion, humanity becomes subjected to new, ficticious means. The states try again to become theocracies which means that they force totalitarian character of the state and block free thinking. Jung admits he is frightened by the fact that people are again ready to kill each other because of childish theories claiming the possibility to create paradise on earth.

Another figure, apart from Gilgamesh and Hiob, that Jung exposes in his descriptions of the adventures of great souls is Friedrich Nietzsche. Diagnosed by him as pathologically identified with archetype of the Old Wise Man, nevertheless with his rich psychic life may represent the paternal signpost for development. Psychic intricacies were something that Nietzsche did not ignore. He claimed culture becomes more and more a desert when there is lack of space for personal development, and when all unique relations of an individual with the external world are conventionally tamed or excluded. M. Heidegger's detailed analysis of the formal structure of Dasein influenced the very conceptual framework of philosophical tradition, but at the same time he contributed to understanding the problem of psychic health in culture. The Heideggerian point of departure was Husserl's phenomenology and Dilthey's hermeneutic, but he also has been studying Nietzsche's texts to understand what were the reasons of the bad state of the European spirit. The philosophy of life by the author of *Joyful Wisdom* completed his conviction that Christianity may be equally the inspiration for spiritual growth as for the spiritual decline of human singularity. Conclusions that he achieved due to many years of interpreting Nietzsche's criticism of Platonism turned his searching into the direction of metamorphoses of language. Linguistic structures can stop development or can powerfully initiate it. Heidegger himself had an inclination to poetic idiom, as more liberating and less oppressive inwardly, but I suppose all kinds of searching within linguistic possibilities should be recommended as the psychic regeneration of the whole culture. The precise and imaginative poetical phrase may serve for the awakening of our mechanistic rituals of everyday life but may also help in the more sublime dimensions of life. Jung is afraid that more and more of God is kept in the prison of human mental images, whereas: "the living body is the originator of God."[15] His criticism of theology, for example, was based on the suspicion that theologians' attitude to their own bodies is not sincere, because they are limited not by discipline generated by their own psyche and nature but by outward religious assumptions. According to

15 C.G. Jung, *Seminar on Nietzsche's Zarathustra. Notes on the Seminar in 1934–39*, ed. J.L. Jarrett (London, 1994), 330.

theses presuppositions, the existence of God and human cooperation with the divine on sphere cannot be dependent on the stories of individual bodies.[16] Official religion and theology seem to Jung the instances of the common, in Europe after the Enlightenment, "mania of reason" which he calls "disoriented state of mind."[17] In such a context, the Swiss psychiatrist refers to the instinctual knowledge of animal bodies. An animal is not conscious, but it "knows better."[18] Jung's remarks of that sort, together with the numerous tendencies within humanities (psychology, anthropology, ethnology, ethology etc.), have helped to overcome humanistic fundamentalism.[19]

It resembles one of Aristotle's classical theses. It sounds as though one who lives beyond society must be an animal or a god, and not a human being. The thesis was interpreted in different ways, the tendency that Jung acquires, suggests a rather antihierarchical interpretation. Aristotle did not mean, according to its reading, that animals are lower than humans and gods, but that consciousness in the case of humans distorts the relation between body and soul. Jung's efforts strive at regenerating that relation in human beings in a more proper direction. When he concludes that "the body is merely the visibility of the soul",[20] new semantic dimensions become uncovered for exploration by researchers and practitioners. Jung combines these two functions when he memorizes his travels. In his memory, the narrative about his travels is being composed with the distinct purpose to combine and integrate the consciousness and unconsciousness. That is why there are references and detailed analyses of dreams as well as courageous attempts to understand impressions that were unclear and only implied. In all the places he visited he sought for an outward look on Europe as well as his personalconfrontation with his unconsciousness.[21]

16 Ibid., 337 ; He writes there about "terribly infantile theologians", who being psychologically immature themselves treat people below their own level. Jung evaluates that as immoral.

17 Ibid., 353.

18 Ibid., 354.

19 Commentators of B. Latour's ANT- theory, use the term "fundamentalist humanism" to name those standpoints that treat as their object of research only human beings and exclude, from investigations, other, beyond human factors. K. Abriszewski, *Poznanie, zbiorowość, polityka. Analiza teorii Aktora-Sieci (ANT) Bruno Latoura (Knowledge, Society, Politics. Analysis of Bruno Latour's ANT – theory)* (Cracow: Towarzystwo Autorów i Wydawców Prac Naukowych "Universitas", 2008).

20 Ibid., 355.

21 Jung's narrative, because these are personal memories, sticks to "personal" dimension. Stanislav Grof writes about transpersonal experiences. The border between them is quite dynamic (Cf. S. Grof books: *Spiritual Emergency: When Personal Transformation Becomes A Crisis* (1989) The *Transpersonal Vision* (1998) and many others).

As he describes, in northern Africa he found our own past, youth, intensity of life.[22]

Among Native American Indians he experienced that they cultivate Pascal's logic of the heart that is different from the logic of reason. He tells the story of sitting with a Native American Indian on the roof. Even when working and being busy, as well as abiding in a block of flats – Natives have the habit to sit on a roof to contemplate the sunset. Jung learns that they perceive white men as cruel and terrible, because they think with their head, not with the heart. The atmosphere of respect, mystery, taboo, when speaking about gods may be connected with the symbolic order of the heart so characteristic for Native American Indian culture. They feel proud of being in mutual ties with gods (gods depend on people and people depend on gods). They prefer to imply something than to express it directly, especially when religious matters are concerned. The sun is God but Indians would not like to talk about it straightforwardly.

4 Overgrowing or Solving the Problem?

The question of the divine dimension may be treated as a good example of the proposed overgrowing, and not solving, the problem. How should we define the very problem in its contemporary shape? In Jung's conception either religion makes people childish or, as he says, "atheism is a neurosis of the great cities."[23] According to Heidegger, mythos and logos, the two narratives that guarantied sense were not in conflict in early Greek culture. But since Roman times and partially due to Christianity the worldview changes, logos becomes the only sovereign dominating kind of knowledge. Heidegger says that mythos stopped to be considered seriously, because gods escaped from humanity. This metaphorical way of speech was connected with Nietzsche's idea which Heidegger, as it seems, continued to some extent. They both considered the dimension of divinity as the most mysterious and not subjected to full explanation. At the same time, European history, strived voluntaristically to articulate the problem of divinity to make it congruent with power and control of society. When Heidegger speaks about escape of gods, he wants to redirect agency. Escape means that we can call them back, we can try to prepare a basis for their return. Nietzsche's and Heidegger's understanding of the relation between gods and humans consists in their mutuality and collaboration. I claim Jung had similar

22 Jung, *Memories, Dreams, Reflections*, 270.

23 Jung, *Psychologia i religia* (*Psychology and Religion*), 110.

attitude to the divine dimension. When he said that atheism is a neurosis of great cities, he realized that resignation of the divine dimension in the human psyche puts it in danger and founds the lack of integration between consciousness and unconsciousness. The memory of his travels helps to recreate elements helping to recognize how to shape that integration individually and for the whole European culture.

In tropical Africa Jung had the occasion to notice the rule: our perception and knowledge create the objective world. What was his important experience in work with psychotic patients appeared to be also the rule among people from tropical Africa. Today we may be a little embarrassed with the frankness of Jung, but he offers a description and not a valuation. It is better to be aware of such general mechanism and then to be able to use it or to avoid it as the demands of the situation may be. It is worse not to see the mechanism of projection and its traps. In tropical Africa Jungexperienced vividly the cosmic meaning of consciousness.[24] In India, Jung says radically, he found the solution of the problem that much worried him much and which seemed to be unsolvable from a European perspective. Evil was ethically excluded in favour of goodness, and the philosophical doctrine of Saint Augustine, that evil is not something existing (positive in a sense) but only the lack of goodness, prevailed in Europe. The solution that he seemed to find in the homeland of Mahatma Gandhi and Rabindranath Tagore,[25] consisted in the fact that only when we accept and not exclude evil, we can choose good again, because the process of uncovering evil as evil (without rationalization and without lies) starts the elaboration – psychic and ethical – the task to transform it. From the experiences that Jung has collected in his psychiatric practice and from the history of the ethical development of humanity in the West, he was convinced that exclusion of evil is not, in psychic economy, a reasonable, path. Excluded evil comes back and torments us from the unconscious level. Jung's as well as Heidegger's observations of the one-sidedness of the European approach to constructive values lead them to accusation of Europe as allowing excesses of voluntarism. That is why, in his memory of meeting in the East with the solution of the problem of evil, Jung emphasizes the catharctic role of uncovering evil (the Shadow) and confronting it, to become complete and mature.

24 Jung, *Memories, Dreams, Reflections*, 284.

25 I mention these two Hindu moral authorities of the twentieth century to underline some of the direct intellectual and moral consequence of the attitude noticed and appreciated by Jung.

In Ravenna Jung had his very personal enlightening experience which caused him to come back frequently to that memory. He named it "meeting as if face to face with his anima" there.

As far as Rome is concerned his premonitions that the thick cumulation of cultural and sublime material and symbolic values there will have a great impact on him, he fainted while buying tickets to Rome. As a result he resigned to go there (1949).[26]

The solution of the problem of European one-sidedness (rationality) could be begun by the psychic act of invitation of the lacking parts: the past, sensual intensity of life, the need of being proud because of mutual relationship with gods (not one direction), contemplation of nature: the sun and elements as supporting psyche etc. after invitation (opening) – its gradual and reasonable integration. Jung's recollection of his past travels becomes a significant lesson for European culture.

M. Heidegger did not travel much. His formulation of the problem and suggestions directed at its solving spring from his deep thinking about European destiny. Today it may and even should be questioned.[27] Was he right? Was his perspective well chosen? Does he not mislead us?

It is easy to qualify Heidegger's protest against systematic non-reflecting on technology as romantic anti-modernism. It is more difficult, and, at the same time, more sensible according to me, to treat his assertions rather as questions, as systematic questioning that takes our essence and the essence of technology into account; and finally, tries to open cooperation between them without pretending they have nothing in common.

Numerous critics (R. Wolin, R. Schuerman, ...) accuse Heidegger of judging negatively and totally the present epoch. The mistake of such an accusation is an effect of their own projections or of the custom of generalization so common among philosophers. Heidegger tries not to overuse generalization, hence his idea of *formale Anzeigen*.[28] When applied, for example, to religious problematic, it would not decide on the ontological issue of the existence or nonexistence of God but it would recommend starting from true religious experience and then, following *formale Anzeigen* building step by step the form

26 Jung, *Memories, Dreams, Reflections*, 319.

27 R. Wolin, R. Schuerman, J. Habermas and many others are severe critics of Heidegger's theses which are treated as harmful illusions (Cf. R. Wolin, *The Politics of Being: The Political Thought of Martin Heidegger* [New York: Columbia Univ. Press, 1990]).

28 M. Heidegger, *Fenomenologia życia religijnego* (*Phenomenology of Religious Life*), trans. G. Sowiński (Cracow: Znak, 2002), 54–58.

of religious life.[29] In such process religion would not acquire the quality Jung exposes – to keep an individual in a childish immaturity.

When we mention here "essence of technology" or "our essence" it is important to remember how revisionistic Heidegger was about the concepts. R. Rorty is right that essentialism is not an adequate standpoint towards the whole net of ties and interrelations that form dynamic character of social and cultural reality. Heidegger's essentialism has, however, a bit different character. The question about our essence and the essence of technology may be understood as the beginning of new ways of dealing with the whole issue of technology. He understands essence in a dynamic way. Essence is a process. It is becoming, growing. That is why it is so important to diagnose where the essential moments are and what future they prepare for us. The problem, if we are to be slaves and servants of technology or if *Gelassenheit* (letting-be, liberation) is possible, requires that essential level of reflection and meditation.

Michael R. Heim, philosopher of cyberspace, writes in *Electric Language* about an epochal shift in relations between thought, language and experience.[30] Christopher Norris in his review of *Electric Language* recalls Derrida's interpretation of writing in Plato's *Faedrus. Farmakon* is at the same time cure and poison. The potential for change that is inherent both in our essence and in the essence of technology, when properly used, may protect us from becoming unconscious slaves of outward conditions.

5 Conclusions

My comparison of these two perspectives aimed at pointing out the necessity of cooperation between psychology and philosophy. When technology more and more strongly shapes our environment, we cannot deny it deserves reflection, both individual and cultural (systematic). Jung and Heidegger address a vast and intricate problem, the one of the one-sidedness of European culture dominated by consciousness (Jung) and by technology (Heidegger). The dynamic character of changes in the world connected with technological progress supports a certain kind of one-sidedness, and at the same time covers the fact, simulating multisidedness. It was described systematically by Heidegger,[31]

29 Ibid., 58–61.

30 M. Heim, *Electric Language: A Philosophical Study of Word Processing*, 2nd ed (New Haven: Yale University Press, 1999).

31 For example in his essays: The Age of World Picture, Science and Reflection, The Question Concerning Technology etc. (Heidegger, *The Question Concerning Technology and Other Essays*).

Jung, in his medical practice had to do with the most sensitive preys of that one-sidedness in dominating culture, that is why he also developed in many of his texts a general view how to overcome it. Both thinkers experience the situation as alarming. They appeal not only to individualized reflection as solving the problem of one-sidedness, although in both cases, they appreciate the possible role of an individual to initiate the influential processes of regeneration. They also point to the systemic necessity to create conditions of transforming one-sidedness. Heidegger' s theoretical discovery of the architecture of habits that stop human beings (Dasein) from living cooperation with the surrounding for the real profit – psychic and moral – of an individual and of culture may become a start of transformation. Each moment/situation when one-sidedness is overgrown may be liberating to multidimensional experience of life. Liberating of what? According to Jung – completeness, fullness. According to Heidegger – balance. According to him, balance is connected with attunement to what we inherited and what can be developed in the inner world within communicational sphere with the real world. That communication demands collaboration of psychology and philosophy in a culture that is not one-sided, by human beings who are now overpowered by their one-dimensionality.

References

Abriszewski, K. *Poznanie, zbiorowość, polityka. Analiza teorii Aktora-Sieci (ANT) Bruno Latoura (Knowledge, Society, Politics. Analysis of Bruno Latour's ANT – theory)*. Cracow: Towarzystwo Autorów i Wydawców Prac Naukowych "Universitas", 2008.

Davis, M. *Planet of Slums.* London; New York: Verso, 2007.

Heidegger, M. *Being and Time.* Translated by J. Macquarrie and E. Robinson. Re-Trans. by J. Stambaugh, Albany: State University of New York Press, 1962. London: SCM Press, 1996. Originally published as *Sein und Zeit* (New York: Harper & Row, 1962).

Heidegger, M. "Conversation on a Country Path about Thinking." In *Discourse on Thinking*, translated by J.M. Anderson and E.H. Freund. New York: Harper and Row, 1966. Originally published as *Gelassenheit* (1959).

Heidegger, M. *Fenomenologia życia religijnego (Phenomenology of Religious Life)*. Translated by G. Sowiński. Cracow: Znak, 2002.

Heidegger, M. *The Question Concerning Technology and Other Essays.* Translated by W. Lovitt. New York: Harper and Row, 1977.

Heidegger, M. *Zollikon Seminars: Protocols, Conversations, Letters.* Edited by M. Boss. Translated by R. Askay and F. Mayr. Evanston IL: Northwestern University Press, 2001.

Heim, M. *Electric Language: A Philosophical Study of Word Processing*. 2nd ed. New Haven: Yale University Press, 1999.

Jung, C.G. *Memories, Dreams, Reflections.* Edited by A. Jaffe. Translated by C. Winston and R. Winston. London: Random House, 1961.

Jung, C.G. *Psychologia i religia* (*Psychology and Religion*). Translated by J. Prokopiuk. Warsaw: Wydawnictwo KR, 1995.

Jung, C.G. *Seminar on Nietzsche's Zarathustra. Notes on the Seminar in 1934–39*. Edited by J.L. Jarrett. London, 1994.

Kępińska, A. *Sztuka w kulturze płynności* (*Art. in the Culture of Fluidity*). Poznań: Wydaw. Galerii Miejskiej "Arsenał", 2003.

Kierkegaard, S. *Bojaźń i drżenie* (*Fear and Trembling*). Translated by J. Iwaszkiewicz. Warsaw, 1972.

Olsen, J.K.B., S.A. Pedersen, and V.F. Hendricks, eds. *A Companion to the Philosophy of Technology*. Wiley-Blackwell, 2009.

Vattimo, G. *The Adventure of Difference: Philosophy after Nietzsche and Heidegger.* Translated by T. Harrison and C.P. Blamires. Baltimore: Johns Hopkins University Press, 1993.

Wolin, R. *The Politics of Being: The Political Thought of Martin Heidegger.*New York: Columbia Univ. Press, 1990.

CHAPTER 4

Is a Jungian Analysis Scientific?

Robert Segal

Abstract

The Jungian community is divided into two camps. The doubtless larger camp has no interest in the scientific status of Jungian psychology. On the contrary, it despises science as narrow, one-sided, and even irrelevant to the depths of the psyche. It revels in THE RED BOOK, where Jung expresses a hostility to science that makes present-day creationists seem like Nobel laureates in physics. This camp sees science as simply an option, which it chooses to spurn. Better for it the religious Jung. The smaller, scientific camp respects science and wants to make Jungian psychology scientific. Whether it succeeds in doing so is the subject of this article.

Keywords

Jung – Psychoanalysis – Religion – Psychology of Religion – Depth Psychology – Science – Religious Studies – The Red Book in Jungian Studies

1 Is a Jungian Analysis Scientific?

For me, Jungian analyses of persons and things are unscientific in four ways. First, the analyses tend to assume Jungian tenets rather than to argue for them. Second, the analyses tend to apply only Jungian theory and to ignore any other theory. Third, the analyses tend to be so malleable that applicability is guaranteed. Fourth, the analyses tend to be *ex post facto* rather than predictive. Indisputably, my objections hold for many other theories as well and certainly in the fields that I know best: mythology and religion. And it is on the application of Jungian theory not to patients but to texts that I will be focusing, though I think that my objections hold for the analysis of persons as well.

 | DOI:10.1163/9789004336636_006

2 Internal Criteria

Put another way, my objections are both internal and external. Internally, Jungian analyses are unscientific because they are rarely tested. There is therefore scant chance that they will be wrong, in which case there is no evidence that they are right.

Testing can take several forms. In the loosest sense, testing means applicability. In the example that I will be using here, the ancient Greek myth of Adonis, applicability would mean the translatability of the myth into Jungian terms. It would mean fit. By no means do all theories of myth fit or fit to the same degree. Applicability does, then, offer testing of a kind.

My objection is that, ordinarily, Jungian applications are offered in isolation rather than in competition with other possible ones. Furthermore, applications often enlist concepts so broad that success is almost certain. An archetype can be found for any character or thing in any myth, and any archetype can evince itself in an endless number of ways.

In a stronger sense of the term, testing means prediction. Take two theories, Freudian and Jungian, that both purport to analyse the place of a character in a myth or, say, a novel. Assume that the theories fit equally well the place of a character – for example, the protagonist's boss. The Freudian analysis is: the character, read symbolically, is the father of the protagonist. The Jungian analysis is: the character, also read symbolically, is the father archetype of the protagonist.

Is any prediction possible? Perhaps one can ask how, for a Freudian or a Jungian, the character, once encountered, would be expected to behave. But this kind of "prediction" does not count since the novel is already finished. True prediction requires new data, such as analyzing an unfinished novel. So one might have done with the serialization of Dickens' novels. While I stated that I find exasperating the tendency of Jungian analyses to be *ex post facto* rather than predictive, I grant that that objection holds less readily for analyzing living persons, whose lives are unfinished, than for analyzing finished novels or finished myths.

3 External Criteria

Even if a Freudian or a Jungian analysis of a novel or a myth could be tested for both applicability and predictability, the test would *assume* the theory. I am most exasperated by the tendency of Jungian analyses to invoke the theory rather than to defend it. Externally, the question is what is the evidence for the theory underlying the analysis. What is the evidence for an Oedipus complex or for a father archetype? Without good evidence, no analysis "holds water."

In the terms that I will be using, an interpretation must be supported by an explanation. Admittedly, the terms "explanation" and "interpretation" are commonly used in varying and confusing ways. In *Explaining and Interpreting Religion*,[1] I distinguish these ways. In the present essay I will not review the options. I will use the terms in one of these possible ways, and will do so to make a single point: that a Jungian interpretation of myth or of religion or of anything else is only as persuasive as the explanation being applied.

Here an interpretation of a myth answers the question of the *meaning* of the myth. An explanation answers the questions of the *origin* and *function* of the myth. Those three questions – of meaning, origin, and function – are the key theoretical questions. By "explanation" I mean the account – of the mind, the world, culture, or society – that is presupposed by the interpretation. Freud and Jung offer explanations of the mind that get applied to the interpretation of myth.

While interpretation and explanation are more often than not deemed incompatible, I maintain that they are not only compatible but, even more, interlocking. An interpretation of Adonis as a puer archetype depends on the existence of the archetype. The interpretation does not stand by itself and makes sense of the myth only if the existence of archetypes is presupposed. To apply a theory without evidence for the theory is to start *in medias res*.

Reciprocally, the applicability of Jungian theory to the myth of Adonis offers support for the theory. After all, not all theories may prove applicable, and some may prove more applicable than others. But the support for a theory offered by applicability is limited. The theory must rest on more than applicability.

4 The Myth of Adonis

The myth of Adonis, the main sources for which are Apollodorus and Ovid, describes the miraculous birth of a preternaturally beautiful human out of a tree, the fighting over him by Aphrodite and Persephone, his annual division of the year into a third with Persephone in Hades and two thirds on earth with Aphrodite, and his eventual death while hunting.[2]

1 R.A. Segal, *Explaining and Interpreting Religion* (New York: Lang, 1992).

2 See Apollodorus, Library, 1.116, 3.182, 183–85; Ovid, Metamorphoses 10.708–39. On both the myth and the cult of Adonis, see D.D. Boederker, *Aphrodite's Entry into Greek Epic* (Leiden:

5 Frazer's Adonis

Of all the interpretations of the myth of Adonis, Frazer's remains the most popular. Frazer writes about Adonis in all three editions of *The Golden Bough* (1890, 1900, 1911–15)[3] and also in his abridged edition (1922), which repeats the chapters from the second and third editions and from which the quotations below are taken. From the second edition on, Frazer works out three pre-scientific stages of culture, and he places Adonis in all three stages: those of magic, religion, and magic and religion combined. Though to differing degrees, in all three stages Adonis, for Frazer, is a mere personification of vegetation rather than a personality. Vegetation does not symbolize Adonis; Adonis symbolizes vegetation.

Frazer locates the potted gardens of Adonis in his first, magical stage. Since in this stage humans believe that impersonal forces rather than personalities cause events in the physical world, Adonis here cannot be a personality.

In Frazer's second, religious stage, Adonis is an outright personality. He is the god of vegetation. Frazer asserts that in this stage rites of mourning were performed for Adonis – not, as in the next stage, to undo his death but to seek his forgiveness for it.[4] For Adonis has died not, as in the third stage, because he has descended to the underworld but because in cutting, stamping, and grinding the corn – the specific part of vegetation he symbolizes – humans have killed him. Yet Adonis is somehow still sufficiently alive to be capable of punishing humans, something that the rituals of forgiveness are intended to avert. Since, however, Adonis dies because vegetation itself does, the god is here really only a metaphor for the element that he supposedly controls. As vegetation goes, so goes Adonis.

In Frazer's third pre-scientific stage, which combines the first with the second, Adonis' death means his descent to the underworld for his stay with Persephone. If in stage two as vegetation goes, so goes Adonis, now as Adonis goes, so seemingly goes vegetation. Frazer assumes that whether or not Adonis wills his descent, he is too weak to ascend by himself. By acting out his rebirth, humans magically facilitate it. In this stage gods still control the

Brill, 1974), 64–67; W. Burkert, *Structure and History in Greek Mythology and Ritual* (Berkeley: University of California Press, 1979), 105–11; *Greek Religion* (Cambridge MA: Harvard University Press, 1985), 176–77.

3 See J.G. Frazer, *The Golden Bough*, 1st ed. (London: Macmillan, 1890), I: 278–96; J.G. Frazer, *The Golden Bough*, 2nd ed. (London: Macmillan, 1900): II: Chapter 3, 115–30; J.G. Frazer, *The Golden Bough*, 3rd ed. (London: Macmillan, 1913), I: Chapters 1–4, 9–10; J.G. Frazer, *The Golden Bough*, abridged ed. (London: Macmillan, 1922), Chapters 29–33.

4 See J. G. Frazer, *The Golden Bough*, abridged ed., 393–94.

physical world, but their effect on it is automatic rather than deliberate. To enact the rebirth of Adonis is to spur his rebirth and thereby the rebirth of vegetation.[5]

Yet even if Adonis chooses to descend to the underworld, he is not choosing infertility, which is just the automatic consequence of his sojourn below. Similarly, even if he chooses to return, he is not thereby choosing fertility, which likewise simply follows automatically from his resurfacing. Adonis proves to be not the cause of the fate of vegetation but only a metaphor for that fate, so that in fact in stage three as well as in stage two as vegetation goes, so goes Adonis. For Frazer, the myth that Adonis spent a portion of the year in the underworld "is explained most simply and naturally by supposing that he represented vegetation, especially the corn," which lies buried half the year and re-emerges the other half.[6]

In a much larger sense Frazer, in all three of his pre-scientific stages, reduces Adonis to the mere personification of vegetation. For even where Frazer does deem Adonis an independent personality, the only aspect of his life he considers is that which parallels the natural course of vegetation: Adonis' death and rebirth. Yet Adonis' life, from his birth to his "permanent" death, is anything but natural.[7] His final death terminates, not perpetuates, the change of seasons. He is killed and in some versions is even murdered – by either a spurned lover, Artemis, or a bested rival, Ares. To be sure, Frazer need not take the myth literally and therefore supernaturally. But he must *translate* the supernatural terms into natural ones. Instead, he ignores them. It is not hard to see why. Only if Adonis is reborn forever can his life symbolize the course of vegetation.[8]

6 Jung's Adonis

Unlike Frazer, Jung himself mentions Adonis only in passing,[9] but he does mention him as an instance of the archetype of the eternal child, or *puer aeternus*.[10]

5 See ibid., 377.

6 Ibid., 392.

7 See R.A. Segal, *Theorizing about Myth* (Amherst: University of Massachusetts Press, 1999), 101.

8 See ibid.

9 See C.G. Jung, "Symbols of Transformation", in *The Collected Works*, vol. 5 (Princeton NJ: Princeton University Press, 1956), paras. 321, 330 nn.32, 392, 530 79; "Answer to Job", in *The Collected Works*, vol. 11 (Princeton NJ: Princeton University Press, 1952), par. 715.

10 See Jung, "Symbols of Transformation", paras. 392, 526; "Psychological Aspects of the Mother Archetype", in *The Collected Works*, vol. 9i (Princeton NJ: Princeton University

That archetype too Jung discusses only in passing, though he does devote many pages to an allied archetype, the Great Mother.[11]

From a Jungian point of view, the myth of Adonis serves as a warning to those who identify themselves with the puer archetype. To live as a puer, the way Adonis does, is to live as a psychological infant and, ultimately, as a fetus. The life of a puer in myth invariably ends in premature death, which psychologically means the death of the ego and a return to the womb-like unconscious.

As an archetype, the puer constitutes a side of one's personality, which, as a side, must be accepted. A puer personality just goes too far: he makes the puer the whole of his personality. Unable to resist its spell, he surrenders himself to it, thereby abandoning his ego and reverting to sheer unconsciousness.

Adonis is a quintessential puer because he never marries, never works, and dies young. He never grows up. His puer personality spans the period from infancy to adolescence. He must first break out of a tree in order to be born. His mother, transformed into the tree, is reluctant to let him out. Like any other mother, she may be overjoyed at his conception; but unlike normal mothers, she wants to hoard him. In Ovid's version, Adonis himself has to find an exit.

No sooner does Adonis emerge from the tree than, in Apollodorus' version, Aphrodite thrusts him back – not, to be sure, into the tree but into a chest. She thereby undoes the birth that had proved so arduous. She tells no one, for she wants Adonis all to herself. When Persephone, to whom Aphrodite has entrusted the chest without revealing its contents, opens it, she likewise falls in love with Adonis and refuses to return him. Each goddess, just like his mother, wants to possess him exclusively. Though Zeus' decision leaves Adonis free for a third of the year, Adonis readily cedes his third to Aphrodite. Never, then, is he outside the custody of these archetypal mother figures.

Seemingly, a Jungian interpretation of the myth faces the same contradiction as Frazer's: that Adonis annually breaks free of the mother yet eventually dies permanently. But a Jungian interpretation need not ignore Adonis' final demise, which is reconcilable with his recurrent revival. For the annual cycle of death and rebirth can symbolize not Adonis' annual liberation from the mother but the opposite: his annual return to the mother, even if that return

Press, 1954), para. 193; *Letters* (Princeton NJ: Princeton University Press, 1976), I: 82. See also M.L. von Franz, *Puer Aeternus*, 2nd ed. (Santa Monica CA: Sigo, 1981); E. Neumann, *The Origins and History of Consciousness* (Princeton NJ: Princeton University Press, 1970). Originally published in 1954, 88–101. Neumann himself uses the term "son-lover" for puer.

11 On the archetype of the Great Mother, see Jung, "Psychological Aspects of the Mother Archetype"; "Symbols of Transformation"; Neumann, *The Origins and History of Consciousness*; *The Great Mother*, 2nd ed. (Princeton NJ: Princeton University Press, 1972).

ends in release. Where a normal child needs to be born only once to liberate himself from the mother, Adonis, as a puer, continually returns to the mother and so must be born again and again. His final death is simply his permanent rather than temporary return to her. It is the culmination of his past returns rather than a break with them. Previously, he had been strong enough to resist the mother temporarily. Now he can no longer do so.[12]

7 Is a Jungian Analysis of the Myth of Adonis Scientific?

7.1 *Interpretation*

The first step in assessing the scientific status of a Jungian analysis of the myth of Adonis is to match it up with other analyses, as I have done with Frazer's analysis, and would be expected to do with other ones. As I stated at the outset, I find exasperating the tendency of Jungian applications to operate in isolation – as if the sole criterion were whether a Jungian approach works.

I have argued that a Jungian analysis of the myth of Adonis works better than Frazer's does. Frazer must turn Adonis, a human being, into a god – the god of vegetation. Adonis can perhaps be said to die insofar he spends a portion of every year in the land of the dead. But gods who die are usually reborn. They do not stay dead. By contrast, Adonis, while dying and being reborn for untold years, is eventually killed while on earth and stays dead forever. If he still returns to Hades, now he does so permanently. Yet as much of a jump the transformation of Adonis from human to god is, even more of a jump is the transformation of Adonis from personality to vegetation itself. All the characteristics that make Adonis a personality, human or divine, a personality thereby get dropped. That Adonis, like vegetation, dies and is reborn is what remains.

The Jungian analysis that I have offered may depart as fully as Frazer's does from the literal meaning of the myth. But it is far more detailed. It delineates the character of Adonis much more closely than Frazer's does. Like Frazer's, it types Adonis: as a puer rather than as a god of vegetation, which really means as vegetation itself. Adonis for Jung is not merely, as for Frazer, someone or

12 To be sure, this negative interpretation of the puer archetype and therefore of Adonis represents only the classical Jungian view. The post-Jungian, archetypal view of James Hillman (J. Hillman, ed., *Puer Papers* [Dallas: Spring Publications, 1979]) and his followers interprets the puer archetype positively and would therefore applaud rather than castigate Adonis for his identification with that archetype. Where for Jung and von Franz the life of a puer ends tragically, if not pathetically, in premature death, for Hillman it ends triumphantly, in a refusal to compromise with the everyday world. The behavior that for Jung and von Franz is childish would for Hillman be childlike.

something that dies and is continually reborn. Adonis is a personality, or more precisely one side of a personality – and of a human personality, not a divine one. Adonis symbolizes not a god but a human being.

7.2 *Explanation*

The second step in assessing the scientific status of a Jungian analysis of the myth of Adonis is tying the interpretation to an explanation. As I stated at the outset, I find exasperating the tendency of Jungian analyses to assume Jungian tenets rather than to argue for them. Applicability of the theory *once* the theory is assumed cannot justify the theory, which must be supported in its own right. Support is required even if there are no rival interpretations. Arguing that the myth of Adonis is illuminated *when* Adonis is taken as a case of a puer personality requires acceptance of the puer archetype and of Jung's whole notion of a collective unconscious.

Like all other theories of myth, Frazer's and Jung's are theories of far bigger domains than myth, which is merely one case in point. Frazer's theory is a theory of culture, of which religion is a part and myth in turn a part of religion. Other parts include magic and science. Frazer's theory is, even more basically, a theory of human nature. All of culture is for him a series of elaborate ways of getting food on the table. Frazer's theory – of myth, religion, culture, and human nature – has been fervently debated. But Frazer does bring to the fore more than a classicist's mastery of a specific myth. He brings a twelve- and really thirteen-volume tome, *The Golden Bough* in its third edition. He enlists information from almost the whole world. Of course, his theory can still be wholly wrong, as many critics have asserted. But his analysis of the myth of Adonis rests on more than the ability to interpret a story.

The same is true of Jung, whose theory of myth is even more fully a theory of human nature. Jung does not, like Frazer, automatically subsume myth, which for him can be secular, under religion. The equivalent for Jung to Frazer's erudition is the findings of modern psychiatry and of depth psychology. Jung's theory, like Frazer's, may be wholly wrong, but a Jungian analysis of the myth of Adonis likewise rests on more than the ability to interpret a story.

Where no one disputes the existence of a need to eat, not quite everyone accepts the existence of an unconscious, let alone of a Jungian variety. Jung's theory of myth presupposes the existence of a collective unconscious. Myth for him operates unconsciously rather than, like myth for Frazer, consciously. Myth originates and functions to fulfil the need to encounter one's unconscious and to evaluate the state of it. Only to the extent that Jung's conception of the unconscious is established is a Jungian analysis of the myth of Adonis plausible.

Frazer's theory of myth does not commit one to more than physicalism. For him, myth arises from observation, hypothesis, and generalisation: from observing, for example, the falling of rain and hypothesizing a human-like rain god and in turn human-like gods generally to account for physical events. But gods can be physical, and the relationship of the mind to the body – of thinking to eating – is readily compatible with physicalism. Frazer does hold to an old-fashioned view of science, which for him parallels myth and, even more, magic. But whatever his views of not only science but also, if any, metaphysics, they are not germane to his theory of myth.

By contrast, Jung's theory of myth presupposes dualism and, for those Jungians who cannot abide the identification of the soul with the mind, the existence of the soul as well as of the immaterial mind and the body. Physicalism is by far the dominant position in science and in philosophy of science. Dualism, let alone substance dualism, is a position held by few, if any, scientists and philosophers of science. And even if one grants substance dualism, what is the evidence for the specific dualist claims made by Jung: that the human mind contains not just an immaterial unconscious but also an unconscious composed of inherited archetypes? How many scientists and philosophers of science take seriously Jung's claims? Even if, once again, a Jungian interpretation of the myth of Adonis is more persuasive than Frazer's is, Frazer's explanation of myth is more persuasive than Jung's is. It is more scientific.

References

Boederker, D.D. *Aphrodite's Entry into Greek Epic*. Leiden: Brill, 1974.

Burkert, W. *Greek Religion*. Cambridge MA: Harvard University Press, 1985.

Burkert, W. *Structure and History in Greek Mythology and Ritual*. Berkeley: University of California Press, 1979.

Frazer, J.G. *The Golden Bough*. 1st ed. London: Macmillan, 1890.

Frazer, J.G. *The Golden Bough*. 2nd ed. London: Macmillan, 1900.

Frazer, J.G. *The Golden Bough*. 3rd ed. London: Macmillan, 1913.

Frazer, J.G. *The Golden Bough*. abridged ed. London: Macmillan, 1922.

Hillman, J., ed. *Puer Papers*. Dallas: Spring Publications, 1979.

Jung, C.G. "Answer to Job." In *The Collected Works*, Vol. 11. Princeton NJ: Princeton University Press, 1952.

Jung, C.G. *Letters*. Princeton NJ: Princeton University Press, 1976.

Jung, C.G. "Psychological Aspects of the Mother Archetype." In *The Collected Works*, Vol. 9i. Princeton NJ: Princeton University Press, 1954.

Jung, C.G. "Symbols of Transformation." In *The Collected Works*, Vol. 5. Princeton NJ: Princeton University Press, 1956.

Neumann, E. *The Great Mother*. 2nd ed. Princeton NJ: Princeton University Press, 1972.

Neumann, E. *The Origins and History of Consciousness*. Princeton NJ: Princeton University Press, 1970. Originally published in 1954.

Segal, R.A. *Explaining and Interpreting Religion*. New York: Lang, 1992.

Segal, R.A. *Theorizing about Myth*. Amherst: University of Massachusetts Press, 1999.

Von Franz, M.L. *Puer Aeternus*. 2nd ed. Santa Monica CA: Sigo, 1981.

CHAPTER 5

Collective Memory and Common Imagination – Archetypes in the Perspective of the Theory of Sign

Anna Olejarczyk

Abstract

In this paper the archetypes are explored as signs of cultural discourse which constitute both the collective memory and common imagination. From this perspective, the archetypes, as primordial images, which give the world the anthropomorphic stamp, and as psychoids which compose the matter of human consciousness and unconsciousness given by human biological nature, are mega-signs of any epistemological model and any cultural narration. Archetypes are pivotal in commemorating the past and inventing the future.

The archetypes are unveiled in anamnetical exploration of collective memory; that leads to revealing the structure collective unconsciousness. They are creations of common imagination. They have a heterogeneous and dialectical nature: archetypes are at the same time natural and cultural phenomena, expressed and perceived by everyone in very personal way, and on a common level by using collective media. An archetype is something which is to be perceived and recognized only by the presence of contents that are capable of conscious perception. So it is clear that archetype is dialectic in another way as well: it is something which has roots in an unconscious layer and something which creates the stratum generated from both the conscious experiences and unconscious feeling. Archetype is dialectic because it is something which should be consciously expressed in signs of a language and symbols of beliefs, and which could only affects the level of associations of subconscious and unnamed emotions.

Keywords

Jung – Platonism – post-structuralism – archetype – sign – anamnesis – noesis – heroisation

 | DOI:10.1163/9789004336636_007

1 Introduction

In this paper I would like to discuss archetype as a sign in the perspective of modern semiotics (especially the one created by Umberto Eco) and the theory of discourse (in the meaning mainly proposed by Michel Foucault – the student of Gaston Bachelard). I strongly believe that the outlook stemming from this methodological point could be a remedy for notoriously ill-defined Jungian vocabulary, and then again it could give a fruitful insight into the cultural phenomenon of archetype. In the first part of the text I am going to reconstruct the notion of archetype by analyzing the synonyms of this term and discussing their contextual and co-situational meanings. I will argue that it is worth exploring the phenomena of collective memory and common imagination which are – as I postulate it – correlated to collective or common unconsciousness and the only way to do it is to expose the Neo-Platonic layer of Jung's thought, especially his use of the concept of *anamnesis*. The second part of the paper consists of extensive analyses of archetypes as signs in correlation to the notion of the Library (or the Bibliotheca) and the concept of possible worlds. Finally, in the third part I am going to discuss archetypes – signs of collective memory and common imagination while using the example of the archetype of a hero (as it is explored by Jung's co-worker Károly Kerényi) and the cultural process of heroisation.

2 The Archetype in the Perspective of Modern Humanities

The notion of archetype is notoriously difficult to define. Jung's personal evolution of thought and the change of the perspective of exploring the collective unconscious is the first obstacle on the way to its precise definition. For example, the shift in emphasis from an image to a structure caused by introducing the term archetype as a synonym of primordial image could be noticed in the essay *Instinct and the Unconscious* written by Jung in 1919.[1] Furthermore, the matter seems to be blurred on purpose: archetype gives the world the "anthropomorphic stamp" but it grounds human existence in nature as well.[2] Hence, archetype could be understood both as "archetypical image" (an element of cultural reality created by man) and as the "psychoid" (an experience or a phenomenon given to man by his biological nature). As the psychoid

1 R. Brooke, *Jung and Phenomenology* (London, New York: Routledge, 1991), 137.

2 C.G. Jung, "The Archetypes and the Collective Unconscious", in *The Collected Works*, trans. R.F.C. Hull, vol. 9 (London: Routledge, 1991), 66.

archetype expresses itself in symbols, signs and rites. As an image it introduces unconscious matter into private consciousness and collective communication. Although Jung warns about confusing the archetypal representation (images and ideas) with the archetypes as such, one finds it very difficult not to ask about the meeting point between culture and nature, or – in other words – between conscious reasoning on the one hand, and free imagination and involuntary remembrance on the other. Are the rules of that expression in ideas and images made or given? Is the way of introduction into the unconsciousness learnt or innate? – these questions mark the perspective of my investigation. I consider archetype understood as primordial image in the realm of signs and at the same time I will discuss archetype – the psychoid as the source of patterns: structures or models of knowledge. I explore the similarities between Jung's theory and Eliade's concept of intercultural, but the most important feature of my standpoint is discussing the archetype in terms of Peirce's triadic conception of sign and semiotics by Eco. In Eco's work the sign is a part of a semiotic space – it creates possible worlds, it opens the universe of mind; by changing the meaning it changes the perception of common creation known as reality. The last (but not least by any meanings) problem I discuss is the ontological status of patterns of knowledge: are they common or collective? To begin with, I understand this difference as a disparity between passive and active. To explore this ontological question I have to take into consideration the epistemological problem of the relationship between imagination and knowledge and the connection between knowledge and memory. These problems were discussed many times by many thinkers; I find the common level with Bachelard when he presents imagination as the source of images of art and terms of science as well.[3] The reflections on memory presented by Ricouer have also influenced my perspective.[4]

3 The Archetype and Its Philosophical Roots

Carl Gustav Jung constructed the notion of archetype and he used it with other synonymous terms to make exploration of the phenomena of the unconscious possible. Unlike Sigmund Freud, Jung found the collective unconscious more interesting than an individual one – he took under his scrutiny something

3 G. Bachelard, "La Notion de profil épistémologique", in *La Philosophie du non. Essai d'une philosophie du nouvelle esprit scientifique*, by G. Bachelard (Paris: Presses Universitaires de France, 1940).

4 P. Ricouer, *La Mémoire, l'histoire, l'oublie* (Paris: Éditions du Seuil, 2000).

which was common on a natural level of species or in a cultural field of tradition. (This distinction between cultural and natural media and factors is an important one and it will be discussed widely later). Jung signalized that preference many times in methodological introductions to his papers on archetypes, e.g. the *Introduction* to *Four Archetypes* he started with the remark:

> At first the concept of the unconscious was limited to denoting the state of repressed or forgotten contents. Even with Freud, who makes the unconscious – at least metaphorically – take the stage as the acting subject, it is really nothing but the gathering place of forgotten and repressed contents, and has a functional significance thanks only to these. For Freud, accordingly, the unconscious is of an exclusively personal nature, although he was aware of its archaic and mythological thought-forms.[5]

While reading this passage we have an opportunity to reconstruct how Jung comprehended the difference between his own and Freud's exploration. As he observed, the main result of this difference of perspectives between his and Freud's approach was that from Freud's point of view the unconscious, even treated as an acting subject, is disordered and chaotically gathered psychotic matter which fills up the reservoir of private experiences. However, at the same time Jung pointed out that even for Freud, who almost exclusively studied what privately was denied or closed, and pushed away into the personal unconscious, the unconscious had also a collective aspect. To express this concept of Freud's theory, Jung used the phrase "archaic and mythological thought-forms" – one of many synonyms and equivalents of the notion of archetype. As a result of setting his mind against Freud's theory, Jung made a dialectical coupling of natural constitution and cultural disposition visible. Freud kept the nature side – in his analyses he explored an individual and private realm of unconscious under the pressure of Eros's and Thanatos's impulses. These two powers are characteristic to human nature taken as the *physis* of species. For Jung the laws of social and cultural phenomena and processes were more important – he had studied the symbols, signs, and narrations in which the powers of nature under the rules of culture were set.

As has already been said, Jung used plenty of synonymous and parallel terms and phrases to express the notion of archetype. For example, while explaining the meaning of this notion, he had given definition: there is "something identical in every man which constitutes a common psychic substrate

5 C.G. Jung, *Four Archetypes. Mother, Rebirth, Spirit, Trickster*, trans. R.F.C. Hull (London: Routledge, 2003), 1–2 [2nd paragraph of Collected Works edition].

of a supranatural nature which is present in every one of us."[6] Which is followed by another explanation: archetype is something of a deeper layer, which is not derived from personal experience and is not a personal acquisition but inborn.[7] He also pointed out the equality of his archetypes and "archaic and mythological thought-forms" by Freud.[8] Those synonyms and definitions show the heterogeneous and dialectical nature of archetypes: they are at the same time natural and cultural phenomena, expressed and perceived by everyone in a very personal way, and on a common level by using collective media.

The next group of synonymic expressions is used to put an emphasis on the subject of the manner in which archetype or its psychic contents are perceived. Archetype is something which is to be perceived and recognized only by the presence of contents that are capable of conscious perception.[9] So it is clear that archetype is dialectic in another way as well: it is something which has roots in an unconscious layer and something which creates the stratum generated from both the conscious experiences and unconscious feelings. Archetype is dialectic because it is something which should be consciously expressed in signs of language and symbols of beliefs, and which could only affect the level of associations of subconscious and unnamed emotions: "an unconscious content that is altered by becoming conscious and by being perceived it takes colours from individual consciousness in which it happens to appear."[10]

By asking a question on the manner of perceiving archetypes, Jung entered the phenomenologist's field of research. He was aware of it – he quoted Kant (who was a predecessor of modern phenomenology) and Hartmann (the Neo-Kantist). He expressed the similarity to psychologists exploring the methods of phenomenology or other contemporary perspectives, for example: Jung quoted the Lévy-Bruhl term "représentations collective" – the term used to denotate the symbolic figures in the primitive view of the world. It means practically the same thing as archetype. In primitive tribal lore thought by tradition archetypes are not a part of the unconscious; they have already changed into conscious formulae.[11] Jung realized that, by discussing the "thought-forms" which worked at the same time as the conscious power of creating an actor and as the unconscious embrace of the passive subject, closely, one can get to the tales of Neo-Platonism and Gnosis. The notion of archetype itself has

6 Jung, *Four Archetypes*, 1–2.
7 Ibid.
8 Ibid.
9 Ibid.
10 Ibid., 3.
11 Ibid.

Neo-Platonic roots – the fact which Jung was well aware of. He has frequently quoted early-Christian Neo-Platonic thinkers like Augustine, Philo Judaeus, Irenaeus, and Dionysius the Areopagite to show the genesis of this term.[12] For example, in Philo Judaeus's works the word "archetype" means the *Imago Dei* – the image of God which is present in every man; for Irenaeus it is the image or formula which exists outside God and which are copied by the Creator to make the things of our world. Dionysius the Areopagite, in the writings quoted by Jung, agreed with this way of understanding of archetypes. In his works this term is connected with an adjective – "immaterial", however, on other hand, it means the etalon set as firmly as in stone – Dionysius used the phrase "Archetypal stone", which fact Jung pointed out. Jung also used the images of "archetypical light" given by the authors of *Corpus Hermeticum.*

These are the reasons why everybody who reads Jung's work notices how difficult his notion of archetype is to define. Roger Brooke suggests that this notion evolved from one giving out the matter to one giving out form. Brooke complains that Jung does not make any clear distinction between "archetype" and "archetype image", that he mixes up "primordial image", "motifs" and "archetype." In the introduction to *The Psychology of the Child Archetype* this policy of changing terms and getting the boundaries blurred is visible:

> [...] typical mythologems were observed among individuals to whom all knowledge of this kind was absolutely out of the question, and where indirect derivation from religious ideas that might have been known to them, or from popular figures of speech, was impossible. Such conclusions forced us to assume that we must be dealing with "autochthonous" revivals independent of all tradition, and, consequently, that "myth-forming" structural elements must be present in the unconscious psyche. These products are never (or at least very seldom) myths with a definite form, but rather mythological components which, because of their typical nature, we can call "motifs", "primordial images", types or – as I have named them – archetypes.[13]

This policy of blurring the boundaries poses the question of: what comes first? Is archetype the result of an image? Or maybe archetype produces images? Maybe image and archetype are equal. Maybe there is a circular motion from

12 Jung, *Four Archetypes*, 3.

13 C.G. Jung, "The Psychology of the Child Archetype", in *Essays on a Science of Mythology. The Myth of the Divine Child and the Mysteries of Eleusis*, by C.G. Jung and C. Kerényi, trans. R.F.C. Hull (Princeton NJ, London: Princeton University Press, 1993), 71–72.

image to archetype, from archetype to another image, in which archetype is incorporated. But this is not the end of our trouble. The carousel of terms and notions, metaphors and allegories clarifying what archetype is, goes round and round.

Jung expressed the connection to many previous thinkers; the list of antecessors of his perspective is long: as he noticed Leibniz, Kant, and Schelling had already pointed very clearly to the problem of the dark side of the psyche which has led up to the formation of the notion of "unconsciousness."[14] The Cartesian distinction between *res cogitans* and *res extensa* was pivotal to Jungian ontology as well as Kantian notions of "phenomenon" and "noumenon" were important for his epistemology. Jung read and quoted philosophers, he discussed philosophical matters, but he put it clearly – he wasn't the scholar of philosophy himself:

> Were I a philosopher, I should continue in this Platonic strain and say: somewhere, in "a place beyond the skies", there is a prototype or primordial image of the mother that is pre-existent and supraordinate to all phenomena in which the "maternal", in the broadest sense of the term, is manifest.[15]

But in this declaration he gave the proof of his deeply rooted Platonic beliefs and by all means Plato is Jung's most beloved predecessor. He referred to Plato and Platonic matter in many ways: literally by using – just like Augustine had done many centuries before – the notion of "archetype" as synonymous to an "idea" (a term which came from Greek words *eidos* and *eikon*), or by quotation from Plato's dialogues and the use of Platonic images. For example, the image of "place beyond the sky" comes from Plato's *Phaidros* and the metaphor of cosmic space (the Greek term *chora*) being like a wet-nurse or breast-feeding mother to the matter of the world comes from Plato's *Timaeus*. He referred to Platonism symbolically and set the broadly taken Platonic tune by using the images of light as true knowledge or beam of light as meaningful existence. He used images which were so well established in popular culture that they turned into archetypes themselves and which had originated from Plato's dialogues despite the fact that almost everybody had forgotten about it. These archetypical metaphors of common imagination are images of "slaves in a cave" and "the reason as a charioteer of soul."

14 Jung, "The Psychology of the Child Archetype", 71.

15 Jung, *Four Archetypes. Mother, Rebirth, Spirit, Trickster*, 8 [149th paragraph of Collected Works edition].

4 The Archetype and Platonic Perspective

Let us have a closer look at and read along other quotations. The presence of Platonic and Neo-Platonic matters and motifs in Jungian theory is evident. Jung quoted Plato contextually as well by presenting ontology and epistemology constructed in Platonic style. He not only preferred to use terms with dialectical notion, but also admired the methods of dialectics.[16] He explored the Neo-Platonic world of early Christianity and Gnosis, he quoted the Neo-Platonic alchemy which was so prominent for Medieval and Renaissance European culture – and he kept Plato's side of the historical battle of perspectives in explaining the reality, or in reasoning what is real. Jung understood philosophy as an endless struggle of two types of philosophical explanation – for him one is represented by Plato, the other by Aristotle. He concluded that the Aristotelian type:

> [...] runs as follows: we accept as valid anything that comes from outside and can be verified. The ideal instance is verification by experiment. The [Platonic] antithesis is: we accept as valid anything that comes from inside and cannot be verified. The hopelessness of this position is obvious. Greek natural philosophy with its interest in matter, together with Aristotelian reasoning, has achieved a belated but overwhelming victory over Plato.[17]

Jung adopted the Platonic solution: the dialectical one. He blurred the limits of a notion as well as he gave them opposite meanings, he used polar perspective to achieve the dialectical tension which he understood not only as a coexistence of Platonic *Monas* (The One – the active principle which makes everything individual and connected in one aggregate at the same time; this principle makes everything to be cognizable) and *aorystos Dyas* (undefined Two – the passive principle; thanks to it everything is in its plurality; hence this principle which is undefined makes all indefinable things possible and all indeterminable phenomenon, as well), but also as Neo-Platonic *coexistentio oppositorum* (the idea of the necessity of existence of two opposite principles). That is why I assume that taking the Platonic ontology and epistemology under scrutiny could be fruitful for Jungian studies.

---

16 Jung, *Four Archetypes*, 4.

17 Ibid., 9 [149th paragraph of Collected Works edition].

5 The Archetype – Common or Collective?

Through the previously mentioned spectrum of nature-culture dialectical coupling, the tension between individual and congregational is to be seen. And it is time to ask, what is the type of group phenomena which were taken into consideration? It seems that for Jung there is no difference between "common" and "collective"; he had used these two adjectives interchangeably. For instance, he wrote

> A more or less superficial layer of the unconscious is undoubtedly personal. I call it the personal unconscious. But this personal unconscious rests upon a deeper layer, which does not derive from personal experience and is not a personal acquisition but is inborn. This deeper layer I call the collective unconscious. I have chosen the term "collective" because this part of the unconscious is not individual but universal; in contrast to the personal psyche, it has contents and modes of behavior that are more or less the same everywhere and in all individuals. It is, in other words, identical in all men and thus constitutes a common psychic substrate of a suprapersonal nature which is present in every one of us.[18]

Jung's concept of the common psychic substrate co-echoed with the contemporary concept of Mirror Stage by Jacques Lacan, who noticed that the differences in chimpanzee and human child development show that some features in human cognition are biological, and some strictly cultural. For instance, young chimpanzees reach the highest point of motion development earlier than human children, however, their motion in front of a mirror stays meaningless. In the same time, in the case of the human child the series of gestures connected his body with the mind, and with his environment; in the play with a mirror the virtual complex and reality reduplicate and create the notion of selfness.[19]

---

18 Jung, *Four Archetypes*, 2 [3rd paragraph of Collected Works edition].

19 J. Lacan, *Le stade du miroir. Théorie d'un moment structurant et génétique de la constitution de la réalité conçue en relation avec l'expérience et la doctrine psychanalytique*, Communication au 14ème Congrès psychanalitique international (Marienbad: International Journal of Psychoanalysis, 1937).
English edition:
J. Lacan, "The Mirror Stage as the Formative of the I Function as Revealed in Psychoanalytic Experience", in *Écrits. The First Complete Edition in English*, trans. B. Fink, H. Fink, and R. Grigg (New York, London: W.W. Norton & Company Inc., 2006), 75–81.

As we see for Jung it is important to distinguish clearly what is congregational from what is individual. However, at the same time, he seems to rate the difference between passive and active ways of participating in reality as significant. He wrote:

> Modern psychology treats the products of unconscious fantasy-activity as self-portraits of what is going on in the unconscious, or as statements of the unconscious psyche about itself. They fall into two categories. First, fantasies (including dreams) of a personal character, which go back unquestionably to personal experiences, things forgotten or repressed, and can thus be completely explained by individual anamnesis. Second, fantasies (including dreams) of an impersonal character, which cannot be reduced to experiences in the individual's past, and thus cannot be explained as something individually acquired. These fantasy-images undoubtedly have their closest analogues in mythological types. We must therefore assume that they correspond to certain collective (and not personal) structural elements of the human psyche in general, and, like the morphological elements of the human body, are inherited. Although tradition and transmission by migration certainly play a part, there are, as we have said, very many cases that cannot be accounted for in this way and drive us to the hypothesis of "autochthonous revival." These cases are so numerous that we are obliged to assume the existence of collective psychic substratum. I have called this the collective unconscious.[20]

I understand that Jung deliberately chose the term "collective" as qualification of unconsciousness and because in my book "collective" means: something which is in common and something which is (e.g. experienced) together but which is actively – for example – constructed, created, redefined, modified, and "common" means something which is obviously in common but it is passively – for example – inherited, inducted, received or given. "Collective" as the active element for me is rather self-awareness; "common" on the other hand is self-oblivion.

6 The Archetype and the Notion of "Anamnesis"

Hence, Jung used Platonic ontological and epistemological perspectives and he used the notion of "anamnesis" to explain the way in which people perceive

20 Jung, "The Psychology of the Child Archetype", 74.

archetypes, it is clear that Plato's view of memory influenced Jung's theory. So it is reasonable to ask if Plato's view on imagination influenced it as well. Anamnesis is a special kind of remembering process – it is the process of the coming of thoughts and psychic matter into the conscious mind from the abysses of unconscious. One should ask what image the anamnetical power possesses and Jung – as I assume – gives the answer: archetype. Hence, I suggest discussing archetype as a sign.

Archetype is a collective and common figure – all people have this image rooted deeply in their unconsciousness to be ready to float out in a sudden act of realization and understanding, or in a sudden stroke of genius, which creates a strong image. Archetype is collective – it is created by collective effort, but it is at the same time common – for everybody it is obvious and understandable without much thinking. Anamnesis is the process in which the mind without the conscious process of thinking reaches the realm of the deep and true structure of reality. Thanks to this process, the mind catches the source and reason for everything. Jung's theory of archetypes, thanks to the use of the motion of anamnesis, explores the collective unconsciousness and the collective memory.

Jung's and Plato's views on memory seem to be alike. It is worth asking if their understanding of imagination is similar, as well. Plato thought of three kinds of imagination – in the seventh book of the *Republic*, while presenting the image of the cave, Plato's Socrates discussed the ways in which the images were perceived by our senses and were created in our minds. He used three terms: *phanthasia*, *eikasis*, and *noesis*. Phanthasia means the imagination which produces images from broken parts of the images previously perceived by a fogged mind. Phanthasia is the source of dangerous *phantasmata* – delusive, unreal images and narration which are very easy to be taken as true ones. Eikasis means everyday imagination – the way in which our mind perceives the phenomena of outside and inside reality. Thanks to eikasis, we are able to connect an image with a notion, a notion with a name, and a name with a sign. Therefore, eikasis is a strong useful power of our mind. It works on the boarders of unconsciousness and consciousness – it could bring out the forgotten or unconscious memories or knowledge by connecting pieces of information and using reasoning and unconscious associations.

Noesis is the source of pure knowledge. The process of real anamnesis opens the prospects of this way of imagining. It is a clear seeing without any distraction from the material world. It is the seeing of pure reason just like seeing the light itself and not only the bright colours. The noetical image is shared with other men – it is collective and common at the same time, since it is both actively achieved and passively accepted. Thus, it is obvious that Jung's archetypes are rather noetical objects, rooted in the connections created by eikasis, rather than objects of common phanthasia.

Archetypes are remembered in the process of anamnesis, which literally means: "bringing back from what is forgotten." They are deeply rooted symbols which rule our cognitive processes, as images, notions, and names, the way of that ruling is embraced by the notion of eikasis. Finally, archetypes are noetical objects which inhabit our common imagination. Therefore, it is time to ask if archetypes were signs in the meaning of modern semiotics.

7 The Archetype in the Perspective of Modern Semiotics

Jung himself used the term "mythologem" while analyzing the specific examples of archetypes. This term shows the well-defined connections with structuralism – one of the basic theories of modern knowledge of language, sign, and communication. Hence, it is reasonable to check if his theory is further liaised with the theory of sign. In the 50's and the 60's, thanks to the works of Roland Barthes and the redefining of the theory of Ch.S. Pierce, the sign started to be understood as a complex phenomenon. For Ferdinand de Saussure every sign was a binary object, consisting of the active signifier and passive signified, for Roland Barthes such a model was too simple: a sign had at least two levels; each of them bipolar and consisting of signifier and signified. In this way a sign started to be understood as a compound structure, in which the first binary nucleus sign became the signifier of the next level; such as the "borrowing" or "robbing" of words could proceed infinitely and, quoted Barthes's phrase, "myth was the borrowed or robbed sign or word."[21] At the same time the triadic model of sign proposed by Ch.S. Peirce was renewed by the next generation of scholars. Jung was aware of all these processes, his writings proved that he was well read. That is why the "mythologems" he discussed should be treated as complex signs. Since '50, simultaneously with very important decades of Jung's activity, it is not difficult to find terms like "myth" or "mythologem", "topos", "philosophem" in the vocabulary of humanists' theories. They mean in general compound signs, signs which despite their complexity and appositional meaning communicate as simply as a nucleolus sign. Every compound sign works like a normal nucleolus sign, but at the same time it has several layers or tiers – each could be connected with a different cultural field, region, tradition. Therefore the "borrowing" or the "robbing" of the sign means translating or incorporating the sign with its previous context and co-situation into a new

21 R. Barthes, *Mythologies* (Paris: Seuil, 1957), 5.

ones, like in the theory of communication functions by Roman Jakobson.[22] Hence, archetype, like every compound sign, could have different meanings and show opposite things at the same time. It is another reason for archetype to be dialectic.

Just like "mythologem" means elemental, but autonomous mythical narration (or part of such narration), and "topos" – the notion which was used in classical hermeneutics already – mean the sovereign topic or repetitive structure in literature, "philosophem" means self-independent notion, topic, or argumentation in philosophy. By comparison "archetype" could be understood as an autonomous image, topic, or notion which is repetitive and could be found in culture, religion or phenomena of everyday life.

Archetype, like mythologem, topos, or philosophem, is a narration which works as a simple sign.[23] Unlike them, archetype tells a different story: while in the notion of topos the regularity of specific narrative structure or image is important, and in "myth" or mythologem the order of fable elements is important, archetype means regularity and specific order in giving the answer to an important question. In this value it is similar to philosophem from which archetype differs in giving images and presenting narration on human nature and the human way of perceiving life – philosophem gives basic ontological or epistemological answers in which the universality of perspective is important.

The ontology and epistemology of Jung is eclectic as Brooke noticed or – using the term of Gaston Bachelard – the "spectrum" of his notion of archetype is constructed with heterogeneous matter. The "epistemological obstacle" and "epistemological break" – the other notions from Bachelard's dictionary work perfectly in context of Jungian thought.[24] These three terms open the door to the archaeology of science by Foucault.[25] Foucault as well as other post-structuralists uses the notions of "encyclopedia" and "library/bibliotheca"[26] (these notions are pivotal for Eco's semiotics)[27] and I would like to introduce these

22 Cf. R. Jakobson, *Selected Writings*, ed. S. Rudy, vol. 1–6 (Paris: The Hague, 1971).

23 It is a very difficult task to point out, who is the inventor or first user of the terms "mythologem" or "philosophem" – the first one was in constant use in structuralist discourse, the second one – is a common tool of the research of post-structuralism.

24 G Bachelard, "La Notion de *profil épistémologique", in Bachelard, "La Notion de profil épistémologique"*, 41–51.

25 M. Foucault, *L'archéologie du savoir* (Paris: Gallimard, 1969).

26 M. Foucault, *Les mots et les choses. Une archéologie des sciences humaines* (Paris: Gallimard, 1966).

27 Cf. U. Eco, *Semiotics and Philosophy of Language* (London: The Macmillan Press, 1984). For the term "encyclopedia" and its use – see: p. 47; for the notion "dictionary" and the relation between "dictionary" and "encyclopedia" – see: p. 68.; for "library-language" – see: p. 177.

terms into our discussion on archetype and collective memory and common imagination.

In the semiotics rooted in Peirce's theory of triadic sign, especially in Eco's theory of possible worlds, the notions of "library" or "bibliotheca" exist.[28] Library is a term used by Michel Foucault, as well. He also used the notion of "archive." Library or bibliotheca, terms used frequently by both post-structuralists and scholars of Peirce – Eco and post-structuralist and successor of Bachelard – Foucault, mean the aggregate of all texts which existed. Library is a collection of books, ranging from any particular set of books to a hypothetical set of every book possible taken into consideration. It is the semiotic space in which all existed or possible narration takes place. Library can denote different levels or layers: it could be the contemporary library (all texts, books, and narration existing now), it could be a medieval one (e.g. all texts, books, and narration which were in use in the times of Thomas Aquinatus). The library has its zones: that is why it is reasonable to discuss the library of Gnosis, or library of Enlightenment. It is possible to differentiate the levels of universality: one could explore the universal library – texts, books, and narration which are in common knowledge, or special library – texts, books, or narration known only for specific groups. It is even possible to use this term in reference to the individual semiotic space of texts, books, and narration which create the sphere of private understanding and experience of the world through the lenses of language and communication.

As was already pointed out, the notion of library explores the realm of knowledge. It puts some light on the subject of collective memory and common knowledge: how does it work?; how is it handed down? In the vocabulary of Eco's semiotics two other notions for signifying the semiotic space are proposed: "encyclopedia" means the aggregate of all theories, definitions, and notions used to explain how reality works; "dictionary" marks a set of every word and its definitions, meanings, both denotated and conotated. Encyclopedia constitutes a set of notions, images and explanatory narrations from any particular set to a hypothetical set of all possible notions, images and narrations. Like library, encyclopedia and dictionary have their layers, levels, zones. Dictionaries and encyclopedias create library. A very similar situation happens with archetypes; as signs they create the semiotics space with a complex structure of connection inside. When one explores that realm one could notice aggregates of archetypes similar to library, encyclopedia, and dictionary mentioned above. Library, encyclopedia, and dictionary are systems of signs,

28 U. Eco, *Role of the Reader. Exploration in the Semiotics of the Texts* (Bloomington: Indiana University Press, 1979), 217–20.

they create the semiotic space in which symbols, icons, and all images could operate, the field on which the narrations could grow. Archetypes, as symbols, images or as narrations, mythologems as well, are incorporated into those systems.

It is worth mentioning, that, Eco – who presents himself as the scholar close to the model of knowledge given by Aristotle, and the researcher of Thomas Aquinas – explains notions of "dictionary" and "encyclopedia" by creating the image of the tree of knowledge, a tree which explodes, during the act of perception, into a "turmoil of infinite accidents." This is a very Platonic, or even Gnostic, image. It gives a dialectical vibe and has an archetypical nature by putting to use the archetype of the cosmic tree.[29]

The notion of Encyclopedia and Library could be considered to be the semiotic universes and, as such, are analogues to the Heideggerian notion of "the world" understood as a set of "things" and the Jungian notion of "the world" as a set of "images." Because I discuss archetype in connection with myth, and from my point of view myth, as meaningful narration which gives the explanation of the experienced world, introduces order into the "things" or "images." Why do I put the sign of equality between these two terms? Roger Brooke points out several similarities between Heideggerian ontological and epistemological resolution and those which Jung's theory of archetypes included. And he suggests that when Heidegger explains the world as consisting of "things", Jung – on other hand – describes it as a coexistence of images.[30] I find that equalization between "things" and "images" useful: it shows how things are at the same time images, how they work as signs and this double existence (as a thing and as a sign) lies in the core of the idea of archetype in which everything is itself and a sign for something else at the same time. Jung noticed:

> Psychic existence can be recognized only by the presence of contents that are capable of consciousness. We can therefore speak of an unconscious only in so far as we are able to demonstrate its contents. The contents of the personal unconscious are chiefly the feeling-toned complex, as they are called; they constitute the personal and private side of psychic life.

29 The image mentioned above is presented in the passage:

> The tree of genera and species, the tree of substances, blows up in a dust of difference, in a turmoil of infinite accidents, in a nonhierarchical network of *qualia*. The dictionary is dissolved into a potentially unordered and unrestricted galaxy of pieces of world knowledge. The dictionary thus becomes an encyclopedia, because it was in fact a disguised encyclopedia

Eco, *Semiotics and Philosophy of Language*, 68.

30 Brooke, *Jung and Phenomenology*, 136–60 [Chapter VIII].

> The contents of the collective unconscious, on the other hand, are known as archetypes.[31]

What are the contents of collective unconscious, one can ask.

8 The Archetypes by Jung and the Greek Mysteries and the Cult of Heroes

Jung analyzed four archetypes: the archetype of the Primordial Child, the Virgin/Mother archetype, the Trickster-Figure, and the Spirit. Although all of them are the potent *topoi* of literature and powerful images in art, only the first two are fully developed mythical narrations which progressed into the opulence of rituals and lore's rules. Jung himself dedicated more time and attention to the study these two archetypes, and for his friend – Kerényi they are pivotal to his reconstruction of Greek beliefs. As every mighty archetype both Primordial Child archetype and Virgin/Mother archetype, it consists of many plots and motives.

The Primordial Child means the immortal child, forever young, or a child who overcomes death. It has the abnormal origin: it could be a child of a god or goddess, it could be born from an element – like sea or stone, for instance, it could come out from a Cosmic Egg or the egg laid by Lea. In myths the Primordial Child can be a hermaphrodite, and as a young adult – bisexual. It is common in many cultures to think of the Primordial Child as the first human being who ever existed. Therefore, Adam, known in Gnosis and alchemic tradition as Adam Kadmos, is the example of the Primordial Child archetype. Many others can be found in Mediterranean cultures: Greek, Minoan, Egyptian. Osiris, Dionysius, Mitra and Jesus are the primordial children. The myths of primordial children tell a story not only about the boys; there are some girls, as well. Kora, the daughter of the goddess Demeter is one of them.

Kerényi studied the story of Kora very closely. In two essays published in a book of collected papers both by Jung and by himself, Kerényi analyzed thoroughly the mysteria in Eleusis and the myths of Kora/Persephone, which were the foundations for rituals conducted in Eleusis.[32] The story goes that Kora, the believed daughter of Demeter – goddess of abundance and all life growing

---

31 Jung, *Four Archetypes. Mother, Rebirth, Spirit, Trickster*, 2 [4th paragraph of Collected Works edition].

32 C. Kerényi, "Kore", in *Essays on a Science of Mythology. The Myth of the Divine Child and the Mysteries of Eleusis*, by C.G. Jung and C. Kerényi, trans. R.F.C. Hull (Princeton NJ, London: Princeton University Press, 1993), 101–55.

from the earth, was seen by Hades – the younger brother of Zeus and the god of the underworld and death. Hades was struck by love and he decided to capture the young virgin. Demeter was furious at first, then she started to mourn deeply: everything growing, flowering, and fruiting became dead. There was eternal winter on Earth. Zeus stepped in and mediated: it was decided that Kora, who in the meantime became Hades's wife under the new name of Persephone, would stay with her husband for one part of the year and would spend the other half with her mother. She would stay with her husband for as many months as the number of grains of pomegranate she ate. That was the beginning of the seasons: when Demeter is happy with her child it is the springtime and summer on Earth, while Kora as Persephone stays with her husband it is the time of winter.

Eleusis was the center of the cult of Demeter and Kora/Persephone because it was believed that one of the caves situated in the vicinity was the entrance to the underworld. In Eleusis all Greeks and all people who spoke Greek met every springtime to celebrate the rebirth of Kora (coming back from the underworld, which was understood as rebirth). These celebrations were extremely popular and had a long history: the last priest who led the mysteries in Eleusis lived in the fifth century A.D. and was one of the scholars of the Fifth Academy – the last Neo-Platonic school in Athens.

It is important for this study to truly understand the meaning of myths told and rituals conducted in Eleusis. According to well-acclaimed reconstruction given by Kerényi, in the core of those mysteries was the ritual of rebirth of everyone who celebrated it. Pilgrims sacrificed suckling piglets to commemorate two goddesses – The Mother and the Virginal Child. In this act of sacrificing the pilgrim became one with the piglet; he or she sacrificed himself or herself to become one with the reborn Kora. That sacrificing took place on the steps of many altars, shrines, and temples built in Eleusis. But inside the main temple, far from the eyes of pilgrims, the priest announced: the child was born. He cried: "korus is born" ("korus" means the boy newly born or child), but he meant that the daughter of Demeter was back. At the same time every pilgrim (men and women alike) whispered into the ear of his or her piglet: "I am the reborn Kora" (using the female grammar form).[33]

The mysteries in Eleusis, the myth of Demeter and her daughter, the archetype of the Primordial Child and the archetype of the Virgin/Mother are truly about immortality and everlasting youth. Kerényi explored the world of Greek

33 See: G. Mylonas, *Eleusis and the Eleusian Mysteries* (Elefsina: Princeton University Press/ Cyceon Tales Publication, 2010).

mythoi and came to the conclusion that the cult of heroes was powerful and meaningful in Greek culture as much as rituals concentrated in Eleusis. Although Jung did not explore myths and rituals on heroes[34] (however Kerényi did),[35] I think, they are worth examining. I believe it is allowed to discuss the Hero archetype, despite the silence of Jung on this subject.

In Greek tradition and myths a hero is a powerful man – king (such Minos was), warrior (such Achilles or Hercules was), or ingenious thinker (Odysseus, for instance), artisan (Dedalus), or healer (Asclepius). The hero was a real man, because of his greatness he was thought to be the son of one of the Olympic gods. He wasn't immortal as such, but he had a gift of everlasting youth and strength, and after his death he joined the gods in Olympus. As archaeological research shows, the real kings and rulers of the Neolithic and Bronze eras became heroes: their graves became the cult centers, the special anthems and poems were composed to glorify them, sports games took place near the grave stones (the roots of the Olympic games were such a cult; ancient Greece has many other sports games commemorating heroes).[36] Ancient and classical Greeks were aware of the beginnings of the cults of heroes – a popular story of four eras of mankind's past: the Golden, the Silver, the Bronze, and the Iron one, give evidence to that. That story was handed down by Hesiod in his poem *Theogony*, and by Plato in his *Timaeus*, hence, it was a part of unwritten and written tradition as well.

The archetypes of the Primordial Child and the Virgin/Mother are still with us as part of Christian beliefs they are still influencing our unconsciousness and are present in our dreams.[37] On the other hand, the stories, and images of heroes are standing strong; they have a powerful impact not only on popular culture, but also on the ways of our reasoning: the genius ones, the gifted ones, the beautiful ones, the young ones, or even just the famous or popular ones still become our heroes. They are almost immortal, after their death they

---

34 He wrote only a few pages on the subject of the hero:
C.G. Jung, "Identification with a Cult-Hero", in Jung, *Four Archetypes. Mother, Rebirth, Spirit, Trickster*, 72.
And he mentioned mysteries of Eleusis twice:
C.G. Jung, "Forms of Rebirth", in ibid., 55.
C.G. Jung, "The Psychology of Rebirth", in ibid., 59.

35 C. Kerényi, *The Heros of the Greeks*, trans. H.L. Rose (London: Thames and Hudson, 1997).

36 R. Osborne, "Monumentality and Ritual in Archaic Greece", in *Greek Ritual Poetics*, ed. D. Yatromanolakis and P. Roilos (Cambridge MA, London: Center for Hellenic Studies, Harvard University Press, 2004), 37–54.

37 As it is visible in analytical practice of Marion Woodman. See: M. Woodman, *The Pregnant Virgin: A Process of Psychological Transformation*. Toronto: Inner City Books, 1988.

are still young and living in our memory. The process of heroisation, as I believe, is the strongest argument showing the rightfulness of Jung's theory of archetypes.

References

Bachelard, G. "La Notion de *profil épistémologique*." In *La Philosophie du non. Essai d'une philosophie du nouvel esprit scientifique*, by G. Bachelard. Paris: Presses Universitaires de France, 1940.

Barthes, R. *Mythologies*. Paris: Seuil, 1957.

Brooke, R. *Jung and Phenomenology*. London, New York: Routledge, 1991.

Eco, U. *Role of the Reader. Exploration in the Semiotics of the Texts*. Bloomington: Indiana University Press, 1979.

Eco, U. *Semiotics and Philosophy of Language*. London: The Macmillan Press, 1984.

Foucault, M. *L'archéologie du savoir*. Paris: Gallimard, 1969.

Foucault, M. *Les mots et les choses. Une archéologie des sciences humaines*. Paris: Gallimard, 1966.

Jakobson, R. *Selected Writings*. Edited by S. Rudy. Vol. 1–6. Paris: The Hague, 1971.

Jung, C.G. *Four Archetypes. Mother, Rebirth, Spirit, Trickster*. Translated by R.F.C. Hull. London: Routledge, 2003.

Jung, C.G. "The Archetypes and the Collective Unconscious." In *The Collected Works*, translated by R.F.C. Hull, Vol. 9. London: Routledge, 1991.

Jung, C.G., and C. Kerényi. *Essays on a Science of Mythology. The Myth of the Divine Child and the Mysteries of Eleusis*. Translated by R.F.C. Hull. Princeton NJ, London: Princeton University Press, 1993.

Kerényi, C. *The Heros of the Greeks*. Translated by H.L. Rose. London: Thames and Hudson, 1997.

Lacan, J. *Le stade du miroir. Théorie d'un moment structurant et génétique de la constitution de la réalite, conçue en relation avec l'expérience et la doctrine psychanalytique*. Communication au 14ème Congrès psychanalitique international. Marienbad: International Journal of Psychoanalysis, 1937.

Lacan, J. "The Mirror Stage as the Formative of the I Function as Revealed in Psychoanalytic Experience." In *Écrits. The First Complete Edition in English*, translated by B. Fink, H. Fink, and R. Grigg. New York, London: W.W. Norton & Company Inc., 2006.

Mylonas, G. *Eleusis and the Eleusian Mysteries*. Elefsina: Princeton University Press/ Cyceon Tales Publication, 2010.

Osborne, R. "Monumentality and Ritual in Archaic Greece." In *Greek Ritual Poetics*, edited by D. Yatromanolakis and P. Roilos. Cambridge MA, London: Center for Hellenic Studies, Harvard University Press, 2004.

Peirce, C.S. *The Essentinal Peirce. Selected Philosophical Writings*. Edited by N. Houser and C. Kloesel. Vol. I (1867–1893). Bloomington, Indianapolis: Indiana University Press, 1992.

Peirce, C.S. *The Essentinal Peirce. Selected Philosophical Writings*. Edited by Peirce Edition Project. Vol. II (1893–1913),. Bloomington, Indianapolis: Indiana University Press, 1998.

Ricouer, P. *La Mémoire, L'historoire, L'oubli*. Paris: Éditions du Seuil, 2000.

Woodman, M. *The Pregnant Virgin : A Process of Psychological Transformation*. Toronto : Inner City Books, 1988.

CHAPTER 6

The Idea of Culture Image Confronted with Psychoanalytic Tradition

Ewa Kwiatkowska

Abstract

The iconic perspective of culture knowledge based on the idea of image activity may be developed in relation to the reflection of Aby Warburg and to other aspects within new Bildwissenschaft, particularly to the assumption about particular autonomic logic of images and their constructive role in thinking and in culture. The assumptions of iconic conceptions of epistems by Gottfried Boehm may form the point of reference for reflections upon the imaginary dimension of knowledge and culture, mutual relations between recognition, imaginatio and image.

Similar issues appear in the context of Jung and Bachelard tradition. Confronting it with the achievements of contemporary *Bildwissenschaft* referring to Warburg conception, reveals the continuity of traditions in dialogue: the one based on culture historic approach to image and the one referring to its unchangeable trans-historic basis of some kind. In spite of obvious fundamental controversies between the two traditions, they nevertheless share some points, namely, the issues of mnestic aspects of image, the idea of specific "energy" or activity of image, and also transferred to culture plane the issue of symptom. The clash between these two different traditions of approach to image and the character of its activity aims at defining critical points in trans-disciplinary research into image.

Keywords

Culture image – structuralism – post-structuralism – image – symbol – iconic turn – iconic epistemes

1 Introduction

One of the starting points for placing psychoanalysis within contemporary humanities may be Paweł Dybel's observation that as a result of poststructuralist interpretations, Freud's concept is recognised not only as a psychological reflection with philosophical implications or a kind of hermeneutics as a method of interpretation, but as a strictly philosophical concept undermining the traditional concepts dealing with human beings and culture.[1] Reservations about the scientific nature of psychoanalysis do not obscure its real role in shaping the humanistic debate, consisting not only in defining the meaning of the unconscious in the human *universum*, but also in introducing a completely new language, which quickly transgressed the boundaries of its discipline. Psychoanalysis as such, as an overt and hidden element of other concepts in the form of "psychoanalytic thinking" and as a negative point of reference has become, as Dybel stresses, an immanent component of many contemporary philosophical concepts and humanistic theories.[2]

As we indicate areas that are of interest to both psychoanalysis and other research traditions, we reveal important issues in the contemporary humanistic debate, potential subjects of transdisciplinary research. A juxtaposition of the issue of pictorial symbol, rooted in the psychoanalytic tradition, with the idea of image active in culture present implicitly in new image studies indicates one of such key areas. In an analysis of the relations between a cultural studies approach and a psychoanalytic approach to any cultural phenomenon, including the image, the fundamental questions are: the issue of "psychoanalytic thinking", and a possibility of applying psychoanalytic concepts (the unconscious, repression, distortion or symptom) in cultural studies. A reconstruction or redefinition of these notions in culture studies goes far beyond the framework of the present analysis; of key significance here is the difference between the psychoanalytic understanding of the unconscious and the understanding of this concept in cultural studies and social sciences.

In addition to significant divergences over conceptuality, there are also other critical points between psychoanalysis and contemporary image studies. This is the objective of the confrontation between the consequences of the iconic interpretation of the unconscious as an anthropological matrix and, more specifically, the concept of *image matricielle* or visual matrix, and the idea of culturally active image developing within theiconic turn, especially in *Bildwissenschaft*. Despite the obvious fundamental controversies between the psychoanalytic tradition and the image studies tradition, they still have some themes in common, themes like mnestic aspects of images, the idea of the "energy" or activity of the image, or the issue of the image as a symptom.

1 P. Dybel, *Okruchy psychoanalizy: teoria Freuda między hermeneutyką i poststrukturalizmem*, Horyzonty nowoczesności (Cracow: Universitas, 2009), 21.

2 Ibid., 26.

2 The Iconic Turn and Psychoanalysis

Proclaimed in the early 1990s, the iconic turn restored to the image its humanities status of both an object and tool of cognition.[3] The iconic turn itself is a transdisciplinary phenomenon. Its main strands,very varied as they are,[4] make no significant reference to psychoanalysis, although the programmatic text of the new *Bildwissenschaft*, Gottfried Boehm's "Die Wiederkehr der Bilder" does refer to Freud and unconscious imagination,[5] and the book *Was ist ein Bild?*, which begins with the above mentioned essay, contains two papers by Lacan. However, both the philosophical provenance and the consequences of the new *Bildwissenschaft* are not only very distant from but even contrary to those of psychoanalysis.

One of the most interesting threads of the iconic turn is the idea – which runs through it but is never completely explained – of an image active in culture. Premises of this idea can be found in some contemporary concepts of image studies; its patrons are Aby Warburg's concept of image-symbol and Walter Benjamin's concept of dialectical image. In the light of the Warburgian tradition, often referred to in image studies, and the Benjaminian tradition, referred to only rarely,[6] a culturally active image can be recognised thanks to its special impact on cultural processes. An important assumption of the concept of culturally active images is recognising that the link between these processes and images is not accidental; on the contrary, it stems from the very essence of the anthropological and cultural relation between humans and images.

3 See G. Boehm, "Die Wiederkehr der Bilder", in *Was ist ein Bild?*, ed. G. Boehm (Munich: Fink, 1995); "Jenseits der Sprache? Anmerkungen zur Logik der Bilder", in *Iconic turn: die neue Macht der Bilder*, ed. C. Maar and H. Burda (Cologne: DuMont, 2005); D. Bachmann-Medick, *Cultural turns: nowe kierunki w naukach o kulturze*, trans. K. Krzemieniowa (Warsaw: Oficyna Naukowa, 2012). Originally published as *Cultural Turns. Neuorientierungen in den Kulturwissenschaften* (Reinbek bei Hamburg, 2006), 421.

4 See Bachmann-Medick, *Cultural turns*, 390–451; for more on the diversity of trends within the pictorial turn see also the correspondence between G. Boehm and W.J.T. Mitchell (G. Boehm and W.J.T. Mitchell, "Briefwechsel: Gottfried Boehm und Tom Mitchell", in *Bilderfragen: die Bildwissenschaften im Aufbruch*, ed. H. Belting [Munich: Fink, 2007], 27–46); especially Mitchell's reply (W.J.T. Mitchell, "Pictorial Turn. Eine Antwort", in *Bilderfragen: die Bildwissenschaften im Aufbruch*, ed. H. Belting [Munich: Fink, 2007], 37–46).

5 See Boehm, "Die Wiederkehr der Bilder."

6 G. Schweppenhäuser notes that the image theory of the Frankfurt School, which for him includes Benjamin, has not been represented in the image studies discourse of recent years, despite the fact that image concepts have played quite an important role in critical theory, and image studies issues in critical theory concern both aesthetics and historiosophy, cultural criticism and theory of cognition (G. Schweppenhäuser, "Überlegungen zum Bildbegriff der Kritischen Theorie", *Zeitschrift für Kulturphilosophie* 4, no. 2 [2010]: 320).

Important points in an analysis of the activity of the image in culture include the dilemma of whether the epistemological and the cultural pictorial experience is primary or secondary with regard to langue, the issue of images being non-reducible to iconic signs, images being characterised by their epistemic, mnemic, performative, symbolic, poietic etc. action.

In such a research field we can ask the following question: What do reflections deriving from the psychoanalytic tradition (and those referring to it through, for example, the notions of the unconscious or archetype, or "psychoanalytic thinking") have to offer to the idea of a culturally active image? The answer is all the more interesting given the fact that the attitude of both pioneers of the idea of culture image, Warburg and Benjamin, to psychoanalytic concepts is still widely discussed in the literature on the subject,[7] and that the *Mnemosyne Atlas* and *Das Passagen-Werk* are regarded, together with Weber's concept and the founding of the Frankfurt School, as belonging to the great enlightenment projects of the first half of the twentith century.[8] Cultural criticism, too, carried out by Freud on the one hand and Warburg and Benjamin on the other encourages reflection on possible parallels between these projects. Today, even more interesting than the relations between these now classic concepts would be a confrontation between the iconic turn and not just psychoanalysis alone, but also research trends referring to it, for instance Gaston Bachelard's concept of material imagination or Gilbert Durand's concept of archetypology of the imaginary.

In the present analysis, of crucial importance is a distinction between two interpretations of the unconscious: one inspired by language theory (of the Frankfurtians, post-structuralist readings of Freud[9]) and one iconic. This distinction corresponds to one of the most important oppositions, not only methodological, in the contemporary humanities: between the linguistic turn and the iconic turn. Worthy of note is the fact that it was precisely the linguistic-semiotic paradigm that contributed greatly to the emergence of

7 See E.H. Gombrich, *Aby Warburg: eine intellektuelle Biographie*, trans. M. Fienbork (Hamburg: Philo Fine Arts, 2012), 543; G. Didi-Huberman, *Das Nachleben der Bilder: Kunstgeschichte und Phantomzeit nach Aby Warburg*, trans. M. Bischoff (Berlin: Suhrkamp, 2010), passim; C. Zumbusch, *Wissenschaft in Bildern: Symbol und dialektisches Bild in Aby Warburgs Mnemosyne-Atlas und Walter Benjamins Passagen-Werk* (Berlin: Akademie Verlag, 2004), 48–97. It is worth noting that Theodore W. Adorno intended Benjamin's concept of dialectical image to be a polemical tool with regard to Jung's concept of archetypal images (see W. Adorno's letter to W. Benjamin and M. Horkheimer in [W. Benjamin, *Pasaże*, trans. I. Kania (Cracow: Wydawnictwo Literackie, 2005), 1046–51, 1082–83]).

8 Zumbusch, *Wissenschaft in Bildern*, 55.

9 By e.g. Roland Barthes, Jacques Lacan and Jacques Derrida.

language-theory-focused interpretations of psychoanalysis,[10] and that post-structuralist interpretations of psychoanalysis today contribute largely to its popularity. However, the structuralist tradition is accused of having a reductive approach to the symbol,[11] of favouring syntactic rules over semantics, while treating psychoanalysis as hermeneutics seems to be increasing the distance between psychoanalysis and semiostructuralism, accused of scientism and neopositivism. This reductive approach of semiotics to the symbol was criticised by Durand, whose *Les structures anthropologiques de l'imaginaire. Introduction à l'archétypologie générale*, published in 1960, was intended as a polemic with Lévi-Strauss' *Structural Anthropology*. By combining some aspects of Bachelardism and Jungism with an anthropology based on reflexology, Durand opened up a field of interdisciplinary studies of the image and the imaginary as an archetype-rooted cultural sphere.

While the post-structuralist interpretation of psychoanalysis is present and well-developed in the literature on the subject,[12] the relation between psychoanalysis and the iconic turn is an issue that is yet to be analysed holistically and systematically, although, as I have already mentioned, there are discussions about the relation between the concepts of one of the pioneers of *Bildwissenschaft*, Aby Warburg, and those of Freud or Jung. Three assumptions present in the psychoanalytic tradition, and reconstructed and adopted by Ilona Błocian, can be points of reference in the endeavour of comparing it with image studies. They are: the unconscious as an anthropological matrix,[13] the iconic interpretation of the unconscious, and the building of a direct bridge between the unconscious and symbolic (pictorial, mythical, metaphorical) thinking.[14] These assumptions require a brief commentary.

10 P. Dybel, *Dialog i represja. Antynomie psychoanalizy Zygmunta Freuda* (Warsaw: IFiS PAN, 1995), 40.

11 See J.-J. Wunenburger, *Filozofia obrazów*, trans. T. Stróżyński (Gdańsk: Wydawnictwo słowo/obraz terytoria, 2011). Originally published as *Philosophie des image* (Paris, 1997), 52.

12 See Dybel, *Okruchy psychoanalizy*, 20–24.

13 Comprising instinctive patterns and, at the same time, a priori universal psychoid forms acting in both the individual and the collective order (I. Błocian, *Psychoanalityczne wykładnie mitu: Freud, Jung, Fromm* [Warsaw: "Eneteia" Wydawnictwo Psychologii i Kultury, 2010], 497–505; "Pojęcie nieświadomości a obraz groty w badaniach nad wyobraźnią G. Bachelarda", *Studia Philosophica Wratislaviensia* VII, no. 3 [2012]: 93, 102); In any case, in the Jungian perspective there is no distinction between these orders, though in Freud's reflection the issue can be interpreted differently (ibid., 114–15).

14 These are the premises of Ilona Błocian's *Psychoanalityczne wykładnie mitu*; see also Błocian, "Pojęcie nieświadomości a obraz groty w badaniach nad wyobraźnią G. Bachelarda", in: "Studia Philosophica Wratislaviensia", Vol. 7, fasc. 3 (2012).

In reconstructing the anthropology of psychoanalysis and examining the activity of the unconscious as an anthropological matrix,[15] Ilona Błocian uses the iconic interpretation of the unconscious. It is expressed in the assumption that the unconscious is recognised primarily through the pictorial basis, that the unconscious is expressed in symbolic images.[16] The bridge that links the concept of the anthropological matrix and the iconic interpretation of the unconscious is the idea of *image matricielle* or visual matrix. Jean-Jacques Wunenburger uses it to designate elementary or primordial images, which for him include the invariable matrices of potential images defined, for instance, by Jungian archetypes.[17]

The consequences of the assumption that the unconscious is an anthropological matrix for an approach to culture depend on, among others, the way the anthropological matrix is interpreted: ontologically and/or epistemologically. The ontological interpretation (naturalist vs. transcendental approach to the unconscious) leads to essentialism, while the naturalist interpretation leads also to reductionism. The epistemological interpretation does not have to carry such a risk, which, however, does not eliminate the distance between psychoanalysis and culture studies or social sciences. The anthropology of psychoanalysis is antinomic or at least inconsistent; its theoretical and non-theoretical roots vary greatly and source writings of its authors lead to antinomic interpretations.[18] An immanent contradiction is also to be found in the psychoanalytic concept of the human being and – consequently – human culture. Reconciling the image studies perspective and the culture studies perspective with the psychoanalytic perspective is impossible, and indicating critical points (contradictions, points of contact) between them makes it

15 We can point to various interpretations of this matrix: what is repressed; what is automatic; what belongs to the activity of archetypes; pictorial thinking; what is mythopoeic; and even, going to the extreme, the unconscious as a hidden basis of reality (Błocian, "Pojęcie nieświadomości a obraz groty w badaniach nad wyobraźnią G. Bachelarda", 92–93).

16 See Błocian, *Psychoanalityczne wykładnie mitu*, passim, especially pp. 507–511.

17 Wunenburger, *Filozofia obrazów*, 40–42; According to Jung, the primordial image is a mnemic deposit or engram of a constantly recurring psychic experience (C.G. Jung, *Typy psychologiczne*, trans. R. Reszke [Warsaw: Wrota, 1997]. Originally published as *Psychologische Typen; Carl Gustaw Jung: Gesammelte Werke* [Walter-Verlag AG, 1994], 465); cf. Błocian, "Pojęcie nieświadomości a obraz groty w badaniach nad wyobraźnią G. Bachelarda", 96.

18 This can be seen, for instance, in the distinction made between two dimensions of Freudian psychoanalysis: clinical and hermeneutic; the variety of interpretations of Jung's concept is linked to its evolution, from biologistic to hermeneutic approaches (Błocian, *Psychoanalityczne wykładnie mitu*, 504).

necessary at least to make their positions more specific and may even lead to mutual inspirations.

Two trends in contemporary image studies: anthropological (Hans Belting's and Didi-Huberman's concepts) and epistemological (Gottfried Boehm's concept of iconic epistemes) can be of particular interest here. In their light we can bring about a confrontation between the approach to the image in the psychoanalytic tradition and in new images studies. Such a confrontation can find its axial themes in the consequences of the epistemological and, at the same time, iconic interpretation of the unconscious vs. the consequences of the concept of iconic epistemes, the issue of *image marticelle* vs. culture image, and imagination as a product of the unconscious vs. product of the collective imaginary (*das Imaginäre*) evolved in a historical-cultural process defined in one way or another. The central idea in a comparison of these two scholarly traditions can be the issue of cultural activity of the image, which implicitly emerges in Warburg's concept.

3 Warburgian Threads and the Psychoanalytic Tradition

The essence of the Warburgian cultural studies project lies in approaching culture from the point of view of the image, through pictorial processes. In today's reception of Warburg's legacy, Warburg is seen primarily as a precursor of the anthropology of the image[19] and the author of the concept of visual cultural memory. Albeit comparable to psychoanalytic concepts, Warburg's concept emerged completely independently,[20] although it drew on analogous, and sometimes the same sources (e.g. Darwin's concept or Semon's biologistic concept of memory). However, unlike psychoanalytic concepts, Warburg's reflection leads to neither reductionism nor any form of essentialism. Its cultural studies potential lies in, among others, the fact that Warburg provided an original counterpoint to his own assumptions expressed in a psychologistic-naturalistic language[21] in the concept of bipolar function of art

19 According to G. Didi-Huberman, for Warburg the image is a completely (totally) anthropological phenomenon, a crystallisation and condensation of an utterance expressing the character of culture (Didi-Huberman, *Das Nachleben der Bilder*, 54).

20 For more on the sources of Warburg's concept, see B. Villhauer, *Aby Warburgs Theorie der Kultur: Detail und Sinnhorizont* (Berlin: Akademie Verlag, 2002), 25–51.

21 R. Kany, *Mnemosyne als Programm: Geschichte, Erinnerung und die Andacht zum Unbedeutenden im Werk von Usener, Warburg und Benjamin* (Tübingen: Niemeyer, 1987), 149.

and, consequently, in the concept of culture polarised between the mythical-magical and intellectual-scholarly aspects.[22]

Three ideas in particular derived from Warburg's legacy can act as guides in a comparison between the contemporary image studies reflection and the psychoanalytic tradition: the idea of mnestic influence of the image, the idea of "energy" of the image, and the idea of the image as a symptom of culture. These threads focus on what can be described as cultural activity of the image. The rule that has to be followed in any search for spheres of this activity is that the definition of the very notion of "image" should be fairly broad and include, in addition to image presented (external image) also imaginary image, and image as an idea (internal image).[23] Taking over the close link between the image and the symbol from the Warburgian tradition makes it possible to place images-symbols in culture. Perhaps it is also the psychoanalytic lesson, inspiring us to include field dreams, ideas and phantasms in our cultural research, that enables us to present such a broad definition of the image.

3.1 *Energy of the Image*

The idea of an active or acting image in contemporary image studies is to some extent associated with the notion of "force", "power" or "energy" of the image, which appeared both in psychoanalysis and in Warburg's concept. Decoding the provenance and content of this notion will become an important moment in understanding what tradition is behind it, what meanings, sometimes contradictory, it may sometimes have.

> The psychoanalytic tradition was the first – in any case the first to do it so clearly – to treat the image as an active phenomenon, a phenomenon to which autonomous power, stemming from the unconscious, was attributed. Through its analysis of dreams and its method of active imagining, psychoanalysis created conditions for the image to happen, for it to be transformed, to disappear, to become blurred, to emerge in new contexts.[24]

---

22 See A.M. Warburg, "Mnemosyne. Einleitung", in *Der Bilderatlas Mnemosyne*, ed. M. Warnke and C. Brink (Berlin: Akademie Verlag, 2008), 3–4.

23 Cf. H. Belting, *Miejsce obrazów*, trans. M. Bryl, Artium Quaestiones, XI (Poznań, 2000). Originally published as *Das Erbe der Bilder. Kunst und moderne Medien in derKulturen der Welt* (Munich, 1998), 324–25.

24 E. Kobylińska, "Psychoanaliza i obrazy"", *Kultura Współczesna. Teoria. Interpretacja. Praktyka*, no. 4 (2006): 78; For more on active imagining in Jung's concept, see E. Więckowska, "Zarys problematyki aktywnego wyobrażania w ujęciu C.G. Junga", in: *Studia mitoznawcze*, ed. I. Błocian and E. Kwiatkowska (Toruń: Wydawnictwo Adam Marszałek, 2010), 215–33.

In Warburg's concept, rooted in Tito Vignoli's naturalistic-evolutionist aesthetics, the notion of energy of the image has a dimension that is by no means metaphoric.[25] Warburg sees the image-symbol as an engram of cultural memory, a trace, an imprint, which houses the energy of a reaction to an event, the energy that, having been latent, can be updated, although the symbol may change its meaning under the influence of cultural-historical demands of the period.[26] The Warburgian image-symbol, as a visual imprint of the primordial trauma, emerges as "canned energy."[27] According to Warburg, mental energy is rooted in human biology and its power stems from the "phobic reflex", a fear of the horror of human existence. The conviction that expressive matrices are drive-motivated is juxtaposed in Warburg's reflection with a conscious distance established in culture with regard to them and to the entire pictorial-symbolic view of the world.

In contemporary image studies the notion of energy or power of the image appears again and again, but its nature is rather metaphoric. The question concerning the content of the image energy metaphor could be answered during an examination of the image's multifaceted activity in culture, for instance, epistemic, mnemic, performative, symbolic or poietic.

3.2 *The Mnestic Nature of the Image*

The issue of the mnestic nature of the image is at the core of the Warburgian reflection and the mythopoeic aspect of the image is intrinsic to its anthropological origins and, consequently, to cultural memory. The understanding of this memory evoked by Warburg's reflection – significantly different from the current dominant understanding emphasising the communicative and social dimension – places its mechanism on the anthropological rather than strictly social level. Warburg's concept draws on the largely unconscious and emotive character of cultural memory.[28] The visual is linked to the mnestic aspect also in psychoanalysis; an image is a memory trace associated with a desire. Before

25 See Didi-Huberman, *Das Nachleben der Bilder*, 467–68.

26 Gombrich, *Aby Warburg*, 463–65; cf. G. Agamben, "Aby Warburg i 'nauka bezimienna,'" in *Konteksty : polska sztuka ludowa : antropologia kultury, etnografia, sztuka.*, vol. 2–3 (Warsaw, 2011). Originally published as *"Potentialities: Collected Essays in Philosophy"* ("Stanford CA": "Stanford University Press", 1999), 281.

27 H. Böhme, "Aby M. Warburg (1866–1929)", in *Klassiker der Religionswissenschaft: von Friedrich Schleiermacher bis Mircea Eliade*, ed. A. Michaels (Munich: C.H. Beck, 1997), 145.

28 Didi-Huberman also points out that the principle of Warburg's Mnemosyne Atlas is modelled on the unconscious and that a historian of culture acts as an interpreter of what has been repressed (Didi-Huberman, *Das Nachleben der Bilder*, 533); see also the analysis of analogies between the concept of Pathosformel and Charcot's studies of hysteria; the Warburg Library housed two works by Charcot (ibid., 319).

it assumed a theoretically more abstract form in which a drive was manifested, the archetype was defined by Jung as an imprint (*typos*), "a definite grouping of archaic character containing, in form as well as in meaning, mythological motifs."[29] This way of understanding the archetype only seems to be analogous with the Warburgian concept of image-symbol as an engram of memory[30]; to look for an analogy between Jung's concept and Warburg's concept seems to be a misunderstanding caused by a superficial reception of either the former or the latter.

An analysis of the "deep structure" of Warburg's concept indicates that his concept of visual cultural memory has its roots in Giambattista Vico's thought.[31] Culture, as an active process of memory contained in language, in both the historical and creative aspect can be regarded as one of the subjects of Vico's *New Science*.[32] Warburg's concept has exactly the same subject; what it changes is just the way in which this memory is objectivised, from linguistic to visual. The term *Nachleben* expresses the idea of inseparability of the image and cultural memory; the very way of producing an image guarantees its mnemic potential. In the origins of an image, imagination, creation and memory are linked in one active cultural process. The image is not a passive means of transmitting memory, but an active participant in or even transformer of the mnemic process. Before they become petrified and start functioning as signs, images-symbols preserve the memory of their magical-mythical stage together with its cultural-historical baggage. Whether the mythopoeic potential of an image is updated or remains only residual – this is determined by cultural circumstances. Referring to Warburg's concept, we can perceive the image as a palimpsest that could be interpreted both historically or chronologically (the image encodes in itself the past of cultural experiences) and synchronously (the image contains a latent mythopoeic layer, which can always be updated).

To sum up, of key importance to the rejection of the thesis that Warburg's concept and Jungism are parallel is the historical-cultural nature of the *Nachleben* of the image,[33] revealing a paradoxically achronological process of a "return to the matter" (i.e. anamnesis, through expression matrices, of the primordial

29 C.G. Jung, *Analytical Psychology*, ed. W. McGuire (Routledge, 2014), 30, see also fn. 19.

30 See fn. 19. According to Jung, the primordial image is a mnemic deposit or engram of a constantly recurring psychic experience (Jung, *Typy psychologiczne*, 465).

31 Warburg's concept is placed in the Vikian mnemonological tradition by R. Kany, see Kany, *Mnemosyne als Programm*, 150.

32 J. Kreuzer, "Die Sinnlichkeit der Sprache", *Zeitschrift für Kulturphilosophie* 4, no. 2 (2010): 285–302.

33 Cf. Agamben, "Aby Warburg i 'nauka bezimienna,'" 282.

conditions of existence imbued with terror).[34] The unconscious and even to some extent automatic operation of visual cultural memory in Warburg's concept does have some Jungian traits, yet both the theoretical starting points and the consequences of these two concepts are completely different. Warburg's universality of expressive matrices is rooted in the anthropological-cultural conditions of existence, while the "survival" of the image is analogous to Vico's concept of recurring barbarism rather than to Jung's concept of transhistorical archetype.

4 The Image as a Symptom of Culture

Today parallels are being pointed out between Warburg's concept and Freud's reflection. Such affinities are revealed by Georges Didi-Huberman, who combines the Warburgian tradition with "psychoanalytic thinking." Of key importance here is the issue of the relation between the anthropological dimension of the image and unconscious memory, and the interpretation of Warburg's concept of the symbol through Freud's *Symptombildung*.[35] According to Ewa Kobylińska, who follows Didi-Huberman in her analysis, Warburg's formulas of pathos and *Nachleben* are opposites of the archetype understood as patterns of generalisation. Being idiomatic, they are closer to Freud's concept; we could point to, for instance, an affinity between *Nachleben* and Freud's *Nachträglichkeit*.[36]

When it comes to the symptomatic nature of the image, it is worth quoting Kobylińska herself:

> the resistant, obsessive, repeatable nature of the symptom refers to something that is beyond semiotics, although it borders on it, but the border is something of an epistemic crack. (…) What for Charcot was still a chaos of hysterical poses and gestures (…) becomes intelligible in Freud's approach.[37]

34 See Warburg, "Mnemosyne. Einleitung", 3–4.

35 See Didi-Huberman, *Das Nachleben der Bilder*, 266–67, 301–14.

36 Kobylińska, "Psychoanaliza i obrazy'", 66; It could also be said that the analogies between the Warburgian and the psychoanalytic approach to memory are largely due to the fact that both are indebted to Richard Semon (see R. Semon, *Die Mneme Als Erhaltendes Prinzip Im Wechsel Des Organischen Geschehens* [Leipzig, 1911]).

37 Kobylińska, "Psychoanaliza i obrazy'", 64.

Kobylińska draws a parallel between Freud's symptomatological model and Warburg's *Pathosformeln*, which crystallise and animate the places of affective (literally "suffering") memory.[38] At the same time, in Didi-Huberman's view the psychoanalytic interpretation, in the face of the dream-work and the work of the symptom, "strips words of their meaning." Freud abandons the stronghold of intelligibility, smashes the whole into pieces in order to be able to start from fragments, convinced that only a "secondary revision" reflects the dream-work.[39]

An important observation comes from these remarks: the image as a symptom is doubly desemiotised: as a symptom (a symptom is not an image) and as an image in itself. More radical trends of the iconic turn find their essence in approaching the image as an image (non-text).[40] In this respect, the image is "overdetermined" by its autonomous ways of working.

The issue of the image as a symptom confronts culture scholars with a challenge linked to the conceptual apparatus of their discipline. Didi-Huberman's or Hans Belting's studies of the phenomenon of the image had to transgress the boundaries of history of art and use a new language to formulate the anthropology of the image project. Similarly, the psychoanalytic inspiration in culture studies requires a rethinking of the consequences of applying psychoanalytic terms in these studies, terms often used outside psychoanalysis without any reflection, without any awareness of the baggage they carry with them. For instance, when speaking of the symptomatic nature of the image in culture, we need to establish how the category of the symptom is understood here. Obviously, the traditional psychoanalytic terms associated with this concept (like drive or desire[41]) cannot be transferred to culture studies. But the definition of the symptom as a "compromise formation", a phenomenon available through hiding-revealing, shifting, distortion, transformation into its opposite,[42] can be heuristically interesting to these studies. The use made of

38 Ibid., 65; for more of the symptomatic nature of Pathosformel, see also Zumbusch, *Wissenschaft in Bildern*, 71–89.

39 G. Didi-Huberman, *Przed obrazem: pytanie o cele historii sztuki*, trans. B. Brzezicka (Gdańsk: Wydawnictwo Słowo/Obraz Terytoria, 2011). Originally published as *G. Devant l' image. Questions posées aux fins d'une histoire de l'art* (Paris, 1990), 109.

40 See e.g. W.J.T. Mitchell, "The Pictorial Turn", in *Picture Theory: Essays on Verbal and Visual Representation* (Chicago: The University of Chicago Press, 1994); H. Belting, *Antropologia obrazu: szkice do nauki o obrazie*, trans. M. Bryl (Kraków: Universitas, 2012). Originally published as *Bild-Anthropologie. Entwürfe für eine Bildwissenschaft* (Munich, 2002), passim; G. Boehm, "Das Paradigma 'Bild.' Die Tragweite der ikonischen Episteme", in *Bilderfragen: die Bildwissenschaften im Aufbruch*, ed. H. Belting (Munich: Fink, 2007).

41 See Dybel, *Okruchy psychoanalizy*, 364.

42 See Kobylińska, "Psychoanaliza i obrazy'", 64.

the notion of symptom by psychoanalysis could be not so much a literal model, but a subject of reflection.

The idea of culturally active images, implicit in the Warburgian tradition, could be analysed through the perspective of *Nachleben* and *Orientierung*,[43] understood as significant cultural processes carried by images, with the relation between these processes and the images not being accidental but stemming from the anthropological essence of the relation between human beings, culture and images. This relation can be expanded in the light of the iconic epistemes concept to include the epistemic aspect.

The terms *Orientierung* and *Nachleben* also express the Warburgian concept of culture stressing the tension between the sphere of affects and drives, and a consciously shaped attitude of human beings to the the world and to themselves. Psychoanalysis approaches the tension between drives and culture in a different manner, defining it as antinomic, while for Warburg it is more bipolar. Giorgio Agamben pointed out that thanks to their definition of conflict as bipolarity, the Warburgian interpretative categories were more subtle than the opposition between rationalism and irrationalism.[44] This leads to another controversy in the contemporary polemic concerning the image – the question of its share in cognition.

5 The Cognitive Aspect of the Image in Psychoanalysis and in the Concept of Iconic Epistemes

The iconic interpretation of the unconscious fits in well with the contemporary polemic surrounding the image. For William J.T. Mitchell the fear of the image is, quite paradoxically, one of the elements of the origins of the iconic turn and the criticism of the "power of images" – as a kind of iconoclasm.[45] The scope of the cognitive role of the image in psychoanalysis depends on our interpretation of the unconscious. In the individualist interpretation, images and symbols provide information about the emotional meaning of human experiences; in this sense they are "meaningful."[46] In the interpretation of the unconscious as an anthropological matrix, the cognitive power of the image is much broader. Psychoanalysis, in its positive valorisation of the image, nevertheless attributes to it the same properties as its critics: irrationality, magic,

43 For more on Orientierung, see Villhauer, *Aby Warburgs Theorie der Kultur*, 114–16.

44 Agamben, "Aby Warburg i 'nauka bezimienna,'" 284.

45 Mitchell, "The Pictorial Turn", 15.

46 See Błocian, *Psychoanalityczne wykładnie mitu*, 135.

aintellectuality (and even anti-intellectuality), spontaneity (and, at the same time, non-intentionality). Thus by positioning itself among "iconophiles", psychoanalysis attributes to the image a number of qualities for which is it criticised by "iconoclasts."[47] Here lies an important sphere of conflict between contemporary images studies and psychoanalysis, and, more generally, irrationalistic concepts of the image. It can be analysed from the point of view of Gottfried Boehm's concept of iconic epistemes providing for an active and constructive role of the image in thinking and cognition.[48]

In its intention it contradicts both the psychoanalytic approach to the image and the Bachelardian approach providing for an antinomy between abstract rationality and pictorial *imaginarium*.[49] In the philosophical tradition to which Boehm refers, image power (*Bildpotenz*) is attributable to philosophical thinking itself, while the image in itself contains an argumentative potential.[50] In the concept of iconic epistemes, unlike in psychoanalysis, images not only are not irrational, as spontaneously generated by drives (instincts, archetypes etc.), which are antinomic to culture, but, creating an epistemic space, are legitimate tools of cognition; moreover, they participate in the formulation of notions. They have their own way of generating sense guided by pictorial logic – entirely different from and even primary in relation to linguistic logic. It works through e.g. indeterminacy, intensity, ambiguity; it refers to diversity, particularity, sensuality, obviousness, energy and affectivity.[51] According to its author, the consequences of the concept are at least as follows:

- it revises one of the oldest foundations of European science, namely that only what can be expressed in sentences can have a meaning or veracity attributed to it;

47 For more on the polemic surrounding the image, see P.J. Bräunlein, "Bildakte. Religionswissenschaft im Dialog mit einer neuen Bildwissenschaft", in *Religion im kulturellen Diskurs. Festschrift für Hans G. Kippenberg zum. 65. Geburtstag*, ed. B. Luchesi and S. Stuckard (Berlin: De Gruyter, 2004), 197–203.

48 See Boehm, "Das Paradigma 'Bild.' Die Tragweite der ikonischen Episteme"; see also "Jenseits der Sprache? Anmerkungen zur Logik der Bilder."

49 For more on this antinomy, see Wunenburger, *Filozofia obrazów*, 58–60.

50 When referring to the crucial points leading to the iconic turn in its philosophical aspect, Boehm cites concepts formulated by Friedrich Nietzsche, Edmund Husserl, Ludwig Wittgenstein, Martin Heidegger and Hans Blumenberg – see Boehm, "Die Wiederkehr der Bilder", 12–16; "Jenseits der Sprache? Anmerkungen zur Logik der Bilder", 36–38; G. Boehm, "Iconic Turn. Ein Brief", in *Bilderfragen: die Bildwissenschaften im Aufbruch*, ed. H. Belting (Munich: Fink, 2007), 28–29.

51 Boehm, "Das Paradigma 'Bild.' Die Tragweite der ikonischen Episteme", 79–82 Both, each in its own way, were juxtaposed with psychoanalytic concepts. Yet they stemmed from theoretical assumptions contrary to Jungism and their theoretical consequences were just as contrary to it.

- the idea of logos as an articulated sense can no longer be equated with language; if we want to continue to speak of the logos, we need to include non-predicative, implicit and deictic knowledge – the content of pictorial experience.

The most important meaning of the concept of iconic epistemes relates to the fact that the power of imagination manifests itself in its entirety in images. The inner proximity between *imaginatio* and *imago* was the basis of mistrust with regard to the cognitive properties of images (images were regarded as misleading, deceitful, far from the truth). According to Boehm, the imaginary (*das Imaginäre*) turns out, however, to be a highly productive (*produktives*) though also risky instrument, which ultimately comes truein reality.[52]

The culturalist turn in philosophy, which makes us realise that culture is an intermediary of cognition, and, consequently legitimises the conviction that culture studies belong to fundamental sciences,[53] may determine the premises of a cultural studies interpretation of the concept of iconic epistemes. This concept is a point of reference for reflections on the imaginary dimension of knowledge and culture,[54] mutual relations between cognition, imagination and images.[55] The asymmetric nature and mutual non-reducibility of the logic of language and the logic of images prompts new questions about the rules of symbolic thinking. Of particular interest here is a similarity between the issue of these rules and the issue of the logic of images and its cognitive role. Thus what we find between the epistemological aspect of the iconic approach and image studies is the issue of relations between the activity and autonomy of images,[56] the logic of images and symbolic (mythical, metaphorical) thinking, the issue of a constructive role of images in thinking, the relation

52 Ibid.

53 A. Szahaj, "Filozofia kultury jako filozofia pierwsza [uwagi wstępne]", in: *Co to jest filozofia kultury?*, ed. Z. Rosińska and J. Michalik (Warsaw: Wydawn. Uniwersytetu Warszawskiego, 2006).

54 The interest of culture studies in the imaginary is emphasised by Birgit Mersmann in her programmatic article "Bildkulturwissenschaft als Kulturbildwissenschaft?", which presents a programme for "imaginology" (B. Mersmann, "Bildkulturwisschenschaft als Kulturbildwissenschaft? Von der Notwendigkeit eines inter- und transkulturellen Iconic Turn'", *Zeitschrift für Ästhetik und Allgemeine Kunstwissenschaft*, no. 1 [2004]).

55 Similar issues can be found in the philosophical tradition from Bachelard to Wunenburger – see Wunenburger, *Filozofia obrazów*, passim.

56 The question of the sources of image activity is raised again by Horst Bredekamp, who refers to two positions: the belief that the action of images is autonomous and nearly magical, and the belief that the activity of images derives from actions of the users of pictorial acts (H. Bredekamp, *Theorie des Bildakts* [Frankfurt: Suhrkamp, 2010], 49 and footnote 74, 343).

between pictorially active thinking acts and the imaginary. One of the most interesting consequences of the concept of iconic epistemes would be to use it to describe the constructive role of images in the historical-cultural process of symbolisation.[57]

The interpretation of iconic concepts in cultural studies should also stress the autopoietic assets of the image as defined first of all culturally. If some images lead to other images, then culture scholars look for cultural-historical links between them. This may be the main signum of the cultural studies approach to the image – treating the logic of the image as an aspect of the autopoiesis of culture.

6 Conclusions: Critical Points in Both Traditions

Given the inner diversity of trends within psychoanalysis, it is difficult to briefly refer to the psychoanalytic approach to the image. On the other hand, it is possible to indicate the main reservations with regard to it from the point of view of culture studies. The basic assumptions of psychoanalytic anthropology are prejudgments. The concept of the unconscious as an anthropological matrix is deterministic, leading ultimately to the belief in the necessity of producing specific symbolic images. In this respect both symbolic thinking and its concrete expressions have the same qualities everywhere. The assumption that symbolic images have an archetypal basis denies them the value of being truly poietic. Thus the psychoanalytic perspective obviously does not give us tools to capture the cultural sources of images. Depending on the interpretation of the unconscious we adopt, it may also be associated with a risk of various versions of essentialism. In its Freudian and Jungian versions dehistorising the pictorial symbol and, consequently, the myth, psychoanalysis deprives us of a possibility of seeing in them products of culture and tools of historical-cultural self-cognition. Contemporary concepts of the unconscious, when analysed in the critical-social perspective in which the image, symbol and myth hide collective traumas,[58] are better suited to starting a discourse with culture studies and social sciences.

57 Several aspects of symbolisation in the context of the iconic turn are examined by Peter J. Bräunlein, who focuses on Susanne K. Langer's distinction between discursive and presentational symbolisation (Bräunlein, "Bildakte. Religionswissenschaft im Dialog mit einer neuen Bildwissenschaft", 210).

58 See Błocian, *Psychoanalityczne wykładnie mitu*, 35.

The mutual untranslatability of the problems of image studies based on psychoanalytic concepts and culture studies concepts thus consists mainly in pointing to different sources of the activity of the image, especially its historical versus non-historical qualities. For example, in the contemporary discourse of cultural memory (including pictorial memory), the attitude to history is a privileged topic. Didi-Huberman, too, referring to the *longue durée* of images, long-lasting anthropological impact of images (e.g. religious images),[59] presents the durability of the image in a historical context, which can be interpreted in the light of the tradition of the *Annales* school. Looking for another interpretation, taking into account the anthropological rootedness and emphasis on the corporeal aspect in the Warburgian reflection, we could refer to Pierre Bourdieu's concept of cultural practices, which has a lot to offer to those who continue Warburg's work today. The transhistoricity of visual matrices can be juxtaposed, on the one hand, with the historicity of culture images and on the other – with their poietic and unpredictable (because of their poietic nature) potential, and the formality ("emptiness") of archetypes – with the concrete nature of cultural-historical practices.

Translated by Anna Kijak

References

Agamben, G. "Aby Warburg i 'nauka bezimienna'." In Konteksty: polska sztuka ludowa : antropologia kultury, etnografia, sztuka., Vol. 2–3. Warsaw, 2011. Originally published as "Potentialities: Collected Essays in Philosophy" ("Stanford CA": "Stanford University Press", 1999).

Bachmann-Medick, D. *Cultural turns: nowe kierunki w naukach o kulturze*. Translated by K. Krzemieniowa. Warsaw: Oficyna Naukowa, 2012. Originally published as *Cultural Turns. Neuorientierungen in den Kulturwissenschaften* (Reinbek bei Hamburg, 2006).

Belting, H. *Antropologia obrazu: szkice do nauki o obrazie*. Translated by M. Bryl. Kraków: Universitas, 2012. Originally published as *Bild-Anthropologie. Entwürfe für eine Bildwissenschaft* (Munich, 2002).

Belting, H. *Miejsce obrazów*. Translated by M. Bryl. Artium Quaestiones, XI. Poznań, 2000. Originally published as *Das Erbe der Bilder. Kunst und moderne Medien in der Kulturen der Welt* (Munich, 1998).

Benjamin, W. *Pasaże*. Translated by I. Kania. Cracow: Wydawnictwo Literackie, 2005.

59 Didi-Huberman, *Przed obrazem: pytanie o cele historii sztuki*, 22.

Błocian, I. "Pojęcie nieświadomości a obraz groty w badaniach nad wyobraźnią G. Bachelarda." Studia Philosophica Wratislaviensia VII, no. 3 (2012): 91–104.

Błocian, I. *Psychoanalityczne wykładnie mitu: Freud, Jung, Fromm*. Warsaw: "Eneteia" Wydawnictwo Psychologii i Kultury, 2010.

Boehm, G. "Das Paradigma 'Bild.' Die Tragweite der ikonischen Episteme." In *Bilderfragen: die Bildwissenschaften im Aufbruch*, edited by H. Belting. Munich: Fink, 2007a.

Boehm, G. "Die Wiederkehr der Bilder." In *Was ist ein Bild?*, edited by G. Boehm. Munich: Fink, 1995.

Boehm, G. "Iconic Turn. Ein Brief." In *Bilderfragen: die Bildwissenschaften im Aufbruch*, edited by H. Belting. Munich: Fink, 2007b.

Boehm, G. "Jenseits der Sprache? Anmerkungen zur Logik der Bilder." In *Iconic turn: die neue Macht der Bilder*, edited by C. Maar and H. Burda. Cologne: DuMont, 2005.

Boehm, G., and W.J.T. Mitchell. "Briefwechsel: Gottfried Boehm und Tom Mitchell." In *Bilderfragen: die Bildwissenschaften im Aufbruch*, edited by H. Belting. Munich: Fink, 2007.

Böhme, H. "Aby M. Warburg (1866–1929)." In *Klassiker der Religionswissenschaft: von Friedrich Schleiermacher bis Mircea Eliade*, edited by A. Michaels. Munich: C.H. Beck, 1997.

Bräunlein, P.J. "Bildakte. Religionswissenschaft im Dialog mit einer neuen Bildwissenschaft." In *Religion im kulturellen Diskurs. Festschrift für Hans G. Kippenberg zum.65. Geburtstag*, edited by B. Luchesi and S. Stuckard. Berlin: De Gruyter, 2004.

Bredekamp, H. *Theorie Des Bildakts*. Frankfurt: Suhrkamp, 2010.

Didi-Huberman, G. *Das Nachleben der Bilder: Kunstgeschichte und Phantomzeit nach Aby Warburg*. Translated by M. Bischoff. Berlin: Suhrkamp, 2010.

Didi-Huberman, G. *Przed obrazem: pytanie o cele historii sztuki*. Translated by B. Brzezicka. Gdańsk: Wydawnictwo Słowo/Obraz Terytoria, 2011. Originally published as*Devant l' image. Questions posées aux fins d'une histoire de l'art* (Paris, 1990).

Dybel, P. *Dialog i represja. Antynomie psychoanalizy Zygmunta Freuda*. Warsaw: IFiS PAN, 1995.

Dybel, P. *Okruchy psychoanalizy: teoria Freuda między hermeneutyką i poststrukturalizmem. Horyzonty nowoczesności*. Cracow: Universitas, 2009.

Gombrich, E.H. *Aby Warburg: eine intellektuelle Biographie*. Translated by M. Fienbork. Hamburg: Philo Fine Arts, 2012.

Jung, C.G. *Analytical Psychology*. Edited by W. McGuire. Routledge, 2014.

Jung, C.G. *Typy psychologiczne*. Translated by R. Reszke. Warsaw: Wrota, 1997. Originally published as *Psychologische Typen;* Carl Gustaw Jung: *Gesammelte Werke* (Walter-Verlag AG, 1994).

Kany, R. *Mnemosyne als Programm: Geschichte, Erinnerung und die Andacht zum Unbedeutenden im Werk von Usener, Warburg und Benjamin*. Tübingen: Niemeyer, 1987.

Kobylińska, E. "Psychoanaliza i obrazy'." Kultura Współczesna. Teoria. Interpretacja. Praktyka, no. 4 (2006).

Kreuzer, J. "Die Sinnlichkeit der Sprache." Zeitschrift für Kulturphilosophie 4, no. 2 (2010).

Mersmann, B. "Bildkulturwisschenschaft als Kulturbildwissenschaft? Von der Notwendigkeit eines inter- und transkulturellen Iconic Turn.'" Zeitschrift für Ästhetik und Allgemeine Kunstwissenschaft, no. 1 (2004).

Mitchell, W.J.T. "Pictorial Turn. Eine Antwort." In *Bilderfragen: die Bildwissenschaften im Aufbruch*, edited by H. Belting. Munich: Fink, 2007.

Mitchell, W.J.T. "The Pictorial Turn." In *Picture Theory: Essays on Verbal and Visual Representation.* Chicago: The University of Chicago Press, 1994.

Schweppenhäuser, G. "Überlegungen zum Bildbegriff der Kritischen Theorie." Zeitschrift für Kulturphilosophie 4, no. 2 (2010).

Semon, R. *Die Mneme Als Erhaltendes Prinzip Im Wechsel Des Organischen Geschehens.* Leipzig, 1911.

Szahaj, A. "Filozofia kultury jako filozofia pierwsza [uwagi wstępne]." In *Co to jest filozofia kultury?*, edited by Z. Rosińska and J. Michalik. Warsaw: Wydawn. Uniwersytetu Warszawskiego, 2006.

Villhauer, B. *Aby Warburgs Theorie der Kultur: Detail und Sinnhorizont.* Berlin: Akademie Verlag, 2002.

Warburg, A.M. "Mnemosyne. Einleitung." In *Der Bilderatlas Mnemosyne*, edited by M. Warnke and C. Brink. Berlin: Akademie Verlag, 2008.

Więckowska, E. "Zarys problematyki aktywnego wyobrażania w ujęciu C.G. Junga." In *Studia mitoznawcze*, edited by I. Błocian and E. Kwiatkowska. Toruń: Wydawnictwo Adam Marszałek, 2010.

Wunenburger, J.-J. *Filozofia obrazów.* Translated by T. Stróżyński. Gdańsk: Wydawnictwo słowo/obraz terytoria, 2011. Originally published as *Philosophie des image* (Paris, 1977).

Zumbusch, C. "Wissenschaft in Bildern: Symbol und dialektisches Bild" in *Aby Warburgs Mnemosyne-Atlas und Walter Benjamins Passagen-Werk.* Berlin: Akademie Verlag, 2004.

CHAPTER 7

Is the Jungian Concept of "Image" Still Relevant in a Modern Psychoanalytic Perspective?

Alessandra De Coro

Abstract

The Multiple Code theory has been elaborated by Wilma Bucci, with the aim of proposing a new model of the mind which – linking together psychoanalytic clinical thought and the more recent perspectives of cognitive science – could explain the analytic process. In this work I will propose some reflections about the concept of "image" as it is used in Jung's and Bucci's theories, underlining differences and similarities between their respective explanations of therapeutic change. Since his very first essays, Jung defines the visual images as "autonomous transformations of elementary stimuli" and indicates their function also in the organization of mnestic material: sometimes, he writes, the images are the result of unconscious association processes, so that, while a person perceives something, the image of an absent object or person "comes to mind".

In this theory, images are conceived as the bridge between the sub-symbolic level of mental activity, that implies a parallel distributing processing of sensory and emotional information, and the verbal symbolic level, where the language organizes meanings through words and their logic rules. In this model, images represent the first form of meaning, which may be elaborated both at an implicit and at an explicit level, and their manifestation in consciousness allows to compact a multiplicity of sensory and emotional data in a piece of information according a sequential modality (symbol formation).

Keywords

Jung – Bucci – psychoanalysis – symbol – image – multiple code theory – symbolic activity – symbol formation

 | DOI:10.1163/9789004336636_009

1 Some Premises

How can we define the main goal of an analytic psychotherapy, that is the highly complex process which Jung used to name the "individuation process"? I suggest provisionally to undertake the definition proposed by Philip Bromberg, when he suggests that the "personality development" is strictly connected with a real paradox: "the paradox of being known remaining private, of being in the world and at the same time separate from it." The analytic situation can so be considered as "a therapeutic relation that is negotiated in order to obtain this integration."[1]

But many questions arise: how can this abstract and multifaceted objective be reached through a "cure by words"? What happens within and through the interaction between the analysand and the analyst? Does change lead to insight or insight to change? What does it mean that patients may feel equally understood by analysts belonging to different schools of thought, despite their divergent and often conflicting views of what is relevant and correct? What is really effective in psychotherapy techniques? Empirical research has definitely shown that there are common (unspecific) therapeutic factors in different therapeutic methodologies: are there also specific factors which produce the therapeutic change in psychoanalysis and in analytic psychotherapy?

For many years, researchers have tried to answer to the question "what works for whom?" through outcome studies that frequently compared the results of different models of psychotherapy on the same type of patients.[2] Far more interesting to clinicians are the process studies, where the main question is: "given a specific definition of the therapeutic change, which are the specific factors that bring the patient to this change?" These studies intended to take a deeper look at the psychotherapy process and technique, in order to assess its effectiveness, and were considered the most appropriate to inquiry in the psychoanalytic process.[3]

Traditionally, in all the forms of analytic psychotherapy, the main objective has been to get a "structural change", so that the patient obtains multiple and stable changes in different aspects of her/his life and this – from a psychoanalytic perspective – can be reached only if unconscious and conscious processes become more easily communicative with each other. There is a general

1 P.M. Bromberg, *Standing in the Spaces. Essays on Clinical Process, Trauma and Dissociation* (New York: The Analytic Press, 1998), 4.

2 See A. Roth and P. Fonagy, *What Works for Whom? A Critical Review of Psychotherapy Research* (New York: The Guilford Press, 1996).

3 H. Dahl, H. Kächele, and H. Thomä, *Psychoanalytic Process Research Strategies* (Berlin, Heidelberg: Springer Verlag, 1988).

agreement, today, that the most important unspecific factor is the therapeutic relation itself. Wachtel[4] writes that a psychodynamic relational therapy "aims *both* to achieve corrective emotional experiences via the therapeutic relationship *and* to foster new ways of interacting with others outside the consulting room that permit the patient's ongoing life experiences to themselves be a key therapeutic agent."[5] In fact, there is still uncertainty and disagreement as to which components of the analytic encounter are responsible for structural change.

In this paper I intend to discuss the way in which the concept of "image" is used in Carl Gustav Jung's theory of the analytic process and in Wilma Bucci's, underlining continuity and discontinuity lines between their respective explanations of therapeutic change.

2 Mental Images in Modern Cognitive Psychology

Wilma Bucci – a New York psychoanalyst who had formerly frequented a doctoral program in cognitive science – has elaborated in the nineties a new theory to explain the psychoanalytic process and the structural changes expected from it. Moving from her original studies with Paivio about the links between verbal and sensory representations, she built a model of the mind based on the construct of "Referential Activity": this concept, rooted in a theory of emotional information processing derived from psychoanalysis and cognitive science, is defined as a cognitive function which organizes sensorial and emotional experience and links it to words through images.[6]

In the last quarter of last century Paivio,[7] as well as other cognitive psychologists,[8] were defined as "psychologists of images" because they argued that images are completely different from propositional representations: cognitive processes underlining images are similar to those underlining perception; images represent objects by analogy of structural relations between their parts; images represent an object or a scene from a specific point of view; an image can be transformed continuously in the mindthrough changes of perspective.

4 P.L. Wachtel, "An Integrative Relational Point of View", *Psychotherapy* 31 (2014): 342–49.

5 Ibid., 342.

6 W. Bucci, *Psychoanalysis and Cognitive Science* (New York: The Guilford Press, 1997).

7 A. Paivio, *Imagery and Verbal Processes* (New York: Holt, Reinehart & Winston, 1971); *Mental Representations: A Dual Coding Approach* (New York: Oxford University Press, 1986).

8 e.g. S.M. Kosslyn, *Ghosts in the Mind's Machine: Creating and Using Images in the Brain* (New York: Norton Press, 1983).

On this basis, Johnson-Laird[9] elaborated the concept of "mental models", as fundamentally different from propositional representations that constitute what we call our thought, essentially based on linguistic structures. Some empirical studies on memory suggest that the substantial meaning of clearly defined descriptions is better recalled than the substance of not clearly defined ones; but the verbatim details of the indefinite descriptions are better recalled than the verbal expressions of the defined ones. Johnson-Laird infers that in the case of a clearly defined description, people build a mental model (that is a sensory based pattern, such as an image can be); instead, in the case of an indefinite description, people build a "superficial propositional representation."[10]

From the point of view of cognitive neuroscience, the concept of image is central also in explaining the formation of consciousness: how does the activation of neural patterns form conscious contents? A number of researchers agree that the brain answers to perceptual stimuli with emotional and motor activation, forming each time specific neuronal configurations which are called "brain images." Mental images are the result of an activity that coordinates together circuits in different areas (including memory processes); recently, many scholars are convinced that this kind of binding is produced through the sincronicity of the activation of different brain areas rich with convergence/divergence zones, and of the posterior-medial cortex, which produces sensory images, in some way connected with the sense of self.[11]

The questions about the formation of consciousness are relevant, in fact, also for the explanation of the therapeutic change. As Fosshage[12] puts it:

> REM, dream, infant, and cognitive research evidence suggests that imagistic symbolic capacity exists at birth. Learning and remembering using imagistic symbolic processing could suggest a more easily translatable connection with later developed verbal symbolic processing and a closer, although varied, interconnection between implicit and explicit (symbolic) memory systems. (…) Implicit mental models, it is proposed, are *variably* modifiable through two different change processes: (1) accommodation or transformation of expectancies through new implicit procedural experience (not requiring explicit focus) and (2) diminished activation and increased capacity to deactivate implicit mental models through

9 P.N. Johnson-Laird, *Mental Models. Towards a Cognitive Science of Language, Inference and Consciousness* (Cambridge: Cambridge University Press, 1983).

10 Ibid., 259.

11 See A. Damasio, *Self Comes to Mind* (New York: Pantheon Books, 2010), chap. 3,9.

12 J.L. Fosshage, "The Explicit and Implicit Domains in Psychoanalytic Change", *Psychoanalytic Inquiry* 25 (2005): 516–39.

> explicit/declarative processing and the establishment of contrasting implicit models through new implicit procedural experience.[13]

Bucci[14] was convinced that the Freudian hypothesis of the existence of two basic modes of cognitive processing (primary and secondary processes of thought, perception, affects) is rooted in a deep clinical insight and that, consequently, it can still be considered – with a reformulation in terms of modern psychological science – as a basic issue in order to explain both the psychopathology of mental functioning and the process of the analytic cure. With this in mind, she referred to cognitive and neurobiological studies about information processing in order to formulate her Multiple Code Theory, that, as she states, is a general theory of emotional information processing, derived from current work in cognitive psychology and affective neuroscience.[15]

According to this theory, there are three basic modes that human beings use to process information (coming from inside or outside the body) and build up representations: sub-symbolic modality, non-verbal symbolic modality and verbal symbolic modality. The first, immediate and subsymbolic mode of processing sensory, motor, visceral and emotional information is analogic and continuous, stored in parallel, so that it can be recalled only at an implicit and bodily level; in the second mode, non-verbal images appear, that chunk subsymbolic information into meaningful discontinuous units, sequentially stored yet still specific for different sensorial aspects: such images, which can be recalled either implicitly or explicitly, are the beginning of the symbolization process; in the third mode, images are processed through the linguistic organization, originating verbal propositions that can be further combined, generating ever new meanings that can be recalled both implicitly and explicitly, and communicated to others in explicit form.[16]

3 Wilma Bucci's Theory of the Psychoanalytic Process

Paivio[17] had observed that people who are more capable of linking images with words can narrate stories in a more clear and detailed way, using more words

13 Ibid., 516–17.

14 Bucci, *Psychoanalysis and Cognitive Science.*

15 W. Bucci and B. Maskit, "Beneath the Surface of the Therapeutic Interaction: The Psychoanalytic Method in Modern Dress", *Journal of the American Psychoanalytic Association* 55 (2007): 1355–97.

16 Bucci, *Psychoanalysis and Cognitive Science*; Bucci and Maskit, "Beneath the Surface of the Therapeutic Interaction: The Psychoanalytic Method in Modern Dress."

17 Paivio, *Imagery and Verbal Processes.*

referring to sensation and a more imaginal language, characterized by metaphors and figurative expressions. Wilma Bucci transferred these observations to the old analytical question: how can we be sure that a patient is speaking about something which is really embodied in her/his emotional experience? Can we understand in what degree a speaker's language is connected to nonverbal experience, including bodily experience, imagery and affect? In order to answer these questions, she applied four scales (0 to 9 point) to the narrative units in the sessions, in order to evaluate the presence in the speaker's language of an activity of "binding" emotional experience with words: this activity – measured through the mean value of the four scales 1 to 9 points – is the Referential Activity (RA).

The four scales evaluate four different (but interrelated) dimensions of the language used in verbal communication between patient and analyst: Concreteness, that is the "perceptual or sensory quality" of the language;[18] Specificity, that is the degree to which a narrative is "detailed and informative", referring "to particular objects, persons, places, times";[19] Clarity, which refers to "the degree to which the speaker appears to be aware, on some level, of the perspective of the listener, and to be attempting to bring the listener where she is";[20] and Imagery, defined as:

> the vividness and effectiveness with which the speaker's language is reflecting and capturing imagery and emotional experience, in any sense modality. The rater judges the degree to which the experience is present and immediate for the speaker and likely to be experienced as immediate by most listeners. (…) We are trying to capture a dimension of language that is very qualitative, but also where the response would be similar for most native speakers. Vivid sensory impressions should be present to achieve a high Imagery score.[21]

In order to illustrate more accurately this dimension of Imagery in the method to evaluate the patient's therapeutic narratives proposed by Bucci and her research group, we present here two examples reported in their scoring manual, respectively for very poor and very good Imagery:

18 W. Bucci, R. Kabasakalian-McKay, and The RA Research Group, *Scoring Referential Activity* (Ulm: Ulmer Textbank, 1992), 45.
19 Ibid., 48.
20 Ibid., 50.
21 Ibid., 53.

> 0.67: Well, he's pretty nice. I get along with him all right. I've always been able to go to talk with him. Sometimes when he gets an idea in his head he's stubborn. I mean, he can really be stubborn when he wants to be, but most of the time I can always go to him and talk to him.[22]
> 8.25: I was sleeping very, very soundly when in my sleep I heard my mother screaming, you know, calling my name very loudly. And screaming. But I – I kind of didn't pay attention to it because she usually wakes me up very early in the morning, and I was not in the mood to be woken up. But something told me that it was urgent screaming. It wasn't just waking me up, and I – she started screaming "Nancy, Nancy, come here. Look what's happened to me!" And I walked in and my mother was lying in a puddle of blood. A pool of blood.[23]

In the Multiple Code Theory, as described before, images are conceived to be a bridge between the sub-symbolic level of mental activity (that operates continuously but off-line) and the symbolic verbal level, where the language organizes meanings through words and their logic rules. So images represent the first form of meaning, which may be elaborated at both an implicit and an explicit level, and their manifestation in consciousness allows us to compact a multiplicity of sensory and emotional data in a piece of information according to a sequential modality (symbol formation). In this sense, images are considered as the indicators of an activation of what Bucci calls "referential activity", which operates by linking together body sensations, emotions and thought. Referential Activity can be used as a measure of trait, indicating how much a person is capable of linking emotions and verbal contents; or else it can be used as a measure of variability, indicating which changes are observable in the course of time in the same person, depending on her/his physiological and emotional conditions and on the interpersonal context.[24]

The higher or lower ability of the patient to communicate to the analyst her/his emotions and vivid sensory experience through images and concrete, detailed and clear linguistic formulations, according to Wilma Bucci, shows the degree of activation of referential activity in the patient's mind: that means

22 The score 0.67 represents the mean value of the scores given by three expert judges on Imagery scale; the value of RA for this narrative unit, however, was 2.25, because the score for Clarity was nearly good (5.67). Overall reliability among the judges was .96. Ibid., 64.

23 The score 8.25 represents the mean value of the scores given by four expert judges on Imagery; the value of RA for this narrative unit was 7.69, lowered by a 7.25 point in Specificity. Overall reliability among the judges was .96. Ibid., 61.

24 W. Bucci, "The Enduring Hope of Shared Creative Exploration: Some Thoughts on the Work of Philip Bromberg", *Contemporary Psychoanalysis* 49, no. 3 (2013): 420–36.

that, when a patient is using a clear, sensory and detailed language, which evokes vivid images also in the listener, then, at the same moment, her or his "real" and "present" emotional, sensory and visceral experience is substantiating her or his words. The "cure of words", in fact, can be effective only in the case that the patient, at least from time to time, through the verbal propositions uttered in a session can evocate emotions in the actual relationship with the analyst, so that afterwards both can reflect together on such experiences and elaborate them.

So, an analytic psychotherapy process (as well as all the forms of the so-called "dynamic psychotherapy"), which implies an activation of what analysts call "a symbolization process", may be read today as a relational interaction that puts into motion the referential activity, in both the patient's and the analyst's mind. Due to the power of the emotional and verbal exchanges in the analytic relationship, the patient may experience old and new emotional situations, that become significant only when images help him to build a bridge between body and mind, between sensations, feelings, visceral movements and verbal thinking.

Bucci proposes that lower levels of RA are the result of a dissociation between words and emotions: all the forms of psychological suffering imply different degrees of dissociation between sub-symbolic and symbolic ways of processing emotional and sensory information. Therefore, psychopathology, at different levels of structural organisation, may be described as a continuum along an axis that goes from the integration to the disintegration (or dissociation) between the three systems of information processing. Such "emotional dissociation" is the result of the interaction of at least three factors: "the intensity of experienced traumatic anxiety in childhood, the degree in which the caregiver has been able to co-regulate the child's negative emotions, the quantity of personal resources, inborn or acquired, of the traumatized child."[25] Pathological and dissociated emotional schemes tend to organise the everyday life of the person in a maladaptive way and continue to activate painful and compulsive feelings, or uncontrollable and threatening expectations, which induce to maintain and to extend the dissociation.

The analytic cure works by repairing the dissociated pathological schemes, through the creation of narratives which re-activate the referential activity; the new links established between emotions, images and words give the patient a new impulse towards the expansion of the self-reflective function.[26]

---

25 W. Bucci, "Varieties of Dissociative Experiences: A Multiple Code Account and a Discussion of Bromberg's Case of William", *Psychoanalytic Psychology* 20 (2003): 549.

26 P.M. Bromberg, "On Being One's Dream: Some Reflections on Robert Bosnak's 'embodied Imagination,'" *Contemporary Psychoanalysis* 39 (2003): 697–710.

Empirical research has shown that referential activity is an important factor in predicting therapeutic change, and that it can be measured studying the quality of the verbal interchanges between patient and analyst. Moving from empirical results obtained in studies with her first methodology, Bucci has formulated the concept of "referential process", showing that in those sessions that clinicians identify as "good hours" the cycle of the linguistic variables studied tends to assume a regular shape: at the opening of the session, a problematic emotion schema is activated, while the verbal language seems dominated by the subsymbolic processing system, so that RA values are prevailingly low (*Arousal* phase). Then, around the middle of the session, a specific experience (e.g. a memory, or a dream) emerges that represents aspects of the problematic schema, which are now verbally told by the patient: through this narrative emotionally charged, images and emotions are elicited in the analyst, so that RA values notably increase, producing the highest peaks in the session (*Narrative/Symbolizing* phase). Finally, in the last period of the session time, a new decrease in RA values occurs, indicating that the analyst's interventions help the patient to become conscious of the emotion schema and to reflect upon the issues that have been expressed (*Reorganizing* phase).[27]

In order to create more accurate measures for the different phases of the sessions and to deepen the exploration of the therapeutic process, Wilma Bucci and Bernard Maskit have developed different computerized measures for the study of linguistic formulations in the course of therapeutic conversation, measures that are now available also for different languages and can be applied both to audio-recorded transcripts and to the therapist's notes.[28]

4 Images in the Individuation Process According to C.G. Jung

We will now turn to discuss synthetically the concept of image in Carl Gustav Jung's theory of mental functioning and in his more or less explicit definitions of the analytical process. I propose to consider that some of the more recent usages of this concept, including Bucci's theory of the therapeutic process, can be viewed as a modern interpretation of Jung's clinical and theoretical intuitions about the role of images in the everyday life and in the individuation

27 W. Bucci, *Psychoanalysis and Cognitive Science.*

28 W. Bucci, B. Maskit, and L. Hoffman, "Objective Measures of Subjective Experience: The Use of Therapist Notes in Process-Outcome Research", *Psychodynamic Psychiatry* 40, no. 2 (2012): 303–40; R. Mariani et al., "Linguistic Measures of the Referential Process in Psychodynamic Treatment: The English and Italian Versions", *Psychotherapy Research* 23, no. 4 (2013): 430–47.

process, even if those intuitions have been largely ignored by the modern psychoanalytic and cognitive literature. The ideas of Jung about images and their function in connecting unconscious and conscious processes in the human mind, for reasons of space, will only be summarized here, just to support their interpretation in the perspective here proposed.

Since his very first essays, Jung defines the visual images as “autonomous transformations of elementary stimuli”[29] and indicates their function also in the organization of mnestic material: sometimes, he writes, the images are the result of unconscious association processes, so that, while a person perceives something, the image of an absent object or person “comes to mind.”[30] In fact, images are the expression of a form of thought that is “not addressed” and runs separately from the present reality, “losing itself in fantasies relative to the past or the future.”[31] But they play an important role in our mental health: because of their analogy with certain mythologems, images allow us to build connections between the individual consciousness and the collective unconscious, so reducing the natural tendency of the human mind to dissociation, and acquiring a “therapeutic value.” The human psyche generates images in order to give expression to the “ample range of archetypal symbolic potentialities, which are latent in the men’s spirit.”[32]

In *Psychological Types*,[33] Jung reformulates his distinction between the “two ways of thinking”, the rational and the irrational: while reason proceeds with seeking the solution “through the rational, consequent and logical path”, the symbol formation produces images that appear “there where it is not expected.”[34] Images are built through a process of abstraction: “the chaotic succession of immediate data” is organized forming “a general abstract image that links in a logic form the impressions”,[35] giving meaning to a chaotic world of perceptions, feelings, intuitions, or thoughts. The internal image, Jung writes,

29 C.G. Jung, “On the Psychology and Pathology of the So-Called Occult Phenomena”, vol. 1, The Collected Works (London: Routledge & Kegan Paul, 1957). Originally published in 1902, 29.

30 C.G. Jung, “Cryptomnesia”, vol. 1, The Collected Works (London: Routledge & Kegan Paul, 1957). Originally published in 1905, 95–96.

31 C.G. Jung, “Symbols of Transformation. An Analysis of the Prelude to a Case of Schizophrenia”, vol. 5, The Collected Works (London: Routledge & Kegan Paul, 1956). Originally published in 1912, 18.

32 Ibid., 442.

33 C.G. Jung, “Psychological Types”, vol. 6, The Collected Works (London: Routledge & Kegan Paul, 1971). Originally published in 1921.

34 Ibid., 270.

35 Ibid., 298.

> *is a concentrated expression of the total psychic situation*, and not only or prevailingly of unconscious contents. It is also expression of unconscious contents, but not of overall contents, yet uniquely of the ones that are constellated in that moment.

That means: it expresses synthetically both the conscious and the unconscious attitudes and emotions which are relevant for the subject there and then:

> The interpretation of its meaning cannot then be proposed neither by the point of view of consciousness alone, nor by the unconscious one; it has to come only from the mutual relationship between conscious and unconscious.[36]

In this sense, the appearance of images in the analytic process can be of help in the task of re-organizing the relation between the ego and the unconscious: both at a personal level, when images present complexual.[37] I would intend: like a new meaning that gives form putting together dispersed (dissociated) elements in the mind. Exactly like the Bionian[38] transformation of β elements in α ones, or the packing together multiple subsymbolic information in an organized emotional meaning, in Bucci's language.

David Tacey,[39] in the chapter titled "*Healing the split*", comments on the seventh part of *Symbols and the Interpretation of Dreams*, underlining the role of the symbols – expressed through dream images – in the process of re-integrating dissociated aspects of our psychical life.

> The man of today – writes Jung in 1961 – is a curious mixture of characteristics acquired over the long ages of his mental development. (…) Skeptical viewpoints and scientific convictions exist in him side by side with old-fashioned prejudices, outdated habits of thought and feeling, obstinate misinterpretations and blind ignorance. Such are the people

36 Ibid., 448–49.

37 C.G. Jung, "The Psychology of Dementia Praecox", vol. 3, The Collected Works (London: Routledge & Kegan Paul, 1960). Originally published in 1907, 1–152; C.G. Jung, "On the Psychogenesis of Schizophrenia", vol. 3, The Collected Works (London: Routledge & Kegan Paul, 1960). Originally published in 1939, 233–49.

38 C.G. Jung, "Flying Saucers: A Modern Myth of Things Seen in the Skies", vol. 10, The Collected Works (London: Routledge & Kegan Paul, 1964). Originally published in 1958, 326–28.

39 D. Tacey, *The Jung Reader* (London, New York: Routledge, 2012).

> who produce the symbols we are investigating in their dreams. In order to explain the symbols and their meaning, it is essential to learn whether these representations are still the same as they ever were, or whether they have been chosen by the dream for its particular purpose from a store of general conscious knowledge.[40]

Archetypal images – as Tacey suggests – may be more effective in healing the gap between what Jung defines as "scientific convictions" and "old-fashioned prejudices", because this kind of images brings in themselves a very powerful emotional impact. Tacey[41] writes:

> We need to risk forging a relationship with the age-old wisdom of the psyche, to listen to an ancient source inside us which sees reality through different eyes.[42]

5 Jung and Bucci: Continuity and Discontinuity

In Jung's quoted definitions we find the central idea that images bring a new meaning into one's mind, giving a coalescent form to fragments of experience before being dispersed and/or dissociated. The clinical experience that this conception is conveying is that, both in the natural mind development and in the psychic growing process of an analytic therapy, a transformation of sensorial and emotional experience is required in order to give it a meaning. Such a description of the development of mind through the psychoanalytic cure corresponds, at least partially, to Bion's conception of a process transforming β elements in α ones. In Bucci's language, which is nearer to the empirical evidence of modern cognition psychology: images pack together the continuous sub-symbolic flow of information (stored in the brain through a parallel distributing processing), giving an organised affective meaning to chaotic sensations and emotions, and so allowing a new integration of affects and thoughts. The therapeutic change requires a further work of reflection about these meanings, in order to modify complex emotional automatized patterns that express themselves in psychopathology through body reactions and/or distorted evaluations of reality.

40 C.G. Jung, "Symbols and the Interpretation of Dreams", vol. 3, The Collected Works (London: Routledge & Kegan Paul, 1976). Originally published in 1961, 256.

41 Tacey, *The Jung Reader*.

42 Ibid., 300.

The central hypothesis in Bucci's theory follows and in some way even amplifies the key Jungian idea conception that images are the essential bridge between inner creative experience and the rational verbal mode of communication between adult people. As Wilma Bucci puts it, without this transition of sensory, motoric and emotional experience through images to words we cannot have a true narrative in analysis and we cannot reach the deep meanings of the patient's suffering. The use of metaphors in the narrative, for instance, has been seen by both Jung and Bucci, as well as by many other analysts indeed, as one of the strongest way of letting deep unconscious insights come to the surface in analytic conversation. Artistic creation is also recognized to have its sources in an inner world "under" the words. Cambray and Carter,[43] underlining the interconnection between implicit and explicit memory both in analysis and in literature, refer to a notation by Virginia Woolf about the rhythm as a source of the literary creation: "...the rhythm (...) is mysterious and goes much deeper than words. A signal, an emotion, creates this wave in the mind, before the appropriate words are formed..."[44]

The most impressive theoretical difference between Jung and Bucci appears to be in the meaning they give to the word "symbolization." Wilma Bucci seems to consider that words are the highest level of the symbolization process, because – following the general framework of evolutionist psychology and of cognitive neuroscience – she refers to human language as the most advanced instrument to generalise information coming from different sources and to communicate knowledge. In order to share personal and interpersonal experience and to create new meanings for it, we need to have an intense and affectively charged interpersonal exchange of verbal formulations, deeply connected with the past and present emotional experience of both interlocutors.

In his essay on the *Transcendent Function*, Jung takes up again the function of images in mental functioning: the expression of affects through images (e.g. in pictorial productions) creates a product that "incorporates the aspiration of the unconscious to emerge to light and the aspiration of the consciousness to the substance."[45] Of course, Jung is speaking here about internal processes in an intra-psychic frame, but how may we interpret this word "substance"? In many passages of his works, Jung seems to consider that the repairing of the split is possible only when the ego consciousness comes into contact with

43 J. Cambray and L. Carter, "Analytic Methods Revisited", in *Analytical Psychology: Contemporary Perspectives in Jungian Analysis*, ed. J. Cambray and L. Carter (New York: Brunner-Routledge, 2004).

44 Ibid., 147.

45 C.G. Jung, "The Transcendent Function", vol. 8, The Collected Works (London: Routledge & Kegan Paul, 1960). Originally published in 1916, 84.

the collective unconscious. In this essay, Jung extends his reflections about the therapeutic importance of a conscious and voluntary activation of images in the patient's mind, in order to evoke universal meanings (mythologems), which are the expression of a sort of trans-generational memory of human mankind. In their paper about the methods of analytic psychotherapy, Jo Cambray and Linda Carter[46] write "inside the Jungian paradigm, the use of the metaphor can be extended to the inquiry into the collective unconscious."[47]

So, the substantial aim of the individual consciousness, in order to accomplish the individuation process, is the expression of all its biological potentialities: this means to bring the ego to confront himself with affects and symbols lying in the collective unconscious, that is in a dimension which transcends the limits of individual separateness in the relation between the individual and his *Umwelt*. In the Jungian approach, therefore, images are conveying symbols not translatable in the language of words: in some way, archetypal images are hierarchically at a higher level of symbolisation with respect to words.

In the language of modern psychology, according to Jung, implicit memory seems to have a longer history than the individual one, containing our roots both in the history of the biological evolution of our brain and in the history of our cultural background. So, while the *coniunctio* between conscious and unconscious contents allows to acknowledge symbolic categories which are deeply rooted in our brain as neural predispositions that must evolve, it also implies an expansion of the individual consciousness through embracing the interpersonal world of a humanity extended across spaces and times, whose cultural potentialities are still pre-conditions and require a spiritual development.

Hogenson[48] clearly indicates the double nature of the "archetype" concept, in some way implied by the distinction between archetypes and archetypal images. This author argues that a revision of these concepts in a modern key requires us to take a position between two possible interpretations: either we put in evidence the neurobiological structure of the human brain as responsible for the recurring of universal images in mythology, art, dreams and hallucinations, or we treat the archetypal images as emergent qualities of the clinical experience of affective mutual exchanges. Even if he seems to think that the ambiguity of Jung's theoretical statements implies a forcing interpretation in

46 Cambray and Carter, "Analytic Methods Revisited."

47 Ibid., 149.

48 G.B. Hogenson, "Archetypes: Emergence and the Psyche's Deep Structure", in *Analytical Psychology: Contemporary Perspectives in Jungian Analysis*, ed. J. Cambray and L. Carter (Hove / New York: Brunner-Routledge, 2004).

both cases, Hogenson prefers the second option, founding this preference also on the recent conceptions of an emergent mind in developmental psychology.

Coming back to Bucci's notion of referential activity, it had originally been proposed as an intrapsychic mental function which links together different internal modes of processing reality. In recent developments of her theory, however, the focus has been progressively oriented towards the activation of this function through the interpersonal sharing of subjective experience.[49] I would say that Wilma Bucci is now nearer to the Boston Group positions about the clinical implications of the results of infant research: see, for instance, Tronick's hypothesis about the emergence of a dual consciousness through the sharing of intense emotional meanings, in both the infant-mother and the analytic couple.

If we interpret Jung's intra-psychic *coniunctio* as corresponding to an expansion of the sense of self in an interpersonal world, transcending the individualistic perspective, it is possible to enhance the social and relational dimension of his definition of the individuation process. So images – rooted in a functional brain predisposition to give meaning to emotions and feelings as well in a millenary cultural *Umwelt* of the human species – may bridge the meanings of individual suffering over a possibility of sharing it with other people, opening the way towards a more universal, really *transcendent*, sense of life.

References

Bromberg, P.M. "On Being One's Dream: Some Reflections on Robert Bosnak's 'embodied Imagination'." Contemporary Psychoanalysis 39 (2003): 697–710.

Bromberg, P.M. Standing in the Spaces. Essays on Clinical Process, Trauma and Dissociation. New York: The Analytic Press, 1998.

Bucci, W. "Pathways of Emotional Communication" 21, no. 1 (2001): 40–70.

Bucci, W. Psychoanalysis and Cognitive Science. New York: The Guilford Press, 1997.

Bucci, W. "The Enduring Hope of Shared Creative Exploration: Some Thoughts on the Work of Philip Bromberg." Contemporary Psychoanalysis 49, no. 3 (2013): 420–36.

Bucci, W. "Varieties of Dissociative Experiences: A Multiple Code Account and a Discussion of Bromberg's Case of William." Psychoanalytic Psychology 20 (2003): 542–57.

49 Bucci, "The Enduring Hope of Shared Creative Exploration: Some Thoughts on the Work of Philip Bromberg"; Bucci, Maskit, and Hoffman, "Objective Measures of Subjective Experience: The Use of Therapist Notes in Process-Outcome Research."

Bucci, W., and B. Maskit. "Beneath the Surface of the Therapeutic Interaction: The Psychoanalytic Method in Modern Dress." Journal of the American Psychoanalytic Association 55 (2007): 1355–97.

Bucci, W., B. Maskit, and L. Hoffman. "Objective Measures of Subjective Experience: The Use of Therapist Notes in Process-Outcome Research." Psychodynamic Psychiatry 40, no. 2 (2012): 303–40.

Bucci, W. Kabasakalian-McKay, R., and The RA Research Group. *Scoring Referential Activity*. Ulm: Ulmer Textbank, 1992.

Cambray, J., and L. Carter. "Analytic Methods Revisited." In *Analytical Psychology: Contemporary Perspectives in Jungian Analysis*, edited by J. Cambray and L. Carter. New York: Brunner-Routledge, 2004.

Dahl, H., H. Kächele, and H. Thomä. *Psychoanalytic Process Research Strategies*. Berlin, Heidelberg: Springer Verlag, 1988.

Damasio, *A. Self Comes to Mind. New York*: Pantheon Books, 2010.

Fosshage, J.L. "The Explicit and Implicit Domains in Psychoanalytic Change." Psychoanalytic Inquiry 25 (2005): 516–39.

Hogenson, G.B. "Archetypes: Emergence and the Psyche's Deep Structure." In Analytical Psychology: Contemporary Perspectives in Jungian Analysis, edited by J. Cambray and L. Carter. Hove / New York: Brunner-Routledge, 2004.

Johnson-Laird, P.N. Mental Models. Towards a Cognitive Science of Language, Inference and Consciousness. Cambridge: Cambridge University Press, 1983.

Jung, C.G. "Cryptomnesia", 1:95–108. The Collected Works. London: Routledge & Kegan Paul, 1957. Originally published in 1905.

Jung, C.G. "Flying Saucers: A Modern Myth of Things Seen in the Skies", 10:307–436. *The Collected Works*. London: Routledge & Kegan Paul, 1964. Originally published in 1958.

Jung, C.G. "On the Psychogenesis of Schizophrenia", 3:233–49. *The Collected Works*. London: Routledge & Kegan Paul, 1960a. Originally published in 1939.

Jung, C.G. "On the Psychology and Pathology of the So-Called Occult Phenomena", 1:3–88. *The Collected Works*. London: Routledge & Kegan Paul, 1957. Originally published in 1902.

Jung, C.G. "*Psychological Types*", Vol. 6. *The Collected Works*. London: Routledge & Kegan Paul, 1971. Originally published in 1921.

Jung, C.G. "Symbols and the Interpretation of Dreams", 3:1–152. *The Collected Works*. London: Routledge & Kegan Paul, 1976. Originally published in 1961.

Jung, C.G. "Symbols of Transformation. An Analysis of the Prelude to a Case of Schizophrenia", Vol. 5. *The Collected Works*. London: Routledge & Kegan Paul, 1956. Originally published in 1912.

Jung, C.G. "The Psychology of Dementia Praecox", 3:1–152. *The Collected Works*. London: Routledge & Kegan Paul, 1960b. Originally published in 1907.

Jung, C.G. "The Transcendent Function", 8:67–91. *The Collected Works*. London: Routledge & Kegan Paul, 1960. Originally published in 1916.

Kosslyn, S.M. *Ghosts in the Mind's Machine: Creating and Using Images in the Brain*. New York: Norton Press, 1983.

Mariani, R., B. Maskit, W. Bucci, and A. De Coro. "Linguistic Measures of the Referential Process in Psychodynamic Treatment: The English and Italian Versions." Psychotherapy Research 23, no. 4 (2013): 430–47.

Paivio, A. *Imagery and Verbal Processes*. New York: Holt, Reinehart & Winston, 1971.

Paivio, A. *Mental Representations: A Dual Coding Approach*. New York: Oxford University Press, 1986.

Roth, A., and P. Fonagy. *What Works for Whom? A Critical Review of Psychotherapy Research*. New York: The Guilford Press, 1996.

Tacey, D. *The Jung Reader*. London, New York: Routledge, 2012.

Wachtel, P.L. "An Integrative Relational Point of View." Psychotherapy 31 (2014): 342–49.

CHAPTER 8

Jung and Social Thought: "The Undiscovered Self"

Ilona Błocian

Abstract

It seems to be a paradox that Jung defined an archetype as a collective pattern however social history was not a subject of his interest and social thought was not a path of his conception. The *Undiscovered Self* and texts from *Civilization in Transition* or some his notices in interviews have undeniable social character; many statements from the studies on religious symbolism, alchemy or on literature contain also clear social dimension. His defense of individual status in contemporary mass societies, attack on non-authentic, alienated, conventional forms of life experiences and existence, on slave-state and logic of great number are very characteristic and they take their own place in the stream of psychoanalytical, neo-psychoanalytical path of social thought corresponding with Frankfurt School reinterpretation Freud's understanding of individual-society relation.

Jung was a critique of mass society and his position in confrontation with social dilemmas was very critical. A negative image of European experiences is based on colonialism, conquests, "blood baths" of conflicts, wars and the violence of missionary activity of the Church. The contemporary society – due to the history of our culture and direction of social development – is largely penetrated by negative forms of mass processes, gradual erosion of individuals and communities.

Keywords

Jung – social thought – unconscious – collective unconscious – shadow archetype – social world of XXth century – individual and society – history of European culture – mass processes – mass-man

1 Psychoanalysis and Social Dimension

Psychoanalysis introduced the social dimension to its research perspectives very early. Freud has referred to the necessity of social life, customs and socio-cultural determinations in his interpretation of dream motives in *Interpretation*

 | DOI:10.1163/9789004336636_010

of Dreams.[1] The interpretation and understanding of dreams are not possible if one does not know the specific social code of meanings within a dream's images. Freud had written that dreams are completely a-historical and that they unveil human egoism; the consequence seems to consider the unconscious as an incapsuled sphere and isolated organic life, monadic island conserving principles of species heredity and forming it anew in every human child. Many researchers followed this pattern of grasping Freudian unconscious. In the procedure of dream interpretation he had, referred to the historic and social dimension, to the customs and habitual ways of understanding events and experiences to grasp the meaning of images and symbols. The imagery material comes often from the nearest direct experiences. One cannot understand them without knowledge about the environment of the individual who created it.

Freud had also written a lot of studies that can be called "social"; he had become gradually more conscious of the importance of that dimension and had considered social phenomena such as war, conflict, leadership, social primeval institutions (totemism, taboo, magical thinking, animism) in the psychological context of some basic processes of the unconscious: incestuous tendency, projection, repression, reactions on inhibition, identification. As a matter of fact he considered human beings in fundamental relation to the anthropological process of becoming – man and socio-cultural inhibitions, factors and phenomena. These were Adler, Fromm and American neo-psychoanalysts who had developed that line of research in partially new frames of references.[2]

2 Social Dimension of an Archetype

Jung's ideas may be conceived as the underlying collective dimension to the unconscious conception.[3] The main category of Jung's thought, alongside the collective unconscious, is an archetype. Both of them are in a close genetic and functional relationship and make a particular trait of his thought. Both of them have inbuilt a collective dimension; however they are called "collective" and not "social." The dilemma of the notion can be interpreted but sometimes – as in E. Mieletinski's study – they are used interchangeably.[4] Mieletinski, noting the collective dimension of the archetype, points also to the attention of the

1 S. Freud, "Interpretation of Dreams", in *The Standard Edition of Complete Psychological Works of Sigmund Freud*, ed. and trans. J. Strachey, vol. IV, V (London, 2001).
2 M. Birnbach, *Neo-Freudians Social Philosophy* (Stanford CA, 1961); R. Saciuk, *Amerykańska psychoanaliza kulturowa* (Wrocław, 1986).
3 I. Progoff, *Jung's Psychology and Its Social Meaning* (New York, 1955), 9.
4 E. Mieletinski, *Poetyka mitu* (Warsaw, 1981).

origin of that concept. Not once did Jung himself, by defining one of its main categories, clearly indicate its origins not only in the philosophical sources, for example Philo Judaeus, Irenaeus of Lyon, Dionysus the Areopagite or Augustin *ideae principales*, but also in the "elementary ideas" of A. Bastian, the French school of sociology, the concept of "categories of imagination", *les représentations collectives* of H. Hubert, M. Mauss and L. Lévy-Bruhl.[5] On that note Jung had most often defined the term archetype as a "category of imagination", derived from the observation of certain classes, groups and ideas occuring with some regularity, that forms the collective imagination activity and the preferences in creation of meaning. I. Progoff wrote that Jung's interpretation of human individuality had been constructed "directly in terms of historical perspective"[6] and his image of man was based on a "social rather than on a biological conception."[7]

It can therefore be concluded that genealogy had to underpin the concept of archetype. The philosophical, sociological, anthropological and psychological dimensions are therefore inbuilt in that notion; they all bind it, though derived from different traditions in studies of phenomena and forms of human activity. This makes the notion stretched to some extent; multiple layers also cause the considerable problems of interpretation, because some of its aspects refer to different references areas:

1. The socio-anthropological aspect refers to research into the history of culture, collective imagination and the comparative method in compiling the images and meanings of symbols and categories of collective imagination;
2. The psychological dimension refers to the biographical material and the individual (often idiosyncratic set of "dictionaries" and dynamics of affective-representative reactions); and
3. The philosophical dimension refers to attempts of researching the unconscious *matrix* that determine the reality.

These are all some levels of concept stratification that are – in Jung's opinion – activated in the psyche of the individual, in social imagination, psyche species, in the mind, in the reality. Here follows the passage from the level of the individual, common for all human psyche forms to the forms ordering reality as such. This spread in its consequences is enormous. Jung's conception is not

5 C.G. Jung, "The Archetypes and the Collective Unconscious", in *The Collected Works*, trans. R.F.C. Hull, vol. 9.1 (New York, 1959), 4; "Psychological Aspects of the Mother Archetype", in *The Collected Works*, vol. 9.1 (New York, 1959), 79.

6 Progoff, *Jung's Psychology and Its Social Meaning*, 6.

7 Ibid., 10.

based in pure psychology *per se* but in the "totality of the personal and historical lives in Western Europeans."[8]

Jung was sometimes moving towards the extraction and strengthening of some of these dimensions, sometimes the concept of an archetype occurs in the context covering their wholeness. Researchers are sometimes deceived by this or that accentuated attempt to interpret and define the concept, treating it, in good faith, as the most monolithic and specifically referring to the idea of the inherited affective-representative pattern (*le moule affectivo-représentatif*[9]), presumably and primarily in the psychological sense. But the notion is most often beyond that way of understanding in all directions, as it relates to his anthropological, social and often philosophical lineage, which all expand its meaning. In this context, the allegations of psychologism and naturalism in their various forms, to a greater extent in relation to the whole concept of Jung, as well as to the various dimensions of his research, are not accurate, and even seem to be collateral to them.

Thus the concept of the collective unconscious and the notion of archetypes are not only forms of psychological activity of the individual mind. They build anthropological structure, but are also the basis of the process of reality development. R. Brooke noticed that Jung's conception of world is ontologically grasped as "a network" of meaningful archetypal relations. One can conceive the archetypes themselves as being-in-the world through body and as a connection through meaning.[10] Archetypes should not be understood as "things in themselves" (*in se*) but as an essential dimension of relating matrices.[11] Jung often mentioned however that an archetype can be conceived as a "thing in itself" and it is still unknowable.[12] There remains the question if Jung is enclosed in substantial logic patterns and he is not able to think in the terms of relation but only in the terms of substance status.[13]

One of the many dilemmas in the interpretation of the archetype is its *a priori* or *a posteriori* character and its relation to the concept of instinct. These are

8 Ibid., 6.

9 G. Durand, *Les structures anthropologiques de l'imaginaire. Introduction à l'archétypologie générale*, 11th ed. (Paris, 1992), 62.

10 R. Brooke, *Jung and Phenomenology* (London, New York: Routledge, 1991), 2,13.

11 Ibid., 41.

12 G. Durand had also observed the relation between Kantian grasp of "thing in itself" and phenomena and Jung's notion of archetype as a bridge between archetype and archetypal image, imagery and rational processes (Durand, *Les structures anthropologiques de l'imaginaire. Introduction à l'archétypologie générale*, 63).

13 Brooke, *Jung and Phenomenology*, 9.

two aspects of the complexity. Z. Rosińska noticed lots of these dilemmas.[14] There are perceptions that emphasize the different ways of understanding referring to his various statements about the pre-experiential character of an archetype. In this context, an archetype is *a priori facultas praeformandi*, an ability or propensity of the mind "according to which the mind organizes its contents."[15]

"There is an *a priori* factor in all human activities, namely the inborn, pre-conscious and unconscious structure of the psyche."[16]

They do not refer however, to reason, but to the imagination. These pre-existential "categories of the imagination", "instruments of pre-rational psyche" taking the form of an image and of the idea catching the image.[17]

"The archetype in itself is empty and purely formal, nothing but a *facultas praeformandi*, a possibility of representation which is given *a priori*."[18]

That way of understanding the notion is clearly perceptible in connection with its philosophical origins, which defines the pre-existential ideas, according to which the world is formed. E. Neumann was, among others, a supporter of that interpretation of the archetype.[19] Jung however, marked that archetypes are not pre-existential ideas, that after the critical philosophy of Kant no one can assume metaphysical statements and believe that there exist "somewhere, in 'a place beyond the skies'"[20] pre-existent and supraordinate factors, the eternal beings. The archetype thus was not created before life, writes Jung, but with life itself, and there is no way to conceive otherwise its origins. The archetype also means the ability to live the life of a strictly human way, a pattern which is the result of the accumulation of the experiences of particular importance for the development of the human species. Therefore it has undeniably an anthropological nature, though in the late writings Jung also introduces the term psychoid, which is responsible for the transgression of archetype to material reality.[21] And in those writings archetype includes explicitly all formative dimensions of reality. Great importance to highlight the philosophical dimension of the concept has Jung's collaboration with W. Pauli and their

14 Z. Rosińska, *Jung* (Warsaw, 1982).

15 C.G. Jung, "Psychological Commentary on The Tibetan Book of the Dead", in *The Collected Works*, vol. 11 (New York, 1958), 517.

16 Jung, "Psychological Aspects of the Mother Archetype", 77.

17 Jung, "Psychological Commentary on The Tibetan Book of the Dead."

18 Jung, "Psychological Aspects of the Mother Archetype", 79.

19 E. Neumann, *The Origins and History of Consciousness* (New York: Princeton University Press, 1954).

20 Jung, "Psychological Aspects of the Mother Archetype", 75.

21 C.G. Jung, "On the Nature of Psyche", in *The Collected Works*, vol. 8 (Princeton, 1969).

theory of synchronicity. The unconscious and the archetypal forms are conceived here as an organizing factor of the dimensions of reality corresponding to "hidden order" in terms of D. Bohm.[22] We cannot claim that this convoluted hidden order is an organizing pre-form in relation to space and temporal reality, but rather that it is a directly elusive, active and structuring effector ordering the non-local and non-causal bond of phenomena.

The archetype can be understood as *a priori* in the sense that it is a potential form, however ordering the whole process of reality with necessity. Jung, like Bohm, gives the example here: the axial system of a crystal which "performs the crystalline structure in the mother liquid, although it has no material existence of its own";[23] Bohm indicates an organization of forms according to the principles of a greater whole that one cannot capture in the course of local transformations.

The development of the archetypal structures, however, is conditioned by a sequence of updating the past, and so the history of human experiences but not so much in the area *in se*, nor in its biologically specific instinctive ground; in either case it would be difficult to imagine, because of the unavailability of the first and immutability of the second. Development of archetype according to the directions of potential factors encounters possible current actualizations, which are the result of the accumulation and transformation of human history, including social history. Development and actualization are therefore associated with certain *a posteriori* formed content. In the works of social character in *Civilization in Transition* one can track not only some collections of permanent meanings of certain symbolic – imaginal formations, but specific aspects of the archetypal activities in the socio-historical environment in a given culture and time, in the unique *hic et nunc*. Thus in Jung's conception, perspective on the unconscious can be conceived as a psychological basis of society.[24] There are therefore well justified reasons that a group of researchers follows the path of emphasizing the *a priori* character of an archetype and may well certify its position in documenting the many statements of this nature of Jung's idea. The understanding of the concept as referring to *a posteriori* accumulated and historically variable contents – it is at the same time also well founded in his perception. The archetype in Jung's conception combines these seemingly antithetical dimensions. Had this historical volatility not existed, it could not be possible in the horizon of Jung's conception to explain cultural

22 D. Bohm, *Ukryty porządek*, trans. M. Tempczyk (Warsaw, 1988). Originally published as *Wholeness And The Implicate Order* (London, 1980).

23 Jung, "Psychological Aspects of the Mother Archetype", 79.

24 Progoff, *Jung's Psychology and Its Social Meaning*, 37.

diversity and multiplicity of symbols, the emergence of new forms, or even the idea of a given European shadow (and therefore specific and possible only in the perspective of European history), which consists of conquest, colonialism and the negative aspects of the Church missionary activity.[25] This form had to grow in the social history area; European colonialism is part of the social history of Europe and even though it is not inherited as part of the heritage of a biological basis, forms of aggression, which take shape in European social history, are active in the individual involved in that given cultural formation. Jung thought, that none of the Europeans was above the "shadow of Europe." It means that it is a part of the inheritance, which is active in shaping the minds and, more broadly, in the formation of the psyche of individuals in that given cultural circle. In this sense, the archetype includes the social dimension in the process of updating in respect for the individual and for the collective transformation of history. In particular, this can be seen not so much in the words of Jung's definitions of archetype but in this analysis, where it is already treated as a research tool for understanding the processes and phenomena. Jung analyzed the contents of a European collective shadow and its symbolic forms, for example in *Answer to Job*[26] or the individual psyche in relation to the history of culture, for example in the *Symbols of Transformation.*[27] Individuation in all its many, multidimensional forms refers to the integration of social contents, and under the influence of various forms of collective and social history.

3 The Concept of Evil and Its Collective Character

Interpretation of social processes in the Jungian conception is involved not only in the fundamental aspects of its archetype and the collective unconscious categories but also in the issues of values and problem of evil. This is evident in his analysis of the previously mentioned European shadow. Social thought in psychoanalysis is marked by criticism grows among others with its particular approach to the problem of evil, which it indicates sometimes in the form of explicit forms, and sometimes implicitly. This is a problem particularly important and distinctive in terms of Jung, although directly devoted to it is his short text *Good and Evil in Analytical Psychology.*[28] Sometimes Jung's conception is

25 C.G. Jung, "The Undiscovered Self", in *The Collected Works*, vol. 10 (London, 1970).

26 C.G. Jung, "Answer to Job", in *The Collected Works*, vol. 11 (New York, 1958).

27 C.G. Jung, "Symbols of Transformation. An Analysis of the Prelude to a Case of Schizophrenia", in *The Collected Works*, vol. 5 (London, 1956).

28 C.G. Jung, "Good and Evil In Analytical Psychology", in *The Collected Works*, vol. 10 (London, 1989).

evaluated as marked by reflection on the archetype of the shadow,[29] which is a major pattern of evil experience. Most of the works of Jung, however, refers to this problem because it is one of the main dimensions of process of individuation. As in many others of Jung's thought perspectives, the concept of evil transcends far beyond the level of individual psychology; evil thus does not only create itself in the experience, does not only refer to the psychological dimension, but also to the anthropological and philosophical ones. In *Good and Evil ...* Jung recognizes that he does not know what good and evil are in themselves, but he knows how they are experienced. This "not-knowledge" of the concepts "in themselves" is also a confession to some extent polemical; Jung doubts that, despite different verbal declarations of philosophical and metaphysical characters, anyone knew it.[30] He presents here to some extent a phenomenological attitude, since he refers to the acts of experience. One does not know what evil is in itself. Individuals call "evil" certain aspects of their experiences. They have, however, the form of archetypes. The archetype of the shadow is a particularly strong factor specifying the individual. One fulfills an active, personal relationship with a very individual form of the experience of evil. General structures of experience as potencies result in personal psyche but it is related to the collective level. The most important for further considerations is Jung's gnostic attitude. Evil is what is experienced and it is considered in the same time as a potential dimension of the psyche. The potency may be actualized and recognized in experiences, may launch the development of the human psyche and spirituality in the course of individual and collective development. It can also remain in the sphere of free choice as a possible focus of being in the world. The same contents related to the archetype of the shadow or negative aspects of other archetypal patterns are not the real evil in terms of Jung. Whatever blocks the mental development, even if it was known and understood as "good", is real evil. Good and evil function within the individual in the logic of process of psychic development. One can only evaluate what is good or bad from the point of view of any given particular development and its purpose, though in its progress it is felt, experienced or understood as completely opposite. Values and counter-values can therefore change their places. There is no external reality to the experience to guarantee values without doubt. The unrecognized and inexperienced contents have the most

29 "The psychology of the shadow" – Z.W. Dudek, *Psychologia integralna Junga* (Warsaw, 1995), 7.

30 I. Błocian, *Dobro i zło w analitycznej psychologii. Jung i problem zła*, in: red. J. Zieliński, S. Barć, A. Lorczyk, *Rzecz piękna, dobra, mądra i wszystko, co takie ....*, Wrocław 2014.

negative and destructive effects. It means that they are rejected and omitted in the develpoment of an individual. Their unconscious position compels them to some kind of realization.

The archetype of the shadow is the Jungian "narrow passage" of the confrontation with the individualized, most personal character of negativity, moral inferiority, subordination to instincts with their chaotic compulsions. "Inferiority" comes from the inadequacy of the biological patterns governing the organic forms of life to the socio-cultural dimension. Thus many forms of aggression are stamped with the adjective "bad" are not "evil" but rather maladjusted to certain forms of social life. However they are the source of the organism's vitality and a kind of its possible self-defense and survival. They become a basis that must be actualized and recognized in its role as a possible self-defense and self-constitution, the role weighty psychologically but socially embarrassing. We call evil the forms of aggression, because they can have a very negative, destructive effect in social interactions. However it is not evil in itself, but rather a tool for individual possible survival and self-constitution. The aggression can bring disruptive or catastrophic consequences in its acute forms in social life. This level of discussion is active in the whole psychoanalytic mainstream,[31] because it is based on the idea of some anthropological "step" of the man's passage from his biological heredity with its goal to survive to a pattern of cultural and social forms of life.[32] The biological level does not generate questions about good and evil; aggression is thought here as a natural and positive factor, and what is more, as a source of vital force of the body, which has a biological potency in terms of survival. The level of socio-cultural and moral consciousness generates the question of good and evil; the forms of aggression are inhibited here by patterns of penality in human cultures,[33] and it is regarded as one of the most threatening forms for social order.

In Jung's conception of evil it becomes more complex. Negative forms of our experience can activize the development to the aim of the individual mental health. From the perspective of psychological development, in which a person was somehow paralyzed by a strict upbringing, the experience of any form of aggression is paradoxically beneficial. The individual code of availability or unavailability of potential mental qualities determines the logic of

31 C. Castoriadis observed in Freud's thought the conflict between primeval drives and social dimension of human life. "The socialization of the psyche, even its sheer survival, requires that that it recognizes and accepts unfulfillability of its nuclear, primeval desires." – C. Castoriadis, "Psychoanaysis and Politics", in *Speculation after Freud. Psychoanalysis, Philosophy and Culture*, ed. S. Shamdasani and M. Münchow (London, New York, 1994), 8.

32 I. Błocian, "Psychoanalityczne koncepcje zła. Freud", in *Psychoanalityczne ujęcie wartości, gustów i upodobań*, ed. I. Błocian and R. Saciuk (Toruń, 2008).

33 A. Wierciński, *Magia i religia. Szkice z antropologii religii* (Cracow, 1994).

the unconscious process and it has also an influence on the possibility to judge what may be called evil, and what may be called good. But it does not lead, contrary to the appearances of Jung's position, to ethical relativism.

> I see it very clearly: this is evil, but the paradox is just that for this particular person in this particular situation at this particular stage of development it may be good.[34]

It might bring good results. The social life forms with its "injunction – and – inhibition" character, the hierarchy of social organization and the normative conventionality generate multiple forms of human suffering, because they go beyond the biological determinants of man, modifies them, provides often a strong challenge for them or demands the complete or partial slow-down of certain potencies. The processes of socialization and education interact in superficial and inauthentic ways. They are based more on wishes with regard to the man's development than on actual human self-knowledge, hence their fiasco and the lack of the individual's adaptation to social life. It has an influence on the consequences of mental disorders, suffering, uncontrolled outbursts of aggression, susceptibility to manipulation and mental illness. This is a formation of a negative image of the "individual-society" relations, destructiveness and specific forms of social negativity.

The entirely freudian mainstream viewed the relation "individual-society" as antagonistic. Psychoanalysis defended the individual and it often warned against the destructive impacts of the social dimension. It tried to protect the status and validity of individual life, expressing an awareness that the relation is a difficult process. The individual changes social reality, creates, enters into it. The full development of mental health is unthinkable without the foundation of this process in a certain balance, which is difficult and often does not happen at all. But the individual "is a social microcosm",[35] "one and only true carrier of reality"[36] and life itself.[37]

Psychoanalysis observes man in this frame process between the individual and the social dimension. It is after all, the state of conflict between desires and their displacement, neuroses, suffering. In terms of the general framework it also functions in Jung's perception – the social dimension, in fact, influences

34 Jung, "Good and Evil In Analytical Psychology", 459 (&899).

35 "He is a social microcosm, reflecting on the smallest scale the qualities of society at large" (Jung, "The Undiscovered Self", 286).

36 Ibid., 252.

37 Ibid.

on the potentiality of man which remains unconscious, and which can be actualized. The unconscious is on the waiting position, sometimes excited, sometimes in anarchic revolt and subversive. It can disrupts the process of adapting the individual to the social reality. Many unconscious drives have quite different orientations than just the adaptation. Learning and imitating, though they can be means of transcending animality, at the same time alienate man[38] and "primeval nature" is replaced by neurosis. Researchers in the neo-psychoanalytical movement underlined anxiety, competition as beginnings of the education process but at the same time as a possible source of neurosis.[39] F. Alexander noticed here the psychological meaning of a necessity to adapt to rapid change of socio-technological conditions.

Mental health for Jung is not only adapting the individual to the world. The pursuit of health often requires a significant disturbance in the process of adaptation. No one could suspect Jung of ideals of simple adaptability.

Jung diagnosed the social dimension in which he lived; he revealed it as a medicine man, a psychotherapist and as a philosopher. The diagnosis is based on several key elements.

4 Mass – Man

Man is a mass man of the contemporary era (*common man*), and as such he is far from the process of individuation. The basis of that process is an authenticity and "becoming oneself." It is conceived as a realization of all potencies in one's own individual circumstances. Mass-man is a completely different pole of humanity. He is a human being reduced to an almost insignificant component of the mass society and social machine. Similiar to Freud, Jung observes a mass on a lower than the individual psychic level of activity. The first smothers the second, its reflection and moral responsibility. Like *animal laborans* in H. Arendt's work,[40] workers resemble working animals, merely slaves of the social machine.

Mass society manages its problems with great difficulty; its ideas are created *ad hoc* for the purpose of the current social trouble. There is an abyss between mass-man and the self; the first is a social being par excellence, because he

38 Ibid., 288.

39 "An anxiety as an educative experience is a reminiscent of Freud's idea of the reality principle supplanting the pleasure principle" – Birnbach, *Neo-Freudians Social Philosophy*, 103.

40 H. Arendt, *The Human Condition* (Chicago, London, 1998).

does not exist individually, but only as part of a mass society. He is an underdeveloped, stunted human form, reduced to the simplest needs, ruled by manipulation tools, opinions and conventions. The diagnosis of mass-man indirectly points to the gap between who a person can be and who he is. However, in this perspective, the inability of individual development is due to participation in the warped, reduced and inauthentic social environment. There is no psychic or spiritual development. It would not be desirable, because it may disturb the adaptation of individuals, burst conformist *persona*, the social mask hiding the lack of human personality. It is difficult to imagine a worse situation from the perspective of the Jungian self and mental health conception. The social dimension of mass society holds individuals in the spiritual stage of "dwarfism." This dimension is not helpful to the individual but it actually destroys the possibility of becoming – a self-process.

5 Authoritarian Tyranny

Jung is not the only critic of the post-war mass society. His voice resonates with many others concerning authoritarian phenomena. They indicate conformity, destruction of interpersonal relationships and the collapse of important values. These are perspective of Fromm, the Frankfurt School and H. Arendt's political philosophy. The analysis of the situation of modern society made by Jung is set in the confrontation of contemporary events of 50th, post-World War II, and therefore in a confrontation with two authoritarian orders of Nazi Germany (which remains in the background of his reasoning), Stalinist Russia and its impact on the countries of Central Europe (marxist state, marxist *Civitas Dei*). Jung writes that they are "modern stables of slaves" so much mentally manipulated into slave ideology, that just barely find opportunity to protest. Authoritarian states are ruled by the oligarchy and support it. Their power is subordinated to ideology ("the all-powerful doctrine of the state"), and the individual is more or less efficiently managed and manipulated. Jung conceived this situation as an archaic social order; the leader only has an individual psyche; the rest is a chaotic mass of people, whose personalities does not develop. The lack of freedom results in a lack of any personal responsibility.[41] Man is completely devoid of even a substitute for the inner critical mentality

41 These notes are very close to Freud's way of understanding psychic quality of a mass (S. Freud, "Group Psychoanalysis and the Analysis of the Ego", in *The Standard Edition of Complete Psychological Works of Sigmund Freud*, ed. and trans. J. Strachey, vol. IV, V [London, 2001]).

(mass – mindedness). This note is very akin to Fromm's diagnosis of contemporary authoritarian order: the absence of critical thinking in the individual. He observed it already in his *Escape from Freedom* in 1941.[42]

Marcusean *One-Dimensional Man*,[43] is a comprehensive study of the lack of freedom in its inner dimension. It was published later than Jung's *The Undicovered...*, because in 1964. These analyses are bonded by strong criticism. Any individual development is nearly impossible in their views upon postidustrial society. Jung was less than Fromm and Marcuse involved in research on social issues, however he noticed rebellions in Hungary and Poland in 1956 (in a footnote to his text).[44]

Mass man is vulnerable to manipulation; his obedience is also integrated with remarkable easy falling into collective mental epidemics, forms of irrational and fanatical passions of powerful resentment. Thus, he is obedient to power and hostile to the indicated enemies. The reason for this vulnerability to psychological hostility is the unconscious priming of an eruption of negative contents and affecting the weak and almost non-existent human "ego." The infantile nucleus is hiding behind the mask of a social role. The misfortune of mass society is precisely characteristic of human underdevelopment, which makes it a plaything to the eruption of the unconscious. For this reason, Jung examines these forms of human activity, which enabled the development of individuals in societies and their cultures, and most of all – religion. Religion is not criticized as such but rather for its lack of fulfillment the function of protection and enabling the possibility of human self-realization. It is not the only one context of the considerations of religion in Jung's conception. Writings on religion are one of the most extensive areas of his interests. Jung examines the religious symbolism, division of science and faith, splits and discussions in the Church, religious forms of Protestantism and Catholicism, the phenomenon of "Christian soul", numinous religious experiences, mysticism, gnosis and Gnosticism, the archetype of God, the status of metaphysics and the confrontation of eastern and western religions. This is a large part of his writings, his attention and one of the favourite subjects of philosophical and psychological reflections. Jung introduces this perspective to his own conception with considerable knowledge of the facts, although it must be admitted that many of his interpretations and analyses raised discussion and controversies.

42 E. Fromm, *Escape of Freedom* (New York, 1971).

43 H. Marcuse, *One-Dimensional Man. Studies in the Ideology of Advanced Industrial Society* (London, 1991). Originally published in 1961.

44 Jung, "The Undiscovered Self", 264.

Religion could be a genuine prospect of the activating process of spiritual development and defense of the individual autonomy, but it is not. Its social role is opposite; it becomes one of the instruments of oppression. It is a conventional, less and less lively, more and more petrified form of social life; its institutionalized character has nothing to do with the need for an authentic living experience of the spirit. It turns into creed ("religious creed") and is far from its source. According to Jung the unconscious is the source of an original numinous experience. The unconscious constitutes for each religion its beginning and the vital principle. The religion becomes the external convention along the process of petrification and it loses its intelligibility and ability to lead internal developments. *Mysterium* becomes external. This externality causes a gradual erosion of religiosity; first, it becomes in terms of Jung's only "creed", next, the pure social convention. Religion could potentially protect the individual, giving it an instrument of self-discovery and self-experience. Psychoanalytic interpretations of such potency are known. For example, B. Bettelheim considered the beneficial function of deeply religious attitudes in concentration camps.[45] The more religion becomes institutionalized, conventional and symbolically "empty", it gradually loses its "souls government."

The psychology and philosophy have also lost or never had the ability to protect human spirituality and self-discovery. Philosophy has lost its influence on human life; instead it has become a purely conceptual, often quite verbal game of rational constructs breaking a relationship with living experience; in addition, it is unresponsive to the impulsive and symbolic dimensions. They have been removed on the margin. They did not lose their strength, on the contrary – an unconscious form of their existence, their anarchy generate "a pressure to appear" in any form of manifestation. Philosophy therefore does not support the individual but rather deforms it precluding self-knowledge.

Psychology is due to the same process. It was formed properly as psychology of conscious ego and awareness; from the heights of research institutions it observes quietly the weakness of the individual, its underdevelopment, its lack of self-knowledge, its faulty, incomplete adaptation to the environment, its unerdeveloped spirituality. As a part of the construction of conceptual and wishful thinking about the psyche it turns out being as helpless as the philosophy.

According to Jung the authentic relationships between individuals are affective ones. There are no ties without affects, only intersection of social roles, of which certainly can arise realization of social goals, but it can have no meaning for the individuals.

45 B. Bettelheim, *The Informed Heart: Autonomy In a Mass Age* (New York, 1960); E. Fromm refers to that study (E. Fromm, *The Anatomy of Human Destructiveness* [New York, 1973]).

What then, would require self-consciousness? The reflection and integration of the shadow. The modern European psyche is connected with the dark pages of European history. Jung, like Freud, points out his version of "horrible catalogue": crimes against other races, conquest, colonialism, along with his exploitation and violence. It was seen a veritable "blood bath" and barbarism of so-called "civilized nations"during the recent wars. The question of the values associated with the progress of civilization becomes grotesque in this context. Values represent today a sort of external, empty staffage. The postulation of them in the external, declarative form only becomes a substitute for the spiritual development of man.

It seems that the whole Jungian analysis involves his conception of human archetypal experience and its confrontation with the social and historical reality. They remain in close relationship. Culturally and socially prepared locks of unconscious drives in the process of human development mean in the perspective of Jung's conception, the necessity to confront negative forms of archetypes. Locked potentialities impact on an interaction unconsciously and in an overwhelmingly negative way. It influences on a gradual erosion of individuals and communities as a result. Jung in *The Undiscovered …* does not consider these phenomena in an ultra-historical perspective but only in the situation of the individual in contemporary mass society and he refers to the historical and social events of the 1950s. The perspective of social history can also be seen in his writings of a religious symbolism and religious imagery. Jung writes, for example, that the necessity of confrontation with the archetype of the shadow is due to the expulsion of evil in the Christian religion. The impossibility of its integration results in an especially dark figure of European history. This collective archetype of the shadow becomes an overwhelming totality, not only a simple premeditation in destructiveness.

Jung's diagnosis of the contemporary situation of an individual seems to be very sharp, uncompromising and pessimistic. But it is a tone that resonates with analyses and diagnoses of social criticism of Fromm and Marcuse. The analyses and forms of criticism are very detailed and uncompromising all of them. The individual is increasingly threatened in the area of self-development, opportunities, the experience of himself. The individual does not understand himself. He is at the mercy of social practices that block the freedom in even the most basic dimensions of its possible experience. Jung was skeptical considering the "liberal dream of a rational world order bringing peace and harmony" (G. Watson).[46]

46 G. Watson, "Introduction", in *Jung's Psychology and Its Social Meaning*, by I. Progoff (New York, 1955).

Jung, like Freud, did not construct an utopia, nor indicate any remedy, beside a renewal of the mental and moral life by means of self-knowledge about the archetypal content still in confrontations with the social horizon.

> The analyst must protect them [individual impulses-I.B.] from the patient's own clumsy recourse to shortsightedness, ruthlessness, and cynicism.[47]

Jung's position is a defense of the value of individual in the social perspective. The individual is considered as the real carrier of life; his self-fulfillment should be the ultimate goal in the sphere of social ideas. Jung's socio-critical thinking is situated in a perspective of a value of individual life.

References

Arendt, H. *The Human Condition*. Chicago, London, 1998.

Bettelheim, B. *The Informed Heart: Autonomy In a Mass Age*. New York, 1960.

Birnbach, M. *Neo-Freudians Social Philosophy*. Stanford CA, 1961.

Błocian, I. *Dobro i zło w analitycznej psychologii. Jung i problem zła*. in: red. J. Zieliński, S. Barć, A. Lorczyk, *Rzecz piękna, dobra, mądra i wszystko, co takie*...., Wrocław 2014.

Błocian, I. "Psychoanalityczne koncepcje zła. Freud." In *Psychoanalityczne ujęcie wartości, gustów i upodobań*, edited by I. Błocian and R. Saciuk. Toruń, 2008.

Bohm, D. *Ukryty porządek*. Translated by M. Tempczyk. Warsaw, 1988. Originally published as *Wholeness And The Implicate Order* (London, 1980).

Brooke, R. *Jung and Phenomenology*. London, New York: Routledge, 1991.

Castoriadis, C. "Psychoanaysis and Politics." In *Speculation after Freud. Psychoanalysis, Philosophy and Culture*, edited by S. Shamdasani and M. Münchow. London, New York, 1994.

Dudek, Z.W. *Psychologia integralna Junga*. Warsaw, 1995.

Durand, G. *Les structures anthropologiques de l'imaginaire. Introduction à l'archétypologie générale*. 11th ed. Paris, 1992.

Freud, S. "Group Psychoanalysis and the Analysis of the Ego." In *The Standard Edition of Complete Psychological Works of Sigmund Freud*, edited and translated by J. Strachey, Vol. IV, V. London, 2001a.

47 Jung, "The Undiscovered Self", 275.

Freud, S. "Interpretation of Dreams." In *The Standard Edition of Complete Psychological Works of Sigmund Freud*, edited and translated by J. Strachey, Vol. IV, V. London, 2001b.

Fromm, E. *Escape of Freedom*. New York, 1971.

Fromm, E. *The Anatomy of Human Destructiveness*. New York, 1973.

Jung, C.G. "Answer to Job." In *The Collected Works*, Vol. 11. New York, 1958a.

Jung, C.G. "Good and Evil In Analytical Psychology." In *The Collected Works*, Vol. 10. London, 1989.

Jung, C.G. "On the Nature of Psyche." In *The Collected Works*, Vol. 8. Princeton, 1969.

Jung, C.G. "Psychological Aspects of the Mother Archetype." In *The Collected Works*, Vol. 9.1. New York, 1959a.

Jung, C.G. "Psychological Commentary on The Tibetan Book of the Dead." In *The Collected Works*, Vol. 11. New York, 1958b.

Jung, C.G. "Symbols of Transformation. An Analysis of the Prelude to a Case of Schizophrenia." In *The Collected Works*, Vol. 5. London, 1956.

Jung, C.G. "The Archetypes and the Collective Unconscious." In *The Collected Works*, translated by R.F.C. Hull, Vol. 9.1. New York, 1959b.

Jung, C.G. "The Undiscovered Self." In *The Collected Works*, Vol. 10. London, 1970.

Marcuse, H. *One-Dimensional Man. Studies in the Ideology of Advanced Industrial Society*. London, 1991. Originally published in 1961.

Mieletinski, E. *Poetyka mitu*. Warsaw, 1981.

Neumann, E. *The Origins and History of Consciousness*. New York: Princeton University Press, 1954.

Progoff, I. *Jung's Psychology and Its Social Meaning*. New York, 1955.

Rosińska, Z. *Jung*. Warsaw, 1982.

Saciuk, R. *Amerykańska psychoanaliza kulturowa*. Wrocław, 1986.

Watson, G. "Introduction." In *Jung's Psychology and Its Social Meaning*, by I. Progoff. New York, 1955.

Wierciński, A. *Magia i religia. Szkice z antropologii religii*. Cracow, 1994.

CHAPTER 9

In a Secular Age: Weber, Taylor, Jung

Roderick Main

Abstract

Sociologists engaging with depth psychology have rarely drawn on the work of C.G. Jung. Part of the reason for this, I suggest, is Jung's seeming tendency to credit, and be informed by, religious and non-rational perspectives. In this chapter I first highlight what sociologists might find problematic in Jung by comparing his views on the desacralisation of the modern world with Max Weber's views on disenchantment. I then argue that Charles Taylor's recent alternative account of disenchantment and secularity provides a framework within which Jung's thought becomes more sociologically creditable despite, and even because of, its approach to matters of religion.

Keywords

Disenchantment – re-enchantment – secularity – religion – Jungian psychology – sociology

1 Introduction[1]

There are good reasons to expect the work of C.G. Jung to be of interest to sociologists and those engaged in psychosocial studies. Even a cursory glance at the contents list of Jung's *Collected Works* reveals the wide range of social themes he addressed, including health, sexuality, gender, families, education, politics, race, religion, national and cultural identities, and the overall nature of modernity. In his book *Jung and the Making of Modern Psychology: The Dream of a Science,*[2] Sonu Shamdasani demonstrates the extent to which

1 Acknowledgement: This chapter originally appeared as an article in *Psychoanalysis, Culture & Society* 18, no. 3 (2013): 277–94. © Macmillan Publishers Ltd. 1088-0763. Reprinted with permission.

2 S. Shamdasani, *Jung and the Making of Modern Psychology: The Dream of a Science* (Cambridge: Cambridge University Press, 2003).

 | DOI:10.1163/9789004336636_011

Jung's psychology was forged out of his attempt to reconcile the conflicting demands of the individual and society, and how he drew for this purpose on the newly emerged social scientific disciplines of anthropology, sociology, social psychology, crowd psychology, and ethnopsychology.[3] Peter Homans, in his earlier, similarly titled book *Jung in Context: Modernity and the Making of a Psychology*,[4] shows both the sociological factors involved in the formation of Jung's thought and that Jung himself can fairly be characterised as a social thinker.[5] Specifically, Homans details the close parallels between Jung's understanding of modern society and the then prevalent theory of mass society[6] as well as, more broadly, the congruence of Jung's understanding of modernity with the views of a variety of twentieth century social theorists.[7]

Despite this promising background, the amount of serious engagement between sociology and Jungian psychology has been slight. Ira Progoff, in his early study *Jung's Psychology and its Social Meaning*,[8] highlights the extent to which Jung's work, while not itself sociology, assumes society and the (Durkheimian) sociological point of view as the basis for its interpretation of individuals.[9] Progoff expresses his belief that a process is beginning that will 'ultimately integrate Jung's perspective into the social thought of our time.'[10] John Raphael Staude, in his paper 'From Depth Psychology to Depth Sociology: Freud, Jung, and Lévi-Strauss,'[11] originally presented at the World Congress of Sociology in Toronto in 1974, suggests that in his work Jung blended German idealism and historicism with French sociological theory and that '[t]his unique amalgam could have led him to elaborate a depth sociology correlative with his depth psychology' had not 'his search for his own historical predecessors led him to investigate the psycho-historical significance of mysticism, spiritualism and alchemy instead.'[12] Richard Gray, in his book *Archetypal Explorations:*

3 Ibid., 271–352.

4 P. Homans, *Jung in Context: Modernity and the Making of a Psychology* (Chicago: The University of Chicago Press, 1979).

5 Ibid., 133–60, 173–82, 193–209.

6 Ibid., 173–82.

7 Ibid., 3–8, 135–40, 148–60; see also R. Main, "The Social Significance of Synchronicity", *Psychoanalysis, Culture & Society* 11 (2006): 36–37, 41.

8 I. Progoff, *Jung's Psychology and Its Social Meaning* (New York: Dialogue House, 1953).

9 Ibid., 162.

10 Ibid., 8.

11 J.R. Staude, "From Depth Psychology to Depth Sociology: Freud, Jung, and Lévi-Strauss", *Theory and Society* 3, no. 3 (1976): 303–38.

12 Ibid., 354.

An Integrative Approach to Human Behavior[13] (originally subtitled *Towards an Archetypal Sociology*), argues that because Jung's work is 'implicitly systems theoretical', 'explicitly cross cultural', and 'carries at its heart assumptions that allow for a smooth transition from the realm of individual experience to the realm of group action' it 'presents a particularly fine groundwork for an approach to sociology.'[14] Focusing on the concept of the archetype, he attempts to use Jung's work as a framework for integrating the approaches of Emile Durkheim, Max Weber, and B.F. Skinner. However, the efforts and suggestions of Progoff, Staude, and Gray do not appear to have been extensively pursued, and it seems safe to say that, while Jungian authors continue to write about social themes, in current sociological and psychosocial studies literature itself, Jung's work and legacy have very little presence, if any at all.

There are many possible reasons for the neglect of Jung by sociologists, but in this chapter I would like to address just one. This concerns Jung's engagement with the area of religion. It is, of course, not Jung's extensive interest in and writing about religion that could be problematic to sociologists. Durkheim and Weber both considered the study of religion fundamental to understanding modern society and wrote texts that have become classics in the sociology of religion.[15] It is rather that Jung, unlike Durkheim and Weber, not only comments on religion but also, it seems, credits and is informed in his thinking by religious and non-rational perspectives. As one sociological commentator suggests: 'Jung's theories have not really become part of the orthodoxy of [critical] theory in the way Freud's have, perhaps because they so often appear to recommend a flight into irrationalism and even mysticism.'[16]

In the following, in order to bring into focus the particular fault-line I am interested in between Jungian psychology and sociology, I first compare Jung's views on the desacralisation of the modern world with Max Weber's views on disenchantment, highlighting some of the critical points on which Jung's response to modernity diverges from Weber's. Then, turning to the contemporary

13 R. Gray, *Archetypal Explorations: An Integrative Approach to Human Behavior* (Hove/New York: Routledge, 1996).

14 Ibid., 7.

15 E. Durkheim, *The Elementary Forms of Religious Life*, trans. J. Swain (London: Allen and Unwin, 1976). Originally published in 1912; M. Weber, *The Protestant Ethic and the Spirit of Capitalism*, trans. T. Parsons (London/New York: Routledge, 2001). Originally published in 1904.

16 D. Macey, *The Penguin Dictionary of Critical Theory* (London: Penguin Books, 2000), 212; cf. D. Jary and J. Jary, *Collins Dictionary of Sociology*, 2nd ed. (Glasgow: Harper Collins, 1995), 344; J. Scott and G. Marshall, eds., *A Dictionary of Sociology*, 3rd ed. (Oxford: Oxford University Press, 2009), 378.

philosopher and social thinker Charles Taylor, I argue that Taylor's alternative account of disenchantment and secularity, especially as articulated in his book *A Secular Age*,[17] provides a significantly different framework from Weber's within which Jung's thought becomes more sociologically creditable – despite, and even because of, its position on matters of secularity and religion. This reframing of Jung's work arguably enhances its relevance for critically engaging with contemporary social and political problems, especially where these involve acute tensions between the sacred and the secular. As an indication of this, I conclude by briefly outlining how Jungian thought might usefully inform analyses of and engagements with religious fundamentalism.

2 Weber and the Disenchantment of the World

In his essay 'Science as a Vocation',[18] Weber famously epitomised his view of secular modernity: '[T]he fate of our times', he wrote, 'is characterized by rationalization and intellectualization and, above all, by the "disenchantment of the world."'[19] For him this meant that in the modern, secular world 'there are no mysterious incalculable forces that come into play, but rather [...] one can, in principle, master all things by calculation. [...] One need no longer have recourse to magical means in order to master or implore the spirits [...].'[20]

The neatness and forthrightness of this formulation should not obscure the complexity of Weber's views on disenchantment. Also in 'Science as a Vocation', he notes that the same process of rationalisation that has led to the disenchantment of the world has also undercut the claims of any viewpoint, including the viewpoint of science, to have ultimate meaning and value.[21] We are confronted with a multiplicity of 'value spheres' which 'stand in irreconcilable conflict with each other.'[22] In a telling, protracted metaphor, Weber refers to the various value spheres as 'different gods' who 'struggle with one another now and for all time to come.'[23] Paradoxically, at the same time as

17 C. Taylor, *A Secular Age* (Cambridge MA: Harvard University Press, 2007).

18 M. Weber, "Science as a Vocation", in *From Max Weber: Essays in Sociology*, ed. and trans. H. Gerth and C. Wright Mills (New York: Oxford University Press, 1946). Originally published in 1918.

19 Ibid., 155.

20 Ibid., 139.

21 Ibid., 143–44.

22 Ibid., 147.

23 Ibid., 148.

rationalisation has disenchanted us, it has also placed us amid a new form of 'polytheism':[24]

> We live as did the ancients when their world was not yet disenchanted of its gods and demons, only we live in a different sense. As Hellenic man at times sacrificed to Aphrodite and at other times to Apollo, and, above all, as everybody sacrificed to the gods of his city, so do we still nowadays, only the bearing of man has been disenchanted and denuded of its mystical but inwardly genuine plasticity. Fate, and certainly not 'science', holds sway over these gods and their struggles. One can only understand what the godhead is for the one order or for the other, or better, what godhead is in the one or in the other order.[25]

In light of this it has been suggested that 'Weber's rationalization thesis can be understood with richer nuance when we approach it as [...] a dialectics of disenchantment and re-enchantment rather than as a one-sided, unilinear process.'[26]

Weber himself, however, does not use the term 're-enchantment.' He is explicit that when he mentions gods he is speaking 'figuratively.'[27] In our disenchanted age, the gods 'take the form of impersonal forces';[28] 'speaking directly', he recognises that they represent only 'the ultimately possible attitudes towards life.'[29] Towards the end of the essay, his position, both intellectual and moral, becomes clear. Disenchantment is described, notably, as 'the fate of our times',[30] that is, as a condition that any intellectually honest person simply has to endure. Weber recognises that some people, unable to bear disenchantment, may prefer to make the 'intellectual sacrifice' of returning to 'the arms of the old churches' which, he notes, 'are opened widely and compassionately' for them,[31] and he says he will 'not rebuke' those who make this decision. But his tone clearly indicates the low opinion in which he holds any person 'who

---

24 Ibid., 147.
25 Ibid., 148.
26 S.H. Kim, "Max Weber", in *The Stanford Encyclopedia of Philosophy*, ed. E.N. Zalta, Fall 2008 (Metaphysics Research Lab, Stanford University, 2008), https://plato.stanford.edu/archives/fall2012/entries/weber/.
27 Weber, "Science as a Vocation", 151.
28 Ibid., 149.
29 Ibid., 152.
30 Ibid., 155.
31 Ibid.

cannot bear the fate of the times like a man.'[32] Similarly, he describes as 'big children' those who still believe that the natural sciences – those paramount drivers of disenchantment[33] – could reveal to us God's plan for the world or 'teach us anything about the *meaning* of the world.'[34]

There is, though, an even more unsatisfactory position than this for Weber. An implication of the 'gods' being in 'irreconcilable conflict' with one another is, for him, that 'the tension between the value spheres of "science" and the sphere of "the holy" is unbridgeable.'[35] Worse, for Weber, than those who make the unmanly choice of attempting re-enchantment are those who, committing neither to science nor to religion, '[lack] the courage to clarify [their] own ultimate standpoint', engage instead in 'feeble relative judgments', and thereby evade 'the plain duty of intellectual integrity.'[36] Weber, it seems, had little regard for those who either aim at re-enchantment or try to acknowledge the claims of both religion and science.

3 Disenchantment and Re-enchantment in Jung

Jung does not use the term 'disenchantment' but he does refer in terms very similar to Weber's to 'the historical process of world despiritualization'[37] and to the condition of the modern world as being 'desacralized.'[38] In many respects his account of the condition of modernity bears close comparison with Weber's.[39] In relation to disenchantment in particular, just as Weber identifies the essential cause of disenchantment as being intellectualization and rationalization, so Jung sees the root cause of desacralisation as being scientific rationalism.[40] Like Weber, Jung recognised that the condition of disenchantment, despiritualisation, or de-sacralisation would lead to a sense of loss not

32 Ibid.
33 Ibid., 139.
34 Ibid., 142.
35 Ibid., 154.
36 Ibid., 155.
37 C.G. Jung, "Psychology and Religion", in *The Collected Works*, 2nd ed., vol. 11 (London: Routledge & Kegan Paul, 1969). Originally published in 1938–1940, para. 141.
38 W. McGuire and R.F.C. Hull, eds., *C.G. Jung Speaking: Interviews and Encounters* (London: Thames and Hudson, 1978), 230.
39 See R. Main, "Ruptured Time and the Re-Enchantment of Modernity", in *Who Owns Jung?*, ed. A. Casement (London: Karnac, 2007), 20–21.
40 C.G. Jung, "The Undiscovered Self (Present and Future)", in *The Collected Works*, 2nd ed., vol. 10 (London: Routledge & Kegan Paul, 1970). Originally published in 1957, paras. 495–97, 501.

only of magic and spirit but also of meaning.[41] Again, Weber predicted that '[r]edemption from the rationalism and intellectualism of science' would be sought in a craving for religious experiences or even just for 'experience as such' and that 'the spheres of the irrational, the only spheres that intellectualism has not yet touched' would be 'raised into consciousness and put under its lens.'[42] Such turns to religious experience, to direct experience generally, and to exploration of the irrational are similarly identified by Jung as responses likely to be prompted by the one-sided rationalism of science.[43]

Notwithstanding these similarities, there is an important difference between Weber's account of the disenchanted modern world in 'Science as a Vocation' and the account that can be gathered from Jung's writings. This difference is less about the actual process that both men perceived to be occurring or about what responses to the process they thought were likely to arise and more about how to evaluate the responses to the process. Specifically, while Weber *observes* the turn to religious experience and concern with the irrational, Jung *makes* and *recommends* this turn. While Weber sees no scope for genuine re-enchantment, Jung positively advocates re-enchantment. In an interview with Mircea Eliade in 1952, Jung clearly stated his position: 'The modern world', he asserted, 'is desacralized, that is why it is in a crisis. Modern man must rediscover a deeper source of his own spiritual life.'[44] The 'must' here signals the moral difference between Weber and Jung: while for Weber it is morally weak to seek re-enchantment, for Jung it is imperative to do so if we wish to address the crisis of the modern world.

In promoting re-enchantment, however, Jung is not naively or straightforwardly religious. As various scholars have noted, there was a deep tension throughout Jung's work between the seriousness with which he took religion and his equal commitment to science.[45] On the one hand, Jung was born of a long line of pastors, had several formative religious experiences in early childhood as well as at various points during his adult life, and remained personally and professionally preoccupied with religion throughout his career, as

41 Weber, "Science as a Vocation", 139–40, 142; C.G. Jung, "The Soul and Death", in *The Collected Works*, 2nd ed., vol. 8 (London: Routledge & Kegan Paul, 1969). Originally published in 1934, para. 815.

42 Weber, "Science as a Vocation", 142–43.

43 Jung, "The Undiscovered Self (Present and Future)"; see also R. Main, *The Rupture of Time: Synchronicity and Jung's Critique of Modern Western Culture* (Hove/New York: Brunner-Routledge, 2004), 117–74.

44 McGuire and Hull, *C.G. Jung Speaking: Interviews and Encounters*, 230.

45 See Homans, *Jung in Context: Modernity and the Making of a Psychology*; Main, *The Rupture of Time: Synchronicity and Jung's Critique of Modern Western Culture*, 100–107.

indicated by his extensive writings on the topic and his correspondence and friendship with religious figures, most notably the Dominican Father Victor White. Jung's interest was not only academic and theoretical. He believed in the vital significance of religion both therapeutically and culturally and, even when he was critical of institutionalised and creedal religion, he remained highly positive and urgent about the need for individual religious experience.[46] On the other hand, Jung was trained in science and medicine and established his early reputation for cutting-edge work in experimental psychology. After he developed his distinctive psychological model, and even when writing specifically on religious topics, he invariably claimed to be a scientist and empiricist, who dealt with actual phenomena (observable behaviours and reportable beliefs and experiences) rather than with philosophical or theological speculations about putative transcendent realities. If he had theologians among his friends and correspondents, so too did he have scientists, including of the calibre of the Nobel Prize-winning physicist Wolfgang Pauli.[47]

The tension Jung experienced between his dual commitments to religion and science shaped many, and arguably all, of his psychological concepts. His mature formulation of the concept of the archetype, for instance, accords it a double nature which relates it to both the physical and the spiritual realms. This is so in two senses. First, Jung characterises the archetype as having both a material, biological pole and an immaterial, spiritual pole.[48] Second, he makes a distinction between experienceable archetypal images and the irrepresentable archetype-in-itself.[49] Of archetypal religious imagery, he writes that 'There is no doubt that there is something behind these images that transcends consciousness';[50] such imagery 'points to' the archetype-in-itself as 'something ineffable', a 'transcendental object', 'the essence of the Unknowable.'[51] A similar doubleness attaches to the concepts of the collective unconscious,

46 Main, *The Rupture of Time: Synchronicity and Jung's Critique of Modern Western Culture*, 100–05, 129–31; R. Main, "Religion", in *The Handbook of Jungian Psychology: Theory, Practice and Applications*, ed. R. Papadopoulos (Hove/Philadelphia: Brunner-Routledge, 2006); A.C. Lammers and A. Cunningham, eds., *The Jung-White Letters* (Hove: Routledge, 2007).

47 Main, *The Rupture of Time: Synchronicity and Jung's Critique of Modern Western Culture*, 100–05, 121–24; C.A. Meier, ed., *Atom and Archetype: The Pauli/Jung Letters 1932–1958* (London: Routledge, 2001).

48 C.G. Jung, "On the Nature of the Psyche", in *The Collected Works*, 2nd ed., vol. 8 (London: Routledge & Kegan Paul, 1969). Originally published in 1947–1954, para. 420.

49 Ibid., para. 417.

50 C.G. Jung, "Answer to Job", in *The Collected Works*, 2nd ed., vol. 11 (London: Routledge & Kegan Paul, 1969). Originally published in 1952, para. 555.

51 Ibid., paras. 555–06.

individuation, the self, and synchronicity, each of which stems from empirical observation and various natural scientific and social scientific assumptions, while at the same time presupposing an aspect of reality that is intelligent, purposeful, and irreducible to material, social, or cultural terms.[52] Other concepts of Jung's, as well as embedding the tension between religion and science, are clearly designed to navigate it: for example, the concept of opposites provides a framework for recognising the inevitability and generative potential of such tensions;[53] the concept of the symbol provides a means by which the complex multi-valence of unconscious psychic contents, including of contents that enfold seemingly opposed materialistic and spiritual positions, can be presented to consciousness;[54] and the concept of the transcendent function provides an account of the process by which this uniting of seemingly irreconcilable opposites in a symbol can take place.[55]

With specific reference to our present theme, the tension Jung experienced between his commitments to religion and science and his attempts to resolve it can be further illustrated by looking at the bearing of his work on disenchantment. Jung was aware not only of the disenchantment of the modern world but also of the fact that psychological work such as his own in an important sense contributed to that disenchantment. Most obviously, Jung's psychology, like psychoanalysis generally, contributes to disenchantment through its recognition of the process of projection and its advocacy of the withdrawal of projections. Thus, Jung notes that the 'hypothesis of invisible gods or daemons' is 'an anthropomorphic projection', and continues:

> since the development of consciousness requires the withdrawal of all the projections we can lay our hands on, it is not possible to maintain any non-psychological doctrine about the gods. If the historical process of world despiritualization continues as hitherto, then everything of a

52 R. Main, "Numinosity and Terror: Jung's Psychological Revision of Otto as an Aid to Engaging Religious Fundamentalism", in *The Idea of the Numinous: Contemporary Jungian and Psychoanalytic Perspectives*, ed. A. Casement and D. Tacey (Hove/New York: Routledge, 2006), 155–56; Main, *The Rupture of Time: Synchronicity and Jung's Critique of Modern Western Culture*, 100–14.

53 C.G. Jung, *Mysterium Coniunctionis: An Inquiry into the Separation and Synthesis of Psychic Opposites in Alchemy, The Collected Works*, 2nd ed., vol. 14 (London: Routledge & Kegan Paul, 1970). Originally published in 1955–1956.

54 C.G. Jung, "On Psychic Energy", in *The Collected Works*, 2nd ed., vol. 8 (London: Routledge & Kegan Paul, 1969). Originally published in 1928, paras. 88–113.

55 C.G. Jung, "The Transcendent Function", in *The Collected Works*, 2nd ed., vol. 8 (London: Routledge & Kegan Paul, 1969). Originally published in 1916.

> divine or daemonic character outside us must return to the psyche, to the inside of the unknown man, whence it apparently originated.[56]

Nevertheless, for Jung this withdrawal of projections was part of a process which could itself lead to a revivified sense of the sacred. For once one identifies religious phenomena as having an intrapsychic source and being expressive of facts about the structures and processes of the mind – for Jung, archetypes, individuation, and so on – then these religious phenomena and the discourses surrounding them become again of vital importance, albeit now psychologically.[57] So while Jung acknowledges the disenchantment attending the withdrawal of projections, he at the same time fosters a kind of re-enchantment by vigorously affirming the reality and importance – albeit psychic reality and importance – of religious phenomena.

Significantly, though, this retrieved sense of meaning is, at least in Jung's earlier work, intrapsychic only, leaving the external world meaningless and void of spirits and in this respect still very like Weber's disenchanted world.[58] Furthermore, it can be argued that, insofar as Jung aspired for his psychology to be seen as a form of naturalistic social science, this reinforces its disenchanting effect. For if Jung's own psychological model can provide a satisfactory naturalistic explanation of religious phenomena, this makes any further explanation of those phenomena in terms of the actual existence of God or other spiritual realities redundant.[59]

A sense of these difficulties may have been one of the factors informing Jung's development late in life of his concept of synchronicity: the idea that inner, psychic events such as thoughts or dreams can be connected with outer, physical events without there being any causal relationship between them.[60] The underlying idea of this concept is that archetypal patterns of meaning can manifest not only intrapsychically in dreams and fantasies (and thence in behaviours) but also, non-projectively, in causally independent external situations

56 Jung, "Psychology and Religion", para. 141.

57 Jung, "Psychology and Religion."

58 Main, "Ruptured Time and the Re-Enchantment of Modernity", 22.

59 R.A. Segal, "Jung as Psychologist of Religion and Jung as Philosopher of Religion", *Journal of Analytical Psychology* 55 (2010): 361–84; R. Main, "Jung's Uncertain Separation of Psychology from Philosophy: A Response to Segal", *Journal of Analytical Psychology* 55 (2010): 385–88; cf. Weber, "Science as a Vocation", 147.

60 C.G. Jung, "On Synchronicity", in *The Collected Works*, 2nd ed., vol. 8 (London: Routledge & Kegan Paul, 1969). Originally published in 1951; C.G. Jung, "Synchronicity: An Acausal Connecting Principle", in *The Collected Works*, 2nd ed., vol. 8 (London: Routledge & Kegan Paul, 1969). Originally published in 1952.

and events. In Jung's paradigmatic example, one of his patients dreamed of being given a jewel in the form of a scarab beetle. While she was recounting this to Jung, there was a tapping at the consulting room window. Jung opened the window and caught an insect as it flew in. It was a scarabaeid beetle, which he handed to the patient with the words, 'Here is your scarab.' In this case, Jung thought that the archetype of rebirth was constellated, since the scarab is a classic Egyptian symbol of rebirth and a process of rebirth is precisely what the patient was undergoing.[61] The significance of this for re-enchantment is that it allows for the possibility that the spiritual values associated with archetypes in Jung's model need not be only intrapsychic but, at least on occasion, can also, non-projectively, be found in the outer world,[62] thereby more fully restoring 'the sacred sense of wholeness and reconciliation between self and world' that was a large part of what was lost in the process of disenchantment.[63] However, even this has its limits, and a detailed examination of Jung's concept of synchronicity in relation to re-enchantment shows that, while synchronicity can go a long way in extending the credibility and scope of re-enchantment, it still falls short of bringing about a return to the kind of enchanted world that prevailed in the pre-modern period,[64] in particular because Jung has no wish to relinquish such defining achievements of modernity as science, differentiated consciousness, and a heightened sense of individuality.[65]

From Weber's perspective, then, Jung seems doubly culpable: first, because, rather than accept disenchantment as the fate of our time, he attempts to re-enchant the world; and second, because, even while advocating this re-enchantment, he attempts to combine religion and science and, as indicated by his struggle over the limits of re-enchantment, remains equivocal about his ultimate standpoint on religious matters. In other words, Weber would fault Jung both for his lingering religiousness and for his lack of clarity and decisiveness about his deepest convictions. Weber's attitude to these matters, though not universally shared among sociologists, is certainly widespread, partly no doubt as a result of Weber's far-reaching influence, but even more, perhaps,

61 Jung, "On Synchronicity", para. 982; Jung, "Synchronicity: An Acausal Connecting Principle", paras. 843, 845; see also Main, *The Rupture of Time: Synchronicity and Jung's Critique of Modern Western Culture*.

62 C.G. Jung, *Letters 2: 1951–1961*, ed. G. Adler (London: Routledge & Kegan Paul, 1976), 541; Main, "Ruptured Time and the Re-Enchantment of Modernity", 25–26.

63 L. Scaff, "Weber on the Cultural Situation of the Modern Age", in *The Cambridge Companion to Weber*, ed. S. Turner (Cambridge: Cambridge University Press, 2000), 105.

64 R. Main, "Synchronicity and the Limits of Re-Enchantment", *International Journal of Jungian Studies* 3 (2011): 144–58.

65 Ibid., 154–56.

because Weber simply articulated a sensibility common among intellectuals of his time.[66] In any case, we can see in this widespread perspective one probable reason for the perceived lack of fit between Jung's work and most classic and contemporary sociology.

4 Taylor and the Secular Age

I would now like to turn to an alternative, contemporary account of disenchantment and secularity in the light of which, it seems to me, Jung's work appears more favourably. This is the account of the Canadian philosopher and social thinker Charles Taylor, above all as articulated in his book *A Secular Age*.[67] Whilst not without its critics,[68] Taylor's account in this book has been widely and favourably discussed and hailed as a major intervention into debates about secularisation.[69] In the course of his book, Taylor provides an expansive historical and conceptual account of what it meant to live in an enchanted world (such as existed in Europe circa 1500). Briefly, for those living in such a world the self was more 'porous' than it is now so that boundaries readily faded between subjects and things, mind and world, inner and outer, physical and moral; meanings existed not only in the human mind but in non-human minds and in things; spirits, demons, and moral forces were acknowledged as real; and it was virtually impossible not to believe in God. In the disenchanted world of modernity, by contrast, the self is much more bounded or 'buffered'; the only locus of meanings is the human mind; the only minds in the cosmos are those of humans; and disbelief in God is not only a readily available option but is for many the only intellectually credible position.[70] Taylor would agree with Weber, whom he acknowledges as one of his sources,[71] that as a

66 See for example S. Freud, *The Future of an Illusion*, Standard Edition 21 (London: Hogarth Press, 1961). Originally published in 1927.

67 Taylor, *A Secular Age*.

68 For example N. Urbinati, "A Secular Age", *Archives of European Sociology* 49, no. 3 (2008): 462–66; J. Butler, "Disquieted History in A Secular Age", in *Varieties of Secularism in a Secular Age*, ed. M. Warner, J. VanAntwerpen, and C. Calhoun (Cambridge MA: Harvard University Press, 2010).

69 Fo example R. Belah, "A Secular Age: Secularism of a New Kind", 2007, http://blogs.ssrc.org/tif/2007/10/19/secularism-of-a-new-kind/; C. Calhoun, "A Secular Age", *Archives of European Sociology* 49, no. 3 (2008): 455–61; M. Warner, J. VanAntwerpen, and J. Calhoun, eds., *Varieties of Secularism in a Secular Age* (Cambridge MA: Harvard University Press, 2010).

70 Taylor, *A Secular Age*, 25–61.

71 Ibid., 156.

result of these transformations the dominant overall framework within which we now live in the modern West is a secular framework of immanence: 'the different structures we live in: scientific, social, technological, and so on', Taylor explains, 'constitute such a frame in that they are part of a "natural", or "this-worldly" order which can be understood in its own terms, without reference to the "supernatural" or "transcendent."'[72]

However, Taylor differs from Weber on a number of important points, and above all in his understanding of the defining condition of secularity. For Weber and most subsequent theorists of secularisation, secularity has essentially been about the privatization or decline of religion.[73] Taylor doesn't deny that in many contexts religion has indeed moved into the private sphere or has declined. But for him secularity is more importantly about religion ceasing to be the default position. Secularity in this sense involves, as he puts it, 'a move from a society where belief in God is unchallenged and, indeed, unproblematic, to one in which it is understood to be one option among others, and frequently not the easiest to embrace.'[74] On this understanding, the immanent frame does not exclude the possibility of religious options: 'this order', Taylor insists, 'of itself leaves the issue open whether, for purposes of ultimate explanation, or spiritual transformation, or final sense-making, we might have to invoke something transcendent';[75] the matter is 'not foreclosed by undeniable arguments.'[76]

Nevertheless, he argues, our experience of the immanent frame tends to be conditioned by certain largely unformulated background 'pictures' (in the Wittgensteinian sense) that hold our thinking captive in what Taylor refers to as 'spins.'[77] These spins can be either open or closed to the possibility of transcendence. But for many, especially in intellectual and academic contexts, the closed spin, that is, a conditioned view of the immanent frame that sees it as closed to the possibility of transcendence, seems 'natural, logically unavoidable', and it is this that 'underpins the power of the mainstream secularization theory, the view that modernity must bring secularity in its train.'[78] Taylor's concern is largely to explain why the 'spin' of closed immanence seems so compelling and to argue that it is nevertheless not inevitable.

72 Ibid., 594.

73 See for example Weber, "Science as a Vocation", 155; S. Bruce, *Fundamentalism*, 2nd ed. (Cambridge: Polity, 2008), 3.

74 Taylor, *A Secular Age*, 3.

75 Ibid., 594.

76 Ibid., 600.

77 Ibid., 549.

78 Ibid., 550.

Central to Taylor's argument about this is his critical view of what he calls 'subtraction stories', that is, accounts of the rise of secularity which assume that once the illusions of religion were removed, what was left was the secular reality that was always there: that in transitioning to the modern, disenchanted world, 'What we got rid of were the illusions, and it took courage to do this; what is left are the genuine deliverances of science, the truth about things, including ourselves, which was waiting all along to be discovered.'[79] Taylor notes that subtraction stories of this kind are 'deeply embedded in modern humanist consciousness.'[80] Not least, they are embedded in the widespread views of secularity as either the privatisation or the decline of religion, both of which views 'tend to think of secularity as simply the absence of religion, not something in itself.'[81]

For Taylor, secular reality, rather than being a natural truth left over when illusions have been subtracted, is itself something that has been historically constructed over many centuries; he describes the idea of a wholly immanent order as '[t]he great invention of the West.'[82] A large part of his almost 900-page book is devoted to tracking this historical development. At the heart of his account is the irony that the process of disenchantment, as of secularisation more generally, was driven by developments that took place within religion itself. Specifically, in extension of the case already famously made by Weber,[83] Taylor argues that the efforts of both Protestant and Catholic reform movements to purge their religion of folk beliefs and practices resulted in the rise of both a new morality governed by self-discipline and an understanding of the natural order as impersonal and as intervened in by God either infrequently or not at all.[84]

For Taylor the powerful attraction of the spin of closed immanence is partly epistemological and partly moral, both of which elements, having been 'naturalised', now operate largely below the level of conscious awareness. Epistemologically, the attraction of closed immanence is based on certain assumed priority relations: the self and its states are prior to external reality and the minds of others, facts are prior to values, the natural is prior to the transcendent. These priority relations tell us 'not only what is learned before what, but also what can be inferred on the basis of what' – with the inference to the

79 Ibid., 575.

80 Ibid., 572.

81 Warner, VanAntwerpen, and Calhoun, *Varieties of Secularism in a Secular Age*, 8.

82 Taylor, *A Secular Age*, 15.

83 Weber, *The Protestant Ethic and the Spirit of Capitalism*.

84 Taylor, *A Secular Age*; Warner, VanAntwerpen, and Calhoun, *Varieties of Secularism in a Secular Age*, 15.

transcendent 'at the extreme and most fragile end of a chain of inferences; [...] the most epistemically questionable.'[85] Taylor notes that these epistemological assumptions have been challenged by phenomenological thinkers such as Heidegger and Merleau-Ponty, who have argued, persuasively for Taylor, that assumptions of the self, of facts, and of the natural only make sense if external reality, values, and even, in the case of late Heidegger, the transcendent are already assumed.[86]

Morally, the attraction of the spin of closed immanence stems from the ethical charge that can attach to secularism, the sense of heroic manliness in facing up to the starkness of a universe without God.[87] This is the kind of morality found in Weber and in Freud. As we have already noted, it is part of Taylor's purpose in his extensive historical discussion to show how, ironically, these moral values underpinning the secular vision have been developed by and inherited from reform movements in both Protestant and Catholic Christianity. Not only are they constructions, they are constructions largely stemming from the very religions against which, in the modern period, they are now turned.

Taylor's arguing against the inevitability of the closed spin doesn't mean he believes there is stronger evidence for an open spin, that is, a view of the immanent frame that sees it as open to the possibility of transcendence. If he doesn't focus on the open spin, it is because this is less dominant in the modern West, particularly in intellectual and academic milieux.[88] He notes, rather, that the whole of modern western culture experiences 'cross pressures, between the draw of the narratives of closed immanence on the one side, and the sense of their inadequacy on the other, strengthened by encounter with existing milieux of religious practice, or just some intimations of the transcendent.'[89] For Taylor, the culture is 'suspended' between the extreme positions of transcendental religion and reductive materialism, even though 'Most people may be ensconced in a relatively untroubled way in one or other position, whether extreme or middle.'[90]

Taylor's understanding of the immanent frame, then, is that, 'properly understood, it allows of both readings [closed and open to the transcendent], without compelling us to either.'[91] In the immanent frame, both open and closed stances involve a leap of faith or, as Taylor attempts to put it more palatably,

85 Taylor, *A Secular Age*, 558.
86 Ibid., 559.
87 Ibid., 575.
88 Ibid., 549, 551.
89 Ibid., 595.
90 Ibid., 598.
91 Ibid., 550.

'a step beyond available reasons into the realm of anticipatory confidence.'[92] In his earlier book *Sources of the Self*[93] Taylor acknowledged that part of his aim was 'to bring the air back into the half-collapsed lungs of the spirit', since 'we tend in our culture to stifle spirit.'[94] To this extent his project was clearly one of re-enchantment or re-sacralisation. In *A Secular Age* he similarly strives to restore credibility to the perspective of spirit, though his aim is not to champion transcendent over immanent views but rather to present both kinds of view even-handedly and to understand both. Insofar as Taylor reveals his own preference, it is for the, as he sees it, difficult position of inhabiting an 'open space' – named 'Jamesian open space' after the thinker who he considers best exemplifies it[95] – wherein the 'cross pressures' of the different views are vividly experienced:

> Standing in the Jamesian open space requires that you [...] can actually feel some of the force of each opposing position. But so far apart are belief and unbelief, openness and closure here, that this feat is relatively rare. Most of us are [...] unable to see how the other view makes sense at all, or else struggling to make sense of it.[96]

Inhabiting this space is difficult because it requires not just grasping the different viewpoints theoretically or intellectually but actually experiencing the sensibility involved in holding them. For Taylor, what he calls 'spin', whether open or closed to transcendence, 'is a way of avoiding entering this space, a way of convincing oneself that one's reading is obvious, compelling, allowing of no cavil or demurral.'[97]

In his epilogue to a book of essays inspired by *A Secular Age* Taylor explained his aim in promoting deeper understanding of the cross-pressured character of modernity and his positive valuation of those who, like William James in his view, can inhabit the 'open space' in which the opposing positions most starkly clash:

---

92 Ibid., 551.

93 C. Taylor, *Sources of the Self: The Making of the Modern Identity* (Cambridge MA: Harvard University Press, 1989).

94 Ibid., 520.

95 Taylor, *A Secular Age*, 549, 551, 592; *Varieties of Religion Today: William James Revisited* (Cambridge MA: Harvard University Press, 2002), 59.

96 Taylor, *A Secular Age*, 549.

97 Ibid., 551.

> a big part of the intellectual agenda of the book is trying to explain the whole phenomenon of secularity and the nova of ever more varied positions in a way in which we could go on having a conversation about it that bridges these differences [among the varied positions].[98]

The kind of conversation envisaged is one that would result not just in intellectual understanding or in 'some kind of middle, compromised solution or synthesis' but in relating to the deep sensibilities and experiences of the other, that is, in 'friendship, which incorporates the kind of understanding where each can come to be moved by what moves the other.'[99] In the kind of inflammatory situations that can so easily arise in and between modern societies, 'If there are enough people here and there who have enough meeting and understanding of the others', writes Taylor, 'they can stand like firebreaks in a forest fire.'[100] Along similar lines, in a lecture at the New School of Social Research in New York in 2009 Taylor argued that his understanding of secularity aims to provide a framework for managing diversity which can ensure three things: maximum freedom for people (believers or unbelievers) to express their deepest convictions, equality of respect among the various positions held, and maximum input by all parties into social, cultural, and political debates.[101]

Taylor does not frame the continuing presence and viability of religious options in terms of either re-enchantment or de-secularisation, since his understanding of secularity already fully recognises and allows for the continued existence and flourishing of concern with the sacred. It is clear, however, that Taylor's work provides an interpretation of secularity that, unlike Weber's, accommodates in a positive way efforts at re-enchantment or re-sacralisation. It is clear, too, that Taylor's work, again unlike Weber's, not only allows for the possibility of acknowledging the claims of both science and religion, or of closed and open stances in relation to the immanent frame, but values especially highly the capacity to do so, for practical as much as for theoretical reasons.

98 C. Taylor, "Afterword: Apologia pro Libro Suo", in *Varieties of Secularism in a Secular Age*, ed. M. Warner, J. VanAntwerpen, and J. Calhoun (Cambridge MA: Harvard University Press, 2010), 320.

99 Ibid.

100 Ibid., 321.

101 C. Taylor, The future of the secular. Keynote address at "The religious/secular divide: The U.S. case" conference at the New School of Social Research, New York, 5–6 March, 2009.

5 Jung in a Secular Age

With these emphases Taylor's understanding of secularity provides a sociological framework in which Jung's work can fit much more comfortably than it can in the Weberian framework. Parallels can readily be found in Jung's work for most of the core claims informing Taylor's view. For Jung, as for Taylor, inhabiting a secular age does not require, or even necessarily tend towards, the foreclosure or devaluing of religious options.[102] Like Taylor, Jung interrogates, albeit more psychologically than philosophically, the assumptions that lead to the naturalisation of reductive materialism and other wholly immanent perspectives. No more than Taylor would he consider such perspectives to have disclosed a natural truth formerly hidden behind the illusions of religion.[103] Though articulated and narrated in different terms, Jung shares Taylor's view that the vision of reality as entirely immanent is itself a historical construction, developed over many centuries by processes in which religion played a significant role.[104] Like Taylor and like James, Jung promotes the religious or spiritual stance, not to the exclusion or depreciation of the scientific or material stance but in order to establish or restore a broad parity between them for the sake of widening overall sympathies. For, above all, Jung, like Taylor, advocates inhabiting a space where the claims of transcendence and immanence, of spirit and matter, can be equally recognised and equally vividly experienced.[105]

In illustrating this last and perhaps most important point we can note also the practical dimension of Jung's concern. 'In practical psychotherapy', writes Jung, 'we strive to fit people for life, and we are not free to set up theories which do not concern our patients and may even injure them.'[106] He continues:

> Here we come to a question that is sometimes a matter of life and death – the question whether we base our explanations on 'physis' or spirit. We must never forget that everything spiritual is illusion from the naturalistic standpoint, and that often the spirit has to deny and overcome an insistent physical fact in order to exist at all. If I recognize only naturalistic values, and explain everything in physical terms, I shall depreciate,

102 Jung, "Psychology and Religion."

103 Ibid., paras. 141–42.

104 C.G. Jung, "Basic Postulates of Analytical Psychology", in *The Collected Works*, 2nd ed., vol. 8 (London: Routledge & Kegan Paul, 1969). Originally published in 1931, para. 649; "Return to the Simple Life", in *The Collected Works*, 2nd ed., vol. 18 (London: Routledge & Kegan Paul, 1977). Originally published in 1941, para. 1345.

105 Jung, "Basic Postulates of Analytical Psychology", para. 678.

106 Ibid.

> hinder, or even destroy the spiritual development of my patients. And if I hold exclusively to a spiritual interpretation, then I shall misunderstand and do violence to the natural man in his right to exist as a physical being.[107]

Recognising these two standpoints, Jung considers that the modern psychologist needs to occupy 'neither the one position nor the other' but to stand 'between the two, dangerously committed to "this as well as that."'[108] He acknowledges the 'very difficult problem' that this presents, for 'How should anything but a formless and aimless uncertainty result from giving equal value to two contradictory hypotheses?'[109] His solution is to appeal to psychic reality as 'our only immediate experience.'[110] From this perspective, physical and spiritual realities can be equally affirmed:

> it seems to us that certain psychic contents or images are derived from a 'material' environment to which our bodies belong, while others, which are in no way less real, seem to come from a 'spiritual' source which appears to be very different from the physical environment. Whether I picture to myself the car I wish to buy or try to imagine the state in which the soul of my dead father now is – whether it is an external fact or a thought that concerns me – both happenings are psychic reality. The only difference is that one psychic happening refers to the physical world, and the other to the spiritual world.[111]

Although Jung's epistemology based on the primacy of psychic reality is not one I think Taylor would share, it is deployed by Jung for a purpose very similar to Taylor's: enabling one to stand in a space equally exposed to both the material and the spiritual, both the immanent and the transcendent.

Jung's practical concern in formulating the above view is focused at the level of the individual psychotherapeutic relationship. But the principles involved can be drawn on to inform psychosocial and other psychologically inflected sociological inquiries. I shall conclude by very briefly outlining how Jung's double perspective might be helpful in one area of inquiry where the tension

---

107 Ibid.

108 Ibid., para. 679.

109 Ibid.

110 Ibid., para. 680.

111 Ibid., 681.

between the sacred and the secular is particularly acute: the study of religious fundamentalism.

The kind of religiousness that is often dubbed 'fundamentalist' typically arises as a reaction against the secularising forces of modernity.[112] It is to be expected, then, that fundamentalists will be hostile to attempts to understand or engage them from the perspective of disciplines based on purely naturalistic, secular assumptions.[113] Conversely, scholars working within purely secular frameworks, as in the social sciences, are likely either to be prejudiced against the supernatural and traditionalist assumptions of religious fundamentalists[114] or at least to find themselves 'so distant from the assumptions and worldviews of fundamentalists that they offer explanations for a phenomenon they have not adequately or fairly described.'[115] From the side of the fundamentalists there is likely to be a disinclination to co-operate with secular scholars,[116] and from the side of the secular scholars there is likely to be a lack of empathy for fundamentalists and even a tendency to stereotype and pathologise them.[117] Clearly this is a situation that could easily lead to distortions in understanding and a lack of conversation, with all that might follow from that at a practical – and ultimately policy – level in terms of limiting the respect and freedom of expression accorded to the other.

For the purpose of trying to advance scholarly engagement with and understanding of fundamentalism, there are at least three ways in which the kind of double perspective found in Jung might be helpful here. First, by dint of genuinely crediting the religious point of view, such a perspective could access a more intimate sense of the motivating power on fundamentalists of their consideration of and commitment to the sacred – a motive surprisingly neglected in sociological and other social scientific research in this area.[118] The insights generated by this empathic access would complement not replace those

112 Bruce, *Fundamentalism*, 15–39.

113 R. Hood, P. Hill, and W. Williamson, *The Psychology of Religious Fundamentalism* (New York: The Guilford Press, 2005), 184.

114 Ibid., 4.

115 Ibid., v.

116 V. Hoffman, "Muslim Fundamentalists: Psychosocial Profiles", in *Fundamentalisms Comprehended*, ed. M. Marty and R. Appleby (Chicago/ London: The University of Chicago Press, 1995), 199.

117 Hood, Hill, and Williamson, *The Psychology of Religious Fundamentalism*, 194–204; Bruce, *Fundamentalism*, 113–22.

118 Main, "Numinosity and Terror", 154; Hood, Hill, and Williamson, *The Psychology of Religious Fundamentalism*, 183–84.

emerging from normally applied social scientific disciplines, which, because the secular point of view is equally respected, would remain fully available.

Second, Jung's double perspective exemplifies the possibility of tolerating the profound ontological ambivalence that, in Taylor's analysis, permeates modern culture as a whole. Wherever and to whatever extent this toleration is realised, it could help to forestall the simplifying but polarising move of exclusively valuing either a sacred standpoint (in the case of fundamentalists) or a secular standpoint (in the case of social scientific scholars).

Third, Jung's double perspective, insofar as it is also part of a depth psychological theory, can articulate important unconscious aspects of the dynamic between fundamentalists and those studying or engaging with them from secular perspectives. It might help to illuminate, for instance, how consciously religious identities can harbour unconscious secular inclinations, and vice versa, and how this unconsciousness, if left unaddressed, might result in fundamentalists and secularists projecting their disavowed secular or religious inclinations onto each other, thereby exacerbating the polarisation between them.

Jungian psychology has many distinctive features beyond those touched on in this paper. If Jung's crediting and being informed by religious perspectives ceases to be a ground for disregarding his theory when seeking depth psychological input into sociological inquiries, and, as I have suggested, may even be seen as especially helpful for some kinds of inquiry, then the way could open to exploring what insights and suggestions these other distinctive features may additionally be able to provide.

References

Belah, R. "A Secular Age: Secularism of a New Kind", 2007. http://blogs.ssrc.org/tif/2007/10/19/secularism-of-a-new-kind/.

Bruce, S. *Fundamentalism*. 2nd ed. Cambridge: Polity, 2008.

Butler, J. "Disquieted History in A Secular Age." In *Varieties of Secularism in a Secular Age*, edited by M. Warner, J. VanAntwerpen, and C. Calhoun. Cambridge MA: Harvard University Press, 2010.

Calhoun, C. "A Secular Age." *Archives of European Sociology* 49, no. 3 (2008): 455–61.

Durkheim, E. *The Elementary Forms of Religious Life*. Translated by J. Swain. London: Allen and Unwin, 1976. Originally published in 1912.

Freud, S. *The Future of an Illusion*. Standard Edition 21. London: Hogarth Press, 1961. Originally published in 1927.

Gray, R. *Archetypal Explorations: An Integrative Approach to Human Behavior*. Hove/New York: Routledge, 1996.

Hoffman, V. "Muslim Fundamentalists: Psychosocial Profiles." In *Fundamentalisms Comprehended*, edited by M. Marty and R. Appleby. Chicago/London: The University of Chicago Press, 1995.

Homans, P. *Jung in Context: Modernity and the Making of a Psychology*. Chicago: The University of Chicago Press, 1979.

Hood, R., P. Hill, and W. Williamson. *The Psychology of Religious Fundamentalism*. New York: The Guilford Press, 2005.

Jary, D., and J. Jary. *Collins Dictionary of Sociology*. 2nd ed. Glasgow: Harper Collins, 1995.

Jung, C.G. "Answer to Job." In *The Collected Works*, 2nd ed. Vol. 11. London: Routledge & Kegan Paul, 1969a. Originally published in 1952.

Jung, C.G. "Basic Postulates of Analytical Psychology." In *The Collected Works*, 2nd ed. Vol. 8. London: Routledge & Kegan Paul, 1969b. Originally published in 1931.

Jung, C.G. *Letters 2: 1951–1961*. Edited by G. Adler. London: Routledge & Kegan Paul, 1976.

Jung, C.G. *Mysterium Coniunctionis: An Inquiry into the Separation and Synthesis of Psychic Opposites in Alchemy, The Collected Works*, 2nd ed. Vol. 14. London: Routledge & Kegan Paul, 1970a. Originally published in 1955–1956.

Jung, C.G. "On Psychic Energy." In *The Collected Works*, 2nd ed. Vol. 8. London: Routledge & Kegan Paul, 1969c. Originally published in 1928.

Jung, C.G. "On Synchronicity." In *The Collected Works*, 2nd ed. Vol. 8. London: Routledge & Kegan Paul, 1969d. Originally published in 1951.

Jung, C.G. "On the Nature of the Psyche." In *The Collected Works*, 2nd ed. Vol. 8. London: Routledge & Kegan Paul, 1969e. Originally published in 1947–1954.

Jung, C.G. "Psychology and Religion." In *The Collected Works*, 2nd ed. Vol. 11. London: Routledge & Kegan Paul, 1969f. Originally published in 1938–1940.

Jung, C.G. "Return to the Simple Life." In *The Collected Works*, 2nd ed. Vol. 18. London: Routledge & Kegan Paul, 1977. Originally published in 1941.

Jung, C.G. "Synchronicity: An Acausal Connecting Principle." In *The Collected Works*, 2nd ed. Vol. 8. London: Routledge & Kegan Paul, 1969g. Originally published in 1952.

Jung, C.G. "The Soul and Death." In *The Collected Works*, 2nd ed. Vol. 8. London: Routledge & Kegan Paul, 1969h. Originally published in 1934.

Jung, C.G. "The Transcendent Function." In *The Collected Works*, 2nd ed. Vol. 8. London: Routledge & Kegan Paul, 1969i. Originally published in 1916.

Jung, C.G. "The Undiscovered Self (Present and Future)." In *The Collected Works*, 2nd ed. Vol. 10. London: Routledge & Kegan Paul, 1970b. Originally published in 1957.

Kim, S.H. "Max Weber." In *The Stanford Encyclopedia of Philosophy*, edited by E.N. Zalta, Fall 2008. Metaphysics Research Lab, Stanford University, 2008. https://plato.stanford.edu/archives/fall2012/entries/weber/.

Lammers, A.C., and A. Cunningham, eds. *The Jung-White Letters*. Hove: Routledge, 2007.

Macey, D. *The Penguin Dictionary of Critical Theory*. London: Penguin Books, 2000.

Main, R. "Jung's Uncertain Separation of Psychology from Philosophy: A Response to Segal." *Journal of Analytical Psychology* 55 (2010): 385–88.

Main, R. "Numinosity and Terror: Jung's Psychological Revision of Otto as an Aid to Engaging Religious Fundamentalism." In *The Idea of the Numinous: Contemporary Jungian and Psychoanalytic Perspectives*, edited by A. Casement and D. Tacey. Hove/New York: Routledge, 2006a.

Main, R. "Religion." In *The Handbook of Jungian Psychology: Theory, Practice and Applications*, edited by R. Papadopoulos. Hove/Philadelphia: Brunner-Routledge, 2006b.

Main, R. "Ruptured Time and the Re-Enchantment of Modernity." In *Who Owns Jung?*, edited by A. Casement. London: Karnac, 2007.

Main, R. "Synchronicity and the Limits of Re-Enchantment." *International Journal of Jungian Studies* 3 (2011): 144–58.

Main, R.. *The Rupture of Time: Synchronicity and Jung's Critique of Modern Western Culture*. Hove/New York: Brunner-Routledge, 2004.

Main, R. "The Social Significance of Synchronicity." *Psychoanalysis, Culture & Society* 11 (2006c): 36–53.

McGuire, W., and R.F.C. Hull, eds. *C.G. Jung Speaking: Interviews and Encounters*. London: Thames and Hudson, 1978.

Meier, C.A., ed. *Atom and Archetype: The Pauli/Jung Letters 1932–1958*. London: Routledge, 2001.

Progoff, I. *Jung's Psychology and Its Social Meaning*. New York: Dialogue House, 1953.

Scaff, L. "Weber on the Cultural Situation of the Modern Age." In *The Cambridge Companion to Weber*, edited by S. Turner. Cambridge: Cambridge University Press, 2000.

Scott, J., and G. Marshall, eds. *A Dictionary of Sociology*. 3rd ed. Oxford: Oxford University Press, 2009.

Segal, R.A. "Jung as Psychologist of Religion and Jung as Philosopher of Religion." *Journal of Analytical Psychology* 55 (2010): 361–84.

Shamdasani, S. *Jung and the Making of Modern Psychology: The Dream of a Science*. Cambridge: Cambridge University Press, 2003.

Staude, J.R. "From Depth Psychology to Depth Sociology: Freud, Jung, and Lévi-Strauss'." *Theory and Society* 3, no. 3 (1976): 303–38.

Taylor, C. *A Secular Age*. Cambridge MA: Harvard University Press, 2007.

Taylor, C. "Afterword: Apologia pro Libro Suo." In *Varieties of Secularism in a Secular Age*, edited by M. Warner, J. VanAntwerpen, and J. Calhoun. Cambridge MA: Harvard University Press, 2010.

Taylor, C. *Sources of the Self: The Making of the Modern Identity*. Cambridge MA: Harvard University Press, 1989.

Taylor, C. The future of the secular. Keynote address at "The religious/secular divide: The U.S. case" conference at the New School of Social Research, New York, 5–6 March, 2009.

Taylor, C. *Varieties of Religion Today: William James Revisited*. Cambridge MA: Harvard University Press, 2002.

Urbinati, N. "A Secular Age." *Archives of European Sociology* 49, no. 3 (2008): 462–66.

Warner, M., J. VanAntwerpen, and J. Calhoun, eds. *Varieties of Secularism in a Secular Age*. Cambridge MA: Harvard University Press, 2010.

Weber, M. "Science as a Vocation." In *From Max Weber: Essays in Sociology*, edited and translated by H. Gerth and C. Wright Mills. New York: Oxford University Press, 1946. Originally published in 1918.

Weber, M. *The Protestant Ethic and the Spirit of Capitalism*. Translated by T. Parsons. London/New York: Routledge, 2001. Originally published in 1904.

CHAPTER 10

Non-fixed Multiple Perspectives in the Japanese Psyche: Traditional Japanese Art, Dream and Myth

Megumi Yama

Abstract

I would like to understand Jung's life as an attempt to be a bridge between the West and the East. Since his early childhood, he seems to have been attracted by and searching for something that compensate for what the West had long devaluated and repressed. For a long time, I have been interested in ego consciousness and the difference between how a subject is established in Japanese versus the Western psyche. In this study, I would like to present some characteristic of the Japanese psyche, firstly through exploring the characteristics of the traditional Japanese arts in a broader sense and secondly, introducing my previous study of a reading of the oldest Japanese myth to explore the way that ego emerges in the Japanese psyche. Later, what the west and Japan can mutually learn from each other is discussed.

Keywords

West and East – Western ego – Japanese psyche – Japanese myth – traditional Japanese art – multiple perspective – garden – picture-scroll – residential building – dream

1 Jung as a Bridge between the West and the East[1]

Since his early childhood, Jung seems to have been attracted by and searching for things that compensate for what the West had long devaluated and repressed. He happened to have his encounter with "the East" while he was confronting images from the unconscious during a period of inner uncertainty and disorientation after the parting ways with Freud.

1 A part of this paper was originally presented at the Annual Conference of the International Association for the Study of Dreams in Virginia Beach, USA in June 2013. It has been largely revised.

 | DOI:10.1163/9789004336636_012

Being engaged in letting the unconscious come through to express itself, Jung drew many mandalas, which he came to find as an expression of "the Self" afterwards. Jung mentions in his *Memories, Dreams, Reflections,*[2] "During those years, between 1918 and 1920, I began to understand that the goal of psychic development is the self. There is no linear evolution. There is only a circumambulation of the self." There is a well-known anecdote that coincidentally or synchronically Jung happened to have a confirmation of his ideas about the mandala and the circumambulation of the center when he received the manuscript of Taoist-alchemical treatise entitled *The Secret of the Golden Flower* and a request for a commentary on it from Richard Wilhelm. In the same way that Jung encountered "the East" within as he was digging into the depths of his own psyche, I would like to argue that Jung himself is a bridge between the West and the East in a more literal sense.

With current rapid globalization, however, it is sometimes said that it may be doubtful that the concepts of "the West" and "the East" are still alive as they were in the past. It is true that we share a lot of news and information simultaneously on the Internet throughout a large part of the world, if not all. But I would like to mention however borderless it seems to be at a superficial level, if we go down to the roots of this, it might be considered that there is a fundamental difference in the structure of the psyche in each culture because originally they are established on a basis of their own characteristic psychological histories and backgrounds that should not be ignored.

In fact, as the idea of modern Western ego has been introduced into Japanese culture rapidly especially since the beginning of the Meiji-era (1868–1912), things are somewhat complicated in the Japanese psyche. Many modern Japanese are disconnected horizontally in a sense. When they think intellectually and consciously, they think in the Western style, but when they live their everyday lives, they unconsciously live a traditional Japanese way of life. They are living a dual process and what is more they are unconscious of this.

Considering the fact that Jung studied alchemy, myth, old rituals and so on in order to explore the unconscious, which were full of primitive or premodern contents as if he was invited to do so by the voice from within, I would like to argue that through studying about the old deep layer of the Japanese psyche, which is not much affected by Western modern ego consciousness, we might be able to get a hint on how we could deal with the unconscious.

Reflecting on my personal history of living in both the West and Japan, I usually experience the difference between these cultures not only on an intellectual

2 C.G. Jung, *Memories, Dreams, Reflections* (London: Harper Perennial, 1995). Originally published in 1961, 222.

level but also at a physical level. It is not only changing my languages from Japanese to English but also I have to change the way I see things and how I grasp the world, as a different structure of a language is based on different thinking patterns, too. Strictly speaking, simple intentionally changing something apparent to adjust to the country where I am is not sufficient at all and it feels that I have to wait until "(I) fundamentally change from the bottom of myself from within." Therefore whenever I go back and forth between the Western countries – UK, US, Australia and other European countries – and Japan I usually suffer from not only jet lag, but also something that has something to do with my existence.

In addition, although psychotherapy was developed in western countries, most of the clients with whom I have sessions in Japan were born and live in Japan. Reflecting on my personal stance of having two different cultural selves; one is the westernized and the other is Japanese, and my experience in practicing psychotherapy for more than 30 years, I would like to argue that we have a lot to learn mutually from either Western/Eastern "wisdom", as we see in alchemy, in which precious materials are produced when opposites meet. Of course we need to be careful not to fall into the trap "only to become a pitiable imitator" as Jung[3] warned in the Introduction to *The Secret of the Golden Flower*.

For a long time, I have been interested in ego consciousness and the difference between how a subject is established in Japanese versus the Western psyche. In this study, I would like to present some characteristics of the Japanese psyche, firstly through exploring the characteristics of the traditional Japanese arts in a broader sense and secondly, introducing my previous study[4] of a reading of the oldest Japanese myth to explore the way that ego emerges in the Japanese psyche. Later, what the west and Japan can mutually learn from each other is discussed.

2 The Ego in the Western and the Japanese Psyche

Before going any further, I would like to present Jung's definition of the ego in *Aion*, which reads as follows,

3 C.G. Jung, *Ougon no Hana no Himitsu*, trans. Y. Yuasa and A. Sadakata (Kyoto: Jinbun-shoin, 1990). Originally published as *Das Geheimnis der goldenen Blüte, ein chinesisch Lebensbuch* (1929), 33.

4 M. Yama, "Ego Consciousness in the Japanese Psyche: Culture, Myth and Disaster," *Journal of Analytical Psychology* 58 (2013): 52–72.

> We understand the ego as the complex factor to which all conscious contents are related. It forms, as it were, the centre of the field of consciousness; and, in so far as this comprises the empirical personality, the ego is the subject of all personal acts of consciousness. The relation of a psychic content to the ego forms the criterion of its consciousness, for no content can be conscious unless it is represented to a subject.[5]

In Western Jungian thoughts, as Edward F. Edinger,[6] mentions briefly, "The ego is the center of the conscious personality...the ego is the seat of *subjective* identity", but as the first Japanese Jungian analyst Prof. Hayao Kawai[7] points out, it does not necessarily apply to the Japanese psyche. The Japanese ego seems to be buried in the unconscious, which has no particular center and is full of narratives with many perspectives, and which doesn't accord to linear thinking. And as it is usually difficult to articulate what is taking place in the unconscious, it may explain why the Japanese seem to be so ambiguous to non-Japanese. It overlaps with the fact that Japanese individuals are buried in a homogeneous collective and they try to hide themselves in the whole for fear that they might be conspicuous. As such a tendency has been acquired over a long time, they are totally unconscious about it.

Hayao Kawai[8] proposed an illuminating model to show the difference between the structures of the Japanese and Western psyche. According to Kawai, in the Japanese psyche, the boundary between consciousness and unconsciousness is much vaguer than in the Westerner's (Fig. 10.1). He adds that in the Japanese psyche, "as the structure of the consciousness is formed with the Self as the center, which is in the unconscious, it is even doubtful whether it really has the center."

To put it very simply, Westerners are much used to being conscious and know much more about the consciousness than the Japanese, and on the other hand, the Japanese prefer to stay in the unconscious, although they are even unconscious of it. Therefore descending to the old and deep layer of traditional Japanese culture, we might find a clue on how we treat what is in the unconscious.

5 C.G. Jung, *Aion* (Princeton: Princeton University Press, 1959). Originally published in 1951, 1.

6 E.F. Edinger, *Ego and Archetype* (New York: Penguin Books, 1972), 3.

7 H. Kawai, *Boseishakai Nihon no Byori* (*Pathology of Japan as a Society of Maternity*) (Tokyo: Chuokoron-sha, 1976).

8 Ibid.

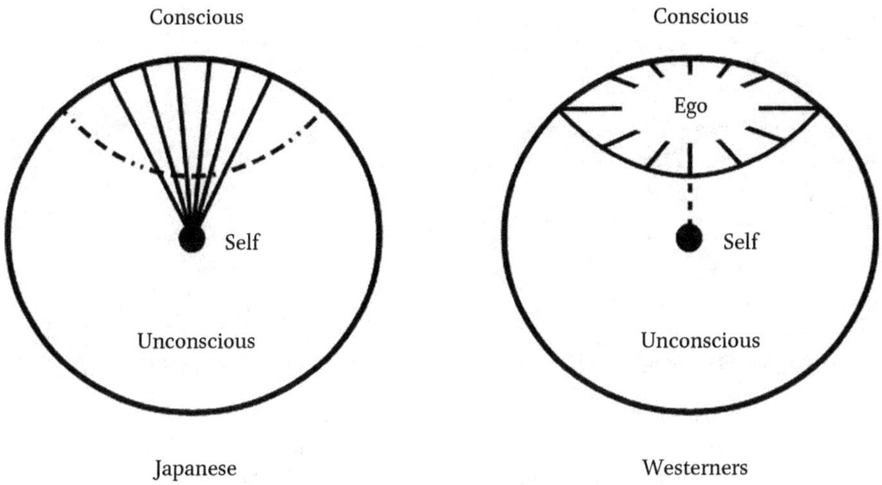

FIGURE 10.1 *Two models of Japanese consciousness and Westerner's consciousness.* Artist: [Megumi Yama]. Retrieved from: H. Kawai, *Boseishakai Nihon no Byori* (*Pathology of Japan as a Society of Maternity*), Tokyo: Chuokoron-sha, 1976. Used with permission from the copyright holder.
Source: Ibid., 176. Hayao Kawai proposed this illuminating model to show the difference between the structures of the Japanese and Western psyche.

3 What I See in Traditional Japanese Arts

Generally, it is considered that the creator's view of the world is reflected in their work. My first attempt is to explore the Japanese psyche in traditional Japanese art through attention to how creators see things and how they are experiencing the world.

3.1 *Rakuchu Rakugai-zu* (*Views in and around the City of Kyoto*)

I would like to give some examples of traditional Japanese-style art. The first one is *Rakuchu Rakugai-zu*, genre paintings from the 16th through 19th centuries (Fig. 10.2). These paintings depicted the town area (inner Kyoto) and suburbs (outer Kyoto) from an overhead view on a folding screen, which consist of several panels. There are several versions, such as the Funaki-version and the Uesugi-version, which have been originally handed down within the Funaki family and the Uesugi family. They were very popular in those days and about hundred of them remain today. Above all, the Uesugi-version is designated as a national treasure.

FIGURE 10.2 *Rakuchu-Rakugai-zu* (*left wing*) *Uesugi version.*
Copyright holder: Yonezawa City Uesugi Museum. Retrieved from: https://commons.wikimedia.org/wiki/File:%E6%B4%9B%E4%B8%AD%E6%B4%9B%E5%A4%96%E5%9B%B3%E5%8F%B3.jpg. Illustration is in the public domain. No permission needed.

As the focus of the painting zooms onto smaller objects (Fig. 10.3), such as the buildings and the people, we come to realize that everyday scenes of life in the city of Kyoto are clearly illustrated. The activities of people from all social classes in various areas, such as in a store or on the street, are depicted in vivid detail. It is a remarkable fact that there may be as many as two thousand five hundred individuals in this painting.

The Japanese art historian Takashina[9] mentions, "The painter does not stay at one point in the air but appears to be looking down while moving freely over Kyoto.... Although the scale is small, [people and scenes in the town] are painted in minute detail, as if they were seen up close and portrayed from an ordinary perspective." The Japanese art critic Teiji Yoshimura[10] also notes the similar point that it is as if the painter is changing their perspectives one after another as necessary, as they fly at a very low altitude. In this way, the painter seems to have been able to paint buildings as they like and depict people as they are leading their lively life in Kyoto. These paintings do not have one specific center but multiple perspectives, which is one of the noticeable characteristics of Japanese-style painting in general.

9 S. Takashina, "The Japanese Sense of Beauty," in *Nihon bijutsu o miru me : higashi to nishi no deai* (*Viewing Japanese Art: Encounters between the East and West*) (Tokyo: Iwanami Shoten, 2011). Originally published in 1983, 11, 12.

10 T. Yoshimura, *Nihonbi no tokushitsu* (*The Essence of Japanese Aesthetics*) (Tokyo: Kashima-shuppankai, 1967).

FIGURE 10.3 *Rakuchu-Rakugai-zu* (*left wing*) *Zooming-up*. Uesugi version. Copyright holder: Yonezawa City Uesugi Museum. Retrieved from Yonezawa City Uesugi Museum. Used with permission.

To the references above as to the movement of perspectives, the Japanese scholar of comparative culture Nobukazu Niigata[11] adds that traditional Japanese-style painters never paint shadows because if they do the perspective of the painter would be fixed at one specific position. Then why do they refuse to have a fixed perspective? To answer to this question, citing the example of Japanese landscape paintings, Niigata[12] comments, "Appreciating landscape paintings does not mean only to look at the painting from the outside, but to enter into it and play there." Zooming in closer to the painting, it felt even as if we are involved in the scene and walking around the city looking at these people depicted in the painting, where we can experience the transition of the time.

In fact, as the French cultural geographer Augustin Berque[13] (1990) mentions, this characteristic applies to Japanese arts in a broader sense, such as gardens, traditional buildings, etc. The theory behind this is also that the Japanese ego develops differently from the way it does in the West, although Japanese individuals have certainly been affected by modern Western ego.

3.2 *The Katsura Imperial Villa*

As the second example, I would like to present some typical western gardens in Europe and compare them with one from Japan, all of which were completed in the 17th century. Fig. 10.4a is the Garden in the Palace of Versailles and Fig. 10.4b is the Palace and the Garden of Schönbrunn in Vienna. Both of these gardens are designed in such a way that the entire panorama is visible from a single fixed point outside of the garden.

The history of the garden in Japan is so long that it is even described in the *Kojiki* (lit. "*Records of Ancient Matters*") and *Nihon-shoki* (lit."*The Chronicle of Japan*") in the 8th century. Originally, Japanese gardens developed under the influence of Chinese gardens, but gradually, by the Edo era (1603–1868), when Japan was adopting a policy of national isolation, except China and Holland under extremely restricted conditions, Japanese gardens begin to cultivate their own appearance.

I would like to present Katsura Imperial Villa in Kyoto (Fig. 10.5a-b), which is regarded as one of the most important large-scale cultural treasures in Japan. The garden in the villa is said to be the masterpiece of Japanese gardening,

11 N. Niigata, *Nihonjin no "Watashi" o motomete* (*Seeking the Japanese "Me"*) (Tokyo: Shinyo-sha, 2007).

12 Ibid.

13 A. Berque, *Nihon No Fukei Seiou No Keikan: Soshite Zoukei No Jidai* (*Japanese Scenery and the Western Vista: And the Age of Landscaping*), trans. K. Shinoda (Tokyo: Kodan-sha, 1990).

FIGURE 10.4A Palace of Versailles.
Photographer: Luca Volpi (Goldmund100). Retrieved from https://upload.wikimedia.org/wikipedia/commons/a/a4/Park_of_Versailles_main_view.jpg. Used with permission of the author.

FIGURE 10.4B *The palace and gardens of Schönbrunn in Vienna.*
Photographer: Gryffindor. Retrieved from: https://commons.wikimedia.org/wiki/File%3ASchloss_Schoenbrunn_August_2006_406.jpg Illustration is in the public domain. No permission needed.

FIGURE 10.5A *The Katsura imperial Villa.* Photographer: Megumi Yama (author). Retrieved from Megumi Yama. Used with permission from the copyright holder.

FIGURE 10.5B *The Katsura imperial Villa.* Photographer: Megumi Yama (author). Retrieved from Megumi Yama. Used with permission from the copyright holder.

which was specifically designed so that the viewers can enjoy constantly changing views as they make their way through the various distinct areas of the garden. Visitors are told to follow the red line on the map (Fig. 10.6). The summary of the Garden reads as follows (partially cited from the official brochure);

> ...In the middle of the villa's grounds, there is a lake with an intricate shoreline and there are five artificial islets of various sizes over which there are bridges made of earth, wood and stone, as well as a boat mooring located near the Shoin [author's note: a style of traditional Japanese residential architecture] and teahouse. There is also a garden, with lanterns and

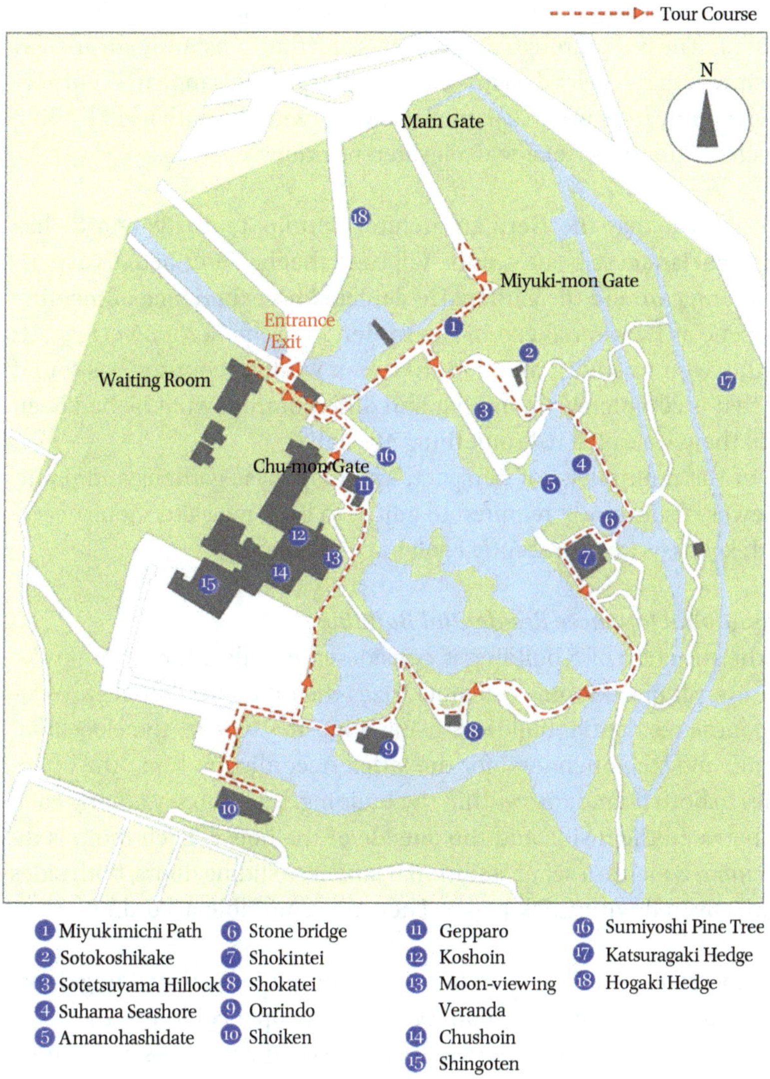

FIGURE 10.6 *Map of the Katsura imperial Villa.*
Designer: The Imperial Household Agency. Retrieved from: http://sankan.kunaicho.go.jp/english/guide/institution_katsura.html. Illustration is in the public domain. No permission needed.

> wash basins in appropriate locations, with pathways laid out in a circuit for strolling.... The walk through the garden is one that constantly surprise[s] the visitor with its clever design – at times, the pond disappear[s] entirely from view, only to return in a panoramic vista, with the path itself leading the visitor from the waterside to elevated positions. ...

It is well known that the German architect Bruno Taut (1880–1938) has found traditional Japanese beauty in the Villa and that he described his experience of wandering around the garden. He depicted his experience of meeting every new scene as he went ahead in the garden in his book *Nippon* (1933). It seems that he, who was born and had lived in a western country, has found something that is completely unfamiliar and different from what he had been used to until then. He called it, "Something eternal."[14]

Because of the multiplicity of perspectives in Japanese gardens and paintings, the viewer is constantly required to adjust to each new situation successively, which keeps us in a constantly evolving movement.

3.3 *Traditional Japanese Residential Buildings*

Generally, the structure of a building is considered to reflect the mentality of its own culture. Shuji Takashina[15] characterizes the difference between Western and Japanese residential buildings using opposites words; "the closeness" for the former and "the openness" for the latter. According to him, "the openness" applies to both boundaries within the building, that is to say among each room, and between the inside and the outside of the house. Each room is divided by *fusuma*, which is a set of traditional Japanese sliding doors, both sides of which are covered with thick paper. They are removable according to the uses of the room.

When many relatives and acquaintances gather in the house, sliding doors were removed to make one large room so that all people could use the same room. Instead of beds, they use *futons,* which consist of a mattress and a quilt. When not used, they are folded up and put away in a closet. They have so few pieces of furniture in each room that all the room can be used for many purposes.

One more important characteristic of the traditional Japanese-style house is that a drawing room is designed as to be able to enjoy the scenery of the

---

14 B. Taut, "Eiennarumono (Something Eternal)," in *Nihonbi no Saihakken* (*A Rediscovery of Japanese Aesthetics*) (Tokyo: Iwanami Shoten, 1981). Originally published in 1939.

15 S. Takashina, *Seiyo no Me Nihon no Me* (*Western Eyes / Japanese Eyes*) (Tokyo: Seido-sha, 2001).

garden if one opens all *amado*, (sliding storm shutters) and *shoji*, (sliding doors made of a wooden latticework over which Japanese paper is pasted). It is as if the drawing room and garden are integrated into one borderless space.

Although most Japanese houses today, especially in urban areas, are quite westernized, native Japanese mentality is apparent in the traditional Japanese-style house. The vagueness of the boundaries between rooms and between the inside and outside of the house suggests that people using the space can go from one room to the other and from inside to outside without being conscious of crossing a border.

3.4 *Emaki-mono (Picture Scroll)*

I would like to present *emaki-mono* (lit.; picture scroll), usually simply called *emaki*, as another good example of traditional Japanese art. It is a horizontal, illustrated narrative form, which first emerged in the Heian era (794–1185). It is viewed from right to left, in the same direction as the Japanese language is written, by unscrolling the scroll little by little and exposing an arm's-length of the scroll at a time.

In the catalogue of the special exhibition, *Emaki Unrolled: Masterworks of Illustrated Narrative Handscrolls* held at the Kyoto National Museum in 2006, it reads, "Forming a unique mode of expression in which a tale unfolds on a long, horizontal sheet of paper, *emaki* parallel modern movies and animation in their spatial and temporal presentation of narrative." It is likely that the origin of the popularity in (animated) cartoons in Japan today can date back to those picture scrolls in the Heian era. We can experience the passage of time and the movement of perspectives as we look at and read them.

3.5 *The Artists' Point of View before and after the Advent of Linear Perspective*

Before going any further, I would like to refer to the difference of an artist's perspective between before and after the development of the technique of linear perspective.

Robert, D. Romanyshyn[16] presents two illustrations of the city of Florence; one is *Panorama of Florence* and dates from 1352, and the other is *Map with a Chain* which dates from about 1490. Sometime between the years in which these two paintings were painted, the technique of linear perspective was developed, where there is an objective with a definite single viewpoint. In *Map with a Chain* this viewpoint is outside of the city, which is expressed symbolically in the painting by a painter sitting outside of the city.

---

16 R.D. Romanyshyn, *Technology as Symptom & Dream* (London, New York: Routledge, 1989).

On the contrary, the earlier painting, *Panorama of Florence*, is its sense of clutter and confusion that is characterized by a multiplicity of perspective simultaneously. Our eyes cannot find any one fixed point from which to view the city, which means that it is very difficult to find the actual center. Consequently and naturally, our eyes are forced to rove through the cityscape.

According to Romanyshyn's keen insight, the reason why we find it confusing is that there is time and body in these paintings, where it felt like walking about in the city. He mentions:

> If we find it confusing, then it is because with the advent of linear perspective vision we have managed to spatialize time, to distance ourselves from the body, and remove ourselves from the midst of things.[17]

A painter who is in the city would be able to feel the atmosphere of the space and may have embodied subjective experiences there, having personal commitment to this environment.

As we have seen above, one of the most important characteristics of traditional Japanese art is that it does not have a linear perspective in the way that post-Renaissance western paintings do. Instead, it employs multiple perspectives and, what is more, there is a definite suggestion of movement, too. It is considered that the development of a linear perspective in art has something to do with the establishment of the modern western ego consciousness, which brought about a definite distinction between "I" as a subject and an object that is to be looked at.

4 Dreams and Japanese Traditional Art

4.1 *Moving Multiple Perspectives*

In personal experience practicing psychotherapy, I have seen that some of my clients report dreams in which they have multiple perspectives, moving from one to another quite naturally. It might be considered a phenomenon quite similar to the characteristics of the Japanese traditional arts.

I would like to relate several dream experiences to explore the characteristics of perspective in dreams. I would like to present a dream of a woman in her late 30s, which shows parallels between dream experience and Japanese traditional art as was described above.

17 Ibid.

Dream 1

> There is a rectangular room. I am in there. Besides me, three or four men and women are sitting on the floor in a circle. It seems that these men and women are willing to kill a man and are talking rather loudly about how to do this. The man in his late 30s, who is to be killed, is standing outside of the room. I am sure he can hear them talking and is listening to that talk. There is a sound of the door unlocking from outside and I know he is coming into the room. I can't understand why he would do this.

Gradually, I begin to stare at a woman who is in an *oshiire* (Japanese built-in-closet next to the room). There is a woman who is combing her hair in the *oshiire*. I am staring at her.... Gradually, I seem to be combing her hair... Then, I realize she is probably me and I might be combing my hair. I feel that this woman might be me, and that it might be my hair that is being combed.

I don't usually presume to try to elucidate everything about clients' narratives in sessions, especially concerning dreams, but I did at that time, because she was smiling bashfully, which, perhaps, implied that she realized something was strange. I asked her how she could see the man outside of the room. After talking for a while, I came to realize that she had had two different perspectives from the very beginning, one was that of the original "I" who is sitting in the room and the other is that of looking down from diagonally above. What is more, the latter perspective was moving around these people who are sitting on the floor, in the same way that a camera pans across a scene. When she hears the sound of the door unlocking, she is in the room, but is also able to see the man unlocking the door from the outside of the room simultaneously.

The "I" in the dream is experienced in two different ways, one is supposed to be experienced as "dream ego" in the room and the other one is moving around the entire space, whose eye is similar to that observed in the *Rakuchu-Rakugai-zu*.

In addition, her description of the first part of the dream is reminiscent of pictures of *The Tale of Genji Picture Scroll*, the oldest surviving picture scroll, which date back to the early 12th century (Fig. 10.7). The depiction of a scene from the upper right side is common in picture scrolls. It is seen from an upper diagonal point of view with the roof, ceiling and sometimes inner partitions removed. Indeed, realism and the detail of architecture is one of the characteristics of scroll painting.

Before exploring the second part of the dream, I would like to present another dream narrative, which also indicates multiple moving perspectives. It is a dream of a woman in her 20s.

FIGURE 10.7 *Genji Monogatari Emaki.*
Published by the Tokugawa Museum in Nagoya, Japan, 1937.
Retrieved from: https://en.wikipedia.org/wiki/Genji_Monogatari_Emaki#/media/File:Genji_emaki_azumaya.jpg.
Illustration is in the public domain. No permission needed.

Dream 2

> A river flows into the sea. A male reporter's voice asks a question "Which way does the river flow?"
>
> I am wondering if we are going to the right. [There is also the viewpoint of a camera eye as seen from a helicopter flying very slowly]. The view goes along the cliff on the side and goes down the river for a while. A lake spreads out on the right. Then the view moves to the left and finally we see the sea. The reporter says, 'There may be remains of an ancient girl' and peeps through the rocks…I look into the crack, too.

It might be considered that this dream employs three different perspectives, namely; that of the dream-ego (I), that of the male reporter and that of the camera eye in the helicopter. At the beginning, the man only gives away his existence through his voice but actually appears in the latter half. The camera eye in the helicopter is like the viewpoint observed in the painting, *Rakuchu-Rakugai-zu.*

4.2 *Merging with the Object (= The "Not-I")*

Returning to Dream 1, in the second part of it, the dreamer is staring at a woman who is combing her hair in the closet at the beginning. Then she seemed to actually become the woman as if they gradually merged into one. This is an example of a blurring the boundary between "I" and "not"-I, in which somehow "I" enters into not-"I" and, perhaps, vice versa, and finally they merge into one.

As the level of consciousness in dreams lowers, the boundary between "I" and "not-I" becomes more obscure, and then we are able to enter another person's perspective as if merging with each other, escaping from an ego-centered one, much more easily than when we are awake. Generally speaking, there are several kinds of perspectives in dreams, such as the ego-centered perspective, (the same perspective as when we are awake and conscious), a looking-from-outside/distant perspective with a vague ego-centered perspective, another person's perspective, and sometimes even the perspectives of an animal or inanimate object.

Here I present a dream of a woman in her 20s, in which the "I (=dream ego)" becomes a dog.

I am taking a dog for a walk. As we walk together, I find myself looking at the road moving very close in front of my eyes. I realize that I am a dog and walking along the road looking down at it from a dog's perspective.

I have also heard of a dream in which the dreamer turned into a cat while she was with some cats. I have heard this kind of dream only from women, so far. I am not certain if on a general scale women report more of these types of dreams than men, or not. This seemingly natural metamorphosis phenomena might be more popular in Japanese dreams than those of Westerners, considering the fact that in Japanese fairy tales the transformation from animal to human is depicted rather naturally, without the use of the magical element, common in western fairy tales. This has been pointed out by Hayao Kawai. I am sure it would be interesting to look deeper into fairy tales from this point of view. I am not certain if identifying oneself with animals or even with substances in the dream is often experienced by Westerners. If so, a discussion of the perspectives from a cultural point of view would also be of interest.

As for the experience of merging into "not-I", the Japanese-style painter, Kayo Yamaguchi (1899–1984), whose motifs were mainly flowers, trees and animals, mentions that he tried to become absorbed in nature, and to talk with objects until he became one with them, meaning the painter and the object he was painting became inseparable and merged with each other.[18] This is not a viewpoint unique to Yamaguchi, but is used generally by other Japanese-style artists as well. This experience is considered to be similar to the concept of *participation mystique*, which Lucien Levy-Bruhl introduced to explain the psyche of primitive people. Of course, it might be said that Japanese painters do so with more intention than these people.

18 K. Yamaguchi, "Hana no kokoro de, doubutsu no kokoro de (By heart of flowers, By heart of animal)," *Yomiuri-shibun* (*Yomiuri-Newspaper*), 1978.

5 Reading Japanese Creation Myth and the Emergence of Ego

5.1 *Beginning of the* Kojiki

My second point is to explore the way that ego emerges in the Japanese psyche by returning to the narrative embedded in the oldest layer of Japanese culture through explication of the earliest myth, the *Kojiki*[19] especially the very beginning, which reads as an extended story of pre-conscious images. I will introduce some of the ideas first mentioned in "Ego consciousness in the Japanese psyche: culture, myth and disaster."[20]

It is well known that Neumann[21] read myth from the standpoint of the development of consciousness. And von Franz, in her book *Creation Myths,*[22] discussed this motif from various examples including Japanese myth. According to von Franz, "stories which are supposed to describe the origin of the real world are completely intertwined and mixed up with factors which we would rather call "stories of the preconscious process about the origin of human consciousness."[23]

The *Kojiki* consists of two parts: the first is the Deity Age, and the second is the Earthly Sovereigns. The former has a very long story with lists of powers, godheads, or primeval powers and finally ends with the beginning of what we call history, where the first earthly emperor appears. There is a long process of descent with many stages. According to von Franz,[24] such lists also appear in many Polynesian and New Zealander cosmogonies. She understands that Japanese civilization has never been cut off from its original primitive roots and mentions that the first deities are completely vague and mist-like, and in each step to the next deity the figure "becomes" more definite, and more specific. This emergence is simultaneous with a process whereby vague images coming out of chaos gradually develop a certain orientation and finally appear with some kind of form or body.

The outline of the earliest sections of the *Kojiki* is as follows: the whole process before the appearance of Japan's First Parents Izanagi and Izanami, who create the land and their offspring, is illustrated in Fig. 10.8.

---

19 Y. Takeda, ed., *Kojiki* (Tokyo: Kadokawa-shoken, 1995).

20 These ideas are discussed in greater detail in Yama, "Ego Consciousness in the Japanese Psyche: Culture, Myth and Disaster."

21 E. Neumann, *The Origins and History of Consciousness* (Princeton: Princeton University Press, 1993). Originally published in 1949.

22 M.L. Von Franz, *Creation Myths* (Boston: Shambhala Publications, 2001). Originally published in 1995.

23 Ibid., 11.

24 Von Franz, *Creation Myths.*

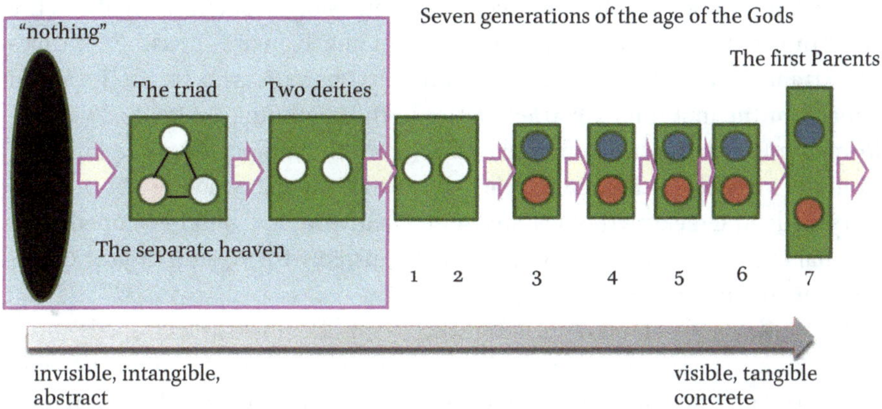

FIGURE 10.8 *The gradual transition from the "nothing" to the concrete.* Designer: Megumi Yama.
Source: Yama, M. (2013) "Ego consciousness in the Japanese psyche: culture, myth and disaster." Journal of Analytical Psychology, 58, 52–72. Used with permission from the copyright holder.
Yama, "Ego Consciousness in the Japanese Psyche: Culture, Myth and Disaster."

This story can be linked to the preconscious process before the emergence of ego and before a subject is established in the psyche. There is nothing in the beginning, then three single deities "became (= came into being)" one by one and disappeared. Deities are not created or produced but just "became" one after another in the seeming "nothingness." According to Masao Maruyama,[25] a Japanese scholar of the history of thought, there are three different patterns of generation in cosmogony. Each of these has a basic verb, "create", "produce", and "become." The first two are more familiar to the western people than "become." As for "become", something manifested itself through the effect of immanent spiritual power within the world, like "mana" in Melanesian myth. Therefore when we use the verb "become", it implies that there is potential for generation within the deity itself and that there should also be some energy to stimulate and encourage the process around it beforehand. At some place and given time, the powers from within and from without are constellated and cooperate to make manifest a physical embodiment. As the verb "become" is considered to show some characteristics of the Japanese language, I would like to refer to it again below.

25 M. Maruyama, *Chusei to Hangyaku* (*Loyalty and Treason*), 7th ed. (Tokyo: Iwanami Shoten, 2006).

The entire process of "becoming" goes on invisibly in silence. Finally, as the seventh generation, the first parents Izanagi and Izanami "became." It takes an extraordinary amount of time until the first parents who create the world appear for the first time. Abstract deities in the beginning are gradually transformed into deities with concrete bodies, from the intangible to the tangible, from the invisible to the visible, from the abstract to the concrete. On the contrary, gods in Greek mythology are more clearly defined and developed. This gradual emergence of consciousness is contrasted with Western myths of origin that are more clear and specific.

Hayao Kawai's[26] statements about the chain of deities are extremely interesting in terms of treating images in psychotherapy. "If we dared to try to verbalize a situation which is difficult to verbalize, it would be the chain of names of the deities as such." He also states, "It is not easy to clearly grasp it, but in fact there is a current which is likely to lead out of chaos and head toward some certain direction."[27] In psychotherapy, especially when we treat unconscious contents such as dreams I think we need to try to understand this dim movement of a current not too clearly but somewhat loosely and vaguely.

5.2 *The Word "Becoming* (Naru:成る)*" in the Japanese Language*

As I touched on above, I would like to add some explanation about the Japanese verb "become", the usage of which may show a uniqueness of Japanese language and culture. In my previous study,[28] I introduced the work of Japanese linguist Takehiro Kanaya[29] who provides good examples to understanding this concept. Kanaya has been living in Canada for about forty years and develops interesting cultural studies from the viewpoint of linguistics. According to him, when someone in Japan sends an invitation to his/her wedding, he/she would write, "became that (we) marry, that is "that marry became (lit. *kekkon suru koto ni narimashita*)": in Japanese language order, on the contrary, in western countries, he/she would say, "We decided to marry" or "We will marry." When you say, "We decided to marry" or "We will marry", there is a clear intention or will of the subject. On the other hand, the Japanese preferred

26 H. Kawai, *Shinwa to Nihonjin no Kokoro* (*Myth and Japanese Psyche*) (Tokyo: Iwanami Shoten, 2003).

27 Ibid.

28 Yama, "Ego Consciousness in the Japanese Psyche: Culture, Myth and Disaster."

29 T. Kanaya, *Nihonngo wa Keigo ga atte Shugo ga nai: "Chijo no Shiten" no Nihon Bunkaron'* (*Honorific but no subject in Japanese language: Japanese culture from "a viewpoint on the earth"*) (Tokyo: Kobun-sha, 2010).

expression "became that marry" means that "the situation has occurred naturally that we marry."

In the Japanese language, it is rarely expressed "who the subject is' or 'one's will or intention." In general, Japanese are not overly concerned about clarification of the subject, and there is a tendency to guess at meaning according to shared context. Perhaps this is a linguistic expression of the lesser value attributed to individuality in Japan when compared to the West.

Returning to the Japanese creation myth, we can understand that this idea of "becoming" implies that the subjects are part of an emerging whole.

5.3 *As If Circumambulating the Self*

Next, let's draw a parallel between the idea of deities "becoming" and disappearing and the way in which new areas of the Katsura Imperial Villa garden reveal themselves in turn.

It seems that we are to experience multiple fragmental perspectives as if they emerge one by one in the garden. But if we understand the garden as a whole, they are not completely fragmental but each scene can be regarded as part of an emerging whole. Suppose that the whole garden is the Self, as Jung defined, this experience of wandering the various stages of the garden is just like circumambulating the Self.

This physical sensation may give us important suggestions when we think of therapy. Reflecting on my personal practice, when we value images of dreams without trying to interpret or understand them, sometimes the dream begins to unfold spontaneously, and this process itself may bring about in a deep sense of healing. In order to make such autonomous movements arise, in which images emerge (or "become" in the Japanese sense) from the vague chaotic unconscious, I would like to emphasize that a protected setting and silence are both essential. Images tend to connect with each other and make complex nets of themselves, which are usually beyond linear understanding. Moreover, these images tend to change their structures every few minutes autonomously. Therefore immediate verbalization about these images often prevents them from amplifying and may even cut their interrelated linkages. Consequently, this might bring about a destruction of the life in the image. As images are usually ambiguous and contain manifold meanings simultaneously, they appear differently according to which perspective we have. This is parallel to strolling in the Katsura Imperial Villa garden, experiencing multiple perspectives on the surroundings.

In therapy, a certain amount of energy is required to bring about such a movement, just as in alchemy, where fire is necessary to encourage the transformative process. The energy is usually produced in a relationship between a client and a therapist.

Hillman[30] insists on the multiplicity of psyche and states, "We can describe the psyche as a polycentric realm of non verbal, non spatial images." Hillman being an American, his slightly poetic expression in the following is interesting, which reminding one of the multiple moving perspectives in Japanese traditional arts as we have seen above. It reads:

> Not monotheistic consciousness looking down from its mountain, but polytheistic consciousness wandering all over the place, in the vales and along rivers, in the wood, the sky, and under the earth.[31]

Recently, establishing the subject is a topic of interest in Japanese psychotherapy due to an increasing number of PDD clients and *hikikomori* people withdrawing from society for an extended period of time. Traditionally and culturally, as the "Mother/Great Mother' has been very strong in Japan, it is quite difficult to become independent and leave warm Mother's warm lap behind. Refusals to attend school and shut-ins have been understood in this context. Japanese people should learn how to establish the subject, however long it takes.

References

Berque, A. *Nihon No Fukei Seiou No Keikan: Soshite Zoukei No Jidai* (*Japanese Scenery and the Western Vista: And the Age of Landscaping*). Translated by K. Shinoda. Tokyo: Kodan-sha, 1990.

Edinger, E.F. *Ego and Archetype*. New York: Penguin Books, 1972.

Hillman, J. *Re-Visioning Psychology*. New York: Harper Colophon, 1975.

Jung, C.G. *Aion*. Princeton: Princeton University Press, 1959. Originally published in 1951.

Jung, C.G. *Memories, Dreams, Reflections*. London: Harper Perennial, 1995. Originally published in 1961.

Jung, C.G. *Ougon no Hana no Himitsu*. Translated by Y. Yuasa and A. Sadakata. Kyoto: Jinbun-shoin, 1990. Originally published as *Das Geheimnis der goldenen Blüte, ein chinesisch Lebensbuch* (1929).

30 J. Hillman, *Re-Visioning Psychology* (New York: Harper Colophon, 1975).

31 Ibid., 33.

Kanaya, T. *Nihonngo wa Keigo ga atte Shugo ga nai: "Chijo no Shiten" no Nihon Bunkaron' (Honorific but no subject in Japanese language: Japanese culture from "a viewpoint on the earth")*. Tokyo: Kobun-sha, 2010.

Kawai, H. *Boseishakai Nihon no Byori (Pathology of Japan as a Society of Maternity)*. Tokyo: Chuokoron-sha, 1976.

Kawai, H. *Shinwa to Nihonjin no Kokoro (Myth and Japanese Psyche)*. Tokyo: Iwanami Shoten, 2003.

Maruyama, M. *Chusei to Hangyaku (Loyalty and Treason)*. 7th ed. Tokyo: Iwanami Shoten, 2006.

Neumann, E. *The Origins and History of Consciousness*. Princeton: Princeton University Press, 1993. Originally published in 1949.

Niigata, N. *Nihonjin no "Watashi" o motomete (Seeking the Japanese "Me")*. Tokyo: Shin-yo-sha, 2007.

Romanyshyn, R.D. *Technology as Symptom & Dream*. London, New York: Routledge, 1989.

Takashina, S. *Seiyo no Me Nihon no Me (Western Eyes / Japanese Eyes)*. Tokyo: Seido-sha, 2001.

Takashina, S. "The Japanese Sense of Beauty." In *Nihon bijutsu o miru me: higashi to nishi no deai (Viewing Japanese Art: Encounters between the East and West)*. Tokyo: Iwanami Shoten, 2011. Originally published in 1983.

Takeda, Y., ed. *Kojiki*. Tokyo: Kadokawa-shoken, 1995.

Taut, B. "Eiennarumono (Something Eternal)." In *Nihonbi no Saihakken (A Rediscovery of Japanese Aesthetics)*. Tokyo: Iwanami Shoten, 1981. Originally published in 1939.

Von Franz, M.L. *Creation Myths*. Boston: Shambhala Publications, 2001. Originally published in 1995.

Yama, M. "Ego Consciousness in the Japanese Psyche: Culture, Myth and Disaster." *Journal of Analytical Psychology* 58 (2013): 52–72.

Yamaguchi, K. "Hana no kokoro de, doubutsu no kokoro de (By heart of flowers, By heart of animal)." Yomiuri-shibun (Yomiuri-Newspaper), 1978.

Yoshimura, T. *Nihon bi no tokushitsu (The Essence of Japanese Aesthetics)*. Tokyo: Kashima-shuppankai, 1967.

CHAPTER 11

Subject Drop and the Japanese Ego

Norifumi Kishimoto

Abstract

With advances in cognitive psychology and cognitive linguistics, the so-called Whorfian hypothesis, that the structure of a language influences its speakers' thoughts and perceptions, has been drawing attention again. In this article, a linguistic structure called subject drop will be discussed. The Japanese language has a strong tendency to omit the subject, which influences the way of being and functioning of ego. Japanese language has a structure which makes the boundary between you and I or between the object and the subject thinner by keeping the subject from becoming apparent. This contributes to form a sense of connectedness with others unconsciously, although it functions as unconscious bonds and sometimes causes troubles. It is necessary to take the linguistic structure and its influence on the ego functioning into consideration if we try to understand the Japanese mind through Jung's concept and theory.

Keywords

Jung – psychoanalysis – unconscious – Whorfian hypothesis – subject drop – structure of language – Japanese ego

1 Influences of Language on Thoughts and Perceptions

The idea that the structure of a language affects its speakers' thoughts and perceptions was first clearly expressed by nineteenth century philosopher and linguist, Wilhelm von Humboldt. He proposed that "the difference between languages is not only in sounds and signs but in worldview" and even claimed that grammatical differences are responsible for shaping these differences in the first place.[1] Edward Sapir advanced this idea and argued that the mother

1 W. Humboldt, "Über das vergleichende Sprachstudium in Beziehung auf die verschiedenen Epochen der Sprachentwicklung", in *Wilhelm von Humboldts Gesammelte Schriften.*

 | DOI:10.1163/9789004336636_013

tongue influences everyday thought and perception as well as philosophical thinking.[2]

Subsequently, Sapir's student, Benjamin Lee Whorf gained popularity when he insisted that a Hopi (a Native American Indian in northeastern Arizona) had no general notion of time since the Hopi language contained no reference to time.[3] However, due to the lack of sufficient evidence, his insistence that language determines thought and that linguistic categories both limit and determine cognitive categories, has been abandoned and criticised over the decades. The dominant view among contemporary linguists is that most of the grammar of language is innate. According to this perspective, at a fundamental level, human beings all think in the same way and "if language influences the way we think, any such influence is negligible, even trivial."[4]

Recently, with advances in cognitive psychology and cognitive linguistics, the so-called Whorfian hypothesis has been drawing attention again, but in its weaker or more elaborate form. For example, research on colour terminology or spatial category demonstrate that our mother tongue can influence thoughts and perceptions. As Deutscher puts it:

> If different languages influence their speakers' minds in varying ways, this is not because of what each language allows people to think but rather because of the kinds of information each language habitually obliges people to think about. When a language forces its speakers to pay attention to certain aspects of the world each time they open their mouths or prick up their ears, such habits of speech can eventually settle into habits of mind with consequences for memory, or perception, or associations, or even practical skills.[5]

Based on these arguments, this article examines the subject drop phenomenon and its influence on Jung's concept of the ego from the standpoint of the weak version of linguistic relativity. My intention is not to insist that subject drop limits a speaker's thoughts and perceptions, but to throw some light on how the habitual use (or disuse) of subject in speaking and writing influences the state and function of the ego.

Herausgegeben von der Königlich Preussischen Akademie der Wissenschaften, ed. A. Leitzmann, vol. 4 (Berlin: B. Behr's Verlag, 1905). Originally published in 1820.

2 E. Sapir, "Conceptual Categories in Primitive Languages", *Science* 74 (1931): 578.

3 B. Whorf, *Language, Thought, and Reality: Selected Writings of Benjamin Lee Whorf* (Cambridge MA: MIT Press, 1956).

4 G. Deutscher, *Through the Language Glass* (New York: Metropolitan Books, 2010).

5 Ibid.

2 The World Looks Different in Other Languages

First, in order to demonstrate the significant impact of subject drop, I focus on the opening sentence of the well-known Japanese novel, *Snow Country* by Yasunari Kawabata, winner of the Nobel Prize for Literature. His work was translated by Edward Seidensticker, a noted scholar and translator of Japanese literature. It begins with the following sentence:

> The train came out of the long tunnel into the snow country[6]

As a reader, what scene can be pictured from this sentence? Probably, the majority of readers will envision a train coming out of a tunnel and heading into a snow country. In fact, most of the English-speaking people in the experiment that Kanaya[7] cited in his book drew pictures that were similar to the figure 11.1. By contrast, those who read the original Japanese sentence drew the scene

FIGURE 11.1 A typical scenery pictured from the opening sentence of the Snow Country translated in English.
Source: Drawn by Ena Kishimoto after the model of the sketch in Kanaya (2004). Used with permission.

6 Y. Kawabata, *Snow Country*, trans. E. Seidensticker (New York: Knopf, 1956). Originally published as *Yukiguni* (Osaka: Sogensha, 1932).

7 T. Kanaya, *Eigo nimo Shugo ha Nakatta* (*There had been no subjects in English, too*) (Tokyo: Kodansha, 2004).

quite differently. Typically, it was a landscape that was seen through the window of a vehicle (Fig. 11.2). These contrasting images suggest that people see the world quite differently from language to language. In addition, what causes such a difference might be in the structure of the languages. If I translate the original Japanese sentence into English as literally as possible, disregarding the grammatical correctness, it will be as follows:

> *Got through the long border tunnel, was a snow country*

In the Seidensticker's translation, the most striking characteristic is the emergence of the subject, i.e. the train. However, there is no subject in the original Japanese sentence. In principle, it is impossible to make a sentence in English without a subject, except for an imperative sentence. In this case, Seidensticker made up for this deficit by adding "train" to the sentence. The original Japanese sentence mentioned above does not describe whether the character is in a train or in a car and we know it while going on reading. Although his interpretation is not incorrect, it is more natural for most Japanese individuals to interpret it as follows: "After I got through the long border tunnel, I found

FIGURE 11.2 A typical scenery pictured from the opening sentence of original Japanese version of the Snow Country.
Source: Drawn by Ena Kishimoto after the model of the sketch in Kanaya (2004). Used with permission.

that there was a snow country." According to this interpretation, it sounds like a description of the scenery from the character's perspective, which will be discussed in detail later.

3 Subject Drop in Japanese Language

Some languages, such as English, German and French, do not permit sentences without subjects and the use of subject pronouns is obligatory. Other languages, such as Polish, Spanish, Chinese and Japanese, allow an independent clause to lack an explicit subject. This phenomenon is referred to as "subject drop" or "null subject." Typically, subject-dropping languages express the person, the number and/or gender agreement with the verb referents. In these languages, one can infer subjects from the verb referents.

By contrast, in Japanese, a subject in a clause can be omitted, despite the absence of verb inflection and the grammatical rule of subject-verb agreement. In addition, in Japanese, it is not rare to see that the subject cannot be determined by the sentence alone. Sentences with subjects, such as "I have money" or "I have a son", are not impossible in Japanese, but they tend to be avoided. In fact, sentences with explicit subjects in Japanese actually appeared in the translations of Dutch texts during the Edo period (seventeenth to nineteenth centuries), although it did not become popular. According to Yanabu,[8] the use of a sentence with a subject in Japan originated with the Constitution of the Empire of Japan in 1889. Almost all the Constitution's articles had the subject-verb-object (SVO) structure in common since they were based on the literal translation of the German draft. This writing style was probably unusual and unnatural for the Japanese at that time. Although the fact that the Constitution adopted this writing style made such an impact that it gradually spread into textbooks, academic articles, novels and translated works, there is still a strong tendency in Japanese for subjects, especially first-person pronouns, to drop in speaking and writing. Moreover, upon comparison of any English translation of a Japanese work, such as a comic, novel or article, with the original one, the missing subjects in the latter are supplemented in the English version quite often.

Although subjects that drop from sentences are not limited to first-person pronouns, this chapter primarily focuses on first-person pronoun drop. More specifically, it compares several simple English sentences with the Japanese

8 A. Yanabu, *Kindai Nihongo no Shiso* (*The Thought of Modern Japanese Language*) (Tokyo: Hosei University Press, 2004).

version. For example, a Japanese expression that corresponds to "I went shopping" is *kaimono ni* (shopping) *itta* (went). In case of sentences that consist of the subject-verb structure, the subject, "I", is usually dropped from the sentence in Japanese. In case of a sentence such as "I understand English", a common Japanese expression will be *eigo* (English) *ga* (postpositional particle) *wakaru* (understandable) of which the literal translation would be "English is understandable." Concerning sentences with the SVO structure, words that are the object in English sentences tend to become the explicit subject because they include the postpositional particle, "*ga*", which is said to be an indicator of the subject. However, they are not real subjects since they are only placed in the position of the subject in order to avoid using the real subject "I", which is dropped from the sentence.

This does not mean that the Japanese have never understood the concept of "I" or a type of ego consciousness. In fact, Eihei Dogen, one of the greatest Zen masters in Japan during the thirteenth century stated, "To get disciplined in the way of the Buddha means nothing other than getting disciplined in properly dealing with your own I."[9] In addition, Ikkyu Sojun, a Japanese Zen master during the fifteenth century, admonished his disciples in a similar manner: "Who or what am I? Search your I from the top of your head down to your bottom."[10] Nevertheless, the Japanese language, which allows subject drop, has forced those who speak Japanese to see and think things in a certain way.

4 Subject Drop and Perspective

What influences does subject drop have on the ego's way of being and functioning? This section focuses on the shift of perspective or literally, the viewpoint of the subject, based upon Kanaya's discussion.[11]

Those who utilise a language that requires overt subjects are consciously and unconsciously forced to make a distinction between "I" and "not I." For instance, when one states, "I see Mt. Fuji", the "I" appears as something independent of Mt. Fuji. Hence, each time the word "I" is spoken, the "I" manifests itself as an objective aspect. In other words, by stating "I", it is objectified as an independent entity. In regard to the components that constitute the sentence, "I" and "Mt. Fuji" are evenly weighed and the viewpoint that makes it possible to simultaneously view both "I" and "Mt. Fuji" should be put outside

9 T. Izutsu, *Toward a Philosophy of Zen Buddhism* (Boulder: Prajna Press, 1977).

10 Ibid.

11 Kanaya, *Eigo nimo Shugo ha Nakatta* (*There had been no subjects in English, too*).

both aspects. Furthermore, when one states, "I see Mt. Fuji", it is assumed that another eye sees both "I" and "Mt. Fuji." In this way, the "I" and "Mt. Fuji" are recognised as separate, distinct entities.

Conversely, the more natural Japanese expression that corresponds to "I see Mt. Fuji" is "Mt. Fuji is visible." In this case, Mt. Fuji is explicitly expressed and the person who sees the mountain, i.e. "I", is implicitly suggested. There is an imbalance between "I" and "Mt. Fuji." The only viewpoint that allows such a perspective is that of the person who sees it, i.e. the "I." On the eye of the "I", what is occurring is that "Mt. Fuji" comes into view and it is no longer necessary to mention "I." In other words, the speaker is inside the scenery and becomes a part of it. In this way, the boundary between "Mt. Fuji" and "I" becomes blurred or vague. Furthermore, "the absence of the first-person pronoun reduces the prominence of the speaker's person, thus reducing figure-ground differentiation"[12] and since the subject is not explicitly mentioned, it is easier for the listener to take the same perspective as of the speaker.

Based on the aforementioned points, the original Japanese sentence, "Got through the long border tunnel, was a snow country", naturally or unknowingly invites readers to see things from the character's perspective. Apparently, it is only a description of a landscape, but the subject drop enables readers to feel as if they are viewing the landscape themselves. Therefore, it is possible to state that the Japanese language consists of a structure that makes the boundary between you and I or between the object and subject thinner by preventing the subject from becoming apparent.

5 Case Presentation

A clinical illustration may help readers understand the subject drop phenomenon and its resulting problems. To bring out the point clearly, I will take up a very simple case. Please note that the following verbatim case records have been literally translated in total disregard of grammatical correctness. In addition, although the sentences lack subjects, they should not be regarded as imperative sentences.

About ten years ago, when I was working at a general hospital's outpatient department of psychosomatic medicine, there was a female patient in her forties who stated:

12 E. Kashima and Y. Kashima, "Culture and Language: The Case of Cultural Dimensions and Personal Pronoun Use", *Journal of Cross-Cultural Psychology* 29 (1998): 461–86.

> Each time conscious of something bad in the body, felt anxious and helpless, and sometimes burst into tears. What to do to deal with this anxiety? Sometimes abdominal pain, which waxes and wanes.

Initially, I understood her statement as:

> Each time (I [= the patient] was) conscious of something bad in my body, (I) felt anxious and helpless, and sometimes (I) burst into tears. What (should I) do to deal with this anxiety? (I have) sometimes abdominal pain, which waxes and wanes.

However, while listening to her, I came to see that the words were not about herself, but about her daughter's neurotic and psychosomatic symptoms. Thus, it should have been understood as:

> Each time (my daughter was) conscious of something bad in her body, (she or I) felt anxious and helpless, and sometimes (she) bursts into tears. What (should I) do to deal with this anxiety? (She has) sometimes abdominal pain, which waxes and wanes.

When I realized that she was talking about her daughter, her manner of speaking (as if she were her daughter) left a significant impression on me. In this case, I believe that she unconsciously identified with her daughter, which was central to the problem. Empirically, since I knew that it was too early to point this out to her, I continued listening to her without making any comments.

One month later, in the fourth session, we came to an important moment. She stated, "There is no change in the situation... By the way, be able to get things in wider perspective." I sensed that the time was right since someone who I could not know was her or her daughter came to have a wider perspective and I asked her, "Who is able to get things in wider perspective?" In her surprise, she replied, "My daughter. Not I." On that moment, she realized that she was speaking as if she were her daughter. With this as a turning point, she slowly recognised that she herself had interfered with her daughter too much and about three months later the problem was resolved. This kind of problem frequently occurs in many situations in Japan. In this case, regardless of whether it can create unconscious bonds and occasional issues, the structure of subject drop prepared those with a certain readiness to empathise with others, which ultimately forms a sense of connectedness between the two parties.

6 The Influence of Subject Drop on Ego Formation

As for psychological aspects of the mother archetype, Carl Jung described as follows:

> The carrier of the archetype is in the first place the personal mother, because the child lives at first in complete participation with her, in a state of unconscious identity... With the awakening of ego-consciousness the participation gradually weakens, and consciousness begins to enter into opposition to the unconscious, its own precondition. This leads to differentiation of the ego from mother.[13]

According to this viewpoint, the therapeutic process of the case mentioned above might be interpreted as that of mother-daughter differentiation and the establishment of ego consciousness. However, I hesitate to give such an explanation since the structure of the ego and its manner of functioning greatly differ between languages of the West (i.e. languages that do not permit subject drop) and Japanese.

A survey of the collected works of Jung reveals that his concept of the ego or ego consciousness did not change throughout his life. In *Aion*, he defined the ego as "the centre of the field of consciousness; and, in so far as this comprises the empirical personality, the ego is the subject of all personal acts of consciousness."[14] Each time one uses "I", as in "I love you", "I play guitar", "I want to be a doctor" and "I have a brother", the boundary between "I" and "not I" is delineated and the ego is established as an integrated and consistent entity. Jung also stated that, "the whole essence of consciousness is *discrimination*, distinguishing ego from non-ego, subject from object, positive from negative, and so forth."[15] In my opinion, this distinction determines the contour of the ego and it also confines Jung's concept of the ego.

In contrast, the Japanese ego is not established in such a manner. For instance, when your boss who really likes baseball asks whether you like baseball, and even if you do not like baseball, you can say, "baseball is liked" in Japanese

13 C.G. Jung, "Psychological Aspects of the Mother Archetype", in *The Collected Works*, trans. R.F.C. Hull, vol. 9.1, Bollinger Series, XX (Princeton NJ: Princeton University Press, 1954). Originally published in 1938.

14 C.G. Jung, "Aion", in *The Collected Works*, trans. R.F.C. Hull, vol. 9.2, Bollinger Series, XX (Princeton NJ: Princeton University Press, 1951).

15 C.G. Jung, "Psychological Types", in *The Collected Works*, trans. R.F.C. Hull, vol. 6, Bollinger Series, XX (Princeton NJ: Princeton University Press, 1971). Originally published in 1921.

without using "I". This is much easier than stating, "I like baseball." In other words, you like baseball in the context of the relationship with your boss and you don't like baseball when you are alone. Thus, the boundary of "I" constantly changes in accordance with the situation. Moreover, while making statements that do not use "I", such as "Mt. Fuji is visible" and "baseball is liked", the relationship between the surroundings (i.e. people and things) configures "I", although somewhat vaguely. This is also reflected in the fact that there are many words that mean "I" in Japanese, including *watashi, watakushi, ore, boku, atashi, uchi* and *jibun*. Therefore, the contour of the Japanese ego continuously changes in accordance with the surrounding situations rather than standing alone.

Thus, subject drop is one of the key factors in Japanese ego formation. It fits well with the "hollow-center" concept of the Japanese ego by Kawai,[16] the first Jungian psychoanalyst in Japan, and the "becoming model" of Japanese myth by Yama.[17] Yama also states, citing from Kawai, that "In the Japanese psyche, the boundary between consciousness and unconsciousness is much more vague than the Westerner's." He adds that in Japanese psyche, "as the structure of the consciousness is formed with the Self as the center, which is in the unconscious, it is even doubtful whether it really has the center."[18] In other words, "the ego is buried in the unconscious depth of psyche. As it is usually difficult to articulate what is taking place in the unconscious, this may explain why the Japanese seem to be so ambiguous."[19]

7 Polyphonic Effect of Subject Drop

Let us return to the opening line from *Snow Country*, "The train came out of the long border tunnel into the snow country" and the original version, "Got through the long border tunnel, was a snow country." As described earlier, this statement could be interpreted as "After I got through the long border tunnel, I found that there was a snow country." However, the subject drop permits another interpretation: "After I got through the long border tunnel, I found that I was in (= came to) a snow country." Although it may appear to be a slight change, the vista given by the phrase is significantly altered. Moreover, the

16 H. Kawai, *Boseishakai Nihon no Byori* (*Pathology of Japan as a Society of Maternity*) (Tokyo: Chuokoron-sha, 1976); "Japanese Mythology: Balancing the Gods", in *Dream, Myth & Fairy Tales in Japan* (Einsiedeln: Daimon, 1995).

17 M. Yama, "Ego Consciousness in the Japanese Psyche: Culture, Myth and Disaster", *Journal of Analytical Psychology* 58 (2013): 52–72.

18 Kawai, *Boseishakai Nihon no Byori* (*Pathology of Japan as a Society of Maternity*).

19 Yama, "Ego Consciousness in the Japanese Psyche: Culture, Myth and Disaster."

character's eyes turn from outward to inward and the landscape of the snow country becomes a reflection in the psyche, an image that manifests itself in the mind of the person who sees it. The phrase could be regarded as describing the landscape in the mind, rather than the actual landscape.

Thus, the phrase eventually depicts the landscape on at least three different levels; i.e. the landscape outside the subject, the landscape to the subject and the landscape in the subject. This is referred to as the polyphonic effect of subject drop since the phrase can simultaneously reverberate in these different layers.

In English, the subject and sentence structure usually determine the perspective or the location where the viewpoint is placed. For a statement such as, "I found that there was a snow country", the eyes turn toward the snow country outside, whereas for "I found I came to a snow country", the emphasis is shifted to "I" or the person who came to the snow country, rather than the snow country itself. Conversely, in Japanese, a sentence usually lacks a subject and it is difficult to determine the perspective only on the basis of the sentence. As a result, the subject remains in a state of suspension until the context becomes clear.

Finally, I want to emphasise that subject drop is only a tiny part of the complexity of the Japanese mind. For instance, there are four syllabaries or four sets of written characters in the Japanese writing system: Hiragana, Katakana, Kanji (Chinese characters), and Romaji (Romanisation of Japanese). Hiragana and Katakana consist of 48 characters each. As for Kanji, Jōyō Kanji (literally, "regular-use Chinese characters") includes 2,136 characters consisting of all 1,006 Kyōiku Kanji characters that Japanese children learn in elementary school, plus an additional 1,130 Kanji taught in junior high and high school. Moreover, each Kanji includes at least two ways to read it, which creates tremendously delicate and rich expressions with both consciously and unconsciously influential visual effects in the Japanese mind.

In conclusion, the subject drop phenomenon and its influence on the ego have been examined from the viewpoint of the weak version of linguistic relativity. The findings show that the structure of certain languages and its influences on meaning is noteworthy, especially when Jungian psychology is applied and translated into other languages.

References

Deutscher, G. *Through the Language Glass*. New York: Metropolitan Books, 2010.

Humboldt, W. "Über das vergleichende Sprachstudium in Beziehung auf die verschiedenen Epochen der Sprachentwicklung." In *Wilhelm von Humboldts Gesammelte Schriften. Herausgegeben von der Königlich Preussischen Akademie der*

Wissenschaften, edited by A. Leitzmann, Vol. 4. Berlin: B. Behr's Verlag, 1905. Originally published in 1820.

Izutsu, T. *Toward a Philosophy of Zen Buddhism*. Boulder: Prajna Press, 1977.

Jung, C.G. "Aion." In *The Collected Works*, translated by R.F.C. Hull, Vol. 9.2. Bollinger Series, XX. Princeton NJ: Princeton University Press, 1951.

Jung, C.G. "Psychological Aspects of the Mother Archetype." In *The Collected Works*, translated by R.F.C. Hull, Vol.9.1. Bollinger Series, XX. Princeton NJ: Princeton University Press, 1954. Originally published in 1938.

Jung, C.G. "Psychological Types." In *The Collected Works*, translated by R.F.C. Hull, Vol. 6. Bollinger Series, XX. Princeton NJ: Princeton University Press, 1971. Originally published in 1921.

Kanaya, T. *Eigo nimo Shugo ha Nakatta (There had been no subjects in English, too)*. Tokyo: Kodansha, 2004.

Kashima, E., and Y. Kashima. "Culture and Language: The Case of Cultural Dimensions and Personal Pronoun Use." *Journal of Cross-Cultural Psychology* 29 (1998): 461–86.

Kawabata, Y. *Snow Country*. Translated by E. Seidensticker. New York: Knopf, 1956. Originally published as *Yukiguni* (Osaka: Sogensha, 1932).

Kawai, H. *Boseishakai Nihon no Byori (Pathology of Japan as a Society of Maternity)*. Tokyo: Chuokoron-sha, 1976.

Kawai, H. "Japanese Mythology: Balancing the Gods." In *Dream, Myth & Fairy Tales in Japan*. Einsiedeln: Daimon, 1995.

Sapir, E. "Conceptual Categories in Primitive Languages." *Science* 74 (1931): 578.

Whorf, B. *Language, Thought, and Reality: Selected Writings of Benjamin Lee Whorf*. Cambridge MA: MIT Press, 1956.

Yama, M. "Ego Consciousness in the Japanese Psyche: Culture, Myth and Disaster." *Journal of Analytical Psychology* 58 (2013): 52–72.

Yanabu, A. *Kindai Nihongo no Shiso (The Thought of Modern Japanese Language)*. Tokyo: Hosei University Press, 2004.

CHAPTER 12

Developing Jung's Theory of Mind in the Light of Evolutionary Psychology

The Theory of Consciousness in the Context of Cognitive Functioning of Individuals with Learning Disability and Pygmy Chimpanzees

Andrew Kuzmicki

Abstract

The goal of this paper is to investigate the nature of consciousness, but also to develop C.G. Jung's "Theory of Mind" in the light of evolutionary psychology. I try to demonstrate here evidence supporting the hypothesis of "continuity" (direct relationship, similarity) between the cognitive conscious processes (for instance on a level of communication) of human beings and other primates – in this case the chimpanzees *bonobo* – but also trying to support the general applicability of the theory of the self in psychological studies.

Nowadays the subject of consciousness still requires new studies and research to let us find out its immanent nature. This paper refers to the theory of consciousness in the context of analysis of cognitive functioning of the individuals with learning disability and cognitive functioning of the apes – pygmy chimpanzees.

Jung once said: "The nature of consciousness is a riddle whose solution I don't know." In this paper we are going to follow this riddle supporting Jung's work and developing our insight into this still not fully understood area.

Keywords

Consciousness – the Self – Damasio – Freud – language – cognitive skills – chimpanzees – bonobo

•••

 | DOI:10.1163/9789004336636_014

> The nature of consciousness is a riddle whose solution I do not know.
>
> C.G. JUNG[1]

∴

1 The Difficulties with Consciousness

What consciousness is and what its role is in the functioning of the mind is still difficult to answer due to the fact that, on one hand, we associate a large set of the psychic functions with it and, on the other hand, it is still difficult to define its core or the borders. As a consequence of these problems some of the models describing the human mind do not require an existence of consciousness at all. In these theories scientists try to explain the processes that are involved in generating plans, realizing tasks, making conscious decisions without consciousness, or – we could say – without the necessity of "freedom of choice" commonly associated with consciousness and without pre-assumed "independency" of human subject/"I"/ego. We have not resolved the problem of the eventual role or necessity of consciousness/awareness in these operations yet.

Firstly, on the basis of the current findings, we cannot establish which part of the brain is responsible for the existence of consciousness and conscious experience. Moreover, the selected functional characteristics of the brain usually associated with consciousness, such as attention, perception or thinking itself, seem to act independently of consciousness, perhaps making it "unnecessary" to some extent. But – finally we still believe that our consciousness and all conscious processes have a key role and are directly involved in all our important choices or decisions and that those processes are the key agents responsible for all our day-to-day life acts, behaviours and self-regulations.

The questions we have to answer are still present:

> Is consciousness a material phenomenon? What is the relationship between consciousness and the brain, and what is its coexistence within the neuro-physiological level of an organism? How can it possibly be homogeneous, consistent or stable at the time of experience by a subject who is experiencing it? Is it possible for this phenomenon to occur outside of the human body? Is it possible for such a function to occur in

1 C.G. Jung, "The Structure and Dynamics of the Psyche", in *The Collected Works*, trans. R.F.C. Hull, vol. 8 (London: Routledge, 1970), para. 610.

> an animal body/brain or in a computer? Does consciousness change anything at all? Does it "do" anything? What does it determine (if anything at all)? How does it influence our thinking and acting in any way? What happens when we are conscious? What determines what will become conscious and what will not? And, if there is such an external thing to our consciousness that determines what and when something can make us conscious (something that is "outside of the consciousness itself"), how can we see consciousness as an autonomous being/function, when it depends on something else? Is consciousness or self-consciousness something more than just a property of mind to receive such meanings (in the immediacy/perception) that relates directly to the shaping of the concept of "ego"/"I"/"self" and to our subjective being with its "first-person" subjective perspective? Does consciousness have separate perceptual apparatus (see so-called: "higher-order perception theories" or "higher-order thought theories") or if it is only a functional addition, an additional level of processing of perceptual data from the internal and external "world"? Is the function of self-reflection or the ability of insight into the subject's own mental states a mechanism of gaining of a self-knowledge and, in further perspective, a mechanism of a self-regulation and ... a foundation of eventual free choice? How can the act of perception be separated from the conscious actor's perception? How can the process of choice be separated from the consciousness of that choice? Do those processes have to take place in a field of consciousness and with direct participation of the consciousness? Or maybe this "factor", the field of consciousness, is unnecessary and superfluous. And finally, as it was in centuries past, the question as to the relationship between psyche and matter is still valid.[2]

Psychoanalytical findings tell us that the conscious processes depend on a hidden psychophysical level of the biological drives and deep unconscious processes. An important factor here is that it is very difficult to determine the moment of their autonomy and the beginning of their influence into the conscious acts of ourselves as the subject. Observations on involuntary, unconscious, automatic behaviour support the hypothesis of luck of the necessity of consciousness in the decision-making process. For example, in research led by Bruce Bridgeman, where he studied the relationship between cognitive processes associated with consciousness and cognition-oriented sensorimotor co-ordination, it turned out that people who had been asked to follow a

2 More on this topic see S. Blackmore, *Consciousness: An Introduction, Hodder Education* (London: Hodder Education, 2007).

moving target did so even when the position changes lasted less than the time of saccadic eye movement, and thus even when the person could not knowingly notice any change. A similar phenomenon can be also observed during a game of professional tennis players. In some moments of the game, when they serve the ball, the ball flies in the direction of the second player with a speed of over 190 km/hour.[3] At that time the conscious cognitive reactions are not quick enough to manage the reactions of the players. The speed of the ball is too fast and makes it impossible to process consciously those senses and the related information. The reactions of the players are automatic, based on the unconscious processes, and to some extent involuntary.

In this paper we cannot approach all of the above questions but we can try to create a bigger picture of the mind and its processes, to let us create a better perspective for the future analysis of those problems. I hope that my efforts will be helpful in that matter and will let us go further towards the final answers referring to the human mind.

Therefore, in this paper I will approach the research in a three-fold way. Firstly, I am going to analyse the research results referring to fully mentally functional (fully developed) people. Secondly, I am going to discuss the observations that apply to the individuals without fully developed mental skills related to conscious experience. Finally, we are going to review the results of the research on the mental cognitive and communicative skills of the pygmy chimpanzees (*Pan paniscus*) also called bonobos. The third group of research results seems to throw additional light on a still very common point of view of animals, including monkeys, who seem not to have sufficiently developed brain processes which are necessary for consciousness to emerge. On the basis of the above perspectives – I hope – we will be able to indicate the processes directly involved in the formation of consciousness – such as: the dimensions determining immediacy, e.g. general "cognitive frame of perception", but also in addition I will try to show how the "handicapped" but still to some extent, functional mechanisms of learning and communicating can be described as integrated into an experience having a feature of conscious being.

2 Conscious – Unconscious According to Freud

Freud was aware of the significance of the topic of consciousness, but for understandable reasons he did not find it problematic and rather thought of it as

3 Cf. B. Bridgeman et al., "Relation between Cognitive and Motor-Oriented Systems of Visual Position Perception", *Journal of Experimental Psychology. Human Perception and Performance* 5, no. 4 (1979): 692–700.

obvious and out of questioning. Instead, he led his research trying to establish a new area of research – the area of research on the unconscious mind and the unconscious processes. We can see that below where Freud writes about the unconsciousness and consciousness in this way:

> there is no need to discuss what is to be called conscious: it is removed from all doubt. The oldest and best meaning of the word 'unconscious' is the descriptive one; we call a psychical process unconscious whose existence we are obliged to assume – for some such reason as that we infer it from its effects – but of which we know nothing. In that case we have the same relation to it as we have to a psychical process in another person, except that it is in fact one of our own. If we want to be still more correct, we shall modify our assertion by saying that we call a process unconscious if we are obliged to assume that it is being activated *at the moment*, though at the moment we know nothing about it. This qualification makes us reflect that the majority of conscious processes are conscious only for a short time; very soon they become *latent*, but can easily become conscious again. […] We call the unconscious which is only latent, and thus easily becomes conscious, the 'preconscious' and retain the term 'unconscious' for the other. We now have three terms, 'conscious', 'preconscious' and 'unconscious', with which we can get along in our description of mental phenomena.[4]

From the above quotation we can see that Freud was focused on the unconsciousness and on its relationship with the conscious mind. The consciousness was to him a background and a wider context to the unconsciousness and the unconsciousness could not exist separately. In other words, their essence and meaning was driven out of their direct relationship, but only the unconsciousness was the centre point of Freud's study. The awareness of their direct relationship and the border between them was always part of his interests and study. In the other fragment of his papers we can see how Freud was describing that border and relationship.

> Under the new and powerful impression of there being an extensive and important field of mental life which is normally withdrawn from the ego's knowledge so that the processes occurring in it have to be regarded as unconscious in truly dynamic sense, we have come to understand the term 'unconscious' in a topographical or systematic sense as well; we have come to speak of a 'system' of the preconscious and a 'system' of

4 S. Freud, *The Standard Edition of the Complete Psychological Works of Sigmund Freud*, vol. 22 (London: Hogarth Press, 1975), 70.

> the unconscious, of a conflict between the ego and the system Ucs., and have used the word more and more to denote a mental province rather than a quality of what is mental. The discovery, actually an inconvenient one, that portions of the ego and super-ego as well are unconscious in the dynamic sense, operates at this point as a relief – it makes possible the removal of a complication. We perceive that we have no right to name the mental region that is foreign to the ego 'the system Ucs.', since the characteristic of being unconscious is not restricted to it. Very well; we will no longer use the term 'unconscious' in the systematic sense ... [...] We will in future call it the 'id'.[5]

In the beginning of the twenty-first century we still discuss and look for the answers to the above questions: *How we should understand ego/I and a consciousness?, How can we understand a conscious being and all different forms of being conscious?* – and finally – *How can we apply Jung's theory of mind to the above questions?* In this paper I will try to look for the answers to these questions and find the answers in Jung's psychoanalytic theory of mind to enrich our understanding of the psychic world of the people with learning disabilities and the apes – particularly bonobo pigmy chimpanzees.

3 Jung – Ego – Consciousness

Jung was a follower of Freud and to some extent Freud's disciple. He knew Freud's findings and inventions. But at the same time Jung led his own studies and had his own point of view regarding the findings and many other subjects. We could say today that they both – Freud and Jung – believed in thedynamic nature of the regulation of the mental processes, they both believed in the quantitative and qualitative character of the mental processes. They also believed in a topographic-structural model of the mind and that consciousness and ego ("I") is a "bridge", an "intermediate entity" between the external world and the realm of the internal psychological life, they believed as well in the dynamic nature of the psychological, partially unconscious psychological life. They believed that ego/"I" emerges from the unconscious. This emergence of the "I"/ego was, according to them, a result of the perception of internal (physiological) stimuli of the body and external stimuli from the surrounding world. But Jung approached the problem of the unconsciousness and, as a consequence of the above, the problem of the consciousness in a different way. He understood the unconscious mind not only as a reservoir of the impulses, instincts and drives, but also as a separate individual, a

5 Ibid., 22:71–72.

separate subject, unconscious but having very often different language and preferences to that we experience consciously. For Jung the unconscious has got a quality similar to some extent to the nature of the conscious subject. That quality is hidden – according to Jung – in the unconscious psychic and processes. Jung called that inner unconscious subject with the term "the Self" (*das Selbst*).

In reference to this we can see now what Jung said about ego and consciousness. In one of his papers we can read about it in the context of the analysis of ego/ "I":[6]

> What do we mean by ego? For all its appearance of unity, it is obviously a highly composite factor. It is made up of images recorded from the sense-functions that transmit stimuli both from within and from without, and furthermore of an immense accumulation of images of past processes. All these components need a powerful cohesive force to hold them together, and this we have already recognized as a property of consciousness. Consciousness therefore seems to be the necessary precondition for the ego. Yet without the ego, consciousness is unthinkable. This apparent contradiction may perhaps be resolved by regarding the ego, too, as a reflection not of one but of very many processes and their interplay – in fact, of all those processes and contents that make up ego-consciousness. Their diversity does indeed form a unity, because their relation to consciousness acts as a sort of gravitational force drawing the various parts together, towards what might be called a virtual centre. For this reason I do not speak simply of the ego, but of an ego-complex, on the proven assumption that the ego, having a fluctuating composition, is changeable and therefore can not be simply the ego.[7]

6 Freud introduced the concept of ego in his earliest writings, using the German word *Ich*, a noun that he coined from the ordinary everyday pronoun *ich* (I), and the translator James Strachey (1987–1967) rendered it as *ego*, wanting to add to that "a veneer of obscurity and technicality" that the original German lacks. From the perspective of the years of developing of the theory of mind that move seems to be a misfortunate one due to the fact that it created that "obscurity" and actually withdrew the psychoanalytic scientists' attention from the main stream university studies on cognitive psychology of the concept of "I" and also divided the scientific society on psychoanalytical and university researchers. The consequence of this move is now leaving the psychoanalytical theory and its findings in the "grey area" of marginal non-main-stream field of studies. Due to the fact of that "obscurity" many contemporary scientists prefer to treat psychoanalytic theory of the "I"/ego and the theory of mind rather as a relic of the history and they don't develop it further.

According to Freud the ego ("I") is a sense organ for perception of both external and internal stimuli. Different factors and ways of "shaping" individual consciousness (psychological perspective).

7 Jung, "The Structure and Dynamics of the Psyche", para. 611.

And further in the same place we read:

> This view of the ego as a composite of psychic elements logically brings us to the question: Is the ego the central image and thus the exclusive representative of the total human being? Are all the contents and functions related to it and does it express them all? We must answer this question in the negative. The ego is a complex that does not comprise the total human being; it has forgotten infinitely more than it knows. It has heard and seen an infinite amount of which it has never become conscious. There are thoughts that spring up beyond the range of consciousness, fully formed and complete, and it knows nothing of them. The ego has scarcely even the vaguest notion of the incredibly important regulative function of the sympathetic nervous system in relation to the internal bodily processes. What the ego comprehends is perhaps the smallest part of what a complete consciousness would have to comprehend.[8]
>
> We could compare consciousness to the beam of a search light. Only those objects upon which the cone of light falls enter the field of perception. An object that happens to lie in the darkness has not ceased to exit, it is merely not seen. So what is an unconscious to me exists somewhere, in a state which is probably no different from what it is when seen by the ego. Consciousness can therefore be understood as a state of association with the ego. But the critical point is the ego. What do we mean by the ego?[9]

As we see above, Jung was aware of the integrating forces that are responsible for creating and establishing the ego structure and how that structure/entity/being is based on and related to the conscious representations of the different body and mind processes. He emphasizes that even more directly saying:

> "Just as the activities of seeing, hearing, etc. create images of themselves which, when related to the ego, produce a consciousness of the activity in question, so the ego, as I have said, can be understood as an image or reflection of all the activities comprehended by it [...] And since man appears to be a living unity in himself, the conclusion would follow that the images of all his psychic activities are united in one total image of the whole man, which if known to him would be regarded as an ego."[10]

8 Ibid., paras. 612–13.
9 Ibid., para. 610.
10 Ibid., para. 616.

In that perspective we can conclude that our conscious life or the life of our subjective consciousness is directly interrelated to the images or sensory representations that appear in the scenery of our being.

4 Preconscious Nature of Ego/I

If we add to what we have said above that many, if not the majority, of the ego/"I"-related processes are not conscious but subconscious, then we will come to the understanding of the preconscious nature of the ego. It becomes, in the first place, a nucleus of subconscious perception, and only then is it a subject of all our personal acts of consciousness. It is the centre of the field of consciousness and all content of that conscious experience appears in a direct relationship to it. The ego is a result of a semi-conscious criterion that makes the conscious being and it is responsible for its further being conscious, the same as without the "I" there will not be conscious content because "to become" conscious means to be in a close/direct relationship with the "I".

From Jung's quotations regarding ego we can also see that Jung's perspective has a structuralist character – with the concept of the complex and the forces that are constellating/structuring/building the individual "I". The "I" here is the complex of conscious (in Freudian perspective preconscious as well) perceptions, which can only become conscious when they are "extracted" by the consciousness. That means, they will either be enough/sufficiently staffed by (associated with) libidinal energy (see: *cathexis*) as wanted by Freud, or they will be significant enough (see: its meaning) and therefore they will be attracted to the relationship with the ego/"I" by the forces of that complex as stated by Jung. For the purposes of this paper I would like to underline that the above energetic/dynamic and semantic criteria should be considered only as one of many hypothetically possible criteria that can potentially participate in the process of the creating of the "I" and the consciousness.

5 The Dimensions of Our Cognitive and Psychic Life

We know from Emanuel Kant's works that the field of our cognition is based on particular dimensions. Space and Time are only two of those dimensions. For instance the three-dimensional observed shapes/objects or the locations of sensed objects are not simply already given by the sensory input but must be reconstructed via active representational processes. Those implicit dimensions create our psychological life, our cognition and experienced meaning. This is important to remember about it, especially for the purpose of this paper, where we discuss different kinds of consciousness and different "ways" of being conscious. When we compare the fully mentally functional human being with the human being without fully developed mental capacity or with the pigmy chimpanzees and their minds we can see how many dimensions we can differentiate in our conscious mental being. I have listed a few perspectives below.

The dimensions defining a structure of our self-image, self-concept:
Self-perception in space
Self-continuity in time
Self-images
Self-impulses
Emotions
Integration of the body/mind perceptions
"The here-and-now" structure of being
Representations of the drives/impulses
Instinctual/archetypal patterns and their interpretations
Memory
Self-concept
Self-knowledge
Wider cognitive representation and wider semantic context
Wider axiological context

The dimensions defining the external structures or mining:
A priori forms of perception: space/time
A priori concepts of thinking: substance, quantity, cause etc.
Semantic context
Axiological context
Projection, projective identification
Instinctual/archetypal patterns of organising perception and patterns of reactions
Unconscious patterns of reactions
The complexes' related reactions
Environmental context
Social context
Axiological context
Paradigmatic context
Cultural context

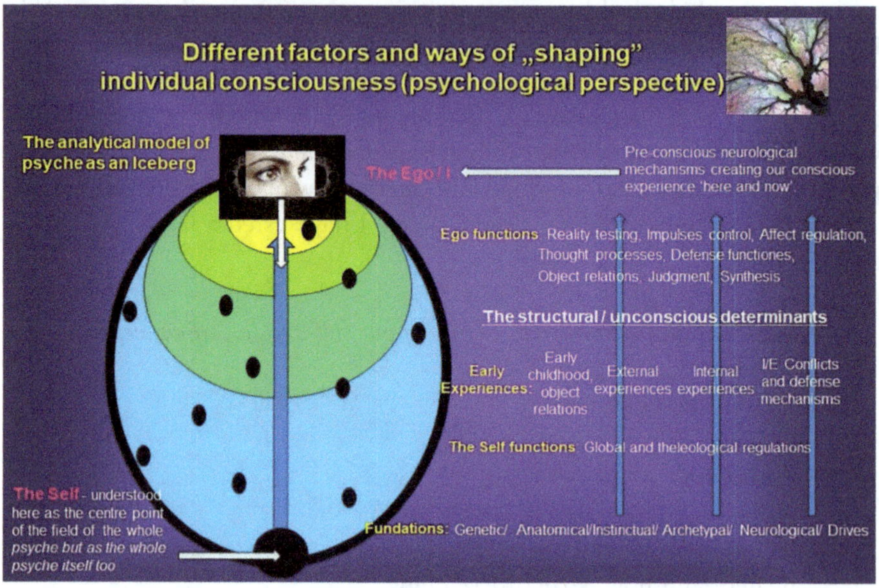

FIGURE 12.1 *Different factors "shaping" the conscious and unconscious processes*. Designer: Andrew Kuzmicki. Retrieved from Andrew Kuzmicki. Used with permission from the copyright holder.

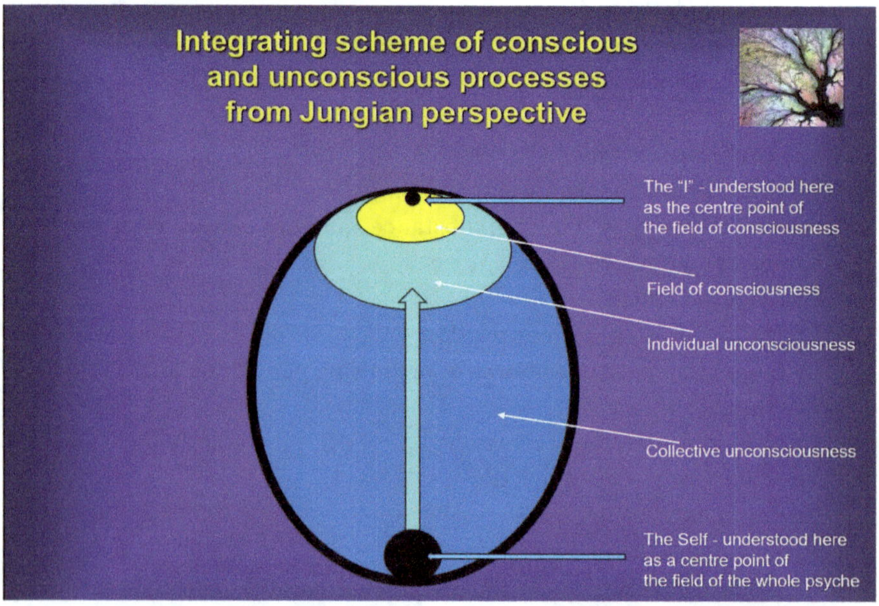

FIGURE 12.2 *Integrating scheme of conscious and unconscious processes from Jungian perspective*. Designer: Andrew Kuzmicki. Retrieved from Andrew Kuzmicki. Used with permission from the copyright holder.

6 The Theory of Consciousness by Antonio Damasio

Above we have described the conscious and semi-conscious processes in the psychoanalytic context. Now we are going to go into the area of the neuropsychology taking into account the theory of Antonio Damasio.

Damasio distinguishes the three main components of consciousness. The first level of it is a "proto-self."[11] On the proto-self is founded the second level of the conscious mind, the so-called "core-self" and on the third and highest level is the "autobiographical-self." "Proto-self" is according to Damasio a biological precursor of the higher forms of "self" being an essentially unconscious representation of the body. This level relates to both of the processes which reflect brain functions and the processes that are involved in maintaining the proper condition of our body (appropriate level of its functioning, stability and functional efficiency that guarantees survival). This unconscious and constantly generated representation that is mapping the internal states of the organism in its basic aspect is just a set of innate mechanisms of the brain whose primary task is to manage the body's vital functions, including chemical and hormonal regulation, coordinating the movements of the internal organs. Its key ingredient and tool is called "neural maps in the brain." The function of reflectivity is a main dimension of the "proto-self" which becomes the foundation and the material of the creation of new forms of conscious mental life.

The next level described by Damasio is "a core consciousness." It is the consciousness that is different from the state of wakefulness or the phenomenon of attention and gives human beings a feeling of being "here and now." Damasio describes that kind of consciousness as the highest level of biological functions of the organism. But, paradoxically, it has also got a clear psychological dimension due to this level containing such (mental) processes as: the integrated field of perception and self-perception that are already non-biological functions of mental life. In contrast to the next, higher level of "expanded"/"wider" consciousness, this phenomenon has only one dimension of organization, but in contrast to "wider consciousness" (in ordinary circumstances) it is always present and "stable" throughout the entire life. There are of course some exceptions to this rule (for instance: epileptic automatism when someone is awake but does not have the feeling of "I").

11 Cf. A. Damasio, "A Neurobiology for Consciousness", in *Neural Correlates of Consciousness*, ed. T. Metzinger (Cambridge MA: MIT Press, 2000), 111–20; A. Damasio, *Tajemnica świadomości* (Poznań: Dom Wydawniczy Rebis, 2000). Originally published as *The Feeling of What Happens: Body and Emotion in the Making of Consciousness* (1999). The reader should be aware that Damasio's term "the self" has got a completely different meaning from Jung's concept of The Self and we should rather associate it with the psychoanalytic concept of ego/I or with its preconscious foundation, preconscious factor.

The core consciousness is associated with the "core-self." It does not depend on long-term memory, or on reasoning or language. The key to this level of consciousness is the concept of "mental image" or neural structure (pattern) that is a "mental pattern in any sensory modality." These structures are collected in a coherent whole and the coordinated adaptive actions of the organism – the main regulative mechanism is a homeostasis. These mental images may reflect any of the "objects" or phenomena – external and internal. They are directly associated with the relationships between the human organism with its psyche and the external and internal environment. The key point here is the relationship: "human mind / cognitive representation ←→ the external/internal objects."

The level of core consciousness is associated with: (1) the integration of perception and (2) the phenomenon, experienced by us, of internal "move-in-the-brain" flowing in our mind and (3) a phenomenon, experienced by us, of qualities perceived by our senses – so called qualia. But still, this level has neither a "past"nor a "future" quality/dimension and all past experiences are present only in a rudimentary form of memory traces that are emerging from the subject's "here and now." On a higher level of extended consciousness all the features are already present.

According to Damasio expanded consciousness has many aspects and sub-dimensions. It is responsible not only for the experience of a sense of individual identity, the extensive (wider, deeper) experience of being a person, but also in a historical, sociological, psychological etc. context. The extended consciousness is associated not only with the functioning of memory, but also with the ability to reason logically and the generation and processing of the complex structures of meanings, including the matter of language with its elements (vocabulary) and its structures (grammar). The expanded consciousness enables us to have the multidimensional experience of ourselves and of the external world.

With both types of consciousness are related the two kinds of "a self"[12]– "the core-self" and "the autobiographical-self." The second of these "selves" described by Damasio can be related to the traditional understanding of "the self" associated with a sense of individual identity and being a unique person with their own history of life. I would add, however, that in my opinion Damasio's understanding of the term "autobiographical-self" relies too heavily on a time-orientated and identity-orientated perspective. That is why at this point I would suggest another term in order to gain a better description of this phenomenon. I suggest the concept of "the understanding-self" – i.e. the self that is directly related and founded on complex mental processes, on understanding

12 We have to remember that all, described by Damasio, the selves are completely different from the Jungian term *the Self*. The Jungian concept is a fully unconscious entity.

of ourselves and the world. This self is fully shaped in a mature man but it develops itself through a whole life by incorporating, gradually, every day further and further perspectives of understanding of the world and human existence. This is confined not only to the autobiographical aspects but to a whole range of meanings that emerge from the activity of our brain itself (for instance the abstract aspects of being in the world).

When we look at all living beings from this perspective we realize that the main criterion of accurate differentiation of the level of conscious experience in living creatures will be the level of their "understanding" of themselves and the world – it will not be the criterion of establishing their existence in the autobiographical or historical perspective.

The ability to acquire language and to perform "semantic marking" of the objects in the world, or – in other words – the semantic differentiation and organization of the subjective experience is one of the key elements defining the psychological development of the subject, but also determines an experience of the consciousness. Of course, language here is not the only dimension that guides and determines the direction of mental development of an individuality, but as each acquired new function is integrated during the development of a child, it affects further development and functioning. Language is in a significant way an instrument of nature which stimulates and directs further development of the living organisms in which it appears or emerges.

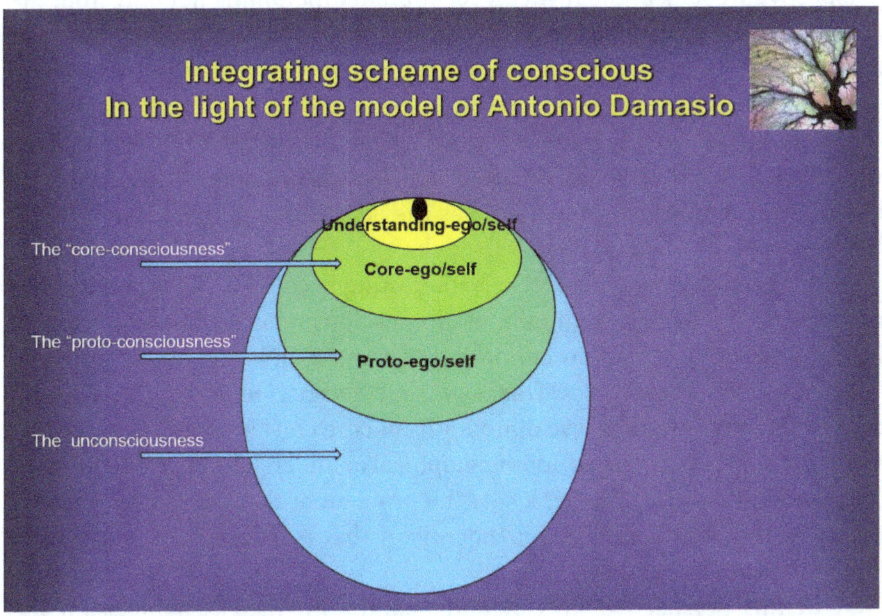

FIGURE 12.3 *Integrating scheme of conscious (Antonio Damasio)*. Designer: Andrew Kuzmicki. Retrieved from Andrew Kuzmicki. Used with permission from the copyright holder.

7 Developing Jung's Theory of "I"/"Ego" and Consciousness

Now let us integrate the aforementioned two theories. "Proto-ego/I" would include all first level mapping structures of the organism with its functions. That level would be closely related to the area of unconsciousness, especially in its biological dimension. "The core-ego/I" would be involved in the building of a conscious "here-and-now" experience on its all levels and aspects. But we can also locate here the first unconscious or pre-conscious influences of the archetypes and collective unconsciousness – especially when we think of them in a perspective of the "shaping" power of archetypal images or instinctual patterns of behaviour. We can locate here as well some of the consequences of an activity of the *psychoid* dimension of the psyche and the matter (here the organism). Lastly, we can locate on that level some influences of the archetype of The Self – understood in Jungian theory mainly as the unconscious factor but acting and influencing conscious states of mind through the modifications on a semi-conscious or pre-conscious level.

But the hypothetical functions of the mind that are associated with the Jungian concept of "The Self" should not be understood only as the functions that operate on a level of "the core-consciousness" because we can assume as well that they are present on a higher level of processing information, on the level of mature reasoning and on the level of the highest insights. In that perspective we look at the higher level of brain functioning not only from the perspective of its manifesting as a conscious being but unconscious too. That means that our higher mental functioning has continuously present two sets of functions: (1) the functions associated with the field of consciousness or the conscious "I" and (2) those functions which operate from out of that field, which the conscious "I" has no access to. The unconscious processes of the higher level can be interpreted here as the adaptive functions related to the higher but unconscious subject – The Self.

The above outlined perspective is interesting because it allows us to better understand the hypothetical mental or conscious reality of a person with a learning disability, the pigmy chimpanzees bonobo and all of us with fully developed conscious processes. This is possible because, in my opinion, just on the border between the above dimensions of core consciousness ("core-self"), extended consciousness and autobiographical or understanding consciousness ("understanding-self") we can locate the problem of the hypothetical mental reality of different beings, independently, if that is an ape, a person with a learning disability or me.

With this perspective we can understand with increased precision the differences in conscious experience specific to those different individuals.

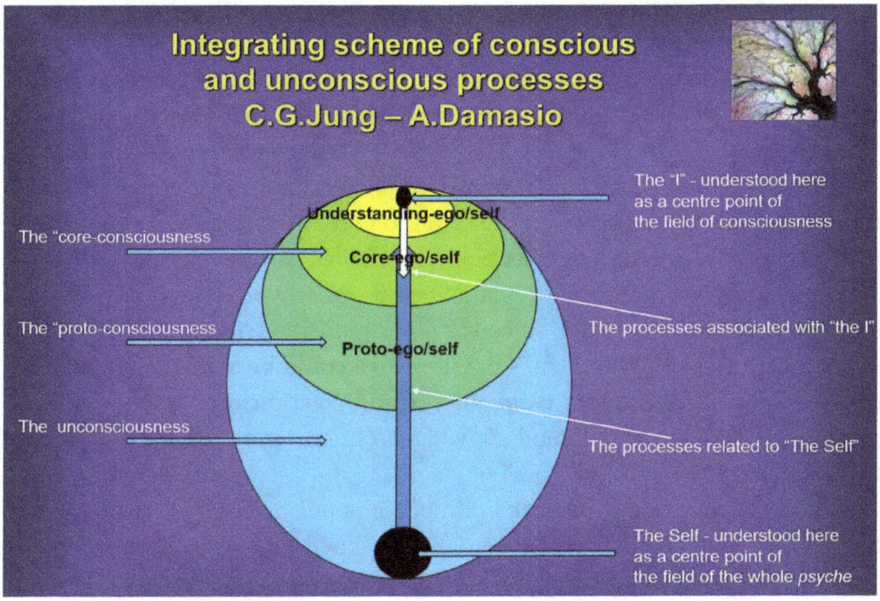

FIGURE 12.4 *Integrating scheme of conscious and unconscious processes – C.G. Jung vs. A. Damasio*. Designer: Andrew Kuzmicki. Retrieved from Andrew Kuzmicki. Used with permission from the copyright holder.

Using this perspective we are able to comment on bonobos, as well as the aforementioned person with some delays in mental development (with some impairments of particular cognitive functions), that they have the "core-self" with the more or less diversified experience "here and now." Conversely, in both examples we can observe the significant lack of important functional features that are characteristic for the higher level of a conscious being of a subject. In both cases, we observe the lack of many of the features specific for the level of an extended, autobiographical, full-of-understanding experience.

8 The Consciousness "not fully functional" – A Person with Learning Disability[13]

When we think of consciousness we usually make an immediate assumption regarding its characteristics and the dimensions associated with it. Of course,

13 In the 1980s, the National Joint Committee on Learning Disabilities (NJCLD) defines the term learning disability as a heterogeneous group of disorders manifested by significant difficulties in the acquisition and use of listening, speaking, reading, writing, reasoning

since Immanuel Kant's works we know that experience of the world (or an object) and our perception is on a primary level based on the *a priori* categories of perception or understanding (In Kant's philosophy, the categories are a pure concept of the understanding). A Kantian category is a characteristic of the appearance of any object in general, before it has been experienced. A category is an attribute, property, quality, or characteristic that can be predicated on a thing. Any particular object that exists in thought must have been able to have the Categories attributed to it as possible predicates because the categories are the properties, qualities, or characteristics of any possible object in general. Kant referred to Aristotle's concept of predicates. Aristotel had claimed that the following ten predicates or categories could be asserted of anything in general: substance, quantity, quality, relation, action, affection (passivity), place, time (date), position, and state. Such dimensions as space or time are hard for us to abstract from.

Then, what happens when the brain of some person is not fully functional and some aspects of their cognition are "switched off" by nature? As an example of this kind of person I would like to give you John, a 25-year-old man, whose mental development did not progress in a standard way and some of his mental functions have not developed and some are not present at all. John cannot properly construct sentences and operate them. He speaks using either the sequences of the key words (for example: "I-shop-Cola"), simple sentences or learned in early childhood, through regular contact with them (For instance: "How are you? What are you doing? Nice shoes.") He finds it very hard to learn new words. For example, his favourite singer, Michael Jackson, is still, as it has been for years, Michael Keks.

Since John's brain has trouble with distinguishing between and integrating stimuli, particularly verbal, so he cannot understand the more abstract or complex sentences. John can understand speech fairly well if it is based on one or two words. He knows hundreds of words and their equivalents in sign language and their pictorial representations. He can understand the messages like: "Well", and "Bad", "Yes" and "No", "Nice", "Fast", "Slow", but he does not understand some of the above messages with negation (for instance: It's not

or mathematical abilities. These disorders are intrinsic to the individual and presumed to be due to Central Nervous System Dysfunction. Even though a learning disability may occur concomitantly with other handicapping conditions (e.g. sensory impairment, mental retardation, social and emotional disturbance) or environmental influences (e.g. cultural differences, insufficient/inappropriate instruction, psychogenic factors) it is not the direct result of those conditions or influences. The NJCLD used the term to indicate a discrepancy between a child's apparent capacity to learn and his or her level of achievement.

nice). In fact, the sentence *"The dog does not go through the pavement."* John understands rather as the sentence: *"The dog goes down the pavement."* or *"The dog goes."*

John's cognition has no fully functional timeline. In arranging the events that are going to come John uses words or concepts associated with the concept of time (such as the days of the week etc.) but he freely (to some extent randomly) chooses them in a situation. When he comes to his support worker he says for example: "Dad, tomorrow", "My birthday, tomorrow", "Christmas, tomorrow." He does not know when these events will take a place. Using the word "tomorrow" expresses rather a desire for that to happen now or in the nearest future. But he understands a difference between "now" and "not-now" e.g. "later." You can see that when he asks for "Shop Now." At that moment he really wants to go to the store now.

John has a very limited time horizon, however it is evident to some degree. We can observe here a particular organization of events. His cognitive apparatus collects some form of symbolic or semantic representation of the world, but it is not able to fully assimilate and develop more abstract dimensions or concepts as time, the concepts of more abstract or subtle feelings and full dimensions of cause-effect thinking.

If we wanted to address the development of John to the child's psychological development theory which was developed by French psychologist Jean Piaget, one could say that John's development, when he was about 2 years old (after having passed the sensorimotor part of his development phase), displayed significant disruption or a blockage of higher cognitive functions, including development of language and complex semantic and symbolic representations of the world.

In John's case not only was the development of the "nominal representation" blocked corresponding to the outside world, but he also did not fully develop such dimensions of understanding and perceiving of the world as: correct integration of complex sensory stimuli, self-perception and causal thinking. John's mind has got an idea of permanence of objects and a form of causality with a result that he can operate quite efficiently with visual objects (for instance: playing video games relatively well – such as: X-Box or Play Station).

John based his actions on the learned earlier structures and, additionally, simple sequencing is a main factor of the organization of his thoughts and actions. His perspective of thinking is strongly associated with his person which can be regarded as an indicator of an unfinished process of crossing the early childhood perspective of self-centeredness. A good example of how John's brain works is a situation when he wants to make tea for someone. He can make tea for himself without problems, but when he makes the tea for someone else he often makes simple mistakes. It is worth mentioning here that in this situation John comes to a particular person many times asking: at first, if that person wants water with the tea, then if he or she wants sugar, and finally if that person wants milk. But finally, when he brings the tea it may not correspond to how the person requested their tea (It is worth noting here that John knows how much one teaspoon of sugar is and the phrase "without milk").

8.1 *Categories of the Faculty of Understanding – Cognitive Representation*

In John's perception we can find the dimensions of such individual perceptual modalities as: sight, hearing, touch, taste, feel heat, proprioception. His brain integrates these sensory data relatively satisfactorily at the level of sensory-motor skills. John also has, to some extent, a symbolic/semantic representation of external and internal reality and language too. His thinking has, however, nominal character and the words which are used by him to describe himself and the world appear as if without broader understanding (awareness) of their deeper meaning (see: "understanding-ego/autobiographic-ego") or wider semantic, grammatical or logical relationships between different concepts/words. Any more challenging abstract concepts and relationships between concepts can't be assimilated by John's brain.

However, we can say that John is to some extent conscious. We can check that, observing the way he directs his attention while performing particular tasks and by watching the way he uses the pronoun "I" and first-person perspective. Seeing a banana he will say, "Me, banana", and if you answer him: "Yes. Take it." then he will reach for the fruit. Or if we ask him: "Do you want to go to the shop?" he will respond: "Yes, buy Coke." Please note here that to answer this question his brain has to have the ability to perform the whole range of the operations: (1) it has to understand and process the message directed to him, (2) it has to understand that the above question was directed to him, (3) it has to select a specific answer, (4) but most importantly, John has to examine what he wants in those circumstances himself (we are assuming here that he has got the ability to determine his "wants" and "wishes", "desires").

Drawing a conclusion from the previously outlined situation it is possible to say that John has a representation of himself, his internal states and desires. Additionally we can say that the objects he desires, at the moment of choosing, are present in the field of his consciousness and attention – we could also say that those objects are in a direct relationship to his "I"/"ego." There is only one question: *Is he aware of that*? Would it be possible for him to do what he did without any consciousness of himself, without a self-consciousness? The answer is: *Yes* and *No*. Yes – because a programmed digital machine (a robot) could probably answer those questions, the same way as John did, giving the observer an impression of adequacy of response. But, on the other hand, such a response from a robot would not come from – we could say – an "infinite" set of hypothetically possible answers, that is a characteristic feature of the human brain. Those answers would come from the smaller set of options provided by the programmer.

So where would the place for the consciousness be? The consciousness would be this kind of "subjective experience" where, either in a human being or in a computer, both are present: (1) the existential cognitive element we call "the I/the ego" and (2) a semantic/symbolic representation of the objective world and subjective reality – external and internal world.

If a human being or a computer did not have a cognitive representation of himself in the first place in the field of consciousness, the whole objective representation of the world would not be possible and affected by that due to the fact that these circumstances would imply a lack of further development of the cognitive representation of the world and lack of further "meanings" and understanding of the reality.

9 The Consciousness "not fully functional"

9.1 *BONOBO – Pygmy Chimpanzees with Ability of Acquiring Language Skills*

The second case I would like to discuss here are the pygmy chimpanzees – bonobo (*Pan paniscus*). I would like to discuss the results of the research conducted on their communication skills. But, before we go further, we have to mention first some of the problems the researchers experienced. They faced three main problems: (1) lack of satisfactory (at least by most of the researchers) "pre-understanding" of the phenomenon of monkeys' mental and cognitive life, (2) some deficiencies in conceptualizing of the observations and finally (3) the problem of being able to adequately describe the bonobo's cognitive and communicative skills – including here a hypothetical usage of the language.

A further significant problem was: How can we bridge the gap between the monkeys' brains and human beings'? And further: Why is it useful to compare the mental or cognitive skills of the monkeys to the human cognition and communication skills while we are trying to answer the question of the nature of human consciousness? The answer to these questions is, in a word, evolution. The mental life of apes is significant to us because that perspective gives us new dimensions of thinking about human beings where we can study, amongst others things, the long-term genetic development of the mind. We underline this because apes have a close genetic relationship to us, especially on the level of their communication and cognitive abilities.

One of the major participants in the study of the communication and behaviour of apes was Sue Savage-Rumbaugh – professor of biology and psychology – who has led her research at Georgia State University Language Research Center in Atlanta since the early 80's. These studies were focused mainly on the broader communication skills of the apes, but in the wider perspective as well, on the process of acquiring language communication skills by human beings. Rumbaugh herself describes their choice of research object (pygmy chimpanzee, bonobos) in these words:

> It had been our hope that by studying a different ape, the bonobo, additional insights into the mysteries of language would be achieved. Because bonobos employed more elaborate gestures in the field, it seemed possible that they had evolved a greater capacity for language than chimpanzees. It was even possible that they utilized a simple language in the wild that no one had been able to recognize.[14]

As a result of a few decades of research and experimentation, Rumbaugh and her team has developed a tool ("lexigram symbols keyboard") for symbolic communication with the bonobos they worked with and additionally she tested the bonobos' ability to participate (understanding) in language-based communication with the humans. She also formulated her own understanding/theory on the process of acquiring of the ability of using a language in both apes and children.

The key point here, as describes Rumbaugh, was a question: Are the pygmy chimpanzees able to assimilate and appropriately use the signs and symbols in communication?

Sue Rumbaugh was also aware that previous researchers had not been successful when trying to understand and develop the symbols used by apes – especially trying to develop and communicate with them using a syntactic structure. Therefore, Rumbaugh directed her research in another direction and headed toward using not sentences but symbols and later words. She was interested in discovering if the chimpanzees have the ability to understand concepts/symbols and are able to use them in communication. In the first part

14 S. Savage-Rumbaugh, S. Shanker, and T. Taylor, *Apes, Language, and the Human Mind* (New York: Oxford University Press, 1998), 18.

FIGURE 12.5
One of the books of Sue Savage-Rumbaugh.

of her research Rumbaugh focused on developing a cognitive structure in the chimpanzees. Her team applied encoding of food with the help of graphic symbols, building in their minds/brains a dyadic relationship between the symbols and real objects (referents) – here in this role food was used. The next step was a gradual enriching of the "mental cognitive net" (cognitive structure of the concepts in their brains) or cognitive representation of the inedible objects (such as a blanket, a key, a sponge, a stick) and more abstract symbols such as a symbol that represented a word "What?", "Outside" etc. Gradually, the researchers began to introduce and develop a symbol communication between monkeys.

For that purpose they used a meal time, when bonobos were encouraged to co-operate in reaching for directly unavailable food. Following a period of this particular type of training, the bonobos mastered this skill and regularly helped each other to reach a food and communicated using a lexigram symbols keyboard. We could say that it was the first purely symbolic inter-individual communication using the implemented system of signs between the individuals of different from the Homo sapiens species. As a result of further research and training, Rumbaugh's team introduced to the communication with bonobos a further set of concepts, but also verbal communication between bonobos and the researchers (the monkeys were taught to recognize verbal content spoken by researchers).

9.1.1 Bonobo's Mental Skills

The bonobos' mind proved to be able to assimilate the symbols and meanings and was able to use them in social communication, including the accomplishment of the specific tasks they were given. Bonobos are able to capture an essence of the relationship between a symbol and wider context of problematic situations or tasks. They are able to coordinate the collective actions / behaviours using abstract symbols (for instance: asking for a particular tool to solve the task etc.).

These symbolic interactions were set up by the researchers with the help of the table with graphic symbols. Later, gradually, the researchers went towards applying spoken words and language. Bonobos have learned to use a couple hundred of the concepts, words, and lexigrams including selected nouns, and verbs, but also adverbs, and adjectives (e.g.: yesterday, tomorrow, good, bad, slow etc.) and prepositions (e.g.: in, on).

When it comes to other cognitive features of the bonobos' brain we can mention here the fact that they are able to recognize their face in the mirror with the understanding that it is themselves. They also have the so-called "theory of mind", that means an ability to understand that someone else may think about the world in a different way than they do. With this feature is associated the ability to understand that others can have different feelings. Bonobos also make an attribution of intentions or feelings of the people watching them and even – which Rumbaugh underlines – they show an ability to understand the difference between what someone else thinks about the situation, and what that situation is in reality (What I think the situation is like. <=> What that situation is objectively.) They have the ability to play games involving pretending and they seem to have developed an ability, that is developed by children at the age of about 4 years, to act out a symbolic game. Bonobos are able to make plans, that means to imagine the events that occur one after another in sequence, and they bring/implement that ability to communication. They express their plans and intentions. They can also tell us, using the combination of several symbols, what had happened earlier before we came. And finally, we need to underline here that according to Rumbaugh's research, bonobos that came under the training were able after some time to understand the spoken language at the level of a 2- to 3-year-old child. For example, in one of the tests a 9-year-old chimpanzee named Kanzi properly understood and then completed (performed) 72% of commands given him when the 2.5-year-old child was able to understand only 66% of them.

In the perspective of this paper it is important to add some additional questions/issues regarding the bonobos' brain, for example, the question of the existence of a consciousness in a hypothetical monkey's brain or mind.

Another question is: does the bonobos' brain have a cognitive structure similar to humans' and do they experience the concept of "ego"/"I"? Do they have self-consciousness and self-reflection? Does their experience have any signs of a subjective quality which is organized around the internal concept of "I"? What can we say about bonobos' mental world?

On the basis of research and observation we can conclude that their cognitive faculty is somewhat similar to ours. They perceive the world in the three dimensions – the dimension of time, memory of events and the ability to predict. They have the ability of cause and effect thinking, they can make wishes and plans, and announce the plans and activities that are going to be realized. They can learn new abstract symbols and meanings, and then introduce them effectively into communication.

The observation of bonobos' communication indicates that they have a certain image of themselves and probably some form of first-person perspective. Additionally, they can supposedly imagine to some degree a perspective experienced by the other individual/person – expectations, emotions and experiences.[15]

But will this be enough for us to start to view the inner world of bonobos as the world of conscious beings? We can answer "Yes" and "No." Yes, because apparently bonobos have, in addition to the integrated sensory-motor structure, an "embryonic" representation of their individual subjective existence that we could call a nucleus of subjectivity. On the other hand, because of the very limited nature of the cognitive structure of their minds (e.g. the structure of the symbols, meanings etc.), we cannot supposedly expect that their inner world can be called the mental world of consciousness seen from the perspective of the characteristic features of human subjective experience – e.g. a conscious, self-reflection and understanding of the broader context of our own existence.

9.1.2 Chimpanzees, Language and Jung's Theory of the Human Mind

From the perspective of the aforementioned we can say that there is enough evidence to accept a close functional relationship between apes' mind and the human mind – particularly with reference to our communicative and to some of our cognitive skills. We now can also describe which dimensions the human mind has acquired additionally – as the abilities that make him the most psychologically developed animal in the animal kingdom.

In the area of consciousness studies we can also use that knowledge about the mental life of the apes to redefine or to better understand the not fully

15 See E.S. Savage-Rumbaugh and R. Lewin, *Kanzi: The Ape at the Brink of the Human Mind* (New York: Wiley, 1994); E.S. Savage-Rumbaugh et al., "Language Comprehension in Ape and Child", *Monographs of the Society for Research in Child Development* 58, no. 3/4 (1993).

developed cognitive experience observed in the individuals with different kinds of learning disability (autism etc.).

But the most important from now would be, looking at what we have described above from the perspective of Jungian studies, to develop further Jung's theory of mind. From that perspective we can differentiate further the Jungian theory of the conscious and pre-conscious mind, especially the Jungian and psychoanalytical theory of ego/"I." To accomplish it effectively we can use here the theory of Antonio Damasio and modify his psychoanalytical model of the mind. We should describe it now as consisting of the following functional levels:

1. conscious, understanding-self
2. semi-conscious core-self
3. non-conscious or semi-conscious proto-self
4. totally unconscious mind, also including The Self understood from Jungian perspective.

References

Blackmore, S. *Consciousness: An Introduction, Hodder Education*. London: Hodder Education, 2007.

Bridgeman, B., S. Lewis, G. Heit, and M. Nagle. "Relation between Cognitive and Motor-Oriented Systems of Visual Position Perception." Journal of Experimental Psychology. Human Perception and Performance 5, no. 4 (1979): 692–700.

Damasio, A. "A Neurobiology for Consciousness." In *Neural Correlates of Consciousness*, edited by T. Metzinger, 111–20. Cambridge MA: MIT Press, 2000a.

Damasio, A. *Tajemnica świadomości*. Poznań: Dom Wydawniczy Rebis, 2000b. Originally published as *The Feeling of What Happens: Body and Emotion in the Making of Consciousness* (1999).

Freud, S. *The Standard Edition of the Complete Psychological Works of Sigmund Freud*. Vol. 22. London: Hogarth Press, 1975.

Jung, C.G. "The Structure and Dynamics of the Psyche." In *The Collected Works*, translated by R.F.C. Hull, Vol. 8. London: Routledge, 1970.

Metzinger, T., ed. *Neural Correlates of Consciousness*. Cambridge MA: MIT Press, 2000.

Savage-Rumbaugh, E.S., and R. Lewin. *Kanzi: The Ape at the Brink of the Human Mind*. New York: Wiley, 1994.

Savage-Rumbaugh, E.S., J. Murphy, R.A. Sevcik, K.E. Brakke, S.L. Williams, D.M. Rumbaugh, and E. Bates. "Language Comprehension in Ape and Child." Monographs of the Society for Research in Child Development 58, no. 3/4 (1993).

Savage-Rumbaugh, S., S. Shanker, and T. Taylor. *Apes, Language, and the Human Mind*. New York: Oxford University Press, 1998.

CHAPTER 13

The Contributions of C.G. Jung and Eugen Bleuler to Psychiatry: Schizophrenia Then and Now

Michael Escamilla

Abstract

This chapter presents an overview of the work that Eugen Bleuler and C.G. Jung collaborated on in the first decade of the 20th century, at the Burgholzli Psychiatric Hospital. This ten year period was one of outstanding creativity for both Bleuler and Jung, and the ramifications of that work continue to influence our approaches to working with individuals suffering from severe mental illness. The chapter discusses the role of the physician psychiatrist, as it had evolved at the beginning of the 20th century, and present Jung and Bleuler's efforts to bring the methodology of medical science to better understand and define the psychopathology of what they would eventual call "Schizophrenia." The attempt to understand the illness "Dementia Praecox" forms the basis of this ten years of scientific work. The critical role of the Word Association experiments is reviewed, as well as how both Bleuler and Jung worked to build a psychological model of the psychotic disorders. This paper presents their work from the standpoint of medical science and attemps to tie in our current understanding of "the schizophrenias" with the theories and insights that Jung and Bleuler developed from 1900 to 1912. Thepaper will also cover how Jung's idea of the human psyche was directly informed by his work at the Burgholzli, in his work with psychotic patients.

Keywords

Jung – Bleuler – psychiatry – schizophrenia – dementia praecox – psychic disorders – Word Associtations Test – Jung's psychiatric studies – Burghölzli Hospital

1 Introduction

As we consider the impact and role of C.G. Jung's theories and ideas in the twenty-first century, a curiously neglected area of current Jungian research and thought is work related to his primary field, psychiatry. In fact, the early

 | DOI:10.1163/9789004336636_015

work of C.G. Jung played a critical role in the development of a new category of psychiatric disease, schizophrenia, which remains one of the most impairing and most studied mental illnesses in the world. In this chapter, I will review the seminal work on this disorder conducted by C.G. Jung and his colleagues at the Burgholzli Clinic in the canton of Zurich, Switzerland from 1900 to 1911. In addition to highlighting the scientific work conducted by Jung during this period, the importance of his mentor, the Swiss psychiatrist Eugen Bleuler, will be reviewed. During this period of time, both Jung and Bleuler were unequivocally working as medical scientists, coming up with theories and hypotheses to describe phenomena which they observed in their patients. Their hypotheses have led to important modern concepts, such as the "disease" of schizophrenia and the theory of unconscious complexes as fundamental organizing functions of human psychological experience. In viewing Jung as a medical doctor who performed scientific work regarding the severe psychotic disorders, we can test his hypotheses in current patients and see what parts of his theories have traction, using methodologies available in the twenty-first century (such as magnetic resonance imaging and validated scales of personality).

2 Jung's Primary Psychiatry Mentor and Collaborator: Eugen Bleuler

There have been numerous publications and papers reviewing the intellectual and professional relationship between C.G. Jung and Sigmund Freud, which encompassed a 5-year period, a few in-person meetings, and a number of letters, between 1906 and 1914.[1] By contrast, the intellectual, professional and scientific collaboration between Jung and his mentor, Eugen Bleuler, has received short shrift. In fact, the engagement of Jung and Bleuler far surpassed that of Jung and Freud, both in length of time (they worked professionally from 1900 to 1909 in the same institute, and continued professional relations beyond 1912), scientific work (papers and books produced by their team at the Burgholzli), and theorizing (theories of complexes in psychology and the psychological understanding and classification of the disorder "schizophrenia").[2] Indeed, Bleuler can be considered to have been the person who most directly influenced Jung in his development as a psychiatrist and as a psychological theorist. As medical doctors, psychiatrists, both forged their careers in hospitals taking

1 W. McGuire, ed., *The Freud/Jung Letters: The Correspondence between Sigmund Freud and C.G. Jung* (Princeton, 1974).

2 M. Escamilla and M. Bleuler, *Jung and the Creation of the Schizophrenias*, in press (Einsiedeln, 2016).

care of the severely mentally ill. Although for Bleuler, this career as a hospital psychiatrist would consume his entire career, for Jung it would consume the first decade of his professional life, and from the experiences he gained in the Burgholzli, and from his conversations and work with Bleuler, would direct the course and influence the rest of his significant opus.

3 Jung's Work at the Burgholzli

From the years 1900 to 1909, Jung worked full-time at the Burgholzli, an in-patient psychiatric hospital that served the canton of Zurich.[3] The hospital itself had been built in the latter part of the nineteenth century as both a hospital to take care of the acutely and severely ill psychiatric patient, and as a teaching and research site for the medical school of Zurich. At the time Jung joined the staff of the hospital (just upon graduating from medical school), the Burgholzli already had an eclectic history. Early directors of the hospital had come from Germany and other parts of Switzerland, and had brought several schools of psychiatric research and theory together. Predominantly, this included the biological, brain-based approach to psychiatry of the German school, which viewed mental illness as physiological, medical disorders, and the French school of thought (led by Janet and Charcot) which had a special focus on hypnosis and "unconscious", dissociated aspects of the personality. Among the early directors of the Burgholzli was the neuroscientist August Forel, whose personal research spanned from detailed study of neurons to the use of hypnosis in psychiatry to the study of the complex social behavior of ants. Although the school most strongly derived its ethos from the German materialistic medical model (the hospital's founder, Wilhelm Greisinger, was a medical internist with a special focus on infectious disease), when Eugen Bleuler became the director of the Burgholzli in 1898, he had studied under the pre-eminent psychiatrists in Germany (including Emil Kraepelin) and France, as well as under Forel in Zurich. Bleuler himself combined a practical, experienced view of psychiatric illnesses (he had lived for many years as a director of a psychiatric clinic outside of Zurich) with a keen interest in psychological models of the mind (learned from the French school) and a grounding in the diagnostic and brain-based viewpoints of German psychiatry. By the time Jung joined the staff of the Burgholzli as a young doctor, Bleuler's studies of psychology had already reached beyond the early quantitative psychology work being done in Germany and the hypnosis/dissociation clinical work being done in

3 G. Palmai and B. Blackwell, "The Burghölzli Centenary", *Med Hist* 10, no. 3 (1966): 257–65.

France to include the study of psychoanalytic methods being developed by Sigmund Freud in nearby Vienna. Bleuler had written a review of Freud's first publications and actually engaged in an extensive correspondence with Freud that both pre-dates and post-dates Jung's own correspondence with Jung.[4] Under Bleuler, the Burgholzli, at the time that Jung arrived there in 1900, was a teaching and research hospital which utilized a diverse approach to understanding psychiatric illnesses. These included understanding and diagnosing patients using standard German based categories for mental illness, post-mortem studies of brains and neurons, intensive discussions and interactions with patients, and the use of psychological theories (including psychoanalysis) to better understand the disorders which the Burgholzli patients had, all embedded in a therapeutic environment which aimed to help patients recuperate in a humane manner.

In this first decade of the twentieth century, Jung not only *worked* at the Burgholzli, but he *lived* at the Burgholzli (along with Bleuler and a staff of a few psychiatrists and many nurses and attendants).[5] The professional approach Bleuler took, and which he demanded of Jung, was that of total immersion in the lives of the patients. As academic psychiatrists (both held appointments at the Zurich Medical University), they not only diagnosed and treated large numbers of patients, but they also conducted research and wrote a significant number of articles and even books on psychiatric topics. Bleuler had a clear focus on studying one type of patient, those with chronic psychotic experiences, who had been recently classified by German psychiatrist Emil Kraepelin as suffering from a disease called "dementia praecox"[6] – a chronic dementing illness which began early in life (as young as the teenage years) and which had accompanying symptoms such as auditory and visual hallucinations, delusions, catatonic behaviors, and disorganized speech and behavior (all occurring in different combinations in different patients). Bleuler was interested in using psychological testing to better characterize the thought and emotional processes of these patients, and he enlisted a young psychiatrist, Franz Riklin (1878–1938) and C.G. Jung to carry out a set of studies using word association testing to attempt to characterize patients with different diagnoses based on their pattern of association to a list of words read to them. This methodology had been used at other psychiatric research centers in recent years (in fact Riklin had practical research experience in carrying out the word association

4 E. Falzeder, "The Story of an Ambivalent Relationship: Sigmund Freud and Eugen Bleuler", *Journal of Analytical Psychology* 52, no. 3 (2007): 343–68.

5 D. Bair, *Jung: A Biography* (Boston: Little, Brown and Co, 2003).

6 E. Kraepelin, *Lehrbuch Der Psychiatrie*, 6th ed. (Leipzig, 1899).

test previous to his coming to the Burholzli), but had had minimal application to patients with "dementia praecox."

The academic work of both Jung and Bleuler was intensive in the period from 1900 to 1912, and encompassed publications in both journals and book form. For Jung, in addition to his thesis, we can count at least fourteen journal publications (two of these did not involve the word association test), a book chapter and two book publications (*Über die Psychologie der Dementia praecox* [*On The Psychology of Dementia Praecox*] in 1906[7] and *Wandlungen und Symbole der Libido* [*Symbols of Transformation*] in 1911[8]). Bleuler wrote fewer journal articles during this time (at least three), but he published three books during this period, culminating in his master tome on "Dementia Praecox," or the Schizophrenias (1911). All of the articles and books (by both Jung and Bleuler) revolve around the study of psychotic patients and, importantly, normal psychological processes, always with an interest in explaining disease processes in a manner that made them part of the continuum with human experience.

4 Complexes and Schizophrenia

The first stage of this work was based on experimental application of the word association test. From 1904 to 1909, Jung, Riklin and a number of other hospital staff carried out a series of experiments using the word association test, leading to at least twelve published articles, with Jung as the lead author on six of the articles.[9] The most intensive, and first of these papers, was co-written by Jung and Riklin and involved the study of a set of non-psychiatric subjects (including doctors and nurses who worked at Burghölzli) to establish baseline patterns of association in control subjects, prior to testing association patterns in persons with dementia praecox and other psychiatric and neurologic conditions.[10] In this paper (published in the *Journal für Psychologie und Neurologie*) Jung and Riklin became captivated by the discovery of emotional "complexes" that were triggered by words and which hinted at semi-conscious or unconscious emotional reactions which could be stimulated by a word (through a network of associations with emotions occurring in the mind and brain). This had, for them, the potential of bringing psychological conflict areas (carried by

7 C.G. Jung, *Über die Psychologie der Dementia praecox: Ein Versuch* (Halle, 1907).

8 C.G. Jung, *Wandlungen und Symbole der Libido* (Leipzig, 1911).

9 C.G. Jung, *Studies in Word-Association: Experiments in the Diagnosis of Psychpathological Conditions Carried out at the Psychiatric Clinic of the University of Zurich* (New York, 1919).

10 C.G. Jung and F. Riklin, "The Associations of Normal Subjects", ibid., 8.

the person) to the surface (where emotions and reactions could be observed). For Jung and Bleuler, the idea of psychological experience arranged around a set of core complexes (memories and emotions organized around topics or experiences which had had a significant impact on the person in the past), became an organizing topology of the psyche which could be used to understand all human beings (i.e. those with and without illnesses such as dementia praecox). For Bleuler, as well as Jung, understanding a person's complexes became the code breaking process which enabled them to understand their psychotic patients' thoughts, behaviors, and expressions.

Although the day to day work of both Jung and Bleuler was in communicating with and treating patients, many of whom were psychotic and suffering from "dementia praecox", both men were interested in general psychological functioning and developed a theory of how the mind works (including in their theory both thought processes and emotional processes) with the concept of complexes as the building block of psychological experience. For both men, the communications of persons with "dementia praecox" were not absurd or erratic, but actually were understandable once the therapist/doctor had an understanding of how complexes organized human thought, feeling, and behavior. Although Bleuler and Jung were interested in Freud's own discoveries regarding unconscious processes, as revealed in dreams and psychoanalytic work, the "complex" theory of psychology was a comprehensive theory which took into account both conscious and unconscious thoughts and feelings, and which could stand on its own, apart from Freud's topologic and philosophic system of the mind.

The year 1906 was a particularly interesting one from the standpoint of publishing their work. In that year, three different books were published, summarizing the ideas of these Burghölzli researchers regarding complex psychology and the psychotic disorders. One of the books (*Diagnostische Assoziationsstudien* [published in English, along with additional articles, as *Studies in Word-Association: Experiments In The Diagnosis Of Psychopathological Conditions*])[11] was essentially a compendium of six articles that had been previously published by Jung, Bleuler, and a couple of other colleagues from the Burghölzli between 1903 and 1906, with a new introduction from Bleuler. Bleuler also published a book (*Affektivität, Suggestibilität, Paranoia*)[12] which pulled together three key areas of theory which he felt were necessary to understanding the psychology of the psychotic mind (building his theory heavily

11 C.G. Jung, *Diagnostische Assoziationsstudien* (Leipzig, 1906).

12 E. Bleuler, *Affectivity, Suggestibility, Paranoia* (Utica, 1912). Originally published as *Affektivität, Suggestibilität, Paranoia* (Halle, 1906).

from an understanding of how emotional affect organized human experience and how unconscious complexes existed below the surface of our awareness). The third book published during this year was Jung's book *Über die Psychologie der Dementia praecox: Ein Versuch*,[13] which essentially expanded the work on word association tests to explain the grand disease of Kraepelin – Dementia Praecox.

Bleuler's book and Jung's book reference each other and present, when reviewed as a whole, a comprehensive theory of both the human mind and insights into the psychotic disease processes. Central to this psychological system was the concept of complexes, defined in later years by Jung as "emotionally-toned contents having a certain amount of autonomy."[14] The concept of the "complex" is key to the psychological theories of both Jung and Bleuler by 1906, and will form the starting point from which all later Jungian theory is based. It is so key to Jung's work that he is known to have considered using the term "complex psychology" to describe his psychological system prior to settling on the term "analytic psychology."[15] The basic idea was that core ideas and memories were organized, at the level of human psychology, by emotions and the combination or cluster of ideas associated with particularly strong emotions – these webs of particular memories, concepts and emotions were felt to be "complexes." Words could trigger complexes and when a particularly strong complex (one with a substantial emotional component to it) was triggered, one could see the effect in how a person responded. For example, the person might flush, or have a change in tone of voice, or a sudden movement. The first set of association experiments was done with non-psychiatric patients as a ground work to see what types of associations non-psychiatric patients had (the idea was to later compare the associations of psychiatric patients and see whether the association test results could help define types of pathology). For Jung, the discovery of complexes (and a scientific methodology of identifying a particular person's complexes), overshadowed any other finding from the experiments and gave him the necessary building blocks to describe key psychological issues which operated within each person, often without their conscious awareness (hence Jung's emphasis on complexes operating autonomously from the person's consciousness).

13 Jung, *Über die Psychologie der Dementia praecox: Ein Versuch.*

14 C.G. Jung, "Psychological Types", in *The Collected Works*, trans. R.F.C. Hull, vol. 6, Bollinger Series, XX (Princeton NJ: Princeton University Press, 1971). Originally published in 1921, 923.

15 S. Shamdasani, *Jung and the Making of Modern Psychology* (Cambridge: Cambridge University Press, 2003).

For Bleuler, and this was echoed in Jung's book *On the Psychology of Dementia Praecox*, the idea of complexes being organized around emotions and affects, allowed him to develop a theory that delusions were particularly strong complexes which a psychotic patient had difficulty integrating with their sense of self (or directing ego).[16] No doubt, through his long experience working with patients with delusions and hallucinations, he had developed an ability to make sense out of delusions and hallucinations, as having something to do with the psychological history of the patient. But now, fueled with the idea of complexes operating outside of the control of one's attention, both he and Jung could start to describe particular cases and make them "understandable" in terms of persons' having had some very strong complexes (often triggered originally by a traumatic event) which developed as almost dissociated parts of the person. Bleuler was convinced that the central problem for the type of patient formerly described as having "Dementia Praecox" (the German psychiatrists' term for chronic psychotic illnesses – i.e. illnesses with chronic delusions, hallucinations, bizarre posturings and emotions) was not that they had typical dementia, and not that many of the patients had hallucinations or delusions, but rather that they had a basic defect in being able to integrate emotional and cognitive processes effectively.[17] The result, in Bleuler's view, was a person who would have trouble effectively interacting with the events and tasks of the outer world, as the neural functions necessary to move down associative trains of thought, to navigate and not be overwhelmed by the complexes within those webs of thought, were defective, in a manner that he felt had to be biological in nature. Bleuler also postulated that whatever the biological defect underlying this splitting of the functions of the mind ("schizo" meaning split and "phrenia" meaning thoughts or mind functions), it seemed to be heritable, as the illness was seen to run in families.[18] In the books published in 1906, Bleuler has not yet made his final conceptualization of the psychotic diseases (this will come in 1911), but he has used the ideas and findings of complexes to build a theory of human psychology and to explain how delusional disorders can be understood from the standpoint of complexes.

Jung, in his 1906 book, *On The Psychology of Dementia Praecox*, reviews a number of recent articles and theories on the disease "Dementia Praecox", which was a relatively newly described illness (Kraepelin first conceptualized

---

16 Bleuler, *Affectivity, Suggestibility, Paranoia.*

17 E. Bleuler, "Dementia Praecox oder die Gruppe der Schizophrenien (Dementia Praecox or The Group of Schizophrenias)", in *Handbuch der Psychiatrie*, ed. G. Aschaffenburg (Leipzig, 1911).

18 Ibid.

this as an illness in the 1890s[19]). Rather than presenting statistical evidence from the association tests, Jung chose instead to present one case in detail and to use his newly developed methodology for identifying complexes to "explain" the behaviors and unusual belief system of the female patient he describes. He does so by describing the complexes the patient has, and he compares his findings to the methodology of the psychodynamic school of Sigmund Freud, although stressing (as did Bleuler in his book *Affektivität, Suggestibilität, Paranoia*) that complexes could be about a number of things and not just about sexual issues (which Freud insisted upon).

With the publication of the books of 1906, the Burghölzli clinic was now firmly on the map of leading centers of psychiatric research. Subsequently, Bleuler and Jung continued to work full-time at the hospital, seeing and treating patients, the majority of whom had psychotic illnesses of one type or another (in current nomenclature, these cases might run the gamut from what we now call schizophrenia, to bipolar disorder, psychotic depression, and schizoaffective disorders). The number of publications by Jung decreased a bit in the next 5 years as Jung's administrative duties increased and he also began to spend more time involved in the budding psychoanalytic movement led by Sigmund Freud. Nevertheless, we know from Jung's later writings[20] that in the period from 1906 to 1912 he was still primarily focussed on working with psychotic patients and trying to better understand the material contained in their "complexes", as he became increasingly intrigued by mythological and symbolic contents within his patients' delusions and hallucinations. Freud was similarly connecting societal myths to the complexes of his patients, although in Freud's view one mythic structure (that of the Oedipal myth) became the one necessary and sufficient myth to explain the unconscious conflict and one primary complex of all human beings. In the case of Jung, he felt there were several types of mythic and symbolic themes which he could uncover in the psychotic material of his patients, which he would eventually describe in his 1912 book *Symbols of Transformation*.

Around this time, Jung also left the Burghölzli to focus on an outpatient practice at his home, with patients who were less severely ill. True to his pattern when doing the word association tests, where he found "complexes" occurred in all humans (i.e. not just those with psychiatric illnesses but in those who were "well") he would spend the remainder of his career studying the mythologic/symbolic forms of thought which he called "archetypes" as they appeared in the unconscious of all mankind. In the patients with psychosis,

19 Kraepelin, *Lehrbuch Der Psychiatrie*.
20 C.G. Jung, *Memories, Dreams, Reflections* (New York, 1961).

he was introduced to the raw material of hallucinations and delusions, which often took on symbolic forms that went far beyond personal historical experiences. Although the material in these delusions or hallucinations were grounded in personal complexes, their content took forms which represented universal human experiences and psychic structures. As complexes built the structure of an individual personality, the universality of particular types of complex (mother complex, self complex, father complex, etc.) organized the structure of the human species' consciousness (and unconsciousness). Jung also introduces in this book his concept that persons with schizophenia might be persons who had an especially strong drive towards introverted thinking processes (attention and libido focussed more on their inner experiences than on external events).[21] Although Jung will not fully develop his ideas about introversion and extraversion until his book *Psychological Types*, he will often mention people with schozophrenia as an example of persons with increased tendency towards introverted thinking.

In the years from 1906 to 1911 Bleuler continued to gather information and details on his patients at the Burghölzli, working towards a new conceptualization of the psychotic illnesses, which he fully described in a textbook in 1911 (*Dementia Praecox or The Group of Schizophrenias*). In this work, Bleuler describes a set of illnesses circumscibed by what he calls a "schizophrenic" psychological structure. In so doing he coined the term schizophrenia, using this to supplant the group of illnesses that Kraepelin had previously classified as Dementia Praecox. Bleuler, like Kraepelin, hypothesized a disease that was biological in nature and in which heredity (rather than events from a person's history or environment) was the major factor, but he emphasized that symptoms such as hallucinations and delusions were "secondary" and not the key feature of the illness. As mentioned above, the key feature of the illness was a dysfunctional integration of thoughts and feelings, which in turn could result in manifestations of complexes which overwhelmed the patient and could not be integrated or processed by the patient. Over the next twenty to thirty years, Kraepelin's disease concept would fall out of favor and Bleuler's "Schizophrenia" would become codified in the modern western diagnostic system to describe persons with chronic psychotic conditions.[22] The diagnosis is still utilized both in European and in American psychiatric classification systems, and is recognized as one of the top ten diseases (in terms of global burder) on the planet as of the dawn of the twenty-first century.[23] Across all countries studied,

21 C.G. Jung, Wandlungen und Symbole der Libido, Leipzig 1911.

22 American Psychiatric Association, *Diagnostic and Statistical Manual of Mental Disorders: DSM-IV-TR* (Arlington: American Psychiatric Association, 1994).

23 "World Health Organization, Schizophrenia and Public Health" (Geneva, 1998).

scientists estimate approximately one out of every hundred persons meets the criteria for this diagnosis.[24]

Jung's work, as mentioned above, shifted in focus after 1912 as he became increasingly interested in the psychological processes of healthy persons (i.e. persons without psychiatric illnesses such as schizophrenia). However, he maintained a strong interest in the topic of schizophrenia, writing several essays or talks on the topic, throughout his life.[25] He would often maintain that persons with schizophrenia had similar unconscious processes to persons without schizophrenia, but that some "toxin" had damaged their brain, leading to the biological defect that Bleuler had postulated.[26] One difference from the standpoint of Jung was that he would hold out the possibility that the "defect" of schizophrenia (the toxic biological process which led to the "split mind" of schizophrenia) might be set in motion by a psychological stress (and not necessarily from something inherited at the cellular level).[27]

5 Recent Research on Complexes and Schizophrenia

Given the fact that schizophrenia is now an esconced diagnosis in psychiatric practice, one hundred years after Bleuler and Jung's seminal work at the Burghölzli clinic, and given advances in research capabilities not available in the first decade of the twentieth century, it now behooves us to test the hypotheses of Jung and Bleuler, to see if their concepts of psychological functioning (complexes) and disease (schizophrenia) remain valid, or, if not, how these concepts should be modified. In this paper I will touch on three particular areas:

> What additional evidence is there for the existence of psychological complexes?
> Is schizophrenia a disease caused by inheritance (genetic) or by psychological stress?
> Is schizophrenia an extreme case of introverted personality (preoccupation with the inner world)?

24 Ibid.

25 Escamilla, *Bleuler, Jung and the Creation of the Schizophrenias.*

26 C.G. Jung, "Recent Thoughts on Schizophrenia", in *Psychogenesis of Mental Disease*, vol. 3, The Collected Works (Princeton NJ, 1960). Originally published in 1956.

27 C.G. Jung, "Letter to the Second International Congress of Schizophrenia (Symposium on Chemical Concepts of Psychosis)", in *Psychogenesis of Mental Disease*, vol. 3, The Collected Works (Princeton NJ, 1960). Originally published in 1957.

The idea of unconscious processes, made popular at the turn of the last century by Freud and soon after by Jung and Bleuler, has continued to be a subject of study by psychologists as well as analysts. From a scientific standpoint, cognitive scientists have defined different types of processes involving different types of memory (verbal, spatial, emotional) and attention. The idea of complexes as defined by Jung and his colleagues at the Burghölzli have largely fallen out of use in modern psychologic studies of unconscious processes (in fact the term unconscious is rarely used, in favor of more specific terms such as implicit memory or internal conflict). Nevertheless, most Jungian training programs still include the teaching of the word association test and how to empirically define complexes using this test, in much the same manner as Jung and Riklin used the test one hundred years ago.

One scientific method to lend support to a theory such as that of Jung's theory of unconscious complexes is to test for validity by looking for biological evidence such as alterations in neural activity levels. Earlier attempts to "visualize" the complexes in the human brain used electroencephalographic readings, but these studies proved inconclusive. More recently, two different sets of experiments have used functional magnetic resonance imaging to identify regions of brain that are activated when a complex is triggered by the word association test. Petchkovsky et al.,[28] working with twelve subjects in Australia were the first group to show evidence of specific brain regions being activated with word stimuli that trigger complexes (bodily reactions, movements, etc. as classically defined). In their findings, which compared the activity of neural regions when the subject read complex triggering words, compared to the activity triggered when neutral words were read, several regions of the brain showed increased activity, including both left and right prefrontal lobes, left and right temporal lobes, and both insula. These brain regions are involved in a number of psychological functions including the processing and association of language, the control of impulses, and the processing (through emotions) of memory. Similarly, a group in El Paso, Texas, completed a similar set of experiments with functional magnetic resonance imaging and a group of 10 subjects.[29][30] In this independent set of experiments, bilateral brain regions were again identified as being stimulated in response to complex generating words, with some, but not complete, overlap with the regions identified by

28 L. Petchkovsky et al., "The fMRI Correlates of Psychological 'Complexes': Exploring the Neurobiology of Internal Conflict", *Journal of US-China Medical Science* 8, no. 11 (2011): 647–60.

29 P. Bechtel, *Thesis* (Zurich: Jung Institute, 2013).

30 H. Sandoval and et al, "Brain Correlates of Psychological Complexes. EEG and fMRI During the Word Association Test" (20th Annual Meeting of the Organization for Human Brain Mapping, Hamburg, 2014).

the Australian research group. The critical finding, however, shared by both groups, was that using brain imaging, there was clear evidence of differentially activated brain regions when complex words were used to trigger responses. Further research by groups such as these should be able to further delineate the biological substrate which underlies the activation of emotional complexes, as defined by Jung, Bleuler and Riklin. With further refinement of what the psychological components of "complexes" are, Jungian psychology should also be able to dialogue with other psychological studies of implicit memory systems. Future research work from a Jungian perspective might include studying how universal complexes are (from a biological perspective) and how complexes operate at individual and group (cultural) levels.

Scientifically, Bleuler's hypothesis that the disease was largely hereditary has also been borne out, as genetic factors (and in particular gene variants) have now been identified which explain much of the risk for who acquires the illness. Some of the groundwork for identifying the genetic factors involved in schizophrenia actually was laid by Eugen Bleuler's son, Manfred,[31] who himself became the director of the Burghölzli hospital after his father stepped down from his work there. Bleuler hypothesized that genetic inheritance was a major risk factor for schizophrenia, and that, at its core, schizophrenia was caused by a biological neural problem which effected proper integration of emotions and thoughts. In the last two decades, researchers using the diagnosis of schizophrenia have used genetic mapping and analyses to investigate whether indeed there were genes that, through being inherited, could cause schizophrenia. The results have been confirmatory, with a large number of genes now identified which, through specific variations, increase risk for schizophrenia,[32] although it has also become clear that schizophrenic symptoms are caused by a combination of genetic risk and an as yet unspecified combination of environmental stressors.[33] While the finding that genes do contribute to schizophrenia (hence heridity does play a role in disseminating the biological underpinnings of schizophrenic processes), confirms Bleuler's (and Kraepelin's, concerning Dementia Praecox) hypotheses, we can also say that Jung's hypothesis that psychogenic stressors could "cause" schizophrenia fits within a diathesis-stress model for schizophrenia. In other words, at the biologic level, due to genetic inheritance, certain persons are predisposed to develop schizophrenia, but only a portion of those with the predisposition go

31 M. Bleuler, *Schizophrenic Disorders: Long-Term Patient and Family Studies* (New Haven, 1972).

32 J. Chen et al., "Genetic Studies of Schizophrenia: An Update", *Neuroscience Bulletin* 31, no. 1 (2015): 87–98.

33 E. Ruby et al., "Pathways Associating Childhood Trauma to the Neurobiology of Schizophrenia", *Frontiers in Psychological and Behavioral Science* 3, no. 1 (2014): 1–17.

on to develop full clinical schizophrenia, and some stressor (which could very well be psychological) must also play a role.

An additional testable hypothesis derived from Jung's observations on schizophrenia is that having an introverted personality can predispose one to schizophrenia. At least two groups have formally tested this in recent years, using currently available scales for measuring personality. The first such group conducted the study in Spain[34] and more recently, this was replicated in El Paso, Texas.[35] In brief, both studies confirmed Jung's hypothesis that schizophrenic subjects showed higher levels of introversion compared to a matched control sample of non-schizophrenic subjects. Interestingly, though, at least in the latter study (El Paso, Texas), it was clear that there was significant variability in terms of the trait of introversion-extraversion, in both schizophrenic subjects and controls. There were non-schizophrenic controls who scored very high on introversion, and a number of subjects with schizophrenia who scored in the extraverted range. One way of interpreting this is that introversion is a trait associated with a tendency towards schizophrenia, but on a case by case basis, introversion is not identical with schizophrenic thought processes. A relative preference and interest in internal thought processes and emotions, rather than in events occuring in the external world, is a human trait that varies in mankind and is not, in itself representative of health or illness. But Jung's intuition was correct in that, *as a whole* (i.e. at the group level), schizophrenic subjects tend to be more introverted in nature.

To summarize, Jung and his mentor Bleuler, made major contributions to practical psychology and psychiatry, through their identification of psychological complexes, and their nosologic construction of a disease entity called schizophrenia. These discoveries have opened the door, in the field of psychiatry, to studies aimed at identifying the biological basis of schizophrenia, with some significant successes, at least with regard to identifying the genetic components of this illness. The environmental, or stress, factors which contribute to bringing out the illness in those who are at genetic risk for it, remain largely unexplored and unidentified. If one can conceptualize schizophrenia using the constructs of Bleuler and Jung, including an understanding that hallucinations and delusions are "secondary" symptoms related to emotional complexes, it may be possible to further advance our understanding of the psychological factors which exacerbate symptoms, leading to the syndrome of schizophrenia.

34 A. Herrán, "Can Personality Traits Help Us Explain Disability in Chronic Schizophrenia?" *Psychiatry Clin Neurosci* 60 (2006): 538–45.

35 Escamilla, *Bleuler, Jung and Creation of the Schizophrenias.*

The evidence that complexes have a biological underpinning, recently seen in the functional magnetic resonance imaging studies conducted in Australia and the United States, lends further empiric evidence to the existence of complexes and, combined with the emerging data from genetic studies of schizophrenia, may help us to understand the biological mechanisms (potentially reversible in some cases) which cause the symptoms of schizophrenia to become fixated, in neural circuits or neural cells, and lead to the dysfunction in the ability to process emotion, thoughts, and memories.

As we move further into the twenty-first century, the discoveries of Jung and Bleuler in the medical sciences can be tested, investigated, and developed further. Certainly, the phenomena of "the schizophrenias" (Bleuler was certain there were many forms of schizophrenia) can continue to teach us about how our minds and brains function, how emotional and semantic memories define our nature and our life experiences, and how these complexes (found within each individual) are at the same time universal (shared by all humans). In the same manner that Jung moved, in his life work, from an understanding of complexes to a conceptualization of archetypes, medical science may one day follow this path in better explaining what is individual and what is universal in our psychology. It is likely that, as in the Burgholzli just over one hundred years ago, psychiatric patients, in particular those suffering from "the schizophrenias" will help lead the way in teaching us not just about their individual maladies, but about the basis of our human nature.

References

American Psychiatric Association. *Diagnostic and Statistical Manual of Mental Disorders: DSM-IV-TR*. Arlington: American Psychiatric Association, 1994.

Bair, D. *Jung: A Biography*. Boston: Little, Brown and Co, 2003.

Bechtel, P. *Thesis*. Zurich: Jung Institute, 2013.

Bleuler, E. *Affectivity, Suggestibility, Paranoia*. Utica, 1912. Originally published as *Affektivität, Suggestibilität, Paranoia* (Halle, 1906).

Bleuler, E. "Dementia Praecox oder die Gruppe der Schizophrenien (Dementia Praecox or The Group of Schizophrenias)." In *Handbuch der Psychiatrie*, edited by G. Aschaffenburg. Leipzig, 1911.

Bleuler, M. *Schizophrenic Disorders: Long-Term Patient and Family Studies*. New Haven, 1972.

Chen, J., F. Cao, L. Liu, L. Wang, and X. Chen. "Genetic Studies of Schizophrenia: An Update." *Neuroscience Bulletin* 31, no. 1 (2015): 87–98.

Escamilla, M., *Bleuler, Jung and the Creation of Schizophrenia*, In press. Einsiedeln, 2016.

Falzeder, E. "The Story of an Ambivalent Relationship: Sigmund Freud and Eugen Bleuler." *Journal of Analytical Psychology* 52, no. 3 (2007): 343–68.

Herrán, A. "Can Personality Traits Help Us Explain Disability in Chronic Schizophrenia?" *Psychiatry Clin Neurosci* 60 (2006): 538–45.

Jung, C.G. *Diagnostische Assoziationsstudien*. Leipzig, 1906.

Jung, C.G. "Letter to the Second International Congress of Schizophrenia (Symposium on Chemical Concepts of Psychosis)." In *Psychogenesis of Mental Disease*, Vol. 3. The Collected Works. Princeton NJ, 1960a. Originally published in 1957.

Jung, C.G. *Memories, Dreams, Reflections*. New York, 1961.

Jung, C.G. "Psychological Types." In *The Collected Works*, translated by R.F.C. Hull, Vol. 6. Bollinger Series, XX. Princeton NJ: Princeton University Press, 1971. Originally published in 1921.

Jung, C.G. "Recent Thoughts on Schizophrenia." In *Psychogenesis of Mental Disease*, Vol. 3. The Collected Works. Princeton NJ, 1960b. Originally published in 1956.

Jung, C.G. *Studies in Word-Association: Experiments in the Diagnosis of Psychpathological Conditions Carried out at the Psychiatric Clinic of the University of Zurich*. New York, 1919.

Jung, C.G. *Über die Psychologie der Dementia praecox: Ein Versuch*. Halle, 1907.

Jung, C.G. *Wandlungen und Symbole der Libido*. Leipzig, 1911.

Kraepelin, E. *Dementia Praecox and Paraphrenia*. New York, 1919.

McGuire, W., ed. *The Freud/Jung Letters: The Correspondence between Sigmund Freud and C.G. Jung*. Princeton, 1974.

Palmai, G., and B. Blackwell. "The Burghölzli Centenary." *Med Hist* 10, no. 3 (1966): 257–65.

Petchkovsky, L., M. Petchkovsky, P. Morris, P. Dickson, D. Montgomery, J. Dwyer, P. Burnett, and M. Strudwick. "The fMRI Correlates of Psychological 'Complexes': Exploring the Neurobiology of Internal Conflict." *Journal of US-China Medical Science* 8, no. 11 (2011): 647–60.

Ruby, E., S. Polito, K. McMahon, M. Gorovitz, C. Corcoran, and D. Malaspina. "Pathways Associating Childhood Trauma to the Neurobiology of Schizophrenia." *Frontiers in Psychological and Behavioral Science* 3, no. 1 (2014): 1–17.

Sandoval, H., and et al. "Brain Correlates of Psychological Complexes. EEG and fMRI During theWord Association Test." presented at the 20th Annual Meeting of the Organization for Human Brain Mapping, Hamburg, 2014.

Shamdasani, S. *Jung and the Making of Modern Psychology*. Cambridge: Cambridge University Press, 2003.

"World Health Organization, Schizophrenia and Public Health." Geneva, 1998.

CHAPTER 14

A Discourse on the Textual-Psychoidal Duality in the Novel *Thorn and Laurel* ["Cierń i laur"] by Wladyslaw Lech Terlecki

Zbigniew Bitka

Abstract

Discourse on textual-psychoidal duality in Władysław Lech Terlecki's novel *Cierń i laur* (*Thorn and Laurel*). The topic of the novel *Cierń i laur* (*Thorn and Laurel*) by Władysław Lech Terlecki (1933–1999) is the fate of Master – a nameless author of historical novels whose real model might be Józef Ignacy Kraszewski (1812–1887) – a nineteenth century author of historical and domestic fiction, well known in Europe of that time. His last romance coincides with his another novel written simultaneously – two fictional perspectives penetrate and illuminate each other. The play of mirror reflections, elements of chest-like composition and duality of inter-textual perspective find explanation in interpretative horizon inspired by concepts of Carl Gustav Jung. The analysis reveals possible references to mythology, Biblical stories and demonology "hidden" in the text, which may suggest archetypal background of Kraszewski's story. In the case of Master it is "all-powerful femininity that inhibits the process of individuation" – the interpretation emphasizes chtonic motif of the archetype of the Great "Devouring" Mother which organizes the essential aspect of psychological problems of the fictional world in *Cierń i laur* (*Thorn and Laurel*).

Keywords

Author as a moral authority – betrayal – sexual obsession – the archetype of the Great "Devouring" Mother – demonology – spy

1 A Writer

A complicated biography of a writer, his views as a thinker, a creator, as well as his feelings – these are frequently used motifs of artistic and literary explorations of an eminent author of contemporary historical novels – Władysław

 | DOI:10.1163/9789004336636_016

Lech Terlecki (1933–1999). Their aim is to find an answer to the question about the sense of life and art, the art frequently involved existentially and politically – literature, in particular – also painting or theatre – a question asked by the author strongly and frequently. Critics and readers usually managed to guess the names of actual writers, proto-models of the heroes of his prose – A. Mickiewicz (1798–1855) (*Zabij cara* [*Kill the Tzar*]), J.I. Kraszewski (1812–1887) (*Cierń i laur*[*Thorn and Laurel*]), St. Brzozowski (1878–1911) (*Zwierzęta zostały opłacone* [*The Animals Have Been Paid For*]), S.I. Witkiewicz "Witkacy" (*Gwiazda piołun* [*The Star Wormwood*]) – to name just the most popular. Historical context and various biographical connections usually directed readers' attention – (according to Terlecki's intention as the author, declared during interviews and statements, i.e. "do homework in history" – to understand historical processes) – and to the role performed in this context by creators, artists and their art. The heroes of his prose: writers and intellectuals are responsible for the shape of social consciousness; often they are active participants of the described processes or events. Terlecki focuses his attention on such writers in his writings. Another important, parallel trend in his creation includes the works in which the writer presents dilemmas and conflicts of the matters and characters directly involved in the struggle for Poland's independence such as, for example, the politicians and leaders from the times of the January Uprising (1863–1864): A. Wielopolski (1803–1877) (*Drezno* [*Dresden*]), S. Bobrowski (1840–1863) (*Spisek* [*The Conspiracy*]), R. Traugutt (1826–1864) (*Liść* [*A Leaf*]). He indirectly implements the ethos of an involved writer, an intellectual taking care of the "Polish cause" – to which he openly admitted at the end of his life.[1] Terlecki's narratives focus on psychological divagations regarding emotional situations (and motivations to act) of characters in difficult, sometimes "border situations" (Jaspers), ethically ambiguous but simultaneously requiring definitions and mental mastering of very difficult, complex and sometimes mysterious problems, which also require ethical evaluation. The author of *Pismak* [*A Hack*] analyses the working of an artist's memory and imagination, which help reenact events or understand their sense (often hidden and secret). A great role is assigned, obviously, to his art – literature, painting, theatre; he devotes many pages of his expression and considerations to these fields, because he sees them as useful "vehicles" in achieving the explication of the complex (although frequently relatively understood) truth of personal and artistic choices, political decisions and historical events. Intertextual

1 During the years 1994–1999 Władysław Lech Terlecki performed socially committed journalism in "Palestra" – a magazine published from 1924 until now. The columnwas published under the title "Władysława Terleckiego BRULION" [Władysław Terlecki's Notebook].

and metaliterary declarations of Terlecki's prose characters can be supplemented with his critical and journalistic opinions (even more so, because the author of *Spisek* [*The Conspiracy*]), expressed his opinions in numerous interviews and articles); the result is disclosure and reconstruction, for example, of a certain type of literary historicism, which he advocated and practised in literature and journalism. That discourse has been analysed many times, by critical and historical – literary arguments[2] and remained within the scientific standard of literature-specialist disciplines. The historical and existential context of the presented world, emotional connections of literary characters form an active, clear background of the cognitive processes and evaluation of the reality. Entering "deeper" into the complex matter of the novel presentations, I can also see the "dark" background of these processes: narrative signals of the unconscious; the presence of "cracks" in the text – images and motifs, which include the content I perceive as archetypal. Zofia Rosińska, a Polish precursor and analyst of the esthetic consequences of Carl Gustav Jung's thoughts[3] with a literary emphasis, emphasized, among others, his differentiation into "visionary" and "symptomatic" works. In artistic visions, the archetypal material is easier to identify according to Jung's categories; Freud's method is better suited to interpret the "symptom" – psychological, literary realism. The "symptomatic" works form a great majority of Terlecki's output. In spite of that, I have been testing in my interpretations the applicability of Jungian inspirations (not forgetting about Freud), because I think that the entire unconscious is hidden by the author of *Cień karła, cień olbrzyma* [*The shadow of a dwarf, the shadow of a giant*] under the surface narrative, the "symptomatic" layer.

2 Psychoidal and Textual

> The psychoidal zone, which transgresses ordinary consciousness and ordinary personal unconsciousness is called the collective unconscious in Jung's psychology (…) Taking into consideration this collective feature of the human psyche, we can assume that one of the objectives of the research of literary output is an analysis of the mythological ('collective') motifs contained therein; mythological symbolism plays an important role in shaping human consciousness, personality and identity.[4]

2 Critical literature is analysed in the monograph: D. Dobrowolska, *Płomień rodzi się z iskry. Twórczość Władysława Terleckiego* (Kielce, 2002).

3 Z. Rosińska, *Jung* (Warsaw, 1982), *passim*.

4 Z.W. Dudek, "Archetypowa interpretacja literatury", in *Psychoanalityczne interpretacje literatury. Freud – Jung – Fromm – Lacan*, ed. E. Fiała and I. Piekarski (Lublin, 2012), 116–17.

By quoting this remark of Zenon W. Dudek, a Polish psychiatrist and a propagator of Jung's ideas, I would like to delineate a certain perspective and a method, which I shall develop further on. "Psychoid" – is a "psyche-like" concept.[5] I think that undertaking an archetypal analysis of a novel requires a metaphorical approach, in which a work of literature not only becomes "alive" in the process of concretisation, which has psychoidal characteristics – its semantic potential can be treated as a reservoir of unconscious "psychic content", complexes and archetypes – not just of a concrete person (for example the actual author), but a linguistically organised narrative subject – on the level of sender and receiver instances of a text – the nearest category would be the "internal author" category. The motivation area of the actions and character of a hero can be approached from the analytical psychology point of view, through a "deep" archetypal analysis, emphasising the presence of the content perceived as a symptom of collective unconscious, and expressed through symbolic structures in various narrations and poetic tropes, which suggest – or generate a form of archetypal images, naturally, a linguistic one. Such content, expressed by mythical, alchemic or gnostic figures – motifs – define a semantic vector, in which a character fulfills the potential of his dramatic (as an "actor" – the subject of actions in the presented world) and simultaneously symbolic activity, meaningful in the open perspective of amplifications performed on the "cracks" identified in the text – in which the interpreted, archetypal sense of the narrative images emerges. This is not just psychoanalysis, in the sense of searching for the sources of compensation and a substitute unloading, through writing, of the "author's" desires and complexes – but rather "extracting" from a literary text its "primal", "archaic" area of its mythical genesis, hidden in metaphors, epithets and images. In other words – discovering in the construction of an individual literary character creation its imaginary MODEL – a mythical, alchemic or gnostic signature – interpreted in the spirit of Jungian amplification hermeneutics. This procedure can be concluded with defining the sources and character of the creative imagination of the internal author, in the Bachelardian and Jungian phenomenological dimension and a description of his (private) "Olympus" as well as "Hades" – a set of mythologically personified archetypes used by the author in the creative process (and their interrelations); this may result in the emergence of a narrative structure, which implements the assumptions of a "personal myth" applicable equally to both the internal author, the narrator and the characters (heroes) of the presented world.

---

5 J. Jacobi, *Psychologia C.G. Junga. Przedmowa Carl Gustav Jung. Wprowadzenie do całości dzieła*, trans. S. Łypacewicz (Warsaw: Wydawnictwo Wodnika, 1993). Originally published as *Die Psychologie von C.G. Jung: eine Einführung in das Gesamtwerk* (Olsen: Walter-Verlag AG, 1959), 67.

The practical reference to Jungian hermeneutics, the "amplification hermeneutics", is the method of search and articulation of the discovered meanings – a reflection resembling the alchemic circulation – *circumambulatio* – "interpretation of an image from different points of view"[6] – concurrent to a certain degree with the classical principle of a "hermeneutic circle." In the motif of a writer-artist, who looks for the truth about man and history (and about himself), which I am interested in, I can see the possibility to describe it within a set of archetypal roles disclosed by mythological or alchemic metaphors[7] of novel narratives; because, according to James Hillman, a pupil and continuator, who developed and transgressed Jung's theory: "Our life imitates the life of mythological characters: we act, think and feel only in the way which is made possible by primary models set in the imaginative world."[8] The composition "network" of literary motifs and "higher semantic systems", dynamically creating the presented world of Władysław Terlecki's historical novels (which are also modern and modernist novels – A. Izdebska[9]) and which can be called, to a certain extent, postmodern (Dobrowolska[10])) enables us to explore, as mentioned earlier, archetype images and symbols, extrapolated from the text and "supplemented" semantically, with the use of the Jungian amplification method. Such an analysis (extended with Jung's personalities, psychic functions and complexes typology and elements of an individualisation process) carried out in different semantic levels of narration, shows an intriguing – because transdisciplinary – field of possible interpretations (literature, history, psychology and anthropology). The interpretations which assume the existence of a "symbolic commentary",[11] "hidden" in the text of the novel, the disclosure and functioning of which is the objective of my hermeneutic actions, as well as the return to literature-specialist strategies.

•••

6 D. Sharp, *Leksykon pojęć i idei C.G. Junga*, trans. J. Prokopiuk (Wrocław, 1998). Originally published as *Jung Lexicon: A Primer of Terms & Concepts* (1991), 46.

7 The contexts of the issued that I discuss were presented extensively in the work of Ilona Błocian, *Psychoanalityczne wykładnie mitu: Freud, Jung, Fromm* (Warsaw: "Eneteia" Wydawnictwo Psychologii i Kultury, 2010), *passim*.

8 J. Hillman, "Pothos: Nostalgia Pueri Aeterni", trans. J. Prokopiuk, *Gnosis*, November 1993, 35.

9 A. Izdebska, *Forma, ciało i brzemię imperium. O prozie Władysława L. Terleckiego* (Łódź, 2010), 8.

10 Dobrowolska, *Płomień rodzi się z iskry. Twórczość Władysława Terleckiego*, 32.

11 The term of W.C. Booth in A. Sobolewska, *Polska proza psychologiczna 1945–1950* (Wrocław, 1979), 34.

Nevertheless, it should be remembered that despite the above-mentioned declarations, Jung made a certain remark during his lectures in Tavistock: "When analysing characters created by a writer, we can read in his soul";[12] the memory about the actual author always, to a certain degree, imposes itself on all psychoanalytical interpretations – in particular when a writer writes about another writer… And this is the context of Terlecki's novel, which I interpret – *Cierń i laur*,[13] which historians connect with the love affair of the sixty-nine-year-old Józef Ignacy Kraszewski (1812–1887) and a twenty-nine-year-old Viennese, Christina del Negro.[14] Agnieszka Izdebska, an expert in Terlecki's literary output, summarises the work in the following way:

> The novel published in 1989 tells a story about the last years of life of a Polish emigrant writer, famous for his prolific literary output; the hero is clearly modelled on Józef Ignacy Kraszewski. The novel's action focuses around several plots but mainly on the late erotic fascination of the hero with a young and beautiful Viennese, a prospective author of popular romances. Another plot concentrates on retrospective scenes from political activity of the main character, prior to his departure from the country after the uprising. An autothematic level is also developed, which contains mainly the hero's meditations regarding his own creation and its relation with his biography. (…) The novel's hero realises that by getting fascinated with a much younger Miss Lili, a literary apprentice, he exposes himself to disappointment and ridicule. However, he offers her financial help and spends a holiday with her and her mother in the south of France, deluding himself: 'who knows, if I will not soon write a short story about myself and Miss Lili.' The reminiscences from the Warsaw past of the hero bring back not only the atmosphere of the city before the outbreak of the uprising, but also episodes from his love affairs (…) and turbulent relations with his wife. The relations with the wife were complex: the wife discovered the husband's affair with the actress so marital relations became tense and formal; however, the wife did not risk a public scandal, which would undermine her dignity and ruin his image of a mentor and a conscience of the nation. (…) The novel ends with a scene

12 C.G. Jung, *Podstawy psychologii analitycznej. Wykłady tavistockie*, trans. R. Reszke (Warsaw, 1995), 96–97.

13 W.L. Terlecki, *Cierń i laur*, 2nd ed. (Warsaw, 2002).

14 A. Trepiński, *Romans Kraszewskiego z wiedenką* (Warsaw, 1970), *passim*.

> in which the hero, tired with ailments and the relationship with Miss Lili, immerses in the sea, leaving behind all his life trials and tribulations.[15]

Izdebska's remarks, in their most general sense, may imply the hypothetical presence of elements of the above-mentioned "personal myth", because biographical narratives are "open to" the mythical horizon of interpretations, in which the mythical model can be read. Literature – a contemporary mythology – can become a path to individuation for a writer. Even more so, because in Terlecki's novel an important narration level is made of "a story within a story" fragment of another novel, a story from the Saxon times created by the hero, largely counterpointing his life and love affairs.

3 Duality, Unity of Opposites, Degraded Mythologies…

Cierń i laur [*Thorn and Laurel*] shares an interesting "intratextual" motif,[16] with the novel *Drabina Jakubowa, albo podróż* [*Jacob's ladder, or a journey*]which I discused elsewhere.[17] A game between one's own texts, frequent and important in Terlecki's prose, is based here on disclosing the creative idea of the hero of *Cierń i laur* [*Thorn and Laurel*], a nameless writer, a refined intellectual, ironic towards himself and others (referred to as the master) – the Master (in order to emphasise the importance of this character, his name shall be capitalised hereinafter), who plans to write a historical novel about a secret mission ordered by the king Stanisław August Poniatowski (1732–1798), which involved sending a dwarf to the court of Catherine II (1729–1796). "During the return boat trip to Dresden he mentioned that he had just discovered very interesting memoirs of the dwarves of the last Polish king. He added that he wanted to write a novel, describing a trip of one of the dwarves to Petersburg, on a very important political mission. That work was to be a kind of a tale, however a different one than those written by Voltaire's friends many

15 Izdebska, *Forma, ciało i brzemię imperium. O prozie Władysława L. Terleckiego*, 62–64.

16 "Many of the phenomena observed here are intertextual, i.e. the author initiates a game with his own texts" (Dobrowolska, *Płomień rodzi się z iskry. Twórczość Władysława Terleckiego*, 172).

17 Z. Bitka, "'Zło rodzi się w nieświadomości.' Archetypy i historia. Dyskurs o nieświadomości w powieści ,Drabina Jakubowa albo podróż' Władysława Lecha Terleckiego, (Evil is born in the unconscious. Archetypes and history)", in *„Między świadomością a nieświadomością" – współczesność w perspektywie psychologii głębi. „Between Consciousness and Unconsciousness – the Present Day in the Perspective of Depth Psychology"*, ed. K. Węgłowska-Rzepa (Warsaw: Don Fredricksen, 2007).

years ago."[18] The story of Alexander, the dwarf, and his friend, the agent of king Stanisław August Poniatowski, the Count (one may suspect that this character was modelled on Jan Potocki (1761–1815) – a famous Polish-French writer) is the topic of the novel *Drabina Jakubowa, albo podróż* [*Jacob's ladder, or a journey*]!

I start my analysis at this point, because I have discovered the first, extra-text, textual signal of "duality." For Jung, duality was one of the most important, basic qualities of psychic characters:

> The basic feature of psychic characters is their duality or, at least, ability to be dual; in any case they are bipolar and oscillate between positive and negative meaning.[19]

For Marii-Louise von Fraz, an eminent pupil of Jung, an analyst working on psychotherapy and literary analyses of novels and fairy-tales – the duality is a signal of "closeness of the consciousness threshold",[20] a possibility of occurrence of a mythological, unconscious motif. Connection between novels opens intertextual spaces and archetypal structures interpreted by myself earlier in *Drabina ...* [*Jacob's ladder...*], which are continued, in my opinion, in interesting biblical and anthropological allusions – in the case of *Drabina jakubowa ...* [*Jacob`s ledder...*] regarding the *Book ofGenesis* and gnosis, and in the case of *Cierń i laur* [*Thorn and Laurel*], – duality marked in the title, which refers to different biblical plots (cierń [thorn]) and to Greek mythology (laur [laurel]), as well as to demonology and secret knowledge. *Cierń* [*thorn*], a symbol conventional and rich in references, mainly biblical (the soil bearing thorns – a punishment for the sin described in the book of *Genesis* – to the crown of thorns worn by Christ from the book of *Gospel*), a signal of suffering[21] and life hardships – together with *laurel*, a sign of glory, praise – (in the novel there continue discussions on how and where to celebrate the Master's creative work Jubilee; how to honour him) – they create a complex "vegetable" metaphor of a

18 Terlecki, *Cierń i laur*, 39–40.

19 C.G. Jung, *O naturze kobiety*, ed. and trans. M. Starski (Poznań: Wydawnictwo Brama, 1992), 53.

20 B. Goetz, "'Królestwo bezprzestrzenne' z komentarzem M-L von Franz", trans. J. Prokopiuk, *Literatura na Świecie*, no. 3 (1978).

21 Zenomena Płużek in *Proces twórczego kształtowania osobowości w świetle teorii C.G. Junga* (Lubin, 2001), 30 writes: "Jung explains the role and source of the suffering, inseparably connected with development. He declares that a person pursuing excellence must accept suffering, which is caused by something, which opposes the development, but which is necessary to achieve fullness. In order to complete that achievement, 'we need a thorn in our flesh' (2 Cor 12,7), and the suffering is caused by experiencing one's own weakness. Without suffering there would be no progress and climbing up."

human and writer's fate, enriched with numerous descriptions of flowers. This is also an image of a certain "unity of opposites"! In this context, *Cierń* [*thorn*] stands for the whole sphere of internal, painful experience, not necessarily "visible", and *laur* [*laurel*] emphasises the external, which in Jungian thought is connected with the archetype of a *persona* – this part of a "personality", which communicates with the society via a public image. It should be added that the title *laurel* is – a holy tree of poets and seers, the tree of the nymph Daphne – a favourite of Artemis and desired by Apollo, which is important for the mythological context of the analysis.

Both novels are connected by demonological allusions (for the Jungian interpreter this is an important signal of the possible symbolism from the shadow archetype area!) – the issue of presence and influence of demons on human reality is undertaken in different ways in the novels. Duality as a trick, a composition "concept" based on the "mirror" game of motifs' reflections, using the popular, in particular since *Rękopis znaleziony w Saragossie* (1810) [*Manuscrit trouvé à Saragosse*; *The Saragossa Manuscript*] by Jan Potocki,[22] composition model of a "story within a story" (also popular in contemporary postmodernist novel[23]) is the basic level of the analysis, due to its dominating composition principle. The images of the "real" characters are connected with it – on the level of the presented world of the novel as well as imaginary characters created by the writer: an old writer, the Master (who almost continuously compares himself with his idol – Victor Hugo (1802–1885) – which sets another "double" perspective!) – writing a novel about the sinful love affairs of King Augustus II the Strong (1670–1773) with his own daughter Anna Karolina Orzelska (1707–1769), and the Master's pupil, a beautiful and young Lili who, in turn, is writing a romance, using his advice and assistance, of a young and innocent Olympia, *nomen omen*, a novel from the life of the upper classes, "in which she wants to show the decay of the contemporary world."[24]

I would like to add that the relation between the Master and Lili becomes at that point also "dual"; the feeling of an elderly man to the young "spiritual daughter" left under his "fatherly" care shows a motif of incest, analogous to the above-mentioned "story within a story" and a potentially wishful love motif in the Freudian sense. The following passage from the novel could be quoted here:

22 (Maybe Jan Potocki himself was a model of the above-mentioned Count from *Drabina Jakubowa* – that would be an example of an even higher level of intertextual games in Terlecki's novels.)

23 See B. McHale, *Powieść postmodernistyczna*, trans. M. Płaza (Cracow, 2012). Originally published as *Die Postmodernist fiction* (1977) in particular, the chapter "Światy szkatułkowe."

24 Terlecki, *Cierń i laur*, 17.

> Lili is also delighted to see the barber's work. She greets him with a careful kiss in the mouth, as if she was afraid that the dye in his beard did not dry yet. – Isn't it true, dear Lili – he says shortly after – that I smell as the largest flower bed in our garden? The pupils of her eyes immediately spark with laughter. Miss Orzelska could have eyes like these – he thought. So big and shiny.[25]

The echo of a mythological and, according to Freud, fundamental Oedipus complex is very clear here (as well as the narcissistic interest in one's own "improved" look after dyeing one's beard)! The name of the heroine (Olympia) of the novel written by "Miss Lili" is a direct reference to mythology, through its semantics. An interesting mixture could be emphasised here – the "upper spheres" are not just a social environment but also an "uranic" zone (as referred to in Mircea Eliade's writings) – the name is connected with the symbolism, which includes the seat of the Greek gods – Mount Olympus. Another, equally meaningful fragment of the novel with "mythological references" is an ironic remark of the Master, regarding his relations with the women invited to the Riviera:

> Between these hours spent together, which I imagined as a foretoken of blissful joy just a short time ago, a gloomy sky full of hidden anger and suspicion grows in the evenings. I am not a god here but my companions. They play their roles of happy goddesses amazingly naturally. Obviously, the mother has more experience.[26]

Entering into the roles of "a god and goddesses", however conventional, evokes mythological and archetypal associations. The background of the developing love affair is (except for the plots regarding art) another, equally "dual" espionage activity of the Master. (In this context it should be mentioned that Miss Lili received several pieces of advice and one suggested, that the novel about the unhappy love of Olympia should contain secret court intrigues, which would make the novel much more attractive). All this because the Polish writer is simultaneously a French intelligence agent, working against the Prussia of Bismarck, who is contacted by his "supervising officer." Also political activity is dual (open) – current (alongside the above-mentioned secret activity) – manifested in journalism; the Master gives interviews; discusses the current situation in Poland after the January Uprising (also in France and Europe); the

25 Ibid., 205.

26 Ibid., 93.

past, also political activity is recalled in reminiscences of the secret actions, preceding the outbreak of the uprising. The Master is obviously "dual" – as he was introduced to the novel (in an absolutely postmodernist style) as his non-literary proto-model, i.e. the very J.I. Kraszewski, with whom the hero of *Cierń ...* [*A Thorn...*] discovers strange similarities![27] The novel scene with the "current" events of the presented world is also dual: the beginning of the novel is the winter Vienna and the meeting of a literary congress devoted, among others, to financial issues (which I regard as an important signal of the potential mythic-archetypal plan in the novel); next the plot moves south, near Nice, to the spring Côte d'Azure, at "Baie des Anges" – the Bay of Angels.[28] Spatial retrospections focus on Warsaw, recalled by the Master, and Ukraine; also Dresden and Paris. All these locations and cities are associated with women – in turn: Lili (Vienna, Nice), the wife and Mrs Keller (Warsaw, Podole), Estera (Geneva, Warsaw, Paris), Marta (Dresden).

The opposition of images, spatial-temporal and geographical motifs may be an important signal of the possible, above-mentioned mythological amplification. Winter – (Thanatos), in Central Europe and spring (Eros) in the Mediterranean, "paradisal", beautiful nature – with colourful flowers and butterflies – a garden-like scenery. One can also notice here another plot with "unity of opposites", important in analytical interpretations. Next to duality, the principle of the "unity of opposites" is an equally clear sign of the presence of archetypal content; both these scopes of concepts, in their Jungian understanding, frequently unite and merge. The mythological amplifications, which I have been applying, are a type of my interpretation "game" with Terlecki's text, discovering mythical features in the characters and situations from his novels. The quoted J. Hillman encourages performing such a literary and analytical game, together with a number of the quoted and non-quoted Jungian female (e.g. J.S. Bolen, M. Hope, and male scholars (T. Moore, Z.W. Dudek). In the cold, winter Vienna people talk about money[29] – writers' royalties, copyrights, financial issues, censorship and politics. The continuous presence of money motifs, "Plutonic" (symbolising, among others, psychic energy, relationships, career[30]) – is a signal of the presence of the Pluto – Hades archetype

27 Ibid., 274.

28 Ibid., 68–69.

29 "Conversations focused mainly on authors' rights. On illegal editions of works, for which authors receive no royalties whatsoever. (...) On prices, profit and interest. (...) Sometimes mediocre authors demonstrated the best business skills, whereas those who deserved better treatment by editors, were extremely shy when financial matters were at stake. He got rid of false timidity long time ago." (ibid., 13–14).

30 See R. Guiley, *Encyklopedia snów*, trans. S. Kiepiel (Warsaw, 1997), 302–03.

in the novel,[31] (politics and secret services can also be connected with Zeus and Hermes). The temporal motifs: winter and spring, family (and erotic) relations: mother and daughter and an elderly, famous and rich writer: the "Master"; geographical and financial motifs – I think that they justify sufficiently the elementary mythological associations with the history of Demeter and Kore (Persephone), Hekate and Hades (Pluto). Archetypal roles can be "played" by other gods, whose "influence" can be seen in the novel characters – the Master: Zeus, Hermes, Lili: Aphrodite, Kore-Persephone, "elderly lady": Demeter, Hekate… Referring to the earlier mentioned principle of unity of opposites – in its mythological and archetypal version, the opposition of the young and old age is worth emphasising, in the archetypes of, for example, *senex* and *puer* i.e. the Master and his young interlocutors: the writer (a clear allusion to Bolesław Prus (1847–1912), the author of *Faraon* [*Pharaoh* 1897]), a journalist; also, of course, a young and old woman. We face here the "degraded mythology" (B. Schulz <1892–1942>), shallow and "deconstructed", in which, according to Jung: "numerous mythological motifs hide under the form of modern images: it is no longer the eagle of Zeus or the Roc bird but an airplane; a fight with a dragon becomes a collision of trains; the hero, who kills the dragon performs as a tenor in a municipal theatre, chthonic mother is a fat vegetable seller; Pluto kidnapping Proserpina – a dangerous driver.",[32] – frequently ironic and even comical. The comedy, known from the early Greek mime artists and old commedia dell'arte, which thematic source is a pitiful passion of a jealous old man to a young and beautiful woman[33] – (it is also one of the motifs of the biblical Book of Daniel! – ("He sees his silhouette in a large mirror. Thin, bony legs. A protruding belly with flab. Sunken chest and inclined arms. Finally his raven black beard. Indeed, he could be a model for a biblical scene, but a completely different one than he desired."[34] It is undoubtedly an archetypal situation, in which the hidden emotions and individual features come to the surface (the Master's personality is obsessed by the archetype of anima, as well as the presence of

31 See J.S. Bolen, *Bogowie w każdym mężczyźnie*, trans. H. Ciszewska and B. Moderska (Warsaw, 2006), 106.

32 C.G. Jung, *Archetypy i symbole. Pisma wybrane*, ed. and trans. J. Prokopiuk (Warsaw, 1976), 417.

33 Recalling his affair with Estera, the Master notices with self-criticism: "The plot as if taken from a boulevard comedy, in which the heroes are an old writer and an actress; so far nobody has been calling him an old man – he started to think of himself that way; the plot is drawn parallel to a great political drama, in which he started participating himself (…)." (Terlecki, *Cierń i laur*, 326–27).

34 Terlecki, op. cit., p. 205.

the archetypes of a shadow and an old sage), and which is a pretext for cruel discrediting of the novel hero.

The Master is the founder of Miss Lili's therapeutic trip (to cure her eyes), her mother's – "the elderly lady" – and his own (the Master cures his bad kidneys and rheumatism) to a French seaside health resort (the hidden objective is, of course, erotic conquest of Miss Lili). The Jungian, although superficial amplification of bodily-health motifs is appropriate here; both eyes and kidneys have numerous, archetypal and symbolic meanings – for example in biblical, mythological or magical symbolism. It should be added that the Master notices the healthy teeth of the "elderly lady" and her surprisingly "young body" during erotic ecstasy, which additionally emphasises the importance of corporal motifs.[35] The greatest number of such motifs, due to the Master's associations, their symbolic manifestation is disclosed in a Messianic, ethical and biblical moment – during discussions at the writers' Congress in Vienna:

> he shall have to listen to all this pretending that he believes in respectful assurances of his moral authority. When the word was heard here the last time – and they could not ignore Poland when speaking about him – he felt constant pain. The left rib, under which a sharp edge is pushed. This comparison is blasphemous, but the pain – similar.[36]

Body as the source of demonstration – theatricalisation and symbolic gestures (e.g. the mentioned dyeing of the beard,[37] the writer's game of "an agent" – in dark glasses,[38] is entered into the presented world of the novel as a prop with a possible, archetypal interpretation of the sense (e.g. persona).

When commenting on the concept of archetype, in many of his works Jung referred to typical symbolic *characters* and *situations*, in which the presence of unconscious content can be recognised.[39] While analysing his patients' dreams and artistic creations, he carried out many complex amplifications,

35 Eyes, kidneys, teeth – amplification of these motifs, interpreted symbolically, is great – it is enough to check this in any dictionary of symbols. For example, eyes are mainly connected with cognition, but also with the Mother Goddess; kidneys with feelings, relationships; teeth with aggression and vitality.

36 Terlecki, *Cierń i laur*, 12.

37 Ibid., 97.

38 Ibid., 173.

39 "As I have been observing and researching for decades the products of the unconscious in the widest sense of the word, i.e. dreams, fantasies, visions and daydreaming, I could not help noticing certain regularities, i.e. types. Therefore, there are types of situations and characters, which reoccur frequently and behave adequately to their attributed meanings." (C.G. Jung, *Archetypy i nieświadomość zbiorowa*, trans. R. Reszke [Warsaw, 2011], 196).

in which he pointed out the presence of motifs – mythologems, which create their visions and images. By inserting dreams into the Greek tragedy structure, he segmented oniric narrations and ordered the unconscious elements in a "theatrical", dramaturgic manner. In the scene of this internal "theatre", uncovered during the analysis, the symbolic characters' images became semantically "deeper", thanks to amplification. Sketches of mythological figures, antique gods, goddesses and daemons become a language, in which the unconscious creates (together with the author?) and transfers its creative energies to the prospective individuation process of – in this case – the textual subject (a character, an internal author), simultaneously "communicating" the subject and the sense of relations and situations, in which the characters from its "internal", psychoid world, the world of archetypes, in which they participate. On the dark background of mythological reflexes, patterns ordering the narration with deep complications appear, independently, to a certain extent, from the composition frames. The unconscious, penetrating through metaphors and allusions, speaks the "language hidden within the language", which creates these patterns and other, wider frames. The drama in this sense is under way in the whole literary output of Władysław Terlecki; this is the internal author's drama of individuation, "transforming" in the spiral, prospective movement of the alchemic, symbolic distillation, which the literary concrete and echo is the intertextual movement of meanings, gaining the sense – and the frames of that sense – through archetypal and mythological amplifications.

Anima, the personified manifestation of the collective unconscious archetype dominates in the symbolically and mythologically[40] interpreted world, presented in the novel *Cierń i laur*[*Thorn and Laurel*]. Its "incarnations" can be seen in the gallery of female characters – current and past lovers – recalled by the Master; the distant, pious but frequently recalled in memories and letters, wife (the jealous Hera but also the modest and spiritual Hestia), the mad actress Estera (Aphrodite), the romantic (and unconquered) Muse – Lili (Persephone, Aphrodite), and her experienced mother, "the elderly lady" (Demeter, taking care of her daughter, but also a lascivious amateur of herbal drinks and spiritualism – the witch Hekate), whom finally the writer fell erotic prey to.

My "gallery" of the female characters from the novel, who can be associated with anima – due to their functions in the world of Terlecki's work – is largely similar to the description of this archetype differentiation, made by Jung himself: "it refers to that primeval image (…) i.e. the idea of a divine whore Eve, Helen,

40 See Z.W. Dudek, Psychologia mitów greckich, interview by M. Jaszewska, 2013.

Mary and Sophia-Achamoth."[41] Anima is also present in a particular way – "a story within a story" – in the novel set in the times of August II the Strong, written by the Master himself, because the historical figure of Mrs Orzelska – a product of his imagination – is simultaneously a compensation; the erotic relation of king August Wettin II with his daughter is a potential expression of the mentioned earlier incestuous complex of the Master, considering his attitude to Miss Lili – protective and seductive at the same time. Another, particularly "ekphrastic" "story within a story" is a motif of a naked woman (anima) and fire[42] (a signal of erotic and destructive emotions) in the picture painted by the writer:

> In the light of a nearby fire, he tried to depict a group of terrified inhabitants of Kiev. The gate was already opened with the use of a ram. Bodies of the defenders killed in battle could be seen between the thick walls. He thought that this yet unpainted picture should include an image of escaping, naked woman. She may be escaping from the fire. She lost her cover in panic.[43]

I have to emphasise that the process of making the historical and battle theme painting ("Seizure of Kiev") is also a type of reflection of the novel making process and psychological transformation of the author. Both acts of creation – literary and painting (another duality) are continuously analysed in the novel by the Master (sometimes in lonely soliloquies, sometimes in dialogues with Lili and other characters) and are an artistic and intellectual discourse about the sense of art in general, which continues in Terlecki's novel (not only this one but also in others). (It is worth adding that the very motif of fire belongs to the most important catalogue of archetypal, "alchemist" images and pictures of the author of *Pożar* [*Fire*] – this is the title of a short story from the collection published under this title.[44]) My associations and connections presented here – pertaining to art – may justify an even deeper, archetypal level of realization of imagination, in which the anima archetype shows its source; Muse will be its mythological equivalent, as an internal "inspirer" of every art; I would declare

41 C.G. Jung, *Typy psychologiczne*, trans. R. Reszke (Warsaw: Wrota, 1997). Originally published as *Psychologische Typen; Carl Gustaw Jung: Gesammelte Werke* (Walter-Verlag AG, 1994), 211.

42 The motif of fire is also an important unconscious, anxious expression: "he dreamt nightmarish images. The King's Castle, synagogue and St Alexander's church were on fire. He wanted to save something from the fire and, at the same time, he felt that nothing could be saved." (Terlecki, *Cierń i laur*, 327).

43 Ibid., 210.

44 W.L. Terlecki, *Pożar* (Warsaw, 1962).

that Muse is archetypal realisation of art; in the novel, the "young lady" Lili is obviously a Muse.[45] Apollonian area of art, "bright" and related to the Muses (and nymphs!), is confronted in the novel with another area, parallel and dark, which is a realisation of the shadow archetype, present in the novel too.

The before-mentioned spiritualism, practiced by the "elderly lady", Lili's mother, creates her dark and daemonic, incredible image. I find an extraordinary description of a seance in the novel – extraordinary also in the sense of the meta-literary game played by the Master:

> he did not suspect (...), that Miss Lili's mother will want him to undergo psychic exercises. He arrived to participate in a séance (...) asked – keeping an impassive face all the time – maybe Augustus the Strong would appear? The elderly lady sitting in front of him asked: 'Who was that?' He answered that this was a king of Poland and Saxony, at the same time. The plate moved. Augustus was informing us about his immaterial presence. The elderly lady said that the spirit wanted to know, why he was being asked to arrive. He asked her whether the spirit could say something about Mrs Orzelska. The plate clattered a few times and froze. He says – the elderly lady whispered after a while – that it is a great secret of his heart... This is great? – he thought. – That was to be expected. As the plate remained motionless, the presiding lady stated that the spirit must have been offended by something. Why was he asked about this lady? – Because he was her father – he responded quietly. – This is not a reason to be offended! – the lady interrupted. – Certainly, madame! – he agreed. – He was also her lover. The lady moaned, covering her eyes. – Pardon! – he apologised.[46]

The writer has also another, dark "alter-ego" – his previously mentioned spy image, familiar to the characters in the novel, who are "behind the scene" and "in the shade" – an informer and an intelligence officer. The cunning delator, his paid informer, the Prussian military, "bloody Kurt" about whom the Master thinks a lot[47] and whose denouncing letters are the source of his intelligence reports, is shown in the novel in an archetypal situation, illustrated with a significant motif of a mirror![48] It is also a French officer, falsely introduced to the

45 Terlecki, *Cierń i laur*, 268.
46 Ibid., 67–68.
47 Ibid., 23.
48 Ibid., 61.

ladies as an "editor" – according to the conspiracy rules. These are not only subsequent "dualities" of the novel perspective, but the traces of deep, unconscious processes regarding self-knowledge and the presence of the elements of the symbolic other, "dark side" of the novel scene: a dark, secret passage of the Polish politics during the partition. I would interpret the "spy" image of the Master as one of the especially important, symbolic roles with archetypal properties, which can be seen as examples of Polish complexes, originating in culture and history, because I can connect them with the complex of a conspirator, a spy – maybe even a complex of Wallenrod- a treacherous, poetic hero of Mickiewicz (*Konrad Wallenrod 1828* – narrative poem), and a complex of the saviour and prophet, Messiah suffering for the whole nation, an icon of the Polish Romanticism.

I would like to emphasise at this point the problem of the ethical consequences of a writer's deeds – his potential, social embarrassment, because he is aware (in Jung's terminology) of the internal split between his social image – a *persona* – "moral authority" ("he shall have to listen to all this pretending that he believes in respectful assurances of his moral authority")[49] and a comical, elderly lover, involved in suspicious love affairs. The Master's (internal) conflict takes place then on the level of his *persona* – the image of a writer known as a "moral authority" and a sexual maniac, almost a "sexoholic" with a Don Juan complex. His emigration is not only a reaction to Wielopolski's suggestions but also an escape from a scandal, which would break out if his wife discovered his love affair with an actress – Estera. Referring to the previous remarks regarding the doubtful "moral authority" of the Master, trapped in erotic snares, betraying and betrayed, I see in this duality – an agent and a spy hidden under the persona of an eminent citizen, a spokesman for the "Polish Cause" – something that in the Polish code of honour is a burden and a disgrace.

Margrave Wielopolski (1803–1877), the Master's rival in sexual conquests, is called Nebuchadnezzar by the narrator:

> Her permanent visitor – there was no other way to describe the nature of these visits, if you wanted to save a bit of respect towards yourself – was then Nebuchadnezzar, by the grace of the tzar, the main Polish advisor as to the tactics used with the parties. The Margrave, in his bear-like appearance, visited Mrs Keller.[50]

49 Ibid., 12.
50 Ibid., 225–26.

Putting aside historical allusions regarding the political argument related to the patriotic journalism of the Master (the actual Kraszewski) and opposition of Wielopolski due to its allegedly rebellious character, I would like to emphasise the biblical sense of the reference to the Book of Daniel. (Margrave:)

> They say he shouted in his study that he is one of those numerous fools, who are allowed to play the role of prophets by the moronic nation! But prophets were stoned already a long time ago. He is ready to use any means, which may be effective. Now he will force the miserable scribe to leave.[51]

A mixture of the motifs of the Babylon king "Nebuchadnezzar" (with a bear-like appearance!) and a "prophet" alludes to the Old Testament Book of the prophet Daniel – a sage and an interpreter of Nebuchadnezzar's dreams, a prophet prophesying annihilation.[52] Is it just an ornament? Of course, the simplest way out is to accept only the rhetorical function of the above-mentioned motifs. One can also refer to the topical motif of a writer – prophet, characteristic for Polish literature, in particular during Romanticism. The Master admits, after all, to his "prophetic vision of history."[53]- this somehow confirms the above-mentioned complexes of Messiah, the prophet. However, the situation in which there starts a conflict between the ruler and a prophet has its strong biblical, thus archetypal, basis. What is also interesting – with a woman in the background. Although it does not refer directly to Daniel, one may recall a story about a love infatuation of king David, who fell in love with the beautiful Bathsheba and, for this love, he cunningly killed her husband – which was disclosed by the king's prophet – Nathan.[54] The New Testament includes a well known story of Salome, Herod and the prophet, John the Baptist. The prophet was beheaded for criticising the sin of Salome's mother – Herodias, who was betraying her husband with the king Herod.[55] In Terlecki's novel, the "prophet" – the Master – is sentenced to exile from the motherland by a jealous lover, a tsarist tyrant with "bear-like" appearance, "Nebuchadnezzar." The fact that there is also a woman involved shows that we face an archetypal situation with power, desire and violence in play. "Nebuchadnezzar" – Wielopolski is a "manic" figure ("a negative aspect of a 'manic personality', which extends human consciousness upwards, towards heaven, and downwards, to

51 Ibid., 223–24.

52 See Dan 1–5, *Biblia Jerozolimska* (Poznań: Pallottinum, 2006), 1243–52.

53 Terlecki, *Cierń i laur*, 382.

54 See Sm 11–12, *Biblia Jerozolimska*, 350–52.

55 See Mat 14, 3–12, ibid., 1379.

animalistic area"[56]) – his power is fuelled by the totemic energy of a "bear" – which can also refer to the archetype of the "Great, Devouring Mother" (in this way Jung interpreted the "bear", theriomorphic symbolism[57] – connecting it with Artemis[58]) – Russia in this case (a bear is its commonly known, "totemic" symbol).

4 Demonology

Mrs Keller, a lover of Wielopolski and the Master, starts fortune telling during his last visit: "she had a meeting with a fortuneteller (...) that evening Mrs Keller was busy with fortunetelling" – one should emphasise this motif, connected to esoteric motifs of the novel; since in the "jewel case", "story within a story", "the novel set in the times of August II" of the Master, astrology is an important element (so valued by Carl Gustav Jung, as the first, ancient forerunner of psychology!). The attempts to foresee the future in the political turmoil situation are common and well known (not only in the figure of the "prophet" – a writer, an archetypal sage) – but the mantic activities of the women connected to the Master can be treated as a signal of the unconscious, personified in the archetype of a "witch" – Hekate. The content of the novel from the Saxon times written by the Master are also demonic and "a story within a story" motifs, present in the game of reflections – also intertextual – between *Cierń i laur*[*Thorn and Laurel*], and *Drabina jakubowa...* [*Jacob's ladder...*] I would like to strongly emphasise the analytical and metaphoric hypothesis, that the Master during writing the novel, performs a symbolic and imaginary *nekyia*. He takes on a journey into the abyss of the Polish, dreadful history. This "descent" into the "dungeons" of history may be metaphorical – "chthonic." One of the characters in the novel, a young priest sent from the Vatican to the court of Augustus II the Strong, observes the lifestyle of the Polish monarch and his court discovers, to his terror, that he is ignorant in demonology, because in his opinion, the concentration of evil and sins in the royal environment can only be explained by the influence of Satan. The demonic motifs are emphasised by the scene of the meeting of the priest with the court astrologist. The apprentice of the secret knowledge hypnotises the priest in order to convince him about his own, true or forced, love feelings towards a king's lover:

56 C.G. Jung, "Psychologiczne aspekty Kory", in*O naturze kobiety*, by C.G. Jung, ed. and trans. M. Starski (Poznań: Wydawnictwo Brama, 1992).

57 Ibid., 66–67.

58 C.G. Jung, *Symbole przemiany. Analiza preludium do schizofrenii*, trans. R. Reszke (Warsaw, 1998), 83.

> He saw an old man, who approached the well. – Are you hungry? ... – No, he answered in Latin. – And not thirsty, either.... The old man seemed pleased. In beautiful, church Latin he explained that the thirsty usually cry by a well. (...) Nevertheless, he decided that the old man deserved to be trusted. He confessed that he was a visitor from Rome. – Oh, yes! – he pulled a face in a quick smile. So it was time for him to introduce himself. He said he was an assistant to the royal astronomer. But his master was residing in Dresden now. Apparently, they prepare better horoscopes for the king there these days. – So the secret knowledge! – he nodded. (...) The old man raised his brows The science, which comes from the stars – he said – should not be read literally. (...) The truth is not often expressed directly. Secret knowledge frequently uses allegory. And for this you need imagination. (...) The old man as if read his thoughts. (...) Could the old man be thinking about him? – he wondered now. He wants to take a look into the depths of his soul.[59]

The demonic court astrologer completes the archetype of an old sage (and a shadow) in its clear but "dark" version – as a teacher, a mentor and a creator; the Master himself remains also on the side of the "manic", „bright" strength of the power of this archetype, as a teacher, a mentor and a creator. A number of his behaviours in the novel can be described, by analogy, in two previously mentioned mythological models: Zeus and Hades, which may suggest a strong constellation of the complex of a "good" and "bad" father, husband, lover; a strong personality of a renowned and rich creator. The encounter and conversation at the well, which evoke in the Vatican envoy the fear of the insight into the depth astrologist's soul and his desires, have an obvious archetypal, biblical and, at the same time, esoteric meaning. (Indirectly it is also proved by the pair of the interlocutors – for the astrologist is the Sage, senex, as the young priest is puer; this kind of relationship takes place in the novel several times.) The conversation about the secret of the fate, astrology, esoteric knowledge is in Terlecki's novel a signal of a deeper, both biblical and „gnostic" initiation into the meaning of history, which we discover in the novel discussed here, and in his other works.

The axis of the biblical allusion in *Drabina jakubowa, albo podróż* [*Jacob`s ladder, or a journey*] referring in this novel to the partition of the Polish state – a special, because paradoxical moment[60] – is a *Genesis* – of our modern, tragic

59 Ibid., 387–88.

60 I see a paradox here in a certain "uncovered" and developed analogy in titles – the fall and loss of independence of the First Republic simultaneously starts the history of its regaining, both in literary projects (e.g. Adam Mickiewicz – see J. Sowa, *Fantomowe Ciało Króla. Peryferyjne Zmagania Z Nowoczesną Formą* [Cracow, 2011]), and in the fight for independence – this is the "Genesis" – Drabina jakubowa; "Apocalypsis" of the next loss of independence is illustrated by the plot and symbolism in Gwiazda piołun.

history (I wrote about an equally paradoxical *Apocalypsis* – September 1939, when interpreting another novel by Terlecki – *Gwiazda piołun*[61][*Star wormwood*] – it can have also a deep archetypal pattern but of a different character than the one currently interpreted. In my opinion, it is worth uncovering here one of the philosophical and historical "seams", which organises and "unifies" the vision of history in the novels of Władysław Terlecki, in whom I discovered deep historical, archetypal and philosophical intuition. A quotation first:

> He reminds me of someone, frozen in that gesture. A certain old man must have looked similar, in the first month of the siege of Hippo by Vandals. **Heroes change but gestures remain the same, I think** [emphasis Z.B.].[62]

Władysław Terlecki in his early stories, in particular the above-quoted *Oblężenie Hippony* [*The siege of Hippo Regius*] (*Sezon w pełni. Opowiadania* [*The season in full swing. Stories*] 1966) as well as in the later *Piasek* [*Sand*] (1996), recalls the figure of the author of the first historical and philosophical work – "The City of God" – Saint Augustine of Hippo (354–430). This intratextual, contextual trope convinced me additionally to assume, in the interpretation of the possible sense, implied by the hidden presence of the meta-historical plot, analogous to the theological formula of "history of redemption" – (or, following the opinion of Cz. Miłosz (1911–2004) about F. Dostoyevsky (1821–1881), that "history has a hidden, metaphysical content"[63]) the metanarration present in the prose of the author of *Czarny romans* [*Black affair*] We perceive, on the background of the above-described demonological allusions, present in the novel written by the Master – the image of the infernal and orgiastic debauchery of Augustus the Strong's court, which is seen in the following way by a young priest, sent from the Vatican as the curial observer: "The image of the court in Warsaw, which he sees after arrival, seems to be the image of hell. (...) the scenes he saw at the king's court could be compared to descriptions of devil's gardens",[64] it seemed, so to speak, as if the moment from the Book of Genesis, prior to creation of man – "angels' rebellion."[65] The times of August the Strong are

61 Z. Bitka, "Alchemiczny mythos ‚Gwiazdy piołun' Władysława Lecha Terleckiego. Perspektywa jungowska (Alchemical mythos of Wormwood Star by Władysław Lech Terlecki. Jungian perspective)", in *Psychoanalityczne interpretacje literatury. Freud – Jung – Fromm – Lacan* (*Psychoanalytical Interpretation of Literature. Freud-Jung-Lacan*), ed. E. Fiała and I. Piekarski (Lublin, 2012), 155–88.

62 W.L. Terlecki, "Oblężenie Hippony", in*Sezon w pełni. Opowiadania* (Warsaw, 1966), 29.

63 See C. Miłosz, *Rozmowy polskie 1979–1998* (Cracow, 2006), 91.

64 Terlecki, *Cierń i laur*, 361.

65 Jewish and Christian exegetes see in the following fragment of the Book of Genesis an allusion to the creation and rebellion of angels: "Then God said, <Let there be light>; and

presented as the "devil's prelude" to the final end, the monstrous "swallowing" of Poland by the occupants (although "it is easier to swallow Poland than to digest it"[66]) – let me remind that the motif of swallowing, in an unnatural, phantasm sexual act, is described in the end of *Drabina jakubowa ...* [*Jacob's ladder...*] The fact that a priest sent from the Vatican associates demonic motifs with corporality – laziness, gluttony and debauchery (and with all the catalogue of cardinal sins) present in the Saxon court, is a relativised opinion about the Polish history.

> Invisible seeds of sin – the Italian thinks. – Its first symptoms regard laziness – he thinks in distress. Those he meets in Warsaw speak most often about food. Those with their bellies already full, dream of some good drink. Satan does not grant good sleep later to all. Some find time for other pleasures. (...) So corporality is their hell. The spirit died a long time ago. Some helpless angels want maybe to bring some life to the dead souls, however, their efforts are too weak for the amount of sin. What kind of fire is needed then, to make people open their eyes and look at the abyss of hell?[67]

The "[i]nvisible seeds of sin" can be associated with unconsciousness, according to the "demonological" interpretation. Spiritual death – corporeality, immersing in the unconscious – can only be stopped by suffering (here: metaphorical fire of purification). These ideas are close to Jung's individuation and its alchemic symbolism!

I have derived the here suggested type of "psycho-historical" or "historical-archetypal" hermeneutics from Jung's remarks, who thought that:

---

there was light. And God saw that the light was good; and God separated the light from the darkness. God called the light Day, and the darkness he called Night. And there was evening and there was morning, the first day." Analysts started to see in that fragment of the beginning of creation a mention of angels, i.e. spirits brought to existence by God. To be more precise, this element was first noticed by Saint Augustine of Hippo, who claimed that the spiritual and intellectual beings created at that time (i.e. angels) were submitted to the test of allegiance of their free will. (...) And their choice was the choice of the good or its rejection. (...) the created light remained with God and spiritual darkness was rejected. This is also referred to as the fall of those angels, who then became the fallen spirits (...) devils (...) demons." (J. Szymański, *Objawienia demoniczne. Prawdziwe historie o diabłach*, vol. 1 [Marki, 2007], 17).

66 This thought of J.J. Rousseau, expressed in Uwagach nad rządem Polski, (see: L. Wiśniewska-Rutkowska, *Nie tylko o filozofii. Ludzie, idee, przemiany* [Toruń, 2010], 193) – due to its importance in archetypal consequences, the content referring (simultaneously) to one of the most important phantasms of Terlecki's prose, will often accompany my interpretations.

67 Terlecki, *Cierń i laur*, 363–64.

> As a doctor, I cannot think that a psychic life of any nation does not follow psychological principles. A soul of a nation is to me a creation, which differs from a soul of an individual only by a little higher degree of complexity. (…) Because there is something in our soul, which is not just individual but represents a nation, some greater whole, even mankind. (…) And similarly as the darkness inside of me, an individual, calls the helping brightness, the same happens in psychic life of nations.[68]

This "helping brightness" may be identified with literature, which can penetrate what "is going on" or what happened "in psychic lives of nations." Following Jung's remark, I would like to emphasise that the figure of a doctor (also present in the analysed novel as an old doctor, professor, with whom the Master consults his ailments) is a permanent motif in Terlecki's prose. "The right medical diagnosis" is, in my opinion, an "epistemological metaphor" – present in his creation and suggesting the possibility to analyse the basic causes of a "disease", and also as a metonymy of the actual political and historical processes. A doctor, a writer and finally a lawyer (an investigating judge, a prosecutor, a barrister) – all three characters from Terlecki's narrative – search for some justification of the situation (disease, history, crime), which they work on. While looking for a solution, they often "open" a meaningful space of not only logical explanations but also unspecified emotions and affectations. The subjective writer's constructions seem to follow the path of "active imaginations" promoted in Jungian psychotherapy; the imagined space shows then the archetypal content of the collective unconscious.

The above-mentioned medical metaphor is also accompanied by the Master's comment, which justifies the topic of the novel in progress:

> He shall write a large cycle about the times of the Wettins, which were an omen of the future captivity. He did not believe in the principle that the sick should not be told about the disease. It is a poor therapy. In order to help – he explained then – one should precisely understand the causes. Only then can the method of therapy be thought of.[69]

Medicine and demonology set a certain horizon for learning about the causes of diseases (and demonic possession), which become metaphorical categories describing historical events (and explaining them to certain extent).

68 C.G. Jung, "Problem psychiki współczesnego człowieka", in *Psychologia a religia. Wybór pism*, by C.G. Jung, trans. J. Prokopiuk (Warsaw, 1970), 82–83.

69 Terlecki, *Cierń i laur*, 382.

5 Spirit of Chthonic Sexuality

There is a stereotype regarding the allegedly belittled role of sexuality in the thought of the Swiss psychiatrist. It is a false stereotype. As Jung explained himself:

> The opinion that I do not notice the meaning of sexuality is a common mistake. Quite contrary; it plays an important role in my psychology as a relevant – although not the only one – expression of the psychic Whole. However, my main objective was to analyse and explain its spiritual aspect and numinotic sense, reaching outside of its individual meaning and biological function and expressing something that fascinated Freud so much, but which he was not able to comprehend. (…) Sexuality as an expression of a chthonic spirit is of greatest importance, because this spirit is the 'other face of God', the dark side of his image.[70]

The key element in the above-quoted passage is of course the "chthonic spirit of sexuality" – connected by Jung and myth and archaic rituals researchers, with the orgiastic cults from the circle of the "Great Mother." Jung carefully analysed "chthonic" archetypes in his most important writings – *Symbols of Transformation* and the works devoted to alchemy. The sexual motifs and images found in dreams of contemporary people, his patients, were frequently repetitions and reconstructions of mythologems known, for example, from classical Greek mythology. In contrast to Freud, Jung did not reduce the occurring phenomena to the "Oedipus complex" but, quite contrary, in his interpretation method of amplification, he tried to explore thoroughly and, using numerous mythological analogies, reach the zone of the collective unconscious – to reach the archetypal core of the "chthonic spirit", "dark face of God."

Jung's modern biographer, Frank McLynn, compared the therapies objectives of the two main protagonists of psychoanalysis:

> Jung's therapy was dedicated to the people in the second part of their life and was a process of internal development. This was what differentiated it so much from Freud's analysis, which at that stage focused mainly on neurotic patients up to thirty-five years of age. The main principle of Freud's therapy was the achievement of 'sociability' or a satisfactory

70 C.G. Jung, *Wspomnienia, sny, myśli. Spisane i podane do druku przez Anielę Jaffé*, trans. J. Prokopiuk (Warsaw, 1976), 201–02.

> heterosexual relationship. Freud declared that the objectives of a normal man are 'honour, power, fortune, fame and love of women [...]'[71]

The objectives enumerated by Freud seem to set the horizon of aspirations of the hero in *Cierń i laur* [*Thorn and Laurel*]. However, considering Jung's idea of "life stages", these objectives shall refer to the first, "natural" phase of an individual's development. Jung describes the second stage in the following way:

> The spiritual objective, which often goes beyond natural tasks of man and its earthly existence, is absolutely necessary for the health of a soul; it is the Archimedean point, from which one can lift the world from its hinges and transform the natural state into the cultural state.[72]

Jung also enumerated the values required for the "health of a soul." This enumeration is not just a positive axiological catalogue – it is simultaneously a polemic with Freud, as well as a definition of the "spiritual objective" direction. In the following quotation, Jung is presented as a psychotherapist, a "doctor of souls": "But what will happen when a patient will all too clearly see the cause of his disease – the fact that he has no *love*, but sexuality, has no *faith*, because he is afraid to get blind, has no *hope*, because the world and life took away all illusions from him, and has no *cognition*, because he did not get to know himself?"[73]

After a failed sexual intercourse with Miss Lili, when he experienced a "rebellion of the body",[74] the depressed Master firstly "retreats into himself", does not leave his room (what is worth emphasising here is that the Master's room is on the top floor of the house; in Jungian symbolism, this spatial image is a sign of consciousness, male logos; ladies live on the ground floor, "closer to the earth"). When, after a few days of "illness" he goes down, he is told by Rozalia, a servant, that Miss has just left for Cannes, with a young Pole (a geographer employed by the Prince of Monaco in his workshop,[75] an ex-insurgent (with whom he had an important, political conversation). (Earlier, during an excursion of the Master and the ladies, when they met the young man, the elderly lady joked that Poles seem to form "a kind of freemasonry" – the joke was

71 F. McLynn, *Carl Gustav Jung*, trans. R. Bartołd (Poznań, 2000), 266.

72 Quoted after Jacobi, *Psychologia C.G. Junga. Przedmowa Carl Gustav Jung. Wprowadzenie do całości dzieła*, 203.

73 C.G. Jung, *Psychologia a religia Zachodu i Wschodu*, trans. R. Reszke (Warsaw, 2005), 339.

74 Terlecki, *Cierń i laur*, 370–71.

75 Ibid., 333.

significant, as it alluded to the dark tradition of secret Polish independence fighters' associations – also Masonic lodges.[76] During his afternoon nap on the same day, the Master:

> Fell asleep quickly. (…) When he opened his eyes, he saw Lili's mother leaning over him. She wore a dressing gown, gaping on her chest. She put her finger on her lips and, before he managed to get up and express his surprise, she leaned against him and took off her silk gown. He did not think she had such a young body. (…) it seemed to him that the presence of the lady is just a dream. But soon he felt a touch. She caressed him with a great skill. (…) When she decided that the right moment has come, she pushed with all her power. Now she was sitting on him, moving violently and resting her arms on his chest. He opened his eyes carefully again. He saw before him large, white breasts and a head thrown back, with eyes closed. She was breathing deeply and he heard her quiet moaning. So this was not a dream, but something that he could never imagine. How did it happen? His recent impotence passed. The strength returned.[77]

The motif of a violent sexual act, even a rape by a dominating woman, connects *Cierń i laur*[*Thorn and Laurel*] with the aforementioned *Drabina jakubowa…*, [*Jacob's ladder…*] by another characteristic intratextual chain of events. From the psychoanalytical point of view, this motif can be interpreted as "obsessive" and meaningful. In both novels, the rapist is an older and dominating woman. In *Drabina jakubowa…* [*Jacob's ladder…*] she is compared to a witch, in *Cierń i laur* [*Thorn and Laurel*] she is a refined lover – an "elderly lady" with an amazingly "young body", healthy teeth and large breasts. Jung emphasised that these features can be interpreted as the attributes of the "Great Mother."[78]

In my remarks regarding the "elderly lady" as well as her daughter Lili, I referred – in line with the accepted interpretation strategy – to those passages of Jung's work, which have been used by archetypal and mythographic criticism. The following passage I regard as particularly important, due to the relations between the mother ("an elderly lady") and the daughter, who confesses everything to her (Miss Lili):

76 Terlecki's last novel, *Wyspa kata*, refers directly to history of Walerian Łukasiński (1786–1868), the founder of National Freemasonry.

77 Terlecki, *Cierń i laur*, 399.

78 Jung, *O naturze kobiety*, 54, 61.

> The figure of Demeter and Kore as a trinity: a maiden, a mother and Hekate, is not only known in depth psychology, but remains even a certain practical problem. 'Kore' has its psychological equivalent in the archetypes, which I refer to as *self* or *manic personality* on one hand, and *anima* on the other.[79]

These relations, in this context, in the plane of mythical allusions connect the Master (Hades, Zeus) with Lili, the daughter (Kore – Persephone) and her mother (caring Demeter and simultaneously a lewd herbalist and spiritualist – Hekate) – in a union, which resembles more chthonic rituals than a Freudian "family drama." One should mainly emphasise the ruthlessly sexual and technical manner, in which the Master was "conquered." Jung's remark about sexuality without love refers firstly to the situation described in the quoted passage. Before reaching certain conclusions, I need to point out a wider problem, connected with the structure of the novel. In a few passages of the novel (selected on purpose), I pointed out the possibility to interpret archetypically mythological signals, which are visible in the narrative. They refer to the two motifs – most important from the point of view of the "sequences" of motifs, oscillating in archetypal "images" and "situations." These are the two thematic axes of the novel: love and mentoring. Love is the relation of the Master with women, which can be interpreted as manifestations of the anima archetype, in its bright and dark, chthonic character; and (basically omitted in these considerations) mentoring: political and artistic relation of the Master with men (usually his juniors), who appear as mythical youths, confronted with the strength of the old sage archetype. These two axis structures are the strongest "mythological – archetypal" (referring to the self archetype) scaffolding of the novel. Returning to the first motif – according to Jung, a "relationship of an old man with a young woman" can be found:

> in many mythical stories. Thus, according to a certain gnostic account, Simon Magus travelled with a young girl, whom he apparently found in a brothel. Her name was Helena – she was thought to be a new embodiment of the Helen of Troy. One could recall here Klingsor with Kundry and Laozi with a dancer. (…) Salome (hereinafter Jung relates his visions; Z.B.) is a personification of anima. She is blind, because she does not see the sense of things. (It is worth recalling, alongside Jung's considerations, the motif of Lili's eye condition, which brings the threat of blindness; concurrence of the novel and archetype motifs is amazingly precise!).

79 Ibid., 51.

> Elias is a personification of an old, wise prophet, symbolising cognition, whereas Salome symbolises eroticism.[80]

The sexual, "chthonic" motif from the above-quoted passage, is the climax of the novel. The solution follows as its consequence – the Master commits suicide. Both axes cross – Lili leaves with a younger man and the Master's impotence is cured by the mother of his lover. In the quoted description of a sexual act, attention is focused on the erotic experience of the "elderly lady" – "she caressed him skilfully" and the half-dream condition (characteristic of the archetypal Hades);[81] the Master wakes up and focuses on the partner's breasts; this motif returns in the Master's recollections of his affair with his Dresden housekeeper, the "good, decent Marta"[82] – "He lay next to her and was delicately touching large, white breasts."[83] More remarks can be added to Jung's previous comments. Analysing only the iconographic material attached to the book written by Jung's pupil, Erich Neumann *The Great Mother*, one may notice numerous images of "busty goddesses" from antic fertility cults; these cults joined – usually in the orgiastic manner – life and death and involved human sacrifice.[84] The picture of erotic conquests of the Master becomes in this context quite "regressive" and "chthonic." Jung analysed on many occasions the regressive and chthonic characteristics of the Great Mother archetype (and of the mother complex). In my opinion, the following remark of Jung's will be a good commentary on the above-quoted erotic scene in the novel:

> At this level of the myth, which renders the idea of the collective unconscious in the best way, the mother is simultaneously old and young, she is Demeter and Persephone, the son is her husband and a sleeping baby;

---

80 Ibid., 217–18.

81 Jean Shinoda Bolen, a Jungian analyst, connects the half-dream, falling asleep and daydreaming with the archetype described as Hades, active in psyche. (See Bolen, *Bogowie w każdym mężczyźnie*) In Terlecki's novel, the hero sometimes falls asleep during conversation, dreams or immerses in reminiscences, which turn into dreams. I refer here to the analytical methods, which characterise the hero on the level of the presented world. Other interpretation possibilities, not mentioned here, which I connect with this archetype and the character of the Master, are not only the allusions to his wealth but also his "invisibility" – as an intelligence agent; invisibility is one of Hades's attributes as the owner of the "cap of invisibility."

82 Terlecki, *Cierń i laur*, 71.

83 Ibid.

84 E. Neumann, *Wielka Matka. Fenomenologia kobiecości. Kształtowanie nieświadomości*, trans. R. Reszke (Warsaw, 2008), in particular the chapter: Negatywny charakter żywiołowy, *passim*.

> this is the state of indescribable fullness, with which imperfections of the real life, efforts and problems of adjusting and the pain of disillusionments absolutely cannot compete.[85]

The fullness becomes a sexual fulfilment to the Master and also the beginning of the road to suicide by drowning in the sea, which can be and, in my interpretation, is the realisation of the other, dark side of the Great Mother archetype as death – the Devouring Mother. In the case of the Master,

> all-powerful femininity slows down the individuation process[86]... Unfulfilled dreams of conquering the young woman end with the Master's paranoid illusion about the women's plot, who wanted to use him- and it was him, who invited them to the trip; he tried to seduce Lili... The plan was discovered. He was to be caught in a net. Concrete demands would be made during the next conversation.[87]

The motif "in a net" may be associated with a spider's web; here, an overinterpretation may be justified – the symbol of a spider is the domain of the Great Mother archetype.[88] Another archetype, which can be seen in his character, i.e. the power archetype – the mythical Zeus – is also dethroned; the young man – a geographer (also related to the Great Mother archetype – the Earth, its area and description) takes away his Lili. Following the teaching of Jonathan Culler, a deconstructionist, I shall introduce another overinterpretation. Lili's eyes are a shade of "violet"[89] – and a violet is a flower, which grew from the blood of Attis, who castrated himself.[90] The amplification of sexual chthonicity in the case of the Master and Lili's relationship is strangely close to the motif of castration – here impotence. (In order to widen the amplification I might add that the clothes of Demeter's priests were violet!) The flower symbolism – in its sexual type – is also discretely present in *Cierń i laur* [*Thorn and Laurel*]– for example the Master admires the blood-red mouth of *nomen omen* Lili, comparing them to a flower [hibiscus – Z.B.]:

85 C.G. Jung, "Syzygia: animus i anima", in*Archetypy i symbole. Pisma wybrane*, by C.G. Jung, ed. and trans. J. Prokopiuk (Warsaw, 1976), 70–71.

86 Ibid., 72.

87 Terlecki, *Cierń i laur*, 400.

88 Neumann, *Wielka Matka. Fenomenologia kobiecości. Kształtowanie nieświadomości*, 183.

89 Terlecki, *Cierń i laur*, 15.

90 P. Grimal, *Słownik mitologii greckiej i rzymskiej*, ed. J. Łanowski (Wrocław, 1987), 11.

> when I was looking at the mouth of the young lady, I started comparing it to the flowers I saw in the garden (...) I realised that when I saw those flowers in the garden (...) I touched them with my lips and the touch aroused the desire to touch the mouth of the lady, who still did not withdraw her hand and was looking at me inquisitively, just like her mother.[91]

For Camille Paglia, who interprets art and literature through psychoanalysis:

> A flower, a mouth, a wound: Gorgon is an asymmetrical image of the Mystic Rose. Female genitals are a furrow in the female earth. The Snake-haired Medusa is a thorny undergrowth of the continuous fertility of nature.[92]

Earlier, Paglia referred to Freud, who interprets looking at Medusa – Gorgon as a fear of castration. The culmination and mixture of chthonic motifs – eyes, flowers, mouth – are quite considerable, assuming Jung's amplification; one may refer here to the research of the above-mentioned Erich Neumann. Jung's pupil wrote in the famous *The Great Mother*, chapter *The Lady of the Plants*:

> the affinity of femininity and plants can be traced by looking at different levels of the spirit symbolism. All which is expressed in the symbols of flowers, lotus, lily and rose, virginity as the flowers of Eleusinian mysteries, are the symbols of a flowering spiritual and psychic evolution process.[93]

The whole ethical context is added to that – betrayal, love, jealousy, domination ... Lili, the daughter of the "elderly lady" is connected with the motif of degrading impotence – a symbolic castration – the Freudian trace of a thanatic trope – with the mother, a refined lover-rapist, the domination motif, "dethroning", and also humiliation. Eros, contrary to his hopes, did not revive the Master; quite contrary – he showed his "chthonic" image: the "violet-eyed" Muse, Kore-Persephone, Miss Lili and the "elderly lady" – Demeter-Hekate led him to paranoia and suicidal death. The path to the death seems also to be marked with archetypal traces. On the train (the first trace – the train motif probably

91 Terlecki, *Cierń i laur*, 97.

92 C. Paglia, *Seksualne persony. Sztuka i dekadencja od Nefretiti do Emily Dickinson*, trans. M. Kuźniak and M. Zapędowska (Poznań, 2006). Originally published as *Sexual Personae* (1990), 45.

93 Neumann, *Wielka Matka. Fenomenologia kobiecości. Kształtowanie nieświadomości*, 266–67.

connected with "acceleration of the individuation process"[94]), in which the Master travels to the bay and meets a strange youth. The young man, reading poetry, reminds him of a Polish insurgent sentenced to death – hanged at a public execution, which he witnessed – this is the second trace.[95] The meaningful recollection of the execution, a violent death of a young man, comes before the actual, or imagined by the author, moment of his own death:

> It is time to die. (...) He was swimming on his back. He saw stars above. (...) Time was returning to its hidden bottom. Memory did not exist. A moment became the eternity. (...) Far away, in the bay, the wave lifted and covered the stars.[96]

I perceive in the mythical and archetypal level a reflection, an echo of an offering to the "good" Great Mother – which will be Poland, for which the young man recalled by the Master, sacrificed his life for freedom, and Russia – the "bad" – Devouring Mother, against whom he fought and by whom he was punished. The amplifications, which I will quote after Jung, are quite curious:

> Attis castrated himself for his mother and, in order to commemorate this, his image was hanged on pine trees; so Christ was hanged on the Tree of Life and Suffering, the tree of Hekate and Mother. (...) Suffering comes instead of pleasure, a whipping-post instead of mother-lover; the union of male consciousness with female unconsciousness – previously felt as delight – now felt as something painful. (...) Using a modern language, one may say that the last projection means the union of consciousness with unconsciousness, i.e. with a transcendent function, characteristic to the process of individuation.[97]

The concurrence of the sacrifice-chthonic and messianic symbolism in the quoted work of Jung particularly corresponds with the problems and ending of Terlecki's novel. As I mentioned before, although in *Cierń i laur* [*Thorn and Laurel*] there is no vision directly evoking an archetypal image, the amassing of the motifs, which can be interpreted as archetypes, is considerable and

94 The motif of a train journey (in a dream) is thus described by O. Vedfelt: "the process was put in motion. The passengers were understood as the unconscious elements, travelling to the light, i.e. forward to consciousness." (O. Vedfelt, *Wymiary snów. Istota, funkcje i znaczenie marzeń sennych*, trans. P. Billig [Warsaw, 1998], 89).

95 Terlecki, *Cierń i laur*, 410–11.

96 Ibid., 413–15.

97 Jung, *Symbole przemiany. Analiza preludium do schizofrenii*, 543–44.

meaningful. Something other than an emblematic presentation principle is applied here – the "dramaturgic" transmission of the collective unconscious is made up indirectly from fragments, as if from "a fallen apart mosaic." The mixing of the motifs of castration, hanging, sacrifice and marriage – both in myths and in the novel (this one and others; for example, in the novel *Rośnie las* [*The Gorest is Growing*] the following words are spoken in the final monologue of a tsarist agent: "More and more gallows will be needed. Let the wood grow."[98]) – convince me about the existence of an archetypal MODEL rooted in Terlecki's creation – a metaphoric, unclear image of fate of Poland. The Great Mother is the Lady of the Plants, and the "Tree of Life, gallows and wood of the cross, are the forms of a maternal tree."[99] The archetypal symbolism of a tree, which is very complex, combines images of life and death. The Great, "Devouring" Mother, in her archetypal and thanatic symbolism (often connected with Russia), dominates in Terlecki's narratives. The death of the Master is preceded by contemplation of nature and reminiscences of youth – the image of the sun brings the premonition of a self; the stars, "covered" by a sea wave – the symbol of overwhelming unconsciousness, directs one's attention to transcendence (the only secret worth knowing, according to the Master.[100] A star is a permanent and frequent symbol in Terlecki's writing; it has numerous meanings. Here, it is close to that, which Jung commented on: "Since the ancient times, every connection to stars symbolised eternity. A soul comes 'from stars' and returns to stars."[101]

•••

The characters from the novel *Cierń i laur*[*Thorn and Laurel*], which I recall, obtained an archetypal signature, duality – additionally "strengthened" with mythological analogies – as a certain dynamic whole, build an internal scene of the individuation drama, carried out in many textual levels of the novel. In one of them, the "elderly lady" and her daughter Lili implement the archetype of Goddess Mother and Goddess Daughter (with mythological analogy as Kore-Demeter – Hekate). The young God is the geographer. The writer – the Master, is an "Old Sage" (Zeus, Hades, Hermes). The Master's shadow is the "delator", "bloody Kurt"; as well as the dark (Hades) realm of his "invisible" (Hades) intelligence activities. This activity described here can be described a metonymic and symbolic requisit – the most essential, also ironic, sign of ambigous duality.

98 W.L. Terlecki, *Rośnie las* (Warsaw, 1977), 135.

99 Neumann, *Wielka Matka. Fenomenologia kobiecości. Kształtowanie nieświadomości*, 257.

100 Terlecki, *Cierń i laur*, 409.

101 Jung, "Psychologiczne aspekty Kory", 67.

> First I found a briefcase, locked – I know that you should not trust any servants – in a travelling, double-bottomed trunk. I had a look at some papers and after a long while I entered the library. My interlocutor was an immaculately dressed, middle-aged man (…) He explained that his boss in Paris was sent on a special mission and authorised him to have this detailed conversation.[102]

The duality of characters in the stylistic novel form (different, but somehow similar to the "trunk"), "a story within a story" set in times of August II, shows an ironically demonic dominant of the shadow archetype with the key characters of the royal astrologist, the young priest (an undereducated demonologist), king Augustus and his daughter-lover. It also offers a possible interpretation towards a psycho, archetypal and historic, with the dominant archetype of the Great "Devouring" Mother, which I emphasise. The unsolved ethical problem of the Master: a false moral authority, who wants to be a teacher and a national writer – therapist – as well as his interrupted individuation – ended with his suicide: – regression but also "run towards fast transformation" (J. Hillman) opens the space for another, axiological interpretation. *Cierń i laur* [*Thorn and Laurel*] is a *double-bottomed* novel indeed.

References

Biblia Jerozolimska, Fifth edition. Poznań: Pallottinum, 2006.

Bitka, Z. "Alchemiczny mythos ,Gwiazdy piołun' Władysława Lecha Terleckiego. Perspektywa jungowska (Alchemical mythos of Wormwood Star by Władysław Lech Terlecki. Jungian perspective)." In *Psychoanalityczne interpretacje literatury. Freud – Jung – Fromm – Lacan (Psychoanalytical Interpretation of Literature. Freud-Jung-Lacan)*, edited by E. Fiała and I. Piekarski. Lublin, 2012.

Bitka, Z. "'Zło rodzi się w nieświadomości.' Archetypy i historia. Dyskurs o nieświadomości w powieści ,Drabina Jakubowa albo podróż' Władysława Lecha Terleckiego, (Evil is born in the unconscious. Archetypes and history)." In *"Między świadomością a nieświadomością" – współczesność w perspektywie psychologii głębi. „Between Consciousness and Unconsciousness – the Present Day in the Perspective of Depth Psychology,* edited by K. Węgłowska-Rzepa. Warsaw: Don Fredricksen, 2007.

Błocian, I. *Psychoanalityczne wykładnie mitu: Freud, Jung, Fromm.* Warsaw: "Eneteia" Wydawnictwo Psychologii i Kultury, 2010.

Bolen, J.S. *Bogowie w każdym mężczyźnie.* Translated by H. Ciszewska and B. Moderska. Warsaw, 2006.

102 Terlecki, *Cierń i laur*, 99.

Dobrowolska, D. *Płomień rodzi się z iskry. Twórczość Władysława Terleckiego*. Kielce, 2002.

Dudek, Z.W. "Archetypowa interpretacja literatury." In *Psychoanalityczne interpretacje literatury. Freud – Jung – Fromm – Lacan*, edited by E. Fiała and I. Piekarski. Lublin, 2012.

Dudek, Z.W. Psychologiamitów greckich. Interview by M. Jaszewska, 2013.

Goetz, B. "'Królestwo bezprzestrzenne' z komentarzem M-L von Franz." Translated by J. Prokopiuk. *Literatura na Świecie*, no. 3 (1978).

Grimal, P. *Słownik mitologii greckiej i rzymskiej*. Edited by J. Łanowski. Wrocław, 1987.

Guiley, R. *Encyklopedia snów*. Translated by S. Kiepiel. Warsaw, 1997.

Hillman, J. "Pothos: Nostalgia Pueri Aeterni." Translated by J. Prokopiuk. *Gnosis*, November 1993.

Izdebska, A. *Forma, ciało i brzemię imperium. O prozie Władysława L. Terleckiego*. Łódź, 2010.

Jacobi, J. *Psychologia C.G. Junga. Przedmowa Carl Gustav Jung. Wprowadzenie do całości dzieła*. Translated by S. Łypacewicz. Warsaw: Wydawnictwo Wodnika, 1993. Originally published as *Die Psychologie von C.G. Jung: eine Einführung in das Gesamtwerk* (Olsen: Walter-Verlag AG, 1959).

Jung, C.G. *Archetypy i nieświadomość zbiorowa*. Translated by R. Reszke. Warsaw, 2011.

Jung, C.G. *Archetypy i symbole. Pisma wybrane*. Edited and translated by J. Prokopiuk. Warsaw, 1976a.

Jung, C.G. *O naturze kobiety*. Edited and translated by M. Starski. Poznań: Wydawnictwo Brama, 1992.

Jung, C.G. *Podstawy psychologii analitycznej. Wykłady tavistockie*. Translated by R. Reszke. Warsaw, 1995.

Jung, C.G. "Problem psychiki współczesnego człowieka." In *Psychologia a religia. Wybór pism*, by C.G. Jung, translated by J. Prokopiuk. Warsaw, 1970.

Jung, C.G. *Psychologia a religia Zachodu iWschodu*. Translated by R. Reszke. Warsaw, 2005.

Jung, C.G. *Symbole przemiany. Analiza preludium do schizofrenii*. Translated by R. Reszke. Warsaw, 1998.

Jung, C.G. "Syzygia: animus i anima." In *Archetypy i symbole. Pisma wybrane*, by C.G. Jung, 70–71. Edited and translated by J. Prokopiuk. Warsaw, 1976b.

Jung, C.G. *Typy psychologiczne*. Translated by R. Reszke. Warsaw: Wrota, 1997. Originally published as *Psychologische Typen; Carl Gustaw Jung: Gesammelte Werke* (Walter-Verlag AG, 1994).

Jung, C.G. *Wspomnienia, sny, myśli. Spisane i podane do druku przez Anielę Jaffé*. Translated by J. Prokopiuk. Warsaw, 1976c.

McHale, B. *Powieść postmodernistyczna*. Translated by M. Płaza. Cracow, 2012. Originally published as *DiePostmodernist fiction* (1977).

McLynn, F. *Carl Gustav Jung*. Translated by R. Bartołd. Poznań, 2000.

Miłosz, C. *Rozmowy polskie 1979–1998*. Cracow, 2006.

Modern polish writer, author of many novels and short stories (i.e. *Cień karła, cień olbrzyma, Czarny romans, Drabina Jakubowa albo podróż, Gwiazda piołun, Piasek, Pismak, Wyspa kata, Zabij cara, Zwierzęta zostały zapłacone*)

Neumann, E. *Wielka Matka. Fenomenologia kobiecości. Kształtowanie nieświadomości*. Translated by R. Reszke. Warsaw, 2008.

Paglia, C. *Seksualne persony. Sztuka i dekadencja od Nefretiti do Emily Dickinson*. Translated by M. Kuźniak and M. Zapędowska. Poznań, 2006. Originally published as *Sexual Personae* (1990).

Płużek, Z. *Proces twórczego kształtowania osobowości w świetle teorii C.G. Junga*. Lubin, 2001.

Rosińska, Z. *Jung*. Warsaw, 1982.

Sharp, D. *Leksykon pojęć i idei C.G. Junga*. Translated by J. Prokopiuk. Wrocław, 1998. Originally published as *Jung Lexicon: A Primer of Terms & Concepts* (1991).

Sobolewska, A. *Polska proza psychologiczna 1945–1950*. Wrocław, 1979.

Sowa, J. *Fantomowe Ciało Króla. Peryferyjne Zmagania Z Nowoczesną Formą*. Cracow, 2011.

Szymański, J. *Objawienia demoniczne. Prawdziwe historie o diabłach*. Vol. 1. Marki, 2007.

Terlecki, W.L. *Cierń i laur*. 2nd ed. Warsaw, 2002.

Terlecki, W.L. *Cień karła, cień olbrzyma*, Warsaw, 1983.

Terlecki, W.L. *Czarny romans*, Warsaw, 1974.

Terlecki, W.L. *Drabina jakubowa, albo podróż*, Warsaw,1988.

Terlecki, W.L. *Gwiazda piołun*, Warsaw, 1968.

Terlecki, W.L. "Oblężenie Hippony." *Sezon w pełni. Opowiadania*. Warsaw, 1966a.

Terlecki, W.L. *Piasek*, Lublin, 1992a.

Terlecki, W.L. *Pismak*, Warsaw, 1984.

Terlecki, W.L. *Pożar.Opowiadania*,Warsaw, 1962.

Terlecki, W.L. *Rośnie las*. Warsaw, 1977.

Terlecki, W.L. *Spisek*, Warsaw, 1966b.

Terlecki, W.L. *Wyspa kata*, Warsaw, 1999.

Terlecki, W.L. *Zabij cara*, Warsaw, 1992b.

Terlecki, W.L. *Zwierzęta zostały zapłacone*, Warsaw, 1982.

Trepiński, A. *Romans Kraszewskiego z wiedenką*. Warsaw, 1970.

Vedfelt, O. *Wymiary snów. Istota, funkcje i znaczenie marzeń sennych*. Translated by P. Billig. Warsaw, 1998.

Wiśniewska-Rutkowska, L. *Nie tylko o filozofii. Ludzie, idee, przemiany*. Toruń, 2010.

CHAPTER 15

Evidence for the Effectiveness of Jungian Psychotherapy: A Review of Empirical Studies

Christian Roesler

Abstract

In the early 1990s the first meta-analyses of empirical studies investigating the effectiveness of psychotherapy were published. Following this several researchers claimed that there were no studies investigating the effectiveness of Jungian psychotherapy and therefore it should be excluded from the field of psychotherapy. This moved several Jungian training institutes to design the first empirical studies in the field of Jungian psychotherapy, namely Zurich, Berlin and San Francisco. Now several of these studies have produced results and the following paper will give an overview of these. The paper will give us not only the overview of Jungian empirical studies and will summarize the results of the research, but also will give us an insight onto so detailed dimensions or outcomes of the therapy as a satisfaction of the patients with the Jungian psychotherapy, a level of reduction in symptoms and if the effects of psychotherapy were long-lasting.

Keywords

Jung – psychotherapy – empirical studies – effectiveness of psychotherapy – reduction in symptoms – meta-analysis

1 Introduction

In the early 1990s the first meta-analyses of empirical studies investigating the effectiveness of psychotherapy were published. Following this several researchers claimed that there were no studies investigating the effectiveness of Jungian psychotherapy and therefore it should be excluded from the field of psychotherapy. This moved several Jungian training institutes to design the first empirical studies in the field of Jungian psychotherapy, namely Zurich,

 | DOI:10.1163/9789004336636_017

Berlin and San Francisco. Now several of these studies have produced results and the following paper will give an overview of these.

From the beginning there were difficulties in recruiting enough practicing analysts to participate in the studies, which is still a problem today, as can be shown in the latest example, the PAP-study Switzerland. One of the main arguments against participating in empirical studies was the assumption, that the research process would interrupt or at least influence the analytic process and the therapeutic relationship in an unfavorable way. Also it was argued that empirical instruments would never be able to catch the complexity of the analytic process. From my point of view these critical positions are based on false ideas about the research process, its capacities and its limitations. Of course any research design to investigate psychotherapy has its limitations and can only analyze certain aspects of the complex interactions taking place in the process of psychotherapy. But empirical research methods offer the possibility to get an insight into the psychotherapeutic work and its effects from a more objective position. We have to consider that our perspective as practicing psychotherapists on our own processes is, and has to be, mainly subjective and is subject to interpretation and also to the possibility of error. On the other hand empirical research can never claim to tell the whole truth about psychotherapy. I think that both viewpoints have their right and should be combined so as to get a richer picture of the subtle process of psychotherapy.

2 Levels of Evidence

In empirical research there is a differentiation between different levels of studies, which is described in the Handbook of psychotherapy and behaviour change.[1] The highest level or Gold Standard is the Randomized Controlled Trial (RCT), with an experimental and a control group and the participants are divided into the groups by chance. Only RCTs can give proof of the efficacy of a psychotherapy method which means that the effects in the patients are a result of the method alone (and no other extratherapeutical factors). In general only RCTs are accepted as a proof for the efficacy of the psychotherapy method. In recent years though there has been a discussion about the validity of RCTs, since their internal validity is high in the described sense but the

1 M.J. Lambert, *Bergin and Garfield's Handbook of Psychotherapy and Behavior Change*, 5th ed. (New York: Wiley, 2004).

external validity, its applicability to everyday practice, is low.[2] Several researchers have argued for naturalistic prospective outcome studies which are conducted in everyday practice and therefore much better applicable to reality conditions. Several of the Jungian studies have applied this design. Generally speaking prospective data are more valid than retrospective even though the two Jungian studies described below that have applied a retrospective design have been very carefully designed.

3 Overview of Jungian Empirical Studies

Prospective, naturalistic outcome studies
- Praxisstudie Analytische Langzeittherapie (PAL) Schweiz (practice study analytical long-term psychotherapy Switzerland)[3]
- San Francisco Psychotherapy Research Project[4]
- PAP-S practice study outpatient psychotherapy Switzerland[5]

Catamnestic/retrospective studies
- Berlin Jungian Study[6]
- Konstanz Study – A German consumer reports study[7]

Small sample and case studies

2 D. Westen and K.H. Morrison, "A Multidimensional Meta-Analysis of Treatments for Depression, Panic, and Generalized Anxiety Disorder: An Empirical Examination of the Status of Empiricially Supported Therapies", *Journal of Consulting and Clinical Psychology* 69 (2001): 875–99.

3 G. Mattanza, T. Jakobsen, and J. Hurt, "Jung'sche Psychotherapie ist effizient", in *Seele und Forschung. Ein Brückenschlag in der Psychotherapie*, ed. G. Mattanza, I. Meier, and M. Schegel (Basel: Karger, 2006), 38–82; G. Rudolf et al., "Effektivität und Effizienz psychoanalytischer Langzeittherapie: die Praxisstudie analytische langzeittherapie", in *Psychoanalyse des Glaubens*, ed. M. Schlösser and A. Springer (Gießen: Psychosozial, 2004), 515–28.

4 S.I. Rubin and N. Powers, "Analyzing the San Francisco Psychotherapy Research Project" (San Francisco, 2005), http://www.sirseth.net/doc/SFresearch.pdf.

5 V. Tschuschke, "Praxisstudie ambulante Psychotherapie Schweiz", accessed November 22, 2009, www.psychotherapieforschung.ch/downloads/Konzept-PAP-S-2007.pdf.

6 W. Keller et al., "On the Efficacy of Outpatient Jungian Psychoanalyses and Psychotherapies", in *Proceedings of the 13th International Congress For Analytical Psychology Zürich 1995*, ed. M.A. Mattoon (13th International Congress For Analytical Psychology Zürich 1995, Einsiedeln: Daimon, 1997).

7 F. Breyer, R. Heinzel, and T. Klein, "Kosten und Nutzen ambulanter Psychoanalyse in Deutschalnd (Cost and benefit of outpatient analytical psychotherapy in Germany)", *Gesundheitsökonomie und Qualitätsmanagement* 2 (1997), 59–73.

On Jungian sandplay therapy, psychosomatic disorders etc.[8]
Qualitative and process studies
On complex theory,[9] picture interpretation method.[10]

4 Praxisstudie Analytische Langzeittherapie (PAL) Schweiz (Zurich)[11]

A group of researchers of the Jung Institute Zurich participated in a larger German study on analytical long-term psychotherapy[12] conducted by the University of Heidelberg. The design was a naturalistic prospective outcome study which means that therapists and patients were monitored from the beginning of therapy in the usual everyday practice context (no control group). Twenty-six therapists with 37 cases were chosen as representative for Jungian psychotherapy in Switzerland and their patients. Fifty-seven percent of these patients suffered from depressive disorders and with 47% of personality disorders in the patients the sample had a considerably high burden of disease. The mean duration of treatment was 35 months with a mean of 90 sessions which is equivalent to a low-frequency treatment. This was a realistic sample representative for Jungian therapy in Switzerland.

Three different perspectives were applied: researchers, therapists and the patients themselves and on each level a set of objective and self-evaluation research instruments.

Researchers:
Operationalized psychodynamic diagnostics (OPD), Jungian adaptation[13]

8 M. Muller, "A Psychosomatic Study of Patients with Vitiligo from an Analytical Approach." (PhD thesis in Clinical Psychology, Pontifícia Universidade Católica de São Paulo, 2001); A. Kleeberg, S. Schreiber, and T. Schwinger, "Symbole als Ausdruck der therapeutischen Beziehung. Eine empirische Untersuchung zur Schattensymbolik in einer jungianischen Psychotherapie", *Analytische Psychologie* 34 (2003): 266–97; M.L. Tavares, "The Patient's Psyche in Cancer Terminal Phase" (Dissertation, Pontifícia Universidade Católica de São Paulo, 2002).

9 D. Heisig, "Wandlungsprozesse durch die therapeutische Beziehung", *Analytische Psychologie* 32 (2001): 230–51.

10 M. Krapp, "Pictorial-Hermeneutic, Qualitative Methods", in *Open Questions in Analytical Psychology*, ed. M.A. Mattoon (Einsiedeln: Daimon, 1997), 581–86.

11 Mattanza, Jakobsen, and Hurt, "Jung'sche Psychotherapie ist effizient."

12 Rudolf et al., "Effektivität und Effizienz psychoanalytischer Langzeittherapie: die Praxisstudie analytische langzeittherapie."

13 M. Junghan, "Die Anwendung der Strukturachse der OPD in der Analytischen Psychologie", in *Die Struktur der Persönlichkeit*, ed. G. Rudolf, T. Grande, and P. Henningsen (Stuttgart: Schattauer, 2002), 90–114.

Psychodynamic focusses (2 interviews)
Changes in personality structure: Heidelberger Umstrukturierungsskala
Therapeutic alliance and transference (SGRT, TAB)
Interpersonal problems (IIP)
Changes in life conduct (research interview)
Therapists:
Physical and psychological symptoms, severity score (BSS), Status and process ratings, ICD-diagnosis
Patients:
Psychological and interpersonal symptoms (SCL-90-R, PSKB-Se-R, IIP), personality (TPF), health insurance data
Results:
Researchers:
- Positive restructuring of patients' personality, effect size: 0,94.
- Positive changes in everyday life, very high effect size: 1,48.

Therapists:
- Global rating of results positive or very positive for 75% of patients
- Cost-effectiveness good, very good or maximum for 55%

Patients:
- Global Severity Index reduced highly significant, very high effect size: 1,31, normal level at end of therapy
- Reduction of interpersonal problems (IIP), medium effect size
- Rating of results over 90% positive, very positive or maximum
- Cost-effectiveness 80% good, very good or maximum, 20% satisfying

follow-up

All results remained stable after 1 year and 3 years. An interesting point is that there are findings for further positive effects between the end of therapy and follow-up which would mean that some effects of the therapy show only after the end of therapy; this is an effect that psychoanalysis has always claimed for. The use of health care services was already low during the course of therapy and remained on a low level until the follow-up.

So this study could give proof for very positive effects, of Jungian psychotherapy in a prospective design, that remain stable over three years after the end of therapy. Jungian therapy leads not only to a significant reduction of symptoms and of interpersonal and other problems but also to a restructuring of the personality with the effect that the patients can deal with upcoming problems much better after the end of therapy. The satisfaction of the patients with the results was extremely high even though most of the patients had to pay for their therapy by themselves.

5 San Francisco Psychotherapy Research Project[14]

Originally this study conducted by the San Francisco Jung Institute was designed as a prospective outcome study with four points of measurement (start of therapy, end of therapy, one-year and five-year follow-up). In many aspects the design of the San Francisco psychotherapy research project is similar to that of the Zürich study. The instruments applied in the research were: SCL-90-R; IIP, GAF (Global Assessment of Functioning, axis V of the DSM); an additional instrument designed by the Institute asking for demographic data, therapy motivation and subjective experience with the therapy; the therapists had an instrument also designed by the Institute called "Portrait of my practice" (POMP). The participants of the study were patients of the outpatient clinic of the San Francisco Jung Institute; of 100 patients of the clinic 57 participated in the study. The participating therapists were 23 professional analysts of the Institute as well as 17 candidates in training and seven psychology interns.

Because of the low participation of analysts from the Institute the project had to be terminated early. Because of these problems the original design had to be collapsed into a one-group pretest-posttest-design. This included 39 of the original 57 patients and only part of these completed follow-up. So the internal validity of the study could not be secured and the statistical results have to be interpreted on that background. Only data from the start of therapy and the end of therapy could be compared. Regarding these limitations the study points in the direction of the effectiveness of Jungian therapy. There were significant reductions in SCL-90-R and IIP.

6 Berlin Catamnestic Study[15]

In the early 1990s the Empirical Psychotherapy Research Group in Analytical Psychology Berlin conducted a nationwide catamnestic, retrospective study.

14 Rubin and Powers, "Analyzing the San Francisco Psychotherapy Research Project."

15 Keller et al., "On the Efficacy of Outpatient Jungian Psychoanalyses and Psychotherapies"; "Empirical Research in Psychoanalysis and Analytic Psychotherapy", in *Destruction and Creation: Personal and Cultural Transformations*, ed. M.A. Mattoon (Einsiedeln: Daimon, 1999), 556–86; "The Berlin Jungian Study: On the Effectiveness and Efficacy of Outpatient (Jungian) Psychoanalysis and Psychotherapy – a Catamnestic Study (BJS)", in *An Open Door Review of Outcome Studies in Psychoanalysis. Report Prepared by the Research Committee of the IPA at the Request of the President*, ed. P. Fonagy (International Psychoanalytical Association, 1999), http://www.ipa.org.uk/research/R-outcome.htm; "Efficacy and

Former patients of Jungian psychotherapies were asked to participate and were tested via questionnaires and interview. All members of the German Society for Analytical Psychology (DGAP) were asked to participate in this retrospective study, 78% responded, 24.6% participated. The reasons for refusal to participate were documented and no bias was found. The participating therapists documented all cases terminated in 1987/88 and gave a global evaluation about the success of therapy. In Germany psychotherapy is financed quite generously by the health insurances (up to 300 hours of analysis); at the beginning of therapy the therapist has to apply for financing. These applications contain numerous data about the health state and symptoms of the patient, the personality, the social context, the psychodynamics and diagnosis. All of this information is stored by the health insurances for decades and the Berlin study made use of these data. Additionally other health insurance data about the patients could be used as for example use of health care services, days in hospital etc. The distribution of symptoms and their severity in the sample were the following: 46% affective disorders, 24% other neurotic and psychosomatic disorders, 17% personality disorders.

The problem with catamnestic studies is the risk of biases through selection effects, but these were tested in the study: of 353 documented cases 111 participated in the study; a bias was found concerning the number of therapy drop-outs which was higher in the sample than in the population; apart from that the sample was representative for the population. The mean duration of treatment was 162 sessions with a frequency of 1 to 2 sessions per week.

Results: Of 60.4% of patients reporting their well-being as very poor (severe set of diagnoses) prior to therapy, 86.6% rated their global well-being at follow-up as very good, good or moderate (well-adjusted close to normal reference group on all scales of psychopathology). Six years after the termination of treatment 70–94% reported good to very good improvements in: psychological distress, general well-being, life satisfaction, job performance, partner and family relations, social functioning. The Global health state of 88% could be described as "normal health." Patients were better off than any of the clinical groups with which they shared diagnoses prior to therapy. Regarding the SCL-90-R Jungian therapy could move the sample of severely disturbed patients even below the cut of where one can speak of psychological health after the end of therapy. All of these results were statistically highly significant. There was also a significant reduction of health insurance claims: the mean number

Cost Effectiveness Aspects of Outpatient (Jungian) Psychoanalysis and Psychotherapy – a Catamnestic Study", in *Longer-Term Psychoanalytic Treatment. Perspectives for Therapists and Researchers*, ed. M. Leuzinger-Bohleber and M. Target (London: Whurr, 2002).

of days lost due to sickness, the mean number of days of hospitalization, the intake of psychotropic drugs and the number of visits to primary care physicians were all significantly reduced even below the level of the average German member of the health insurance system. Other interesting findings are the relation between improvement and treatment length and again there are indicators for further improvements after termination of therapy (between post- and follow-up).

Summarizing the results it can be said that there was not only a high satisfaction of the patients with the Jungian psychotherapy but there was also a reduction in symptoms which moved the patients into the area of normal health. The effects of psychotherapy were long-lasting and touched all areas of the life of the patients so that even the use of health care services was so drastically reduced that Jungian therapy was also cost-effective in the long run. These results have to be interpreted on the background of limitations of the design even though the study made great efforts to control biases and secure the representativeness of the sample.

7 The Konstanz-Study – A German Replication of Seligman's Consumer Reports Study[16]

The study conducted in Konstanz/Germany is a replication of the famous Consumer Reports Study done by Seligman applied to therapies from several psychodynamic schools and in its design comparable to the above mentioned Berlin study. Ninety psychotherapists distributed 979 questionnaires to former patients of whom 66% participated in the study. There were no systematic biases found in the sample. About a fifth of the participating therapists had a Jungian background and it could be shown that there are no systematic differences between this subgroup and the overall sample so that the study is representative for psychoanalytic practice in Germany in general and for Jungian psychotherapy.

The results are very much comparable to those of the above-mentioned Berlin study, in all dimensions the study found significant benefits in health and well-being. There were again significant changes between end of therapy and follow-up. As in the Berlin study health insurance data were used and a highly significant reduction in health utilisation parameters was found. All of these results remained stable in a six-year follow-up. A special aspect of this study is

16 Breyer, Heinzel, and Klein, "Kosten und Nutzen ambulanter Psychoanalyse in Deutschalnd (Cost and benefit of outpatient analytical psychotherapy in Germany)."

the conduction of a cost-benefit computation: there were significant savings accrued as a result of individual and group psychotherapy in the first two years after therapy. These were significantly higher in relation to the severity of the health status of the patient at the beginning of therapy.

As this study is a retrospective study the results have to be interpreted on the background of risk of biases but these were controlled for as far as possible.

8 Praxisstudie Ambulante Psychotherapie Schweiz (PAP-S)[17]

This study realized a quasi-experimental design which is the highest level of all the studies described here. The design is comparable to that of the Zurich Jungian study but additionally it has a parallel control group. In Switzerland all the different psychotherapeutic schools are organized in the Charta for Psychotherapy and this was the organizer of the PAP-study. The choice of measures applied followed the recommendations given by the Society for Psychotherapy Research and includes outcome as well as process variables. Measures to be filled out by patients: self-rating of therapy outcome (OQ 45), symptoms (BSI), depression (BDI), Sense of Coherence (SOC-9), congruence (K-INK), therapy motivation (FMP). Researchers: Standardized Clinical Interview for DSM (SKID), Global Assessment of Functioning Individual (GAF) and Relationships (GARF), Operationalized Psychodynamic Diagnostics (OPD). The study ran 7 years (2006–2012) including therapies and follow-up.

The participating psychotherapists were coming mainly from psychodynamic and experiental approaches. The problem was that even though the Swiss Jungian Association paid the largest part of the study there were only four Jungian cases participating in the study which is far too small a number to compute a result for Jungian therapy alone. This is a major disaster since the chance to participate in such a high-level study will not come back in our lifetime. Even though all the Swiss Jungians were asked to participate the majority was reluctant.

Nevertheless the study produced some interesting findings. Generally all the participating schools were successful in improving the health status of the patients and can be seen as effective. A part of the study consisted in describing the interventions in detail that are applied by the different schools.

17 Tschuschke, "Praxisstudie ambulante Psychotherapie Schweiz"; V. Tschuschke et al., "Fundamental Reflections on Psychotherapy Research and Initial Results of the Naturalistic Psychotherapy Study on Outpatient Treatment in Switzerland (PAP-S)", *International Journal for Psychotherapy* 14, no. 3 (November 2010).

In the study therapies were videotaped and external raters evaluated which of the described interventions were practically applied. This may be the most interesting finding of the whole study: in every school the majority of interventions applied was not school-specific but either general or stemming from a different school. Only about 15% of the interventions came from the specific background of the therapist. This of course automatically puts the question whether there even is a specificity in the practical therapeutic work of Jungian therapists and what that would be. Maybe in the future it would make more sense not to investigate schools and their differences since the so-called "Dodo-verdict" already showed that in studies comparing schools all seem to be equally effective but instead to look at differences between therapists and investigate what they actually do when they "do therapy."

9 Summary

When we put the studies on Jungian therapy in the matrix of evidence-based therapy we get the following:

> Level I (randomized controlled trials): no studies
> Level II (quasi-experimental studies: prospective naturalistic outcome studies): PAL-Study,[18] San Francisco Research Project[19] (with limitations); PAP-S Study[20] (Tschuschke 2010) (with control group)
> Level III (retrospective studies): Berlin Jungian Study and Konstanz Study with very high methodological level
> Level IV (case studies etc.): positive effects through sandplay therapy, in psychosomatic disorders etc.

As there are up to now no level I studies (RCTs) there is no proof of efficacy of Jungian psychotherapy, but the effectiveness of Jungian psychotherapy is now on the base of the above-mentioned studies empirically proven; the same can be said for the cost-effectiveness. As most of the studies are naturalistic designs it can be assumed that they give a realistic picture of Jungian therapy in everyday practice. All of the studies report positive effects in a wide

18 Mattanza, Jakobsen, and Hurt, "Jung'sche Psychotherapie ist effizient."

19 Rubin and Powers, "Analyzing the San Francisco Psychotherapy Research Project."

20 Tschuschke et al., "Fundamental Reflections on Psychotherapy Research and Initial Results of the Naturalistic Psychotherapy Study on Outpatient Treatment in Switzerland (PAP-S)."

variety of disorders with good or very good effect sizes on: symptom reduction, well-being, interpersonal problems, change of personality structure, reduction of health care utilisation, changes in everyday life conduct. All of these effects are stable in follow-up up to seven years after therapy. There are even further positive changes between termination and follow-up. With an average of only 90 sessions Jungian therapy is a very time- and cost-effective form of psychodynamic psychotherapy. All the studies realized a high methodological standard with objective measures, different research perspectives (patient, therapist, researcher), control of biases. The most convincing results concerning the effectiveness of Jungian psychotherapy in the overview of all studies is that their results all point in the same direction. Nevertheless the efficacy of Jungian psychotherapy is still to be proven in a randomized controlled trial design. We also have to note that in all studies 10–20% of patients do not profit from Jungian therapy. This should be subject to further research aiming at finding markers for personalities expected to profit from Jungian psychotherapy.

Another severe problem that comes to light in the overview of the studies is the fact that Jungian analysts tend to be very reluctant to participate in empirical studies to an extent that leads almost to the breakdown of studies. From my point of view this should be a point of discussion in the Jungian community whether we want to be part of the health care system and how far we are willing to adapt to the relevant quality standards. At least it can be said now that the point that was often made by critics of empirical research in the Jungian community that empirical methods would interfere with the special situation of the analytical relationship has been falsified by the above studies: in no study there was any hint of a negative interference into the psychotherapeutic process; some studies made great efforts to adapt or even develop research measures which catch aspects special to the Jungian background as for example changes in personality or the adaptation of psychodynamic diagnostics.[21] On the other hand we as Jungians can now offer empirical results about the effectiveness of our psychotherapy method and are no longer subject to the critique that our method is not effective or empirically proven.

10 Prospects: Currently Ongoing Studies in Germany

The German Association of Analytical Psychology has formed a research platform (www.cgjung.de/forum) which is currently planning to conduct several studies in the field of Jungian psychotherapy. The training institutes are

21 Junghan, "Die Anwendung der Strukturachse der OPD in der Analytischen Psychologie."

working on an agreement that future training candidates will have to apply a couple of empirical measures (symptoms, life satisfaction, Operationalized Psychodynamic Diagnostics) to their training cases in order to form a database and to make ongoing quality management possible. In the long run this aims at creating a more open attitude to empirical research in the coming generations of Jungian analysts. On the other hand this process aims at stabilizing the currently comfortable position Jungian therapy has in the German health care system for the future by delivering empirical results about the effectiveness of the methods and applying standard quality management processes.

Structural dream analysis: I have developed a narratological qualitative research method for analyzing dream series and extracting the core process of change in the course of the psychotherapy.[22] At the moment a number of dream series from Jungian psychotherapy processes is analyzed using this method in a research project at the University of Basel. After the Structural Analysis of a dream series is completed the results are confronted with the report from the psychotherapist about the process of the therapy. This project aims at building a corpus of cases which would enable us in the long run to show that the unconscious produces therapeutic change via dreams in the course of an analytic therapy.

In another project I have developed a documentation scheme for the systematic documentation of synchronistic events taking place in psychotherapy.[23] This documentation scheme is now distributed in the German Jung Association and practicing analysts are invited to document relevant events to build up a corpus of cases which will be subject to further analysis. This project aims at building an empirically based theory of synchronicity in psychotherapy.

References

Breyer, F., R. Heinzel, and T. Klein. "Kosten und Nutzen ambulanter Psychoanalyse in Deutschalnd (Cost and benefit of outpatient analytical psychotherapy in Germany)." *Gesundheitsökonomie und Qualitätsmanagement* 2 (1997): 59–73.

Heisig, D. "Wandlungsprozesse durch die therapeutische Beziehung." *Analytische Psychologie* 32 (2001): 230–51.

22 C. Roesler and N. Götz, "Manual zur Strukturalen Traumanalyse", 2012, www.cgjung.de/forum/.

23 C. Roesler, "A Research Frame for Investigating the Appearance of Synchronistic Events in Psychotherapy.", in *The Pauli-Jung Dialogue and Its Impact Today*, ed. H. Atmanspacher and C. Fuchs, In Print (Exeter: Imprint Academic, 2013).

Junghan, M. "Die Anwendung der Strukturachse der OPD in der Analytischen Psychologie." In *Die Struktur der Persönlichkeit*, edited by G. Rudolf, T. Grande, and P. Henningsen, 90–114. Stuttgart: Schattauer, 2002.

Keller, W., R. Dilg, G. Westhoff, R. Rohner, H.H. Studt, and Empirical Psychotherapy Research Group in Analytical Psychology Berlin. "On the Efficacy of Outpatient Jungian Psychoanalyses and Psychotherapies." In *Proceedings of the 13th International Congress For Analytical Psychology Zürich 1995*, edited by M.A. Mattoon. Einsiedeln: Daimon, 1997.

Keller, W., R. Dilg, G. Westhoff, R. Rohner, H.H. Studt, and Empirical Psychotherapy Research Group in Analytical Psychology Berlin. "The Berlin Jungian Study: On the Effectiveness and Efficacy of Outpatient (Jungian) Psychoanalysis and Psychotherapy – a Catamnestic Study (BJS)." In *An Open Door Review of Outcome Studies in Psychoanalysis. Report Prepared by the Research Committee of the IPA at the Request of the President*, edited by P. Fonagy. International Psychoanalytical Association, 1999a. http://www.ipa.org.uk/research/R-outcome.htm.

Keller, W., S. Stehle, R. Dilg, T. Grande, G. Rudolf, C. Oberbracht, G. Mattanza, M. Junghan, and M. Krapp. "Empirical Research in Psychoanalysis and Analytic Psychotherapy." In *Destruction and Creation: Personal and Cultural Transformations*, edited by M.A. Mattoon, 556–86. Einsiedeln: Daimon, 1999b.

Keller, W., G. Westhoff, R. Dilg, R. Rohner, H.H. Studt, and Empirical Psychotherapy Research Group in Analytical Psychology. "Efficacy and Cost Effectiveness Aspects of Outpatient (Jungian) Psychoanalysis and Psychotherapy – a Catamnestic Study." In *Longer-Term Psychoanalytic Treatment. Perspectives for Therapists and Researchers*, edited by M. Leuzinger-Bohleber and M. Target. London: Whurr, 2002.

Kleeberg, A., S. Schreiber, and T. Schwinger. "Symbole als Ausdruck der therapeutischen Beziehung. Eine empirische Untersuchung zur Schattensymbolik in einer jungianischen Psychotherapie." *Analytische Psychologie* 34 (2003): 266–97.

Krapp, M. "Pictorial-Hermeneutic, Qualitative Methods." In *Open Questions in Analytical Psychology*, edited by M.A. Mattoon, 581–86. Einsiedeln: Daimon, 1997.

Lambert, M.J. *Bergin and Garfield's Handbook of Psychotherapy and Behavior Change*. 5th ed. New York: Wiley, 2004.

Mattanza, G., T. Jakobsen, and J. Hurt. "Jung'sche Psychotherapie ist effizient." In *Seele und Forschung. Ein Brückenschlag in der Psychotherapie*, edited by G. Mattanza, I. Meier, and M. Schegel, 38–82. Basel: Karger, 2006.

Meier, I., and M. Schegel. *Seele Und Forschung. Ein Brückenschlag in Der Psychotherapie*. Basel: Karger, 2006.

Morrison, K.H., R. Bradley, and D. Westen. "The External Validity of Controlled Clinical Trails of Psychotherapy for Depression and Anxiety: A Naturalistic Study." *Psychology and Psychotherapy: Theory, Research and Practice* 76 (2003): 109–32.

Muller, M. "A Psychosomatic Study of Patients with Vitiligo from an Analytical Approach." PhD thesis in Clinical Psychology, Pontifícia Universidade Católica de São Paulo, 2001.

Roesler, C. "A Research Frame for Investigating the Appearance of Synchronistic Events in Psychotherapy." In *The Pauli-Jung Dialogue and Its Impact Today*, edited by H. Atmanspacher and C. Fuchs. In Print. Exeter: Imprint Academic, 2013.

Roesler, C. (2018): Jungian dream interpretation and empirical dream research. In: Roesler, C. (ed.): Research in Analytical Psychology. London. Routledge.

Rubin, S.I., and N. Powers. "Analyzing the San Francisco Psychotherapy Research Project." San Francisco, 2005. http://www.sirseth.net/doc/SFresearch.pdf.

Rudolf, G., R. Dilg, T. Grande, T. Jakobsen, W. Keller, B. Krawietz, M. Langer, S. Stehle, and C. Oberbracht. "Effektivität und Effizienz psychoanalytischer Langzeittherapie: die Praxisstudie analytische langzeittherapie." In *Psychoanalyse des Glaubens*, edited by M. Schlösser and A. Springer, 515–28. Gießen: Psychosozial, 2004.

Tavares, M.L. "The Patient's Psyche in Cancer Terminal Phase." Dissertation, Pontifícia Universidade Católica de São Paulo, 2002.

Tschuschke, V. "Praxisstudie ambulante Psychotherapie Schweiz." Accessed November 22, 2009. www.psychotherapieforschung.ch/downloads/Konzept-PAP-S-2007.pdf.

Tschuschke, V., A. Crameri, M. Koemeda, P. Schulthess, A. von Wyl, and R. Weber. "Fundamental Reflections on Psychotherapy Research and Initial Results of the Naturalistic Psychotherapy Study on Outpatient Treatment in Switzerland (PAP-S)." *International Journal for Psychotherapy* 14, no. 3 (November 2010).

Westen, D., and K.H. Morrison. "A Multidimensional Meta-Analysis of Treatments for Depression, Panic, and Generalized Anxiety Disorder: An Empirical Examination of the Status of Empiricially Supported Therapies." *Journal of Consulting and Clinical Psychology* 69 (2001): 875–99.

CHAPTER 16

How Can We Objectify a Study on Analytical Psychology?

The Sense of Applying Statistical Methods in Qualitative Research

Jolanta Kowal

Abstract

The methodology of classic statistics can be successfully applied to qualitative research, which creates a basis for posing hypotheses, questionnaire formulation or for the preparation of a projection (forecasting) method.

The aim of the qualitative research lies very often in the preparation of a questionnaire, which is designed as a tool for further wide- ranging research (Kowal, 2012). Chosen respondents are asked to give answers to posed questions. Respondents are supposed to answer verbally (this procedure can be recorded on a tape), in written form on a piece of paper or on a computer. They may draw a picture or choose an illustration symbolizing certain content.

This method allows us to carry out qualitative socio-economical research among consumers or sellers, as they are connected to market segmentation.

Keywords

Methodology – scientific research – statistics – qualitative vs quantitative research – socio-economical research – Jungian research – experiment planning – Anima – Animus – Shadow – Great Mother – Wise Old Man – the Self

1 Introduction

Scientific research can be understood as studies with the aim of obtaining objective responses and formulating laws. Scientific study starts by formulating the research problem, which can be understood as "a certain question or set of questions, the answers to which will deliver the test." The importance and

 | DOI:10.1163/9789004336636_018

validity of research depends on the proper selection of methods, techniques and research tools.[1]

The research test method is the strategy for the investigation of the results from the philosophical assumptions by the research project, specifying the particular object of study, its purpose, objectives, questions and hypotheses, the target population, and how to collect and analyze data. The method is a term used interchangeably with the terms "cognitive model" or "research methodology." It usually refers to a group of general assumptions about the method of the study, adapted to its object and purpose. The research technique (always associated with specific method) is a way to implement the desired tasks, practical activities, and carefully regulated elaborated directives that will help to achieve optimal verifiable information, opinions, and facts.[2] Research tools [are] the medium of choice for delivering technology research, e.g.: questionnaires, interviews, observations, official data, publications, and personal documents.[3] Methods and techniques do not exclude each other but stay in a close relationship and complement each other, whereas research tools (e.g. questionnaires, surveys, interviews, observations, statistical data, publications, personal documents) are instruments used in order to realize a chosen scientific technique.[4]

Scientific methods are classified in different ways but one of the most general is a division into qualitative and quantitative research.[5]

---

1 J. Kowal, "Selected Theoretical and Practical Aspects of Stastistical Methodology of Qualitative Research in Information Systems.", in *Proceedings of the International Conference on ICT Management for Global Competitiveness and Economic Growth in Emerging Economies* (ICTM *2012*), ed. J. Kowal and N. Roztocki (Wrocław: Wyższa Szkoła Zarządzania „Edukacja", 2012), 27–41.

2 A. Kamiński, "Metoda, technika, procedura badawcza w pedagogice empirycznej", in-*Metodologia pedagogiki społecznej*, ed. R. Wroczyński and T. Pilch (Wrocław: Ossolineum, 1974); J. Kowal et al., "Gender versus Women's Management Competencies on the Example of Poland (a Research Results Survey)", in *The Proceedings of the 5th European Conference on Management Leadership and Governance*, ed. J. Politis (Hellenic American University, the Atexcelixi Conference Centre Athens: Academic Publishing Limited, 2009).

3 T. Pilch, *Zasady badań pedagogicznych* (Warsaw, 1977), 116; R.E. Stake, "Case Studies", in *Handbook of Qualitative Research* (Thousand Oaks: Sage Publications, 1994); M.D. Myers and D.E. Avison, eds., *Qualitative Research in Information Systems* (London: A Reader, Sage Publications, 2002); Kowal et al., "Gender versus Women's Management Competencies on the Example of Poland (a Research Results Survey)."

4 Kowal et al., "Gender versus Women's Management Competencies on the Example of Poland (a Research Results Survey)"; Kowal, "Selected Theoretical and Practical Aspects of Stastistical Methodology of Qualitative Research in Information Systems."

5 Myers and Avison, *Qualitative Research in Information Systems*; Stake, "Case Studies."

The majority of researchers decide to choose only one sort of method: either qualitative or quantitative research, although there is also a group advocating the use of both at the same time during the same examination.[6] Apart from the diversification of the research into either a qualitative or a quantitative one, inter alia, the division can also be made between:

- research that considers external perspectives (etic, outsider and researcher's perspective and taken from this perspective theory, for instance in a psychology case study, psychographic method, psychological model) and an internal perspective (emic, participant's perspective and his system of subjective meanings, for instance in psychology hermeneutical dialogue, autobiographical method.[7]

Research may be:

- qualitative (Jungian are mainly qualitative) and quantitative;
- objective and subjective (Jungian studies);[8]
- related to the discovery of general laws (nomothetic, more often concerned with statistics) and the uniqueness of each situation (idiographic research, case study, mainly Jungian studies);
- research aimed at the clarifying and understanding of phenomena, which are a consequence of the prognostic (predictive) study, whose purpose is to describe, predict and modify (Jungian studies).[9]

The examples of qualitative methods could be many, such as action research, case study research or ethnographic research. The sources of qualitative data are many: observation or participant observation, surveys and questionnaires, documents, texts, opinions, participants' monologues, or impressions and reactions of a researcher.

From the beginning of the 1970s qualitative methods did not belong to the mainstream of research, nevertheless they were most often applied in social or

---

6 G. Gable, "Integrating Case Study and Survey Research Methods: An Example in Information Systems", *European Journal of Information Systems* 3, no. 2 (1994): 112–26.

7 B. Bartosz, "Metody jakościowe – rodzaje, dylematy i perspektywy", in *Metody jakościowe w psychologii współczesnej*, ed. M. Straś-Romanowska (Wrocław: Uniwersytet Wrocławski, 2000); M. Straś-Romanowska, "Hermeneutyka w psychologicznych badaniach jakościowych", in *Hermeneutyka a psychologia*, ed. A. Gałdowa (Cracow: Wydawnictwo Uniwersytetu Jagiellońskiego, 1997), 143–57.

8 G. Burrell and G. Morgan, *Sociological Paradigms and Organizational Analysis* (Heinemann, 1979).

9 Bartosz, "Metody jakościowe – rodzaje, dylematy i perspektywy"; Kowal, "Selected Theoretical and Practical Aspects of Stastistical Methodology of Qualitative Research in Information Systems."; Straś-Romanowska, "Hermeneutyka w psychologicznych badaniach jakościowych."

pedagogical work or in research examining human resource management, informatics, medicine or in other fields. There were also other, alternative qualitative methods designed which put emphasis on the issues of reliability and analysis of data as essential factors in exploratory studies.[10]

Quantitative methods began to be used in life sciences, notably in physical phenomena analysis. At present quantitative methods are only applied in socio – economical and psychological sciences, e.g. in survey measures, in experiments carried out in laboratory environments in so-called formal methods (that includes econometrics among others) or in methods of mathematical modeling.[11]

In many information systems (IS) qualitative research is presented within the context of philosophical assumptions, however most commonly it appears as studies in which qualitative data (such as interviews, surveys, documents, results of observations or case study) are analyzed in a substantive way.

In such a perspective the aim of qualitative research is to gather an understanding and explaination of socio-economical or psychological phenomena. In qualitative psychological research, in the hermeneutical version, understanding is perceived as a form of explanation called explanatory, deductive or instrumental understanding.[12] Qualitative research allows us to give answers to such questions as "why", "for what reason", "which are", "what are", after the analysis of individual, free statements of respondents, and an analysis of behavior, gestures or creations. Such analysis is an arduous and time-consuming procedure, thus qualitative research is often carried out on a small scale, but can serve as grounds to formulate hypotheses which then can be verified in quantitative research realized on big populations (see table 16.1). In socio-economical studies the most frequently used qualitative research is the focus group interview (FGI), or in-depth interview (IDI). They are usually used to characterize some community (target group of for instance some market segment), not only in reference to inner motivations or emotional sensitivity threshold but also to attitudes, assessment of some phenomena or higher-order needs.

10 Myers and Avison, *Qualitative Research in Information Systems*; Stake, "Case Studies."

11 D. Straub, D. Gefen, and M.C. Boudreau, "The ISWorld Quantitative, Positivist Research Methods Website", 2004, http://dstraub.cis.gsu.edu:88/quant/.

12 M. Straś-Romanowska, "O metodzie jakościowej w kontekście rozważań na tożsamością Psychologii", in*Metody jakościowe w Psychologii współczesnej*, ed. M. Straś-Romanowska, Prace psychologiczne 53 (Wrocław: Wydawnictwo Uniwersytetu Wrocławskiego, 2000), 16–32.

TABLE 16.1 Comparison of quantitative and qualitative research

Qualitative research	Quantitative research
Aims of the research	**Aims of the research**
1) *Theoretical aims:* They result from substantive assumptions of a research problem concerning a studied field, expressed in the language of words or pictures: 1) understanding, agreement, explanation (understanding, deductive, instrumental) and phenomena interpretation; 2) defining the object of research; 3) defining the cognitive and practical aim; 4) posing cognitive questions concerning: a) features (properties) of examined phenomena (objects) b) the kinds of relationships between features of phenomena c) the correlations between examined phenomena d) formulating complementary questions of a creative character (beginning with such expressions as "what", "with what reason", "what are", "which", etc., with structures which do not include information about a researcher's thesis, but nevertheless requiring elaborate answers.[a]	1) *Theoretical aims:* The main aim of scientific cognizance is to gain the most compact, reliable, general, simple knowledge that contains the maximum information.[b] On the basis of such cognizance it is possible to prove certain regularities and laws that govern them.[c] The aims of quantitative research result from the aims defined earlier on the basis of qualitative research and proper substantive assumptions expressed in the language of logics and mathematics: 1) Description of object population, phenomena, their features and dependencies between them with use of mathematical, statistical functions, numbers; generalization of results to general population 2) Explaining and forecasting formulation of directional "wh-questions" (also starting with auxiliary verbs – do, does, etc., and "whether", "why", "how") whose aim is to confirm or deny given thesis
2) *Practical aims:* Expansion of consciousness, improvement in quality of life	2) *Practical aims:* Control, interference in the course of events, forecasting
3) Subject matter: The world of human spirit, thoughts, facts of culture[d]	3) Subject matter: The world of nature, facts of nature, natural, physical and socio-economical phenomena

Qualitative research	Quantitative research
4) Method of formulating scientific hypothesis. This method gives answers to complementary questions; "what", "for what reason", "why", "in what way", "what are", "which", etc., but first of all they deal with "why-questions"[e] but in an understanding and interpretive approach, without references to numbers	4) Method of formulating scientific hypothesis. This method gives answers to directional "wh-questions" (also starting with auxiliary verbs – do, does, etc., and "whether", "why", "how") in reference to numbers, in the language of logics and mathematics: – which mathematical or statistical functions characterize objects, phenomena, their properties and dependencies between the features or groups of phenomena, – whether representative of general population data, gathered in quantitative research, confirm hypothesis posed on the basis of qualitative research – how we can interpret the obtained quantitative result?
5) Character of cognition: Contextual, historical (ascribing sense) cognition[f]	5) Character of cognition: Linear, sequential (describing causes) cognition
6) Size of examined population Usually small population, rarely random, chosen in purposeful manner	6) Size of examined population Usually statistically large object samples, chosen randomly, according to defined scheme
7) Connection type: Sense (semantic association: part – whole)	7) Connection type: Cause and effect, correlation, symptomatic
8) Criterion of truth: Phenomenological, semantic	8) Criterion of truth: Empirical, statistical
9) Generalizing of results to general population:	9) Generalizing of results to general population:

TABLE 16.1 Comparison of quantitative and qualitative research (*cont.*)

Qualitative research	Quantitative research
In interpretive approach the results are usually not generalized to population. Whether the interpretive, semantic cognition is authentic can be decided on the basis of mutual understanding (between the researcher and the participant, the text recipient and its author) or the feeling of conviction of interpretation accuracy towards defined sense relationship drawn from epistemological experience, knowledge, intuition, insight, authority (subjective criterion). The method of subjectivization is helped by [?] competent judges (competent interpreters) who must reach consensus in interpretations.[g] The results can be objectively generalized to population only under certain conditions, which enable application of methods of statistical inference or statistical optimization.[h]	Numerical results can be generalized to the general population with previously assumed probability, on the basis of methods of statistical inference (point estimation, confidence intervals, verification of statistical hypothesis).
10) Research scenario: Flexible scenario, dependent not only on research method but also on situation, mood or instant idea of researcher or examined person.	10) Research scenario: Most commonly based on secondary sources, physical measures or structured questionnaire in which respondents tick the answers on scales e.g. Likert, Thurstone, Stampil scale, etc.
11) Influence of researcher on course of research – quite big	11) Influence of researcher on course of research – substantially smaller, as the research should take the course defined by created phases of the project. In the realization process there are at least a few thoroughly qualified persons employed.
12) Character of interpretation of results - Big objectivism not only of the researcher but also of participants (especially in hermeneutical approach)	12) Character of interpretation of results – the interpretation is more objective, usually based on methods of statistical inference.

Source: own work on the basis of literature and own research.

a Ibid.; T. Pilch and T. Bauman, *Zasady badań pedagogicznych. Strategie ilościowe i jakościowe* (Warsaw: Wydawnictwo Akademickie Żak, 2001); J. Such, *O uniwersalności praw nauki. Studium metodologiczne*, 2nd ed. (Warsaw: PWN, 1972), 398; K. Ajdukiewicz, *Główne zasady metodologii nauk i logiki formalnej. Skrypt autoryzowany* (Warsaw, 1928).

b Such, *O uniwersalności praw nauki. Studium metodologiczne*, 398.

c Pilch, *Zasady badań pedagogicznych*, 116.

d Straś-Romanowska, "O metodzie jakościowej."

e Cf. Ajdukiewicz, *Główne zasady metodologii nauk i logiki formalnej. Skrypt autoryzowany*.

f Straś-Romanowska, "O metodzie jakościowej."

g Ibid.

h J. Kowal, "Wielozmiennowe modele regresji w badaniach jakościowych w warunkach małej próby", in*Metody jakościowe w psychologii współczesnej*, ed. M. Straś-Romanowska, Prace psychologiczne (Wrocław: Wydawnictwo Uniwersytetu Wrocławskiego, 2000), 83–101.

i J. Kowal et al., "Gender versus Women's Management Competencies on the Example of Poland (a Research Results Survey)"; J. Kowal, "Selected Theoretical and Practical Aspects of Stastistical Methodology of Qualitative Research in Information Systems"; J. Kowal, "Możliwości zastosowań w badaniach jakościowych wybranych metod statystyki klasycznej i planowania eksperymentów optymalnych."

j Ajdukiewicz, *Główne zasady metodologii nauk i logiki formalnej. Skrypt autoryzowany*; J. Brzeziński, *Metodologia badań psychologicznych* (Warsaw: PWN, 1997); Kowal, "Wielozmiennowe modele regresji w badaniach jakościowych w warunkach małej próby"; J. Paluchowski, "Metodologiczne problemy analizy treści", in *Metody jakościowe w psychologii współczesnej*, ed. M. Straś-Romanowska, Prace Psychologiczne, LIII (Wrocław: Wydawnictwo Uniwersytetu Wrocławskiego, 2000), 55–57; Pilch and Bauman, *Zasady badań pedagogicznych. Strategie ilościowe i jakościowe*; Straś-Romanowska, "O metodzie jakościowej"; Such, *O uniwersalności praw nauki. Studium metodologiczne*, 398.

The methods of classic statistics can be successfully applied to qualitative research, which creates a basis for posing hypotheses, questionnaire formulation or a preparation of a projection (forecasting) method.

This methodology allows us to carry out qualitative socio-economic research, even of a Jungian type, among consumers or sellers, as they are connected to market segmentation, for instance on the subject of an efficient way of presentation by sales representatives of preferred products. That is to say: why is it better to cooperate with some representatives and not with others; what features of character, qualifications, knowledge and the attitude of sales agents enable us to cooperate with them; what was the factor that made the client interested in the preferred product; and what should the personality of a worker be from a given branch that would make him successful? Other questions might be what motivates us to work better; what financial conditions, securities, and kind of management are optimal; and how can we define frames of self-presentation in constructing persuasive messages by the method of competent judges?[13]

Good qualitative research practice should include such topics as: how to go about research; the literature review; finding a research question; producing a research design; capturing, managing and analysing the data; producing findings; and interpreting the findings and understanding the limitations of the research.[14] The research question is the central issue – it suggests the methodology. If we decide to conduct qualitative research it is necessary to remember the skills of the researcher and the physical constraints.

In a good quantitative research process researchers should formulate research questions, collect evidence, process evidence and produce findings. During qualitative research, researchers should formulate questions, collect evidence, and try to understand the questions. The process must be concerned with the question of understanding, if there are doubts it is neccessary to consider the research question again (see Figure 16.1)

In the presented paper the problems connected with "qualitative research" are considered in reference to applied methods, techniques and examination tools, with correlation to Jungian studies and information systems.

The class of an IS system is defined as a human activity system, thus a social system constituted not only by people but also by artificial (data, technical means) and abstract components (methods, organization).[15]

Qualitative research is carried out in a Jungian way, but more within the [?] socio-economical, humanities sciences and practical sense [?] using different theoretical approaches (positivist, interpretive or critical) and with the use of miscellaneous methods and techniques (most frequently in focus group interviews, brain storming, individual in-depth interviews, copy tests, experiments or observations).[16]

---

13 A. Kuzio, "Frames of Self-Presentation in Constructing Persuasive Messages: A Study of Polish and American Political Discourse", *Rocznik Kognitywistyczny* 6 (2013): 23–36.

14 D. Remenyi, *Case Study Research: The Quick Guide Series* (Academic Conferences Limited, 2013).

15 Cf. J. Kowal, "Wybrane aspekty badań jakościowych w systemach informacyjnych", in*Wokół jakości życia*, ed. B. Bartosz and J. Klebaniuk (Wrocław: Wydawnictwo „Jakopol", 2006), 173–203.

16 Kowal, "Selected Theoretical and Practical Aspects of Stastistical Methodology of Qualitative Research in Information Systems."

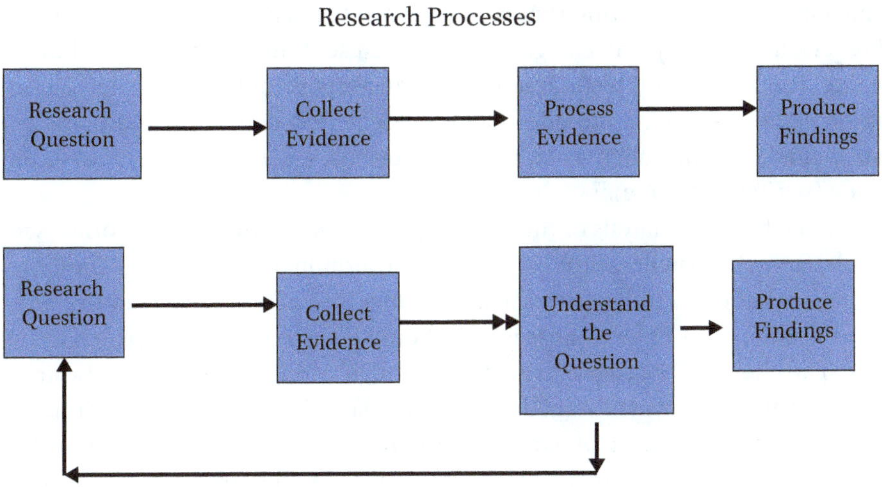

FIGURE 16.1 The stages of research process (from Remenyi, 2013).

This process can be seen in information systems on the Internet, where in Web sites we can encounter the advertisements of firms, public opinion research centers that offer qualitative marketing research, the creation of new looks for companies, products, or the forecasting of changes in management and organization.

2 Manners of Objectivization of Qualitative Research Results as a Method of Competent Judges

From a psychological point of view the reaction of respondents can be analyzed with the use of projection methods – for instance the examinees watch a set of prepared illustrations and their task is to define answers to such questions as: which pictures are the best and why; which bring certain associations; can they represent some features of character; with what do we associate them; and what dreams or feelings can they evoke, etc.

A group of competent judges (according to the rules of classic statistics – at least four, if we assume randomization in sampling) analyzes so-called qualitative material, and on its basis formulates names of a verbal category to which a given answer may be qualified. Next, the judges define to what extent a given "object" (expression, illustration, product, etc.) "fits" a given category. It is worth noting that a given "object" might not always be unambiguous and fit only one category; it can represent an ambiguous symbol or content. A very useful technique to scale answers is multi valued logics, and in order to give answers to questions the judge may simply mark a point on an ordinal or continuous scale, e.g. on a Stevens, Likert, Stapel or Thurstone scale (see Table 16.2a–c).[17]

On the basis of analysis of the answers, the judges formulate categories (see Table 16.2b). It is usually a time consuming and arduous process. It might be done in a way that every judge formulates his categories after having read the text, then together they choose those which should later be used in a research exercise. The choice of answers can be done through voting (the majority of voices decides) or on the basis of statistical analysis results (see Table 16.3: algorithm of elimination of ambiguous objects), which depends on the weight and scale of the ambiguity of the subject matter. If the researcher decides to choose a statistical procedure, judges will individually give a certain number of points (e.g. from 1 to 5 on a Likert scale). The rest of the answers are, in a statistical sense, the most homogenous, with the largest mean and median, and largest first quartile and smallest variation (e.g. a small variation coefficient – less than 100%). After summarizing all the results it is possible to check whether the judges are unanimous on the basis of, for instance, the Friedman Test and Kendall's W coefficient.

On the basis of definitions or expressions which, in the judges' opinions were most frequently repeated, and in whose assessment the judges were the most unanimous, it is possible to prepare a questionnaire to pilot a qualitative study devoted to bigger populations. This would verify the appropriateness of its construction (it is called a process of questionnaire validation).

Example 1 (From Psychological Examinations)[18]

A group of competent judges consisting of psychology students equipped with knowledge from the field of Jungian psychoanalytic theory, especially concerning symbols and archetypes, looked through image advertisements

17 See "Example 1" and "Example 2" in J. Kowal, *Metody statystyczne w badaniach sondażowych rynku* (Warsaw, Wrocław: PWN, 1998).

18 Part of source materials on which the results in the article were created: J. Kowal and K. Węgłowska-Rzepa, "Symbole w reklamie a preferencje konsumentów", in *Psychospołeczne i etyczne aspekty badań rynkowych*, ed. J. Kowal and K. Węgłowska-Rzepa (Wrocław: Wyższa Szkoła Zarządzania „Edukacja", 2002), 209–26.

and assessed what was the strength of "a load" of six archetypes in a chosen photograph on a scale from 1 to 5 (on a Likert scale).

Manner of formulating of questions for competent judges: Define to what extent the below presented picture can be defined in terms of each of the named archetypes: The Shadow, The Animus, The Anima, The Great Mother, The Wise Old Man, The Self:

1	2	3	4	5
Definitely not	Rather not	At medium level,neither yes, nor no	Rather yes	Definitely yes

TABLE 16.2A Matrix of experts' answers[a]

Judge number	The Shadow symbolism	The Animus symbolism	The Anima symbolism	The Great Mother symbolism	The Wise Old Man symbolism	The Self symbolism
1	4	5	1	1	1	1
2	3	5	1	1	1	1
3	4	5	1	1	4	2
4	4	3	1	1	1	1
5	4	5	1	1	4	2
6	4	5	2	1	1	1
7	3	5	2	1	1	1
8	4	3	1	1	3	1
9	4	5	1	1	1	1
10	5	4	1	1	1	1
11	2	5	2	1	1	2
12	5	4	1	1	1	1
13	5	1	4	1	2	1

a The Figure 16.2 demonstrates the Animus symbolism.

FIGURE 16.2 Title: Animus. Photographer: Jolanta Kowal. Retrieved from Jolanta Kowal. Used with permission from the copyright holder.

Example 2 ***(From Socio-economical Research)***

The created examination aims at conducting an opinion poll among representatives of small and medium business (SMB) in the Lower Silesia region concerning the possibility of SMB development in Poland, and getting knowledge concerning this development (e.g. how to make use of assistance programs, fears and perception of threats resulting from economic relationships with the EU, hopes for benefits which result from economic ties with EU2). In order to prepare a questionnaire, there was an introductory qualitative examination prepared with the participation of representatives of SMB drawn from the Lower Silesia region. This laid out what, according to them, were the most important threats and benefits resulting from Poland's accession to the EU.

After having carried out the research, competent judges (scientists and students of WSZ Edukacja) analyzed the qualitative empirical material, and with the use of the brain storming method, prepared a list of expressions – categories (presented in the third column of matrix 1–3). In the next step each of the judges forecasted to what extent the answers matched each category.

TABLE 16.2B Answer matrix for every competent judge. Assessment of judge number 1

Number of interviewee (respondent whose answer will be qualified by judge under one of the mentioned categories)	Interviewee opinion	Fears of interviewee resulting from Poland's accession to the EU	Define percentage with which the expressions from the text match the below presented categories
1	I think that Germans will try to buy our land for nothing, the same as industrial plants. The Polish countryside will run to ruin. With EU competition there is no place for Polish culture, tradition or religion in the countryside. We will have more losses than benefits.	Purchase of industrial plants by foreign capital	80%
		Bankruptcy of many small and medium firms	10%
		Purchase of Polish land by foreigners	90%
		Increase in smuggling	0%
		Loss in industrial competition in EU	100%
		lower than expected Financial help for Poland	20%
		More loss than benefits	100%

TABLE 16.2B Answer matrix for every competent judge. Assessment of judge number 1 (*cont.*)

Number of interviewee (respondent whose answer will be qualified by judge under one of the mentioned categories)	Interviewee opinion	Fears of interviewee resulting from Poland's accession to the EU	Define percentage with which the expressions from the text match the below presented categories
		German supremacy in Europe	98%
		Restructuring of Polish agriculture, mine and steel industry	0%
		Decline of Polish countryside	5%
		Disappearance of Polish religious and cultural traditions	100%
		Loss of national identity	20%
		Increase of unemployment	0%

TABLE 16.2C Assessment of judge number 2

Number of interviewee (respondent whose answer will be qualified by judge under one of the mentioned categories)	Interviewee opinion	Fears of interviewee resulting from Poland's accession to the EU	Define percentage with which the expressions from the text match the below presented categories
2	Germans will be trying to realize their "Drang nach Osten" ("drive towards the East"). That's all.	Purchase of industrial plants by foreign capital	80%
		Bankruptcy of many small and medium firms	
		Purchase of Polish land by foreigners	100%
		Increase of smuggling	
		Loss in industrial competition in EU	
		lower than expected Financial help for Poland	
		More loss than benefits	
		German supremacy in Europe	100%
		Restructuring of Polish agriculture, mine and steel industry	
		Decline of Polish countryside	
		Disappearance of Polish religious and cultural traditions	
		Loss of national identity	
		Increase of unemployment	

3 Comments Concerning Sampling Methodology and Some Methods of Statistical Optimization Useful in Qualitative Research

The majority of the results of a general character in socio-economical research are drawn on the basis of samples whose number is far greater than one hundred. Among scientists there is a widespread assumption that only the examinations carried out on statistically large random populations lead to proper conclusions and forecasts.

Another common opinion concerning scientific methods, resulting from assumptions based on [?] classic statistics, refers to proportions between the number of examined objects and the number of analyzed properties in the frames of multivariate analyses, for instance in multiple regression or factor analyses. In order to avoid a so-called "information glut", multivariate models are realized on big populations of random character. In such a case the number of observations is three, five or even ten times greater than the number of variables in the model. Large random samples are undoubtedly representative, but nevertheless quite expensive to carry out [?].

There are also situations in which the target general population is sparse, for instance in a market of peculiar services, rarely ordered products, within a population of managers of specific qualifications, or among people with particular abilities required in certain professions. Reaching every individual which is a subject matter of research, can be quite complicated and expensive. Conducting this research usually requires the analysis of many variables at the same time. It is a problem quite often met by psychologists who carry out qualitative analyses. They work with a small group of people over a longer period of time, with descriptive materials; nevertheless, they are afraid to generalize the conclusions because of the small number of the research population.

It seems that in order to solve the above mentioned problem, we have two options. One can apply modern methods of experimental statistics, based on the theory of optimal experiment planning,[19] first proposed in the 1920s by R.A. Fisher. Another option is a snowball sampling method utilized in research by S. Sudman and Blair[20] in connection with sequential sampling.[21]

19 J. Wawrzynek, "Uwagi o efektywności planowania eksperymentów", in *Przegl. Statyst.*, vol. XXVI, 1977, 111–25.

20 S. Sudman and E. Blair, "Sampling in the Twenty-First Century", *Journal of the Academy of Marketing Science* 27, no. 2 (April 1, 1999): 269–77.

21 Kowal, *Metody statystyczne w badaniach sondażowych rynku*; "Wielozmiennowe modele regresji w badaniach jakościowych w warunkach małej próby."

4 Some Methods of Sampling in Qualitative Research

Sudman S., Blair E.[22] and Kalton G. et al.[23] created network sampling techniques which allow researchers to obtain good samples, that are representative of a general population, e.g. chain referral sampling or respondent – driven sampling, sometimes called "snowball sampling." The above mentioned method of selection allows us to get a good representative sample if the subject studies are small, specific populations. The mentioned method of sampling was created on the basis of the theory which says that "individuals attract individuals" and create a hierarchical network structure. This is especially in the case of people with uncommon opinions or unusual interests, performing certain professions, working on particular positions in their field.

The surveyor starts sampling from a few respondents who are characterized by features determined with in the aim of the survey (certain attitude, profession, position), but at the same time are substantially different from one another. Then the respondents are asked to give a list of people with similar features (differentiating the chosen group according to the aim of the survey) inside a precisely defined network structure (for instance acquaintance managers in firms, or people in different positions but belonging to a national minority) who will be contacted in later research. Respondent – driven sampling is based on asking respondents to find and name a network of people characterized by similar features who can be contacted by the surveyor in the future. When utilized in a proper way this kind of method allows for sampling in which different groups of typical objects are substantially different from one another in reference to chosen features.

Sequential sampling is an approach which can bring reliable data to surveys at a very low cost. In this method a surveyor introduces new individuals into a population of randomly chosen respondents and checks the results after such an operation. When sampling results satisfy the requirements of the surveyor (for instance a certain range of feature value, structure of variables, distribution of certain properties) then we stop the procedure. Sequential sampling can be utilized in order to collect objects (people, institutions) of qualitative properties, for instance when the surveyor would like to collect information about problems connected with the introduction of new questionnaires in HR verifying qualifications of candidates in managerial positions.

---

22 Sudman and Blair, "Sampling in the Twenty-First Century."

23 G. Kalton, M. Collins, and L. Brook, "Experiments in Wording Opinion Questions", *Applied Statistics* 27 (1978): 149–61.

5 Elements of Experiment Planning Theory in Qualitative Research

In order to solve some problems connected with qualitative research one can apply modern methods of experimental statistics, based on the theory of optimal experiment planning,[24] or the sociological theory of respondent – driven sampling, in connection with sequential sampling. The surveyor, under certain conditions, instead of carrying out costly examinations on a large random sample, can successfully experiment on a small sample using an optimal planning theory experiment, which can be utilized in two specific cases:

1) when the number of n experiments in a test is statistically small ($n < 30$)
2) when we deal with a saturated or almost saturated experiment where the number of trials in n test is statistically big ($n > 30$) but the number of parameters which must be estimated equals, or is a little smaller than, the planned number of n experiments.

In the conducted qualitative research, the planning of experiments has a great importance in the case of small samples. A specific meaning is ascribed to some kinds of discrete plans where the frequency of the appearance of different objects in a sample has a discrete character, whereas the properties of objects are measured on non-continuous scales (e.g. the attitudes of consumers towards advertised products, some sorts of behavior of individuals, lifestyle, different symbols, etc.), mostly on qualitative and ordering ones.

Research methods can be adjusted to such situations in which the surveyor already works with a small, often specific trial population and often cannot increase it significantly, and where the aim of the research is, for example, to define a cause and effect correlation between dependent variables (for instance between the efficiency of advertisement and its positive reception by consumers) and a group of independent variables (market segment, kinds of applied props, symbols, colors, etc.). Optimal experiments theory allows researchers to check what the value of the sample is, taking into consideration the obtained results or structure, and to which large random sample it can be compared. If certain conditions are not yet satisfied, then a few units can be put to a test, at best with the method of respondent – driven sampling in connection with sequential sampling; then the structure of an analyzed population can be checked. The procedure is repeated until we obtain the desired

24 J. Kowal, ed., "Wybrane zagadnienia weryfikacji reprezentatywności prób w społeczno-ekonomicznych badaniach jakościowych. Metody i oprogramowanie komputerowe.", in*Zeszyty Naukowe*, vol. 12 (Wrocław: Wyższa Szkoła Zarządzania „Edukacja", 2002); Wawrzynek, "Uwagi o efektywności planowania eksperymentów"; G. Taguchi and Y. Wu, *Introduction to off-Line Quality Control* (Japan Quality Control Association, 1979).

values of the chosen function optimality criterion, and (or) until the moment when a sample will be representative with respect to structure and dependencies of certain control features (for instance with reference to age and sex). For a chosen set of variables, the researcher counts the value of the criterion function, which informs him whether the population is optimal or whether new units must be added.

The mentioned criterion function can be, for instance, a function of A- or D- optimality; the sample is ideally optimal if A- or D- efficiency reaches value 1 but is not optimal when values are close to zero. If proper mathematical requirements are satisfied, the researcher can start an estimation of variables with the regression method. It is crucial in this method that the units in a sample constitute a good (adequate) representation of a certain problem of social, psychological or economic character.[25]

6 Sample Representativeness Verification

In the above mentioned research connected to advertisement there were algorithms and software applied;[26] this was the statistical package – SRV- Sample representativeness verification. This facilitated the construction and verification of representatives for the general population, allowing [?] inexpensive, statistically small samples for qualitative research. The created application can be utilized also in cases of small and statistically small and large researched populations, as it can help in the verification of sample population representativeness in a widely understood socio-economical qualitative research project.

The aim of qualitative research in a statistical sense can be to search for covariance relationships or cause/effect relations between different variables, measured on different scales, or the description of certain phenomena which are not always measurable in a mathematical sense. These kinds of examinations are usually carried out over a longer period of time on a certain population, which in sociology is called a research panel. It happens that the population cannot be very numerous due to the character of the research (for instance in the case of some psychological long-term qualitative examinations) or because of restricted access to a general population. In such situations the researchers are reluctant to generalize the results for the general population.

25 Kowal, "Wielozmiennowe modele regresji w badaniach jakościowych w warunkach małej próby."

26 Kowal, "Wybrane zagadnienia weryfikacji reprezentatywności prób w społeczno-ekonomicznych badaniach jakościowych. Metody i oprogramowanie komputerowe."

Programs used to verify sampling structures, for instance SRV- Sample representativeness verification,[27] can help in making certain research decisions.

A "sampling structure verification" program takes into consideration not only methodological, but also ethical, aspects of sample representativeness research.[28] It allows researchers to eliminate cases with missing data from analyses, compare sample structures (in connection with a few control features and relationships between them) dedicated to analyses with ideal or desired structures, known for instance from professional literature or from annuals and reports by The General Registry Office (GRO). The user of such a program can create a set in a separate file and prepare a few smaller samples in a random way, which will be ideal in structures related to certain fixed control variables, such as the age or sex of those surveyed, which are often used in public opinion polls to "sample overbalancing". Then the researcher can search for cause/effect relationships between a few independent sample populations and compare the obtained results. The sampling structure verification application also enables us to compare the percentage distribution of certain qualitative features originating from the empirical population, with the theoretical distribution of this feature known from professional literature or GRO reports, taking into consideration control variables. The program can be utilized in the case of small and big samples.

An "optimal experiment planning" program using some elements of optimal experiments planning theory, allows researchers to examine the research population optimization in situations in which the surveyor is searching for some cause/effect correlation between the dependent variable (for instance the efficiency of managerial activities) and the group of independent variables (for instance the number of completed courses, type and level of education, work experience, some psychological features like extroversion, intelligence quotient, etc.). The theory can also be used in [?] estimates of linear dependency, and in decisions to use methods of multiple regression. The program includes options enabling appropriate variable coding measured on different type scales (e.g. nominal, ordinal, interval or quotient scales) in a way that all variables can be put through a regression equation to check what the valuablity of a data set is, in the sense of its optimal use in estimations. The program can be used in cases of both small and big samples with special consideration

27 Ibid.

28 J. Kowal, "Niektóre etyczne, metodologiczne i pragmatyczne aspekty badań statystycznych", in *Psychospołeczne i etyczne aspekty badań rynkowych*, ed. K. Kowal and K. Węgłowska-Rzepa (Wrocław: Wyższa Szkoła Zarządzania „Edukacja", 2002), 143–59.

of so-called saturated experiment plans, where the number of examined objects equals the number of estimated regression parameters, or is only a little smaller.

7 Chosen Statistical Methods in Qualitative Research in Advertising

There was advertisement research carried out in which the variables creation was based on Fromm's and Jung's psychoanalytical concept concerning symbols and archetypes. The aim of the research was to examine the influence of symbols of an archetypal character (the Great Mother, The Anima, The Animus, The Shadow, The Wise Old Man and The Self) in advertisement on different aspects, not only of product or services' reception but also on programs of socio-political interaction.[29] The aim of this qualitative research also defined in what way the symbols of an archetypal character seen in advertising can influence the behavior of consumers (through the creation of individual and social awareness). In other words, if it can cause a desire to change lifestyle through gaining new experiences, getting new qualifications, aiming at universal values. The research results put a foundation to create efficiency, advertisements that bring positive results concerning not only goods, sales and the financial success of companies, but also social and educational advertisement supporting different institutions in business, social or political activities in specific communities, for instance among the unemployed or national minorities.[30]

In the research a planned projection method was used based on one of C.G. Jung's archetypal concepts[31] in which a notebook with eighteen illustrations was used.[32] Chosen pictures represent six basic archetypes e.g. The Shadow,

29 Kowal, "Wybrane zagadnienia weryfikacji reprezentatywności prób w społeczno-ekonomicznych badaniach jakościowych. Metody i oprogramowanie komputerowe."

30 K. Węgłowska-Rzepa et al., "Archetypal Symbols, Their Reception and Meaning for Polish and Korean Societies – Comparative Research", in *2nd International Academic Conference of Analytical Psychology & Jungian Studies* (Texas A & M University, 2005).

31 C.G. Jung, "Mysterium Coniunctionis", in *The Collected Works*, vol. 14 (Princeton NJ: Princenton University Press, 1963); "Psychological Types", in *The Collected Works*, vol. 6 (Princeton NJ: Princeton University Press, 1971). Originally published in 1921; J. Jacobi, *Psychologia C.G. Junga. Przedmowa Carl Gustav Jung. Wprowadzenie do całości dzieła*, trans. S. Łypacewicz (Warsaw: Wydawnictwo Wodnika, 1993). Originally published as *Die Psychologie von C.G. Jung: eine Einführung in das Gesamtwerk* (Olsen: Walter-Verlag AG, 1959).

32 Kowal and Węgłowska-Rzepa, "Symbole w reklamie a preferencje konsumentów"; J. Kowal et al., "The Cultural Symbolism, Integration and Education of Different National

The Animus, The Anima, The Great Mother, The Wise Old Man and The Self. The choice of illustrations, from a collection of 150 pictures, was made by competent judges who knew the Jungian archetypal concept, the content, and the symbols describing each archetype.

The choice of pictures was made on the basis of an activity scheme which I called an algorithm of elimination of "ambiguous" objects (see Table 16.3). This was based on statistical methods excluding given illustration from belonging to a different archetype. This algorithm can also be used to create questionnaires in public opinion polls denoting a certain object's property, for instance diagnostic questions in questionnaires which create foundations for proper public opinion polls or diagnostic questions in addiction questionnaires.[33] The created projection method allows researchers to answer certain questions in further research on larger populations. These questions are: what symbolism is included in photographs; are there any archetypal symbols in illustrations; which symbols of an archetypal character are preferred by their recipients.

8 Creation and Application of Research Methods – Qualitative and Quantitative

The nature of the first phase of research was a choice of photographs in which symbols of one of the six Jungian archetypes was dominant e.g. The Shadow, The Animus, The Anima, The Great Mother, The Wise Old Man and The Self (see Table 16.2a, Example 1 of current chapter). Experts (students of the fourth and fifth grade of psychology) were randomly divided into five subgroups of seven people. Each judge from a group assessed to what extent each photograph can be characterized with symbols representing the six archetypes on a scale of 1 to 5 (on Likert scale). Separate points on the scale meant:

1. photograph symbolism does not represent given archetype
2. photograph symbolism represents given archetype to a very small extent
3. photograph symbolism represents given archetype to such an extent that it is neither "yes" nor "no"

Groups – Comparative Research of Polish, Korean and Philipino's Archetypal Imagery", in *Eksploracja Przestrzeni Historycznej*, ed. T. Leniartek (Wrocław: Wyższa Szkoła Zarządzania „Edukacja", 2008), 261–84.

33 J. Keplinger and J. Kowal, "Kwestionariusz typu S- R do badania poczucia wstydu, Prace Psychologiczne XXXVIII", in *Perspektywy Rozwoju Psychologii w Uniwersytecie Wrocławskim. Preferencje i zróżnicowanie podejść badawczych*, ed. M. Dąbek, Acta Universitatis Wratislaviensis (Wrocław: Wydawnictwo Uniwersytetu Wrocławskiego, 1995), 311–320.

4. photograph symbolism may represent given archetype
5. photograph symbolism definitely represents given archetype.

Each competent judge ascribed 6 grades to the photographs. The grades include information as to what extent a given picture represents the archetypal symbol of The Shadow, The Animus, The Anima, The Great Mother, The Wise Old Man and The Self.

One hundred and fifty advertisement pictures were analyzed (photos, illustrations) in their reference to archetypal material. Out of 150 there were 18 illustrations chosen on the basis of statistical analysis. There were 3 pictures chosen for each archetype. The chosen illustrations were then verified one more time by another group of competent judges consisting of 13 persons. The same statistical procedure was applied, whose steps are presented below (see Table 16.3).

On the basis of the assessment of competent judges the measures of statistical description were counted as: minimum, maximum, mean values, standard deviation, skewness, kurtosis, and variable coefficient for mean. The judges'

TABLE 16.3 The algorithm of "ambigous objects" – The statistical procedures to choose pictures for projective method

Step	Aim of analysis phase	Applied measurement of statistical description or test	Which pictures are selected
1	Random choice of competent judges group (at least 3), Introduction of theoretical basis of methods, creation of grading scale, at best continuous (e.g. Likert, Thurnstone scale, graphic scale from 0 to 10 or form 0 to 1)		
2	Examination of normality of distribution of variables (assessments of the level of saturation the picture with archetypal symbolism of The Shadow, The Animus, The Anima, The Great Mother, The Wise Old Man and The Self) to further choice of proper test	For instance chi-square-test, Kolmogorov, Smirnov, Lilliefors test.	

TABLE 16.3 The algorithm of "ambigous objects" (*cont.*)

Step	Aim of analysis phase	Applied measurement of statistical description or test	Which pictures are selected
3	Comparison of average measures	Arithmetic mean, mean rank, median, dominant	Selection of illustrations with one high value, not smaller than e.g. 4 on a Likert scale ("probably yes")
4	Comparison of variation coefficients	Coefficient of variation to mean, coefficient of variation to median	Selection of illustrations for which variation coefficient does not exceed 0,3
5	Comparison of skewness	Coefficient of skewness α3, coefficient of assymetry based on mean and median	Selection of illustrations with left skewed distribution of assessment ($\alpha 3<0$; mean smaller than median) what indicates dominance of high results
6	Comparison of kurtosis	Kurtosis coefficient α4>3t	Distribution of property should be more concentrated around mean than in a ideal normal distribution
7	Comparison of means for given archetype with other means of the same picture	Test of differences significance for dependent measures, comparison of assessment of pairs of archetypes for the same picture (e.g. t-student test for continuous variables, signed-rank test, Wilcoxon paired samples sequence test – depending on variables distribution	Selection of illustrations whose mean (equaled at least 4) for one archetype is statistically higher than other means

Step	Aim of analysis phase	Applied measurement of statistical description or test	Which pictures are selected
8	Analysis of Pearson's or Spearman correlation coefficients for all assessment pairs of archetypes' assessment in each picture	Pearson's or Spearman's correlation coefficients, test of relevance of correlation coefficient	Selection of illustrations for which correlations for two of any archetype are either statistically not relevant or negative. Statistically relevant correlations for a pair of archetypes indicate that the same people similarly assess two archetypes.
9	Verification of competent judges agreement	*S* Friedman's test for many dependent samples or parametric analysis of variance ANOVA with repeated measures. Calculation of Kendall's coefficient of concordance and Spearman's mean ranks correlation coefficient r_s	Test *S* should show relevance of differences in distribution of many variables designating assessment of saturation the picture with every archetype. Selection of illustrations to which assessments of judges are unanimous. W Kendall's coefficient should be bigger than 0,5
10	Qualification of all selected pictures to clusters	K-means method, hierarchical cluster analysis, agglomeration method, method of comparsison of rank distribution	Selection of illustrations with the highest mean, equaling at least 4,0 and variation coefficient not higher than 0,3
11	Random choice of a new group of competent judges who assess the pictures chosen in point 8 as representative for archetypes	Implementation of procedure on the scale of 1 to 10 points	Selection of pictures chosen by group I and II of competent judges

Source: own materials. Cf. J. Kowal, "Wybrane aspekty badań jakościowych w systemach informacyjnych"; J. Kowal, "Możliwości zastosowań w badaniach jakościowych wybranych metod statystyki klasycznej i planowania eksperymentów optymalnych."

sample was small (13 persons), thus the distribution of individual archetypes can be approximated on the basis of normal distribution. The distribution of a majority of the assessments was not close to a normal one, therefore in the course of the procedure there were non-parametric tests applied.[34]

It was assumed initially that one picture can represent one defined archetype if the mean for the archetype equals at least 4 (4 on a Likert scale means "probably yes"). At the same time though, it is higher than the rest of means and considerably different from them (what was checked on the basis of Wilcoxon pairs sequence test – Table 16.5), and the variation coefficient testifies to at least a moderate variation (Vm<0,3, Table 16.4). The skewness coefficient demonstrated a dominance of high results ($\alpha 3$<0), whereas kurtosis indicated a strong concentration around the mean ($\alpha 3$> = 3).

It was also checked whether competent judges are compatible in their assessments. The S Friedman test, W Kendall correlation coefficient and Spearman's rank correlation coefficient were applied. The pictures, whose assessment was made by competent judges, was compatible (W>0,5), and were left for further analysis.

The r Pearsons correlation coefficients were also analyzed with means of the students' t-test. Only those illustrations were selected for which correlations for any two archetypes were not statistically relevant or were negative. Statistically relevant positive correlations for archetypes pairs mean that the

TABLE 16.4 Descriptive statistics for saturation of picture 1 with symbolism of each archetype

Symbol	*N* important	Mean *m*	Median	Min.	Max.	Standard deviation *s*	Skewness *α*3	Kurtosis *α*4
The Shadow	13.00	3.92	4.00	2.00	5.00	0.86	−0.76	0.85
The Animus	13.00	4.23	5.00	1.00	5.00	1.24	−1.77	2.96
The Anima	13.00	1.46	1.00	1.00	4.00	0.88	2.33	5.90
The Great Mother	13.00	1.00	1.00	1.00	1.00	0.00		
The Wise Old Man	13.00	1.69	1.00	1.00	4.00	1.18	1.42	0.43
The Self	13.00	1.23	1.00	1.00	2.00	0.44	1.45	0.09

Source: own research and own analyses (Kowal, 2009)

34 Kowal, *Metody statystyczne w badaniach sondażowych rynku.*

same people assess them in a similar way, which should eliminate the picture from further analyses.

The example of picture elimination due to ambiguity.

On the basis of measures analysis of statistical description concerning one of the illustrations (pic.1) it was initially assumed that the photo may symbolize The Animus, since the arithmetic mean for the symbol was quite high ($m = 4{,}2$). The variation coefficient demonstrated moderate diversity ($Vm = 0{,}29$), the skewness coefficient demonstrated a dominance of high results $\alpha 3 = -1{,}8$, whereas kurtosis indicated a definite concentration around the mean ($\alpha 3 = 3$, see Table 16.4).

Nevertheless, on the basis of the results of the test of the significance of differences for dependent measures one can notice that the mean for the level of saturation of The Animus symbol was the highest, but not significantly different from The Shadow symbol ($m = 3{,}9$, $Vm = 0{,}22$, $T = 33$, $Z = 0{,}87$, the observed level of significance equaled $p = 0{,}38 > \alpha = 0{,}05$; see Table 16.5). This fact eliminates the picture from further analyses.

Based on correlation coefficients analysis, it is possible to notice that the same people do not assess The Shadow and The Animus in the same way (correlation coefficient for the Animus and the Shadow equals $r = -0.5$

TABLE 16.5 Wilcoxon (paired samples) sequence test

Symbol	*N* important	T	Z	P-value
The Shadow & Animus	13.00	33.00	0.87	0.38
The Shadow & Anima	13.00	0.00	3.06	0.00
The Shadow & The Great Mother	13.00	0.00	3.18	0.00
The Shadow & The Great Mother	13.00	0.00	2.93	0.00
The Shadow & The Self	13.00	0.00	3.06	0.00
The Animus & The Anima	13.00	5.50	2.80	0.01
The Animus & The Great Mother	13.00	0.00	3.06	0.00
The Animus & The Wise Old Man	13.00	2.00	2.90	0.00
The Animus & The Self	13.00	0.00	3.06	0.00

Source: own research and own analyses. Kowal et al., "Gender versus Women's Management Competencies on the Example of Poland (a Research Results Survey)."

and is statistically significant, $p<0.1$; Table 16.7). Friedman's ANOVA and Kendall's coefficient of concordance prove that competent judges are quite equal in their assessment of the picture (*Chi square* = 45.83; $p < 0.000001$; coefficient of concordance $W = 0.71$; mean ranks correlation coefficient $r_S = 0{,}68$). However, the fact that there was an identical distribution of assessment for the Shadow and The Animus (Table 16.5 ($T = 33$, $Z = 0.87$, observed probability $p = 0.38$) indicates an ambiguity towards the symbols. Thus, in accordance with the assumptions of Table 16.3, illustration number 1 is eliminated from further analyses.

The same methods were applied in the case of every picture. Only the pictures assessed in a unanimous way by competent judges were selected for further analyses. This is the reason for the application of Kendall's coefficient of concordance for competent judges. Only the photographs for which the coefficient of concordance equaled at least 0,75 and was statistically significant, were chosen. It is known that the coefficient W ranges from "0" (no agreement) to "1" (complete agreement). The high significant result W denotes the fact that the judges agreed on the criteria that were used during the assessment. In order to calculate the percentage of total variance (variation) of the assessments by competent judges by the given value of W coefficient, an average rank correlation of the assessment was calculated.[35] Only the illustrations where the agreement was higher than 50% were selected.

TABLE 16.6 Friedman's ANOVA and Kendall's coefficient of concordance

	Mean rank	**Rank sum**	**Mean**	**Standard deviation**
The Shadow	5.23	68	3.92	0.86
The Animus	5.35	69.5	4.23	1.24
The Anima	2.85	37	1.46	0.88
The Great Mother	2.12	27.5	1	0
The Wise Old Man	2.92	38	1.69	1.18
The Self	2.54	33	1.23	0.44

Chi square = 45.83; $p < 0.000001$; coefficient of concordance $W = 0.71$; mean ranks correlation coefficient $r_S = 0.68$

Source: own research and own analyses. Kowal et al., "Gender versus Women's Management Competencies on the Example of Poland (a Research Results Survey)."

35 Brzeziński, *Metodologia badań psychologicznych*, 500–505; G.A. Ferguson and Y. Takane, *Statistical Analysis in Psychology and Education*, 6th ed. (New York: McGraw-Hill, 1989), 423.

TABLE 16.7 Pearson's correlation coefficient r for picture 2 (number $N = 13$)

	Statistics	The Shadow	The Animus	The Anima	The Great Mother	The Wise Old Man	The Self
The Shadow	*r*	1	−0.5	0.1	0	0.1	−0.4
	p	—	0.1	0.9	1	0.7	0.2
The Animus	*r*	−0.5	1	−0.6	0	−0.1	0.4
	p	0.1	—	0	1	0.8	0.2
The Anima	*r*	0.1	−0.6	1	0	−0.1	−0.1
	p	0.9	0	—	1	0.8	0.8
The Great Mother	*r*	0	0	0	1	0	0
	p	1	1	1	—	1	1
The Wise Old Man	*r*	0.1	−0.1	−0.1	0	1	0.6
	p	0.7	0.8	0.8	1	—	0
The Self	*r*	−0.4	0.4	−0.1	0	0.6	1
	p	0.2	0.2	0.8	1	0	—

r – Pearson's correlation coefficient
p – observed level of significance test (two-tailed test)
Source: own research and own analyses. Kowal et al., "Gender versus Women's Management Competencies on the Example of Poland (a Research Results Survey)."

TABLE 16.8 Variables in concentration 1 (pictures) with the highest and most moderate variability

Picture code	Mean rank	Rank sum	Mean	Standard deviation
E3	9.12	118.50	4.77	0.44
E6	8.81	114.50	4.69	0.63
D11	8.46	110.00	4.69	0.48
C9	9.00	117.00	4.62	1.12
B14	8.88	115.50	4.62	1.12
C13	8.46	110.00	4.54	1.13

TABLE 16.8 Variables in concentration 1 (pictures) with the highest and most moderate variability (*cont.*)

Picture code	Mean rank	Rank sum	Mean	Standard deviation
B5	8.35	108.50	4.54	0.97
C15	8.42	109.50	4.54	0.97
C12	7.31	95.00	4.46	0.66
C17	8.65	112.50	4.46	1.20
A18	8.00	104.00	4.46	0.97
B2	7.04	91.50	4.23	1.24
E10	7.19	93.50	4.15	1.14
C18	7.31	95.00	4.15	1.34
F7	5.00	65.00	4.08	0.64

Source: own research and own analyses. Kowal et al., "Gender versus Women's Management Competencies on the Example of Poland (a Research Results Survey)."

Photographs were grouped in clusters on the basis of six features (average intensity of the archetypal symbol of The Shadow, The Animus, The Anima, The Great Mother, The Wise Old Man and The Self) with the use of a comparison of the rank distribution method, based on the S Friedman test (Table 16.6). For the projection method, out of 150 illustrations, there were 15 selected from one cluster for which the average value exceeded 4 and where the variation coefficient was smaller than 0,3. Friedmans test showed identical distributions (*Chi square* = 9,24174; *p* = 0,15592), which in this case equaled high saturation with one archetype.

9 Summary

Application of two types of reasoning – not only deduction but also induction – allows researchers to explain the qualitative changes of analyzed phenomena. In the context of scientific philosophy both research paradigms are in fact qualitative paradigms. The utilization of quantitative methods makes sense in qualitative research if it is substantially justified from the perspective of subject matter. The description of a research population with the use of numbers and statistical functions, defines certain relationships or assignments between figures or functions on numbers. But it is a substantial analysis, called a qualitative or "deductive" analysis by scientists, that allows researchers to interpret the results and put them in a logical order.[36] It is possible that the researcher did not define any hypothesis, only deduces, and observes the phenomena, and in descriptions uses only verbal categories. This then appears in the analysis as the expression "change of A is usually (or often) accompanied by B", which denominates certain phenomena of a qualitative, statistical character.

References

Ajdukiewicz, K. *Główne zasady metodologii nauk i logiki formalnej. Skrypt autoryzowany*. Warsaw, 1928.

Bartosz, B. "Metody jakościowe – rodzaje, dylematy i perspektywy." In *Metody jakościowe w psychologii współczesnej*, edited by M. Straś-Romanowska. Wrocław: Uniwersytet Wrocławski, 2000.

Brzeziński, J. *Metodologia badań psychologicznych*. Warsaw: PWN, 1997.

Burrell, G., and G. Morgan. *Sociological Paradigms and Organizational Analysis*. Heinemann, 1979.

Ferguson, G.A., and Y. Takane. *Statistical Analysis in Psychology and Education*. 6th ed. New York: McGraw-Hill, 1989.

Gable, G. "Integrating Case Study and Survey Research Methods: An Example in Information Systems." *European Journal of Information Systems* 3, no. 2 (1994): 112–26.

Jacobi, J. *Psychologia C.G. Junga. Przedmowa Carl Gustav Jung. Wprowadzenie do całości dzieła*. Translated by S. Łypacewicz. Warsaw: Wydawnictwo Wodnika, 1993. Originally published as *Die Psychologie von C.G. Jung: eine Einführung in das Gesamtwerk* (Olsen: Walter-Verlag AG, 1959).

Jung, C.G. "Mysterium Coniunctionis." In *The Collected Works*, Vol. 14. Princeton NJ: Princenton University Press, 1963.

Jung, C.G. "Psychological Types." In *The Collected Works*, Vol. 6. Princeton NJ: Princeton University Press, 1971. Originally published in 1921.

Kalton, G., M. Collins, and L. Brook. "Experiments in Wording Opinion Questions." *Applied Statistics* 27 (1978): 149–61.

Kamiński, A. "Metoda, technika, procedura badawcza w pedagogice empirycznej." In *Metodologia pedagogiki społecznej*, edited by R. Wroczyński and T. Pilch. Wrocław: Ossolineum, 1974.

36 J. Kowal, "Niektóre zagadnienia optymalizacji statystycznej w jakościowych badaniach społeczno-ekonomicznych", in*Rysunek projekcyjny jako metoda badań psychologicznych*, ed. M. Łaguna and B. Lachowska (Lublin: Towarzystwo Naukowe KUL, 2003), 57–87.

Keplinger, J., and J. Kowal. "Kwestionariusz typu S- R do badania poczucia wstydu, Prace Psychologiczne XXXVIII." In *Perspektywy Rozwoju Psychologii w Uniwersytecie Wrocławskim. Preferencje i zróżnicowanie podejść badawczych*, edited by M. Dąbek, 311–320. Acta Universitatis Wratislaviensis. Wrocław: Wydawnictwo Uniwersytetu Wrocławskiego, 1995.

Kowal, J. *Metody statystyczne w badaniach sondażowych rynku*. Warsaw, Wrocław: PWN, 1998.

Kowal, J. „Możliwości zastosowań w badaniach jakościowych wybranych metod statystyki klasycznej i planowania eksperymentów optymalnych." In *Psychologia ilości, psychologia jakości: uzupełniające się spojrzenia*, edited by A. Oleszkowicz and P. Zdybek, 49–69. Wrocław: Oficyna Wydawnicza ATUT, 2009.

Kowal, J. "Niektóre etyczne, metodologiczne i pragmatyczne aspekty badań statystycznych." In *Psychospołeczne i etyczne aspekty badań rynkowych*, edited by K. Kowal and K. Węgłowska-Rzepa, 143–59. Wrocław: Wyższa Szkoła Zarządzania „Edukacja", 2002a.

Kowal, J. "Niektóre zagadnienia optymalizacji statystycznej w jakościowych badaniach społeczno-ekonomicznych." In *Rysunek projekcyjny jako metoda badań psychologicznych*, edited by M. Łaguna and B. Lachowska, 57–87. Lublin: Towarzystwo Naukowe KUL, 2003.

Kowal, J. "Selected Theoretical and Practical Aspects of Stastistical Methodology of Qualitative Research in Information Systems." In *Proceedings of the International Conference on ICT Management for Global Competitiveness and Economic Growth in Emerging Economies (ICTM 2012)*, edited by J. Kowal and N. Roztocki, 27–41. Wrocław: Wyższa Szkoła Zarządzania „Edukacja", 2012.

Kowal, J. "Szanse rozwoju dla małych i średnich przedsiębiorstw w Polsce Unii Europejskiej." In *Związki gospodarcze i grupy producenckie*, edited by D. Knecht, 239–51. Wrocław: Wyższa Szkoła Zarządzania „Edukacja", 2005.

Kowal, J. "Wielozmiennowe modele regresji w badaniach jakościowych w warunkach małej próby." In *Metody jakościowe w psychologii współczesnej*, edited by M. Straś-Romanowska, 83–101. Prace psychologiczne. Wrocław: Wydawnictwo Uniwersytetu Wrocławskiego, 2000.

Kowal, J. "Wybrane aspekty badań jakościowych w systemach informacyjnych." In *Wokół jakości życia*, edited by B. Bartosz and J. Klebaniuk, 173–203. Wrocław: Wydawnictwo „Jakopol", 2006.

Kowal, J., ed. "Wybrane zagadnienia weryfikacji reprezentatywności prób w społeczno-ekonomicznych badaniach jakościowych. Metody i oprogramowanie komputerowe." In *Zeszyty Naukowe*, Vol. 12. Wrocław: Wyższa Szkoła Zarządzania „Edukacja", 2002b.

Kowal, J. "Organizational Ethics and Job Satisfaction of Information Technology Professionals in Poland." In *Proceedings of the Nineteenth Americas Conference on Information Systems*. Chicago, 2013.

Kowal, J., and N. Roztocki. "Business Competency of IT Professionals and Job Satisfaction in Transition Economies: Insights from Poland." In *Proceedings of the Eighteen Americas Conference on Information Systems*. Seatle WA, 2012.

Kowal, J., and K. Węgłowska-Rzepa. "A Vision of Oneself and of the World – Constructive and Reconstructive Function of Narrative Stories." In *Gospodarka, Rynek, Edukacja*, edited by Z. Knecht, 10:6–12. Wrocław: Wydawnictwo Wyższej Szkoły Zarządzania, 2005.

Kowal, J., and K. Węgłowska-Rzepa. "Conscious and Unconscious Influences in Internet Advertising in Transition Economies." In *Proceedings of the Second International Conference on ICT Management for Global Competitiveness and Economic Growth in Emerging Economies*, edited by J. Kowal, N. Roztocki, and H.R. Weistroffer, 37–67. Wrocław: Wyższa Szkoła Zarządzania „Edukacja", University of Wrocław Institute of Psychology, AIS Special Interest Group on ICT and Global Development (SIG GlobDev), 2013.

Kowal, J., and K. Węgłowska-Rzepa. "Symbole w reklamie a preferencje konsumentów." In *Psychospołeczne i etyczne aspekty badań rynkowych*, edited by J. Kowal and K. Węgłowska-Rzepa, 209–26. Wrocław: Wyższa Szkoła Zarządzania „Edukacja", 2002.

Kowal, J., and K. Węgłowska-Rzepa. "The Methodological Aspects of Creating the New Research Method Based on Choosing of Pictures and the Analysis of Creative and Recreative Functions of Narrative Stories." In *Gospodarka, Rynek, Edukacja*, edited by Z. Knecht, Vol. 10. Wrocław: Wydawnictwo Wyższej Szkoły Zarządzania, 2006.

Kowal, J., E. Parka, A. Kwiatkowska, and K. Węgłowska-Rzepa. "Gender versus Women's Management Competencies on the Example of Poland (a Research Results Survey)." In *The Proceedings of the 5th European Conference on Management Leadership and Governance*, edited by J. Politis. Hellenic American University, the Atexcelixi Conference Centre Athens: Academic Publishing Limited, 2009.

Kowal, J., K. Węgłowska-Rzepa, H. Park, H. Lee Kuy, and S. Soon. "The Cultural Symbolism, Integration and Education of Different National Groups – Comparative Research of Polish, Korean and Philipino's Archetypal Imagery." In *Eksploracja Przestrzeni Historycznej*, edited by T. Leniartek, 261–84. Wrocław: Wyższa Szkoła Zarządzania „Edukacja", 2008.

Kuzio, A. "Frames of Self-Presentation in Constructing Persuasive Messages: A Study of Polish and American Political Discourse." *Rocznik Kognitywistyczny* 6 (2013): 23–36.

Myers, M.D., and D.E. Avison, eds. *Qualitative Research in Information Systems*. London: A Reader, Sage Publications, 2002.

Paluchowski, J. "Metodologiczne problemy analizy treści." In *Metody jakościowe w psychologii współczesnej*, edited by M. Straś-Romanowska, 55–57. Prace Psychologiczne, LIII. Wrocław: Wydawnictwo Uniwersytetu Wrocławskiego, 2000.

Pilch, T. *Zasady badań pedagogicznych*. Warsaw, 1977.

Pilch, T., and T. Bauman. *Zasady badań pedagogicznych. Strategie ilościowe i jakościowe*. Warsaw: Wydawnictwo Akademickie Żak, 2001.

Remenyi, D. *Case Study Research: The Quick Guide Series*. Academic Conferences Limited, 2013.

Stake, R.E. "Case Studies." In *Handbook of Qualitative Research*. Thousand Oaks: Sage Publications, 1994.

Straś-Romanowska, M. "Hermeneutyka w psychologicznych badaniach jakościowych." In *Hermeneutyka a psychologia*, edited by A. Gałdowa, 143–57. Cracow: Wydawnictwo Uniwersytetu Jagiellońskiego, 1997.

Straś-Romanowska, M. "O metodzie jakościowej w kontekście rozważań na tożsamością Psychologii." In *Metody jakościowe w Psychologii współczesnej*, edited by M. Straś-Romanowska, 16–32. Prace psychologiczne 53. Wrocław: Wydawnictwo Uniwersytetu Wrocławskiego, 2000.

Straub, D., D. Gefen, and M.C. Boudreau. "The ISWorld Quantitative, Positivist Research Methods Website", 2004. http://dstraub.cis.gsu.edu:88/quant/.

Such, J. *O uniwersalności praw nauki. Studium metodologiczne*. 2nd ed. Warsaw: PWN, 1972.

Sudman, S., and E. Blair. "Sampling in the Twenty-First Century." *Journal of the Academy of Marketing Science* 27, no. 2 (April 1, 1999): 269–77.

Taguchi, G., and Y. Wu. *Introduction to off-Line Quality Control*. Japan Quality Control Association, 1979.

Wawrzynek, J. "Uwagi o efektywności planowania eksperymentów." In *Przegl. Statyst.*, XXVI:111–25, 1977.

Węgłowska-Rzepa, K., and J. Kowal. "The 'Symob' projective Method and Its Possible Applications in the Labour Market: The Basis for the Method's." In *Functioning in the Workplace: Quantitative and Qualitative Psychological Research*, edited by B. Mróz. Warsaw: SCHOLAR Publishing House, 2012.

Węgłowska-Rzepa, K., J. Kowal, P. Bem, and H. Park. "Archetypal Symbols, Their Reception and Meaning for Polish and Korean Societies – Comparative Research." In *2nd International Academic Conference of Analytical Psychology & Jungian Studies*. Texas A & M University, 2005.

Węgłowska-Rzepa, K., J. Kowal, H. Park, and H. Lee Kuy. "The Presence of Spiritual Archetypes Among Representatives of Eastern and Western Cultures." *Jung Journal* 2, no. 3 (2008): 62–76.

Index

Abraham, Carl 29
absolutism
 of the ideal 62
 of the doctrine 62, 69
Adam Kadmos 111
advertising 338
Agamben, Giorgio 128
aggression 158, 160, 161
aims of the research 322
Aion 78, 195, 224
alchemic symbolism 290
alchemy 19, 74, 103, 152, 170, 194, 195, 213, 292
amplification(s) 54, 55, 272, 273, 279, 281, 282, 292, 297–299
Anima 47, 68, 82, 280, 282, 283, 295, 318, 329, 330, 338–340, 343–346
Animus 47, 68, 318, 327, 329, 330, 338–340, 343–346
anthropology 4, 7, 17, 42, 51, 67, 79, 120–122, 127, 131, 170, 273
anthropomorphic stamp 96, 97. *See also* archetype(s)
anxiety 35, 43, 52, 53, 142, 162, 223
Aphrodite 88, 91, 280, 282
apodictic 40, 52, 60, 63
Apollo 173, 277
Apollodorus 88, 91
archetypal images 146, 148, 176, 242, 272, 299
archetype(s) 2, 5–8, 17, 20, 47, 61, 66, 78, 87, 88, 90, 91, 93, 94, 96–114, 119–121, 125, 126, 129, 132, 148, 152–160, 164, 166, 171, 176, 178, 179, 224, 242, 261, 267, 269, 272, 273, 277, 279–284, 287, 288, 292, 295–297, 299–301, 329, 338–343, 345
Arendt, Hannah 5, 8, 162, 163
Aristotle 43, 44, 63, 64, 79, 103, 110
astrology 287
Augustin, Saint 43, 81, 101, 102, 154, 289
Augustus II The Strong (Elector of Saxony, King of Poland) 277, 284, 287, 289, 301
authoritarian 7, 163*n*

Bachelard, Gaston 97, 98, 108, 109, 116, 119
Bair, Deirdre 13, 15
Barthes, Roland 107
Bastian, Adolf 154
Baudrillard 40
Baynes, Cary 19
Belting, Hans 122, 127
Benjamin, Walter 43, 118*n*
Berque, Augustin 200
Bettelheim, Bruno 165
Binswanger, Ludwig 12, 15
Bismarck von, Otto 278
Bleuler, Eugen 9, 15, 253–267
Błocian, Ilona 5, 8, 120, 121
Boas, Franz 16, 17, 26
Bobrowski, Stefan 270
Boehm, Gottfried 7, 116, 118, 122, 129, 130
Bohr, Niels 16
Bolen, Jean Shinoda 279
Bonobo 228, 231, 233, 242, 247*n*
Bonpland, Aimé 23
Borges 40
Bourdieu, Pierre 132
bourgeois 42, 44, 56
Bowen, Margarita 24
Bridgeman, Bruce 9, 230
Brooke, Roger 2, 101, 108, 110, 155
Brzozowski, Stanisław 270
Burgholzli Clinic 9, 14, 15, 253–267

cardinal sins 290
Cartesian distinction (res cogitans, res extensa) 102
Catherine II 275
chaos 18, 19, 40, 52, 56, 65–67, 69, 126, 210, 212
 edge of 39, 48, 50, 57–59
Charcot, Jean-Martin 126, 255
Christ 276, 299
chtonic 269
circumambulating the Self 213
circumambulatio 194, 273
Cognition 236*n*, 237, 244*n*
collective unconscious 2, 17, 26, 31, 93, 96–98, 104–106, 111, 144, 148, 152, 153, 155, 158, 176, 242, 271, 272, 282, 291, 292, 296, 300

complex 2, 66, 88, 104, 110, 146, 177, 196, 234–237, 254, 257–267, 272, 273, 278, 283, 285, 286, 288, 292, 296, 307
consciousness 1, 4, 8, 9, 17, 27, 37, 39–41, 60, 61, 66, 71, 72, 74, 77, 79, 81, 83, 96, 98, 100, 106, 110, 135, 138, 141, 144, 145, 147–149, 160, 166, 175–177, 179, 182, 193–197, 206, 209–212, 214, 221, 224, 225, 228–251, 259, 262, 270–272, 276, 287, 293, 299, 322
Copernicus 37, 40, 41
core-self 239, 240, 242, 243, 252
Corpus Hermeticum 101
Cosmic Egg 111
Côte d'Azure 279
cross pressures 183, 184
Crusoe, Robinson 47
Culler, Jonathan 297

Damasio, Antonio 9, 29, 228, 239–243, 252
Darwin, Charles 24, 122
deduction
  linear chain of logical 55
  essentialist 50*n*
del Negro, Christina 274
dementia praecox 12, 13, 15, 253, 256–260, 262, 265
Demeter 111–112, 280, 282, 295–298, 300. *See also* Virgin/Mother archetype
demonology 269, 276, 287, 291
demons/daemons 173, 177, 180, 277, 281, 282, 290
desacralisation 169, 171, 174
Descartes 35–69
descriptive statistics 343
despiritualisation 174
Deutscher 8, 217
diagnosis 162–164, 166, 258, 262, 263, 265, 291, 308, 310
Dickens, Charles 87
Didi-Huberman, Georges 122, 126, 127, 132
Dionysius the Areopagite 101
Divine Child, Child Archetype 18, 101
Dobrowolska, Danuta 273
doctrine 47, 48, 50, 52–54, 57–62, 68, 69, 77, 81, 163, 177
Dōgen, Eihei 221
dogmatic 35, 40, 50, 51, 53, 62, 68, 72
dogmatism 66
Dostoyevsky, Fyodor 289
dream(s) 2, 3, 14, 18, 19, 47, 48, 54, 56, 57, 59, 60, 65, 69, 73, 77, 79, 105, 113, 123, 127, 138, 143, 145, 148, 152, 153, 166, 169, 178, 193, 194, 206, 207*n*, 212, 213, 258, 281, 282, 286, 290, 292, 294, 297, 315, 328
Dresden 270, 275, 279, 288, 296
dual/duality/dualistic 8, 74, 94, 149, 176, 194, 269*n*
Dudek, Zenon Waldemar 272, 279
Durand, Gilbert 119, 120
Durkheim, Emile 5, 8, 17, 171
Dybel, Paweł 116, 117

Eco, Umberto 5, 97, 98, 108–110
Edinger, Edward 196
ego consciousness 147, 193–195, 206, 210, 211, 221, 224
ego/I 5, 8, 44, 51, 53, 66, 68, 76, 91, 145, 148, 164, 165, 193–187, 200, 206–211, 216, 217, 221, 224–226, 229, 230, 233–236, 242, 246, 247, 251, 252, 260, 284
ego Japanese 196, 200, 216, 224, 225
Eliade, Mircea 98, 175, 278
Elias 296
empathy 188
empirical 3, 5, 6, 9, 21, 30, 41, 43, 44, 46–48, 53–55, 57, 59–62, 64, 68, 72, 136, 138, 143, 146, 177, 196, 224, 304–306, 309, 314, 315, 323, 330, 337
empiricism 23, 44, 46, 64
enchantment 169, 173–175, 178, 179, 184, 185
epistemological 2, 20, 35, 47, 53, 61, 67, 68, 96, 98, 105, 108, 110, 119, 121, 122, 130, 182, 183, 291, 324
epistemology 36, 40, 42, 43, 48, 51, 55, 62, 67, 102–104, 108, 187
equality 100, 110, 185
essence 48, 50, 52–54, 75, 82, 83, 118, 122, 127, 128, 176, 224, 232, 250
ethical 37, 81, 161, 183, 270, 281, 285, 298, 301, 336
Evil 8, 43, 62, 81, 158–161, 166, 287
extremes 50–52, 54, 62, 66

Fantasies 18, 28, 54, 105, 144, 178
fate 13, 37, 73, 90, 172–174, 179, 269, 277, 300

Ferenczi, Sandor 15
First Meditation 44, 45, 56
first principles 63–65
first-person pronoun drop 220
Fordham, Michael 11–13, 15, 17, 58, 62
Forster, Georg 22, 23
Foucault, Michel 38, 97, 108, 109
fractal 36, 46, 54, 62
Franz von, Marie-Louise 1, 16, 210
Frazer, James Sir 89–94
freedom 69, 163, 164, 166, 185, 188, 229, 299
Freud, Sigmund 5, 6, 11, 12, 17, 36, 39, 42, 45–50, 52–54, 56–62, 64, 66, 68, 69, 87, 88, 98–100, 117–120, 126, 127, 152, 153, 162, 166, 167, 170, 171, 183, 193, 228, 231–233, 236, 254, 256, 258, 261, 264, 271, 278, 292, 293, 298
Fromm, Erich 5, 8, 153, 163, 164, 166, 338
fundamentalism 8, 79, 172, 188

Galileo 37, 41, 57
Garden of Schönbrunn 200
Garden of the Palace of Versailles 201
Gnosis 100, 103, 109, 111, 164, 276
God(s)/Goddess 40, 43, 48, 49, 60, 63, 64, 66, 67, 77–80, 82, 89, 91–94, 101, 111–113, 164, 172–174, 177, 178, 180–183, 211, 212, 278, 280, 282, 289, 292, 300
Goethe, Johann 21
Gray, Richard 170*n*
Great Mother 91, 214, 292, 294, 296–300, 318, 329, 330, 338–340, 344–346

Haeckel, Ernst 22
Hartmann, Nicolai 100
Heidegger, Martin 6, 44, 71–78, 80–84, 110, 183
Heim, Michael 83
hermeneutic circle 273
hermeneutics 44, 108, 117, 120, 272, 273, 290
  historical-archetypal 272
hero(s) 7, 17, 24, 97, 111, 113, 270, 272, 274, 275, 279–281, 285, 289, 293
heroine 278
heroisation 7, 96, 97, 114
Hesiod 113
Hillman, James 26, 214, 273, 279, 301
Holy, the 174, 277

Homans, Peter 170
Hooker, Joseph Dalton 24
Hope, Murry 279
Hubert, Henri 5, 17, 154
Hugo, Victor 277
Humboldt (von), W. 216
Humboldt Aleksander von 5–6, 8, 17, 21–27
Husserl, Edmund 44, 78

ideal 41, 43, 47–48, 53, 55–57, 59–64, 69, 103, 162, 337, 341
idealism 2, 44, 52, 66, 170
Ikkyu, Sojun 221
image 4–5, 7, 18–19, 25–26, 29, 44, 47, 49, 54, 56, 59–60, 62, 78, 96–98, 101–102, 105–111, 113, 116–132, 135, 137–149, 152–154, 161, 176, 187, 193, 210, 213–214, 219, 226, 234–237, 240, 242, 251, 271–273, 277, 279–280, 282–285, 289, 292–293, 295, 298–300, 329
imagination 2, 7, 9, 17–19, 23, 26–27, 29, 67, 96–99, 101–103, 105–107, 109, 111, 113, 118–119, 122, 125, 130, 154, 156, 270, 272, 283, 288, 291
Immanence 181–183, 186
Individuality 154, 179, 213, 241
individuation 2, 54, 69, 74, 136, 143, 148, 149, 158, 159, 162, 177, 178, 269, 275, 282, 290, 297, 299–301
induction 55, 347
infinite 49–52, 54, 62–67, 107, 110, 235, 247
instinct 18, 61, 79, 97, 129, 155, 157, 160, 234, 237, 242
Intellectualization 172, 174
interpretation 2–3, 5–7, 9, 20, 37, 59, 76–77, 79, 83, 88–89, 91–94, 117, 119–122, 126–128, 130–132, 143–145, 148, 152–156, 158, 164–165, 170, 185, 187, 219–220, 225, 237, 269, 271, 273–275, 279, 281, 289–290, 292, 294, 297, 301, 305, 307, 322–324
intuitus 35, 43, 50–53, 62
Irenaeus 101, 154
Irrational, the 144, 175
irrationality 66, 128

Jakobson, Roman 108
James, William 17, 22, 184, 186
Janet, Pierre 3, 255

Japanese art 193, 195, 197, 198, 200, 205, 206
Japanese culture 194, 196, 210
Japanese ego 196, 200, 216–219, 221, 223–225, 227
Japanese psyche 8, 193–197, 210–211, 225
Jaspers, Karl 270
Jones, Ernst 15
Jung Institute Zurich 307
Jungian psychotherapy 9, 14, 291, 304–309, 311, 313–315

Kanaya, Toshiyuki 212, 218, 221
Kant, Immanuel 44, 100, 102, 156, 236, 244
Kawabata, Yasunari 165
Kawai, H. 150, 159, 161, 171
Kerényi, Karoly (Carl) 97, 101–102, 107, 109–113
Kobylińska, Ewa 126–127
Kojiki 200, 210
Kora/Persephone 88, 89, 91, 111–112, 280, 282, 295, 296, 298. *See also* Divine Child, Child Archetype; Virgin/Mother archetype
korus 112
Kraepelin, Emil 256, 259–260, 262, 265
Kraszewski, Józef Ignacy 269–270, 274, 279, 286

Lacan, Jaques 104, 118
  mirror stage 104
Laozi 295
learning disability–case study 223, 242–243, 252
Leibniz, Gottfried Wilhelm 43, 102
Lévi-Strauss, Claude 120, 170
Lévy-Bruhl, Lucien 100, 154, 209
logic 5, 8, 13, 18, 55, 72, 80, 116, 129–131, 135, 141, 144, 152, 155, 160, 162, 181, 235, 240, 246, 291, 322–323, 328, 347
Lyell, Charles 24

mandala 19, 28, 194
Marcuse, Herbert 5, 8, 164, 166
Maruyama 211
Masonic lodges 220, 294
mass
  man 8, 152, 162–164
  processes 7, 152
  society 8, 152, 162–164, 166, 170
materialism 183, 186
mathematics 44, 49, 51, 55, 59, 322–323
matter 3, 16, 41, 52, 60, 62, 67, 80, 96–99, 101–103, 106, 108, 125, 169, 172, 179, 181, 186, 230–231, 240, 242, 270–271, 322, 329, 333, 347
Mauss, Marcel 17, 154
McLynn, Frank 292
Merleau-Ponty, Maurice 183
methodology 9, 36, 68–69, 143, 253, 256, 259, 261, 318–319, 325–326, 332
metonymy 291
Mickiewicz, Adam 270, 285
Miłosz, Czesław 289
Mitchell, William John Thomas 128
modernity 42, 169–172, 174, 179–181, 184, 188
Moore, Thomas 279
morality 61, 182–183
Multiple Code 7, 135, 139, 141
mysticism 6, 164, 170–171
myth 5–6, 71, 73–74, 80, 87–94, 193–195, 210–213, 225, 261, 273, 275, 296, 300

nekyia 287
Neo-Kantism 100
Neo-Platonism 100
  coexistentio oppositorum 103
Neumann, Erich 156, 210, 296, 298

objectivization 328
Olsen, Jan Kyrre Berg 75
ontological ambivalence 189
ontology 47, 50, 64, 68–69, 102–103, 108
opposites 126, 177, 195, 204, 275, 277, 279, 280
Orzelska, Anna Karolina 277–278, 283–284

Pagalia, Camille 298
Pascal 6, 35–39, 41–47, 49–53, 55, 57–59, 61–69, 80
Pauli, Wolfgang 20, 156, 176
Peirce, Charles Sanders 98, 107, 109
persona 47, 51, 68, 163, 277, 281, 285
personal myth 273, 275
phenomenology 7, 78, 100
Philo Judaeus 101, 154
Planck, Max 16
Plato 43–44, 50, 102–103, 106, 113
Platonism 96, 102
pleasure principle 48, 61

polarisation 189
Poniatowski, Stanisław August 275–276
Popper, Karl 7, 57
post-structuralism 96, 108–109, 116
Potocki, Jan 276–277
primordial image. *See* archetype(s)
Progoff, Ira 153–154, 157, 166, 170–171
projection 8, 59, 81, 153, 177, 237, 299, 318, 325, 328, 338–339, 345
projective method 340
proto-self 9, 239, 252
Prus, Bolesław 280
psychoanalysis 3, 7, 9, 11–12, 25, 45, 58, 69, 72, 86, 116–121, 123–124, 128–129, 131, 135–137, 152, 158, 161, 216, 256, 272, 292, 298, 308
psychoid(s). *See* archetype(s)
psychosocial studies 169, 171
psychotherapy 4–5, 8–9, 58, 136, 142, 148, 195, 206, 212, 214, 291, 304–315

qualitative methods 320–321
quantitative methods 321, 347

Rakuchu Rakuagai-zu 197–199, 207–208
rationalization 81, 172–174
reactive formation 43
rebirth 89–91, 112, 179
re-enchantment 169, 173–175, 178–179, 184–185
regression 58, 301, 333, 336–337
religion 8, 47, 56, 59, 77, 79, 80, 83, 86, 88–89, 93, 108, 164–166, 169, 171–172, 174–177, 179, 181–183, 185–186, 331
représentation collective 100, 154
re-sacralisation 184–185
Ricouer, Paul 98
Riklin, Franz 256–257, 264–265
Romanticism 11, 20–21, 29, 63, 285–286
Romanyshyn, Robert 2
Rosiska Zofia 155, 271

Sacred, the 8–9, 172, 185, 188
sage 281, 286–288, 295, 300
Salome 286, 295–296
San Francisco Jung Institute 309
Sapir, Edward 8, 216–217
Saussure de, Ferdinand 107
Savage-Rumbaugh, Sue 248–249
Schelling von, Friedrich Wilhelm Joseph 102
schizophrenia 8–9, 15, 253–254, 257, 261–263, 265–267
Schulz, Brunon 280
science 1–7, 11, 13–17, 19–22, 24–25, 27–29, 31, 37–38, 40–41, 45, 53, 57, 62, 74–75, 77, 86, 93–94, 98, 108, 117, 121, 128–131, 135, 137–139, 164, 169, 172–179, 182, 185, 188, 253, 267, 288, 320–321, 328, 347
Scientific 1, 4–7, 11–15, 17, 20–24, 26, 28–30, 35, 42, 53, 56–57, 60, 62, 68, 86–87, 89, 91–95, 117, 145–146, 170, 174, 177, 181, 186, 188–189, 253–254, 259, 264–265, 271, 318–319, 322–323, 332
secular age 169, 171–173, 175, 177, 179–181, 183–187, 189, 191
secularisation 180–182, 185
secularity 169, 172, 180–182, 185–186
Seidensticker, Edward 218–219
Selbst 234
Self 51, 60, 329*n*
self/Self 8, 26, 27, 51, 60, 68, 74, 138, 149, 152, 162, 163, 177, 179, 180, 182–184, 194, 196–197, 213, 225, 228, 230, 234, 239–242, 260, 262, 295, 300, 329*n*
semiotics 5, 7, 97–98, 107–109, 120, 126
Semon, Richard 122
shadow(s) 50, 51, 68, 81, 152, 158–160, 166, 200, 271, 277, 281, 284, 288, 300, 301, 318, 329, 330, 339–341, 344–348
Shamdasani, Sonu 3, 13, 17, 19, 169
sign(s) 54, 58, 72, 96–98, 106–110, 244, 276, 279, 293
Simon Magus 295
Skinner, Burrhus Frederic 171
social science 5, 117, 121, 131, 188
social thought 7, 152–153, 155, 157–159, 161, 163, 165, 167, 170
society 4, 5, 8, 37, 79–80, 88, 152, 157, 161–164, 166, 170–171, 181, 197, 214, 277, 310, 312
sociology/sociological 4–5, 8–9, 17, 154, 169–171, 180, 336
Solomon 63
spirit, spiritual 51–52, 69, 74, 75, 77, 78, 111, 144, 148, 159, 163, 165, 166, 172, 175–181, 184, 186, 187, 211, 272, 277, 282, 284, 290, 292, 293, 298, 322

spirit/spirits 51–52, 78, 111, 144, 165, 172, 175, 178, 180, 184, 186, 272, 284, 290, 292, 298, 322
spirituality 74, 159
statistical methods 318, 339, 340
Staude, John Raphael 170–171
subject drop 216–218, 220–226
subjectivity 29, 43–44, 56, 66, 251
sub-symbolic 135, 139, 141–142, 146
suicide 296–297, 301
Supernatural, the 90, 181, 188
symbol 22, 53–54, 60–61, 69, 116–118, 120, 123–126, 128, 130–131, 135, 141, 144, 177, 179, 249–250, 276, 287, 297, 300, 339, 343–345
symbolism 152, 164, 166, 271, 277–278, 281, 290, 293, 297–300, 330, 339–340, 343
symptom 7, 12, 75, 116–117, 123, 126–128, 272, 314
synchronicity 19–20, 27, 156, 177–179, 315

Takashina, S. 198, 204
Taut, Bruno 204
Taylor, Charles 169, 172, 180–189
Terlecki, Władysław Lech 9, 269–301
The East 8, 74, 76, 81, 193, 194, 333
The Secret of the Golden Flower 19, 194, 195
The West 8, 81, 181–183, 193, 194, 200, 213, 224
theory of discourse 7, 97
theory of sign 96, 107
Thomas Aquinas 43, 110
Thomas Aquinatus 109–110
traditional Japanese art 193, 195, 197, 198, 200, 205, 206
transcendence/the transcendent 18, 60, 147, 177, 181–184, 186, 187
transcendent function 18, 60, 61, 147, 177, 299
Traugutt, Romuald 270
Trickster-Figure 111
truth 37, 40, 43, 50, 52, 59, 62–66, 68, 69, 72, 74, 130, 182, 186, 270, 273, 288, 305, 323
typology 42, 44, 52, 64, 273

unconscious/unconsciousness 2, 3, 7–9, 12, 15, 17–20, 22, 26, 28, 31, 35, 36, 39, 40, 47, 48, 50, 53, 57, 58, 60, 61, 65, 66, 77, 79, 81, 83, 91, 93, 94, 96–102, 104–106, 110, 111, 113, 117–124, 126, 128, 131, 135, 136, 144, 145, 147, 148, 152–158, 160–162, 164–166, 176, 177, 189, 193, 194, 196, 197, 212, 213, 216, 221, 223–226, 230–235, 237–240, 242, 243, 252, 254, 255, 257–259, 261–264, 271, 272, 276, 281, 282, 285, 287, 290–292, 296, 299, 300, 315
universe 25–17, 37, 56, 67, 98, 110, 183
unscientific 86, 87

Vattimo, Gianni 72
Velázquez, Diego 38
Vico, Giambattista 43, 44, 125, 126
Vignoli, Tito 124
Virgin/Mother archetype 111–113

Waddington, Conrad Hal 30
Wager argument 64
Warburg, Aby M. 116, 118–120, 122–128, 132
Weber, Max 8, 119, 169, 171–175, 178–183, 185
Wegner, Alfred 13
Western ego 8, 193, 194, 200, 206
Western psyche 193, 195–197
White, Victor Francis 176
White, Wiliam Alanson 12
Whorf, Benjamin Lee 8, 217
Whorfian hypothesis 216
Wielopolski, Aleksander 270, 285–287
Wilhelm, Richard 19, 21, 194
William, James 17, 184
Wise Old Man 78, 318, 329, 330, 338*n*
Witkiewicz, Stanisław Ignacy "Witkacy" 270
Wittgenstein 3, 42, 49, 52, 55, 66, 181
Wolin, Richard 82
word association test 256, 257, 259, 261, 264
Wunenburger, Jean-Jacques 121

Yamaguchi, Kayo 209
Yanabu, Akira 220
Yoshimura, Teiji 198

www.ingramcontent.com/pod-product-compliance
Lightning Source LLC
LaVergne TN
LVHW011109300926
849160LV00008B/317